Handbook of Philosophy

About the Author

The late Albert E. Avey received his B.A., M.A., and Ph.D. from Yale University and also studied at the University of Berlin. He taught at The Ohio State University for thirty-seven years and was Chairman of the Department of Philosophy from 1942 to 1952. The author also taught at Bryn Mawr College, Florida State University, the University of Pittsburgh, Cottey College, Pierce College (Greece), and The College of Wooster. In addition, he wrote the following: *Rethinking Religion, The Function and Forms of Thought,* and *Historical Method in Bible Study.*

EVERYDAY HANDBOOKS

Handbook of Philosophy

SECOND EDITION

Albert E. Avey

BARNES & NOBLE, INC. • NEW YORK

PUBLISHERS • BOOKSELLERS • SINCE 1873

L. C. Catalogue Card Number: 61-8331

SBN 389 00090 6

Formerly published under the title

HANDBOOK IN THE HISTORY OF PHILOSOPHY

Manufactured in the United States of America

To Anna Cornuelle Avey

Preface

It is often useful for students of philosophy merely to locate a thinker in time and space and to review his fundamental tenets without dwelling long upon him. Philosophers, like other human beings, live at definite times and in particular places; their ideas are necessarily affected by environmental influences. Furthermore, though their thinking is sometimes intricate, there are certain basic conceptions which lie at the heart of their theories.

Many writers of textbooks in philosophy begin with a brief summary of the history of philosophy. But the expression of the personal perspective of each writer as he looks at such a history is an extra-textual concern. An impersonal presentation of the general features of the history should be the starting point for personal interpretation and emphasis. Such a presentation could serve as background for many individual developments. A writer of the history of thought should not confine himself to those points of view that he personally finds convincing. He should know the views he does not accept as well as those he does, for the sake of fairness to all and for the sake of the contrasts which result from comparing the acceptable with the unacceptable. A number of recent texts in philosophy begin with a point of view which is not universally accepted and which makes them difficult to use except as a set of theses to be combated. These texts may provide excellent presentations of particular points of view, but not equally good presentations of contrasting viewpoints.

This volume offers a survey of the course of western philosophic thought, which may be used to accompany textbooks in a special field of interest and to supply historical background for any point of view an instructor may wish to develop.

The presentation is in rather strict chronological sequence in order to give a more accurate impression of the actual course of history. It is customary for works, even on history, to move back and forth in time, in order to keep intact certain relations of thought. This practice is based upon the notion that a history must be a work of art and present certain unities. But history is not primarily artistic; and it is worthwhile to maintain crude actuality rather than to try to improve upon it by substituting aesthetic unity for real occurrence. If the result is less artistic, at least it is more realistic, more true to fact. Thoughts logically relevant to each other often occur independently, to be related later in a mind that surveys the past. This can be done here, too; it can be done even better when the one who does it sees clearly that he is doing it. The order of succession in this volume has been based upon the date of publication of the writer's most characteristic work or the earliest work in which his position is clear. In earlier periods in which dates are not definite it is assumed that the individual was flourishing at about the age of forty.

The procedure adopted gives a clearer sense of the relative richness and poverty of different periods. It has also led to the mention of some names hardly known at all, in order to show that at least a minimum of philosophic interpretation was occurring at all times, constituting the means of continuity by which the torch of learning was handed on. The effort for the most part has been to catch the general spirit and point of view of each thinker, as presented in one of his main works, yet also, in the case of especially important men, to suggest their intellectual biographies as indicated by the chronological succession of their writings, and so to indicate important transitions in their thinking, as in the case of Plato, Aristotle, Augustine, Kant, and others. More than average space has been allotted to those works which are recognized classics and the influence of which upon the history of philosophy has been outstanding. As time has passed, there have been many noble teachers who have carried on the tradition, but who have not proved decidedly original or influential. Yet their names are met now and then, and the reader will doubtless welcome a brief identifying statement about them.

Prefixed to each chapter is a short summary of the content of the section. The reader scanning these summaries may obtain a very succinct survey of the course of western thought.

For further information readers may consult the list of useful books in the Appendix.

The writer gladly acknowledges debt to his colleagues for many valuable suggestions, but exonerates them of any responsibility for defects. He wishes also to express appreciation for the very helpful advice given by the consultants of Barnes & Noble. Inc.

Table of Contents

CHAPTER   PAGE

Preface vii

1. **Early Reflective Thought** 3

 B.C. 3500—*Book of the Dead,* Priest of Seneferu, Ptahhotep
   2400—*Babylonian Tablets, Tablets from Nippur, Gilga-mesh Epic,* Ipuwer, *Eloquent Peasant,* Baba
   1400—Amenemope, *Codes of Law,* Ikhnaton, *Hittite Code, Two Brothers*
   800—*Hebrew Patriarchal Stories,* Amos, Hosea, Isaiah I, Micah
   700—*Assyrian Tablets,* Zoroaster, *Book of Deuteronomy,* Zephaniah, Habakkuk, Jeremiah

2. **The Pre-Socratic Period** 10

   600—Thales, Anaximander, Anaximenes, Isaiah II, Pythagoras, Xenophanes
   500—Heraclitus, Parmenides, Zeno of Elea, Empedocles
   450—Anaxagoras, Archelaus, Philolaus, Melissus, Leucippus, Protagoras, Gorgias, Hippias, Prodicus

3. **The Classic Period** 20

   425—Socrates, Democritus, Euclid, Antisthenes, Cratylus
   400—Aristippus, Plato, Xenophon, Eudoxus, Diogenes of Sinope, Speusippus, Xenocrates
   350—Aristotle, Theophrastus

4. **The Early Hellenistic Era** 38

   350—Pyrrho, *Book of Job,* Epicurus
   300—Zeno of Citium, Euhemerus, Strato, Arkesilaus, Cleanthes, Timon
   250—Chrysippus, Zeno of Tarsus
   200—Carneades, *Ecclesiastes,* Aristobulous

CHAPTER   PAGE

   B.C.   150—Clitomachus, Panaetius
          100—Posidonius, Andronicus, Lucretius, Cicero, Aene-
                sidemus
           50—Q. Sextius, Sotion

5. The Early Christian Centuries   **48**
   A.D.   1—Philo Judaeus, Jesus
           50—Paul, Seneca, Barnabas, Pliny the Elder, *Gospels,*
                Plutarch, Clement, Epictetus
          100—Ignatius, Polycarp, Papias, Nicomachus, Marcion,
                Justin
          150—Numenius, Marcus Aurelius, Lucian, Tatian,
                Galen, Irenaeus, Sextus Empiricus, Clement of
                Alexandria, Tertullian
          200—Alexander of Aphrodisias, Ammonias Saccas, Dio-
                genes Laertius, Origen, Sabellius, Cyprian, Plotinus
          250—Amelius Gentilianus, Mani, Porphyry, *Hermes*
                Trismegistus
          300—Arnobius, Lactantius, Eusebius, Jamblichus, Chal-
                cidius, Arius, Athanasius
          350—Apollinaris, Aphraates, Victorinus, Julian, Am-
                brose, Jerome, Jovinian, Donatus, Plutarch of
                Athens, Macrobius, Augustine, Pelagius
          400—Hypatia, Martianus Capella, Nestorius
          450—Proclus, John Stobaeus, *Pseudo-Dionysius the*
                Areopagite
          500—Dionysius Exiguus, Boethius, Cassiodorus, Da-
                mascius, Simplicius
          550—Evagrius, Gregory of Tours, Gregory the Great
          600—Isidore, Maximus the Confessor

6. From Mohammed to Anselm and Aquinas   **76**
          650—Mohammed, Severus Sebokht, Aldhelm
          700—Bede the Venerable, John of Damascus
          750—Paul the Deacon, Alcuin
          800—Rhabanus Maurus, Paschasius Radbertus, al-Kindi,
                Gottschalk
          850—Erigena, Photius, Eric of Auxerre, Remi of Auxerre

900—al-Farabi, Saadia ben Joseph

950—Suidas, Gerbert

1000—Avicenna, Berenger, Bahya, Peter Damian, Lanfranc

1050—Constantine the African, Gabirol (Avicebron), Anselm, Manegold, Odo, Roscelin, al-Ghazali

1100—William of Champeaux, Adelard, Abelard, Bernard of Chartres, Gilbert de la Porrée, Theodoric of Chartres, William of Conches, Judah ha-Levi, Abraham ben Ezra, Hugh, Peter the Lombard

1150—Abraham ben David, Gerard, John of Salisbury, Richard of St. Victor, Averroes, Alan, Maimonides, Joachim, Amalric

1200—Grosseteste, William of Auvergne, Bartholomew, Alexander of Hales, David of Dinant, Adam Marsh, Albert the Great

1250—R. Bacon, William of Moerbeke, John of Fidanza (Bonaventure), Thomas Aquinas, Witelo, Peter of Spain, Siger of Brabant, Raymond Lully, Peckham, Matthew of Aquasparta, Olivi, Dietrich of Freiberg, Peter of Abano, Eckhart

7. The Transition to Modern Philosophy 106

1300—Scotus, Marsilius of Padua, Nicholas of Autrecourt, William of Ockham, Levi ben Gerson, John of Jandun, Buridan, Tauler, Nicholas of Oresme.

1350—John Wycliffe, Hasdai Crescas

1400—Gerson, Huss, d'Ailly, Marsilius of Inghen, Raymond of Sabunde, Joseph Albo, à Kempis, Nicholas of Cusa

1450—Biel, Ficino, Abarbanel, da Vinci, John Pico, Agostino Nifo

1500—Erasmus, Machiavelli, Pomponazzi, Thomas More, Zwingli, Martin Luther, Paracelsus, Franck, Calvin, Petrus Ramus

1550—Girolamo Cardano, Telesio, Sozzini, Montaigne, Bruno, Zabarella, Weigel, Patrizzi, Suarez

8. Early Modern Thought   124

    1600—Charron, Boehme, F. Bacon, Campanella, Herbert,
          Grotius, Galileo, Jansen, Descartes, Digby, Which-
          cote, Gassendi
    1650—Hobbes, Harrington, Pascal, Boyle, Glanvil, Ar-
          nauld, Sergeant, Geulincx, Henry More, Cumber-
          land, Pufendorf, Malebranche
    1675—Spinoza, Cudworth, Fox, Newton, Locke, Bur-
          thogge, Toland, Bayle

9. The Enlightenment   145

    1700—Norris, Clarke, Mandeville
    1710—Berkeley, Cooper, Collier, Collins, Leibniz, Wolff
    1720—Wollaston, Vico
    1730—Tindal, Gay, Butler, Hume, Bolingbroke
    1740—Montesquieu, La Mettrie, Hartley, Swedenborg
    1750—Baumgarten, Home, Edwards, Diderot, Condillac,
          Hutcheson, Burke, Boscovich, Helvétius, d'Alem-
          bert, Adam Smith, Voltaire, Rousseau
    1760—J. H. Lambert, Reid, Lessing, Mendelssohn
    1770—Baron d'Holbach, Beattie, Euler, Priestley, Mon-
          boddo (Burnett), Price
    1780—Kant, Allen, Herder, Jacobi, Cabanis, Bentham
    1790—Maimon, Stewart, Fichte, Schelling, Schleier-
          macher, Schlegel

10. Nineteenth Century: First Half   176

    1800—Hamann, de Tracy, Paley, Fries, Herbart
    1810—Krause, Maine de Biran, St. Simon, Hegel, Cole-
          ridge, de Maistre, Schopenhauer
    1820—Jefferson, Beneke, Cousin, James Mill, Hamilton
    1830—Rosmini-Serbati, Mackintosh, Comte, de Lam-
          menais, Carlyle, Strauss, Emerson, Poisson, Bol-
          zano, Whewell, Ruge, Gioberti
    1840—Trendelenburg, Bauer, Feuerbach, Parker, Cour-
          not, J. S. Mill, Kierkegaard, Engels, Stirner,
          Vischer, De Morgan

CHAPTER   PAGE

11. Nineteenth Century: Second Half   **195**

      1850—Moleschott, Gobineau, Boole, Thoreau, Renouvier,
             Fischer, Büchner, Bain, Lotze, Ritschl, Buckle,
             Mansel, Darwin

      1860—Fechner, Spencer, Lassalle, Helmholtz, Huxley,
             Ueberweg, J. Grote, Dühring, Lange, Marx, Por-
             ter, Ravaisson, von Hartmann

      1870—Newman, De Sanctis, Taine, Ardigò, Lachelier,
             H. Cohen, Dedekind, Spir, Sigwart, Janet, Teich-
             müller, Jevons, Brentano, Fiske, Boutroux, Lewes,
             Müller, Sidgwick, Stephen, Michelet, Pope Leo
             XIII, Wright, Peirce, Clifford, Balfour, Frege

      1880—Wundt, Venn, Jodl, Dilthey, Green, G. S. Morris,
             Stumpf, Martineau, Abbot, Mach, Nietzsche, Vol-
             kelt, Tönnies, Bosanquet, Avenarius, E. Caird,
             Deustua

      1890—Harris, Fouillée, James, Schroeder, Simmel, Brad-
             ley, Durkheim, Blondel, Windelband, Peano,
             Ostwald, Ladd, Cantor, Plekhanov, Stout, Rickert,
             Hobhouse, McTaggart, Lipps, Ehrenfels, Hodg-
             son, Creighton, Lloyd, Haeckel, J. Ward, Hilbert

12. Twentieth Century: First Half   **238**

      1900—Howison, Höffding, Eucken, Planck, Husserl,
             Royce, Poincaré, Croce, Schiller, Taylor, Russell,
             Moore, Foerster, Zermelo, Santayana, Cassirer,
             Meinong, Rashdall, Bergson, Calkins, Adler,
             Bowne, Tufts, Driesch, Brouwer, Muensterberg,
             Brunschvicg, Lenin

      1910—Natorp, Dewey, Haeberlin, McDougall, Boodin,
             Vaihinger, Hocking, Grabmann, Perry, Werthei-
             mer, Külpe, Unamuno, Watson, Spranger, Macin-
             tosh, Freud, Scheler, Gentile, Jung, Pringle-
             Pattison, R. Otto, Geyser, Stern, Schlick, Turro y
             Darder, Jaspers

      1920—Alexander, Weber, Morgan, Lévy-Bruhl, Leighton,

Table of Contents

Korn, Wittgenstein, Berdyaev, Ortega y Gasset,
P. E. More, Montague, Nuñez Regüeiro, Broad,
Koffka, Woodbridge, Hartmann, Heidegger,
Xirau, Whitehead, Lewis, Köhler

1930—Huizinga, Lovejoy, Brightman, Muirhead, M. R.
Cohen, Ramsey, Gödel, Stace, Tarski, Carnap,
Mead, Quine, Temple, Reichenbach, Ayer, Gilson,
Vasconcelos, Pratt, Maritain, Romero, Barth, Ross

1940—Blanshard, Frank, Sartre, Kallen, Murphy, Lepley,
Northrop, Mumford, Blau, Wild, Ryle, Feigl,
Black, White

13. Twentieth Century: Second Half   **287**

1950—Einstein, Bridgman, Lamprecht, Boas, Weiss,
Hook, Miller, Mayer, Ducasse, von Mises, Tillich,
Marcel, Goodman, Flew, Balz, Baumgardt, Mc-
Keon, Moore, Sellars, Radhakrishnan, Levinson
Toulmin, Sheldon, Toynbee, Niebuhr, Nagel,
Wiener, Robinson, Wolfson, Schneider, Woodger,
Morris, Luce, Pepper, Schilpp, Randall, Adler,
Kaufmann, Pap

Appendix   **307**
   Schools of Philosophy and Their Adherents   **309**
   Reference Books   **319**
   Index   **324**

Handbook of Philosophy

I   Early Reflective Thought

Philosophy, as William James suggested, is "our more or less dumb sense of what life honestly and deeply means." It moves around certain crucial questions, according to Immanuel Kant, such as: What can I know? What ought I to do? What may I hope? The first is the basic theoretical question. The second is the practical one. The third question involves the issue of the nature of the universe, in which we find ourselves, and our relation to it. Men have pondered such questions from the time of the earliest records. The answers were at first intuitive rather than analytic in character. It was easier to pose superficially plausible answers than it was to arrive at answers based upon convincing reasons. Nevertheless, intuitive conclusions constituted the first steps in the process of giving some formulation to the meaning of life.

We must bear in mind that the records of the early ages of man are very incomplete and that the impression we receive of the evolution of ideas is spasmodic. There was not an even, steady progress in the flow of ideas. They arose as particular occasions demanded. Only later reflection began to weave them into ordered systems. This is true to some extent even today. For not all minds build complete structures. Human thought is still episodic, uneven, and disconnected. Consequently, in order to give an accurate impression, the story of human beliefs must depict this uneven and unsystematic character of experience.

For the earliest picture of the principal aspects of western thought, we turn to the Near East—the civilizations of the Nile and the Tigris-Euphrates valleys. It is impossible to say which of these was the earlier civilization. But the majority of the oldest relevant records, which have survived to the present time, have come from Egypt, with supplementary records emanating from Babylonia. The

Egyptians, beginning perhaps as far back as the First Dynasty, had an interest in the final destiny of the individual and a belief in immortality. They believed that an essential condition for approval in the hereafter was the living of an upright life on earth. There are, accordingly, statements regarding conduct from both the collective or social and the individual points of view. Interest in theology was connected at first with the destiny of the individual, but in time it resulted in a more independent appreciation of the goodness of the Divine Being and, finally, a sense of communion with and a personal closeness to God.

The Babylonians supplemented this trend in Egyptian thought with the question of the origins of things, stories of a disastrous flood, and formulation of codes of laws for the regulation of human relations.

In the middle of the eighth century B.C., Hebrew written literature began to appear, originating with men in prophetic circles who correspond to the preachers of the present day—men who were concerned to know the will of God, to interpret the meaning of history, and to formulate principles of ethical conduct. They saw in the great personalities of Hebrew tradition inspiring examples of character which future generations would strive to emulate. These writers set forth the principle of social justice and the idea that benevolence is the essence of God's relationship to man. They saw in the events of history signs of the judgment of God upon nations, although more and more they questioned suffering as a punishment for sin both for nations and for individuals; also, the work of individuals rather than that of national groups seemed to stand out prominently against the background of ruined national independence.

The sense of struggle in life, in fact in all the universe, received systematic formulation in the thinking of Zoroaster about 700 B.C., and it exerted a great influence on later thinking.

Book of the Dead (3500 B.C.). The earliest concern of mankind, as revealed by ancient records, was with the destiny of the human being through eternity. A chapter (LXIV) in the Egyptian Book of the Dead, which dates from the First Dynasty, shows this interest, not as a problem but as a positive conviction regarding the immortality of the soul. As the individual's destiny is dependent upon his conduct in this life, the question What ought I to do? is of paramount importance and has application in both the social and the individual senses.

Priest of Seneferu (*c.* 2900 B.C.). Social ethics appeared as a topic for consideration at a very early date. The reason for considering rules of conduct was dissatisfaction with the social situation. A priest living during the reign of King Seneferu complained of the confusion in the land; due to the lack of rules for social conduct, plundering was common and business was ill-managed.

Ptahhotep (*c.* 2600 B.C.) [Egypt]. Rules for individual conduct were stated by Ptahhotep, counseling how one should conduct oneself in the presence of a man of superior wisdom and in the presence of an equal who speaks evil; indicating one's proper attitude to a social inferior if he shows ability; advising cultivation of the truth and uprightness in fulfilling the duties of one's office. Another in Ptahhotep's long list of suggestions states that one should encourage tranquility among the populace and should not induce fear in them. Each suggestion stands alone, applicable to the particular occasion for which it is appropriate; it is not systematized, not reduced to theory. Each is an example of practical ethics, reflecting the mental attitude of those who examine daily conduct for the purpose of evaluating it.

Babylonian Tablets (*c.* 2400 B.C.). More than four thousand years ago, reflective minds in Babylonia were inquiring about the origin of the universe. A clay tablet from the ancient city of Nippur recorded speculation on this point in polytheistic terms. Also at that time, explanations were sought for the origins of familiar things, such as trees, fields, flocks, grain, houses, temples, men, clothing, and irrigation. Numerous clay tablets show that the creation of man was a favorite subject for thought and that the purpose of his existence was a theme that needed statement. Man was early believed to have been formed from the blood of a god and to have been assigned the fundamental task of worshiping the gods.

Tablets from Nippur (*c.* 2200 B.C.). A story on tablets from Nippur tells of the destruction of man and animals by a flood, with a subsequent renewal of life and a fresh beginning. The people attempted to gain desired ends by conjuring. The granting of immortal life to a hero is recorded. The tablets also tell of the origin of a city and treat the introduction of agriculture at some length. The consideration of the problem of death was begun. Plants were used for medicinal purposes. The problems that life presents—especially the question of the reason for difficulty, suffering, and disaster —became of pressing concern. There resulted a literature of prayer: appeal to the gods for forgiveness for man's shortcomings, and for health and prosperity, and a type of adoration of the high powers of the gods.

Gilgamesh Epic (*c.* 2000 B.C.) [Babylonia]. Meditation upon the meaning of life led the author of the *Gilgamesh Epic* to suggest that the best way to live life's brief span is to relinquish the search for immortality, to eat and be merry day and night, to enjoy bright garments, and to live happily with one's wife and family.

Ipuwer (2000 B.C.) [Egypt]. Statements of dissatisfaction with the social order continued with *Admonitions of Ipuwer.* Ipuwer wrote that religious skepticism was rife. The author even wished for an end to the human race. He asserted that men are lazy. He believed that a leader was needed who would be the shepherd of his people, stop evil, and bring peace of mind to his followers.

Eloquent Peasant (1800 B.C.) [Egypt]. The demands of Social Conscience also were reflected in *Story of the Eloquent Peasant,* which criticized the unscrupulousness of petty officials and the delays in the justice executed in the courts.

Baba (1600 B.C.) [Egypt]. Baba in the Eighteenth Dynasty proclaimed the virtue of his conduct, his attitude toward his parents and relatives, his punishment of evil doers, and his preparations against days of famine ahead.

Amenemope (1400 B.C.). Amenemope described the practical ethics of his time in *Wisdom of Amenemope,* which warned against robbing the poor, failing to aid the aged, becoming haughty, exposing people to unnecessary risks, returning evil for evil, etc. Amenemope enjoined respect for the temple and for the property of a neighbor.

Codes of Law (1400 B.C.). Social relations were regulated by codes of law. One code, found in Assyria, deals with the conduct of women and men's relations with them. It deals also with matters of real estate and cultivation of the ground.

Ikhnaton (*c.* 1375 - *c.* 1358 B.C.) [Egypt]. Surviving to us from El Amarna are protestations of loyalty and upright conduct which originated in a series of letters from officials in the region of Palestine. These letters were written to the King of Egypt, Amenophis IV—who had changed his name to Ikhnaton (Aton is satisfied)—in connection with his efforts to supplant the complex priestly system at Thebes with a monotheistic conception of a benevolent deity, represented by the sun's disc (aton). The latter was believed to be interested in the welfare of all his creatures throughout nature. Ikhnaton had also built a new capital on the Nile, halfway between Thebes and Memphis. His reform proved temporary; it was out-of-tune with his age.

Hittite Code (1350 B.C.) [Asia Minor]. At Boghaz Koi, a code of laws was found which deals with women, bandits, leased lands, damages, and numerous other matters common in the activities of Hittite society.

Two Brothers (1200 B.C.) [Egypt]. One aspect of the problem of conduct is shown in *Tale of the Two Brothers,* depicting in concrete form the characters of an upright young man and the well-intentioned but deluded brother and the improper conduct of an elder brother's wife.

Hebrew Patriarchal Stories (800 B.C.). In the eighth century Hebrew ethical sense became embodied in literary form in the stories of the patriarchs, in the accounts of creation and the flood, in accounts of the origins of human institutions, and in portrayals of the Hebrew people as found in the Jewish Bible—the Christian Old Testament. Contemporary records, later re-edited many times, have survived to us from the Hebrew Prophets Amos, Hosea, Isaiah I, and Micah.

Amos (750 B.C.) [Tekoa, Bethel]. Several significant conceptions came from Amos: the law of the inevitable consequences of conduct, as it operates in life; the rule that as a nation sows so hall it reap; the superiority of ethical over formal religion; the essential status of justice in society; the moral responsibility of nations as well as individuals; and the unity of the Divine Being.

Hosea (740 B.C.) [Jerusalem]. Hosea repeated the suggestion of King Ikhnaton (Amenophis IV) in which God is conceived as a benevolent deity loving his people as a true husband loves even an unfaithful wife, or as a father loves his son.

Isaiah I (737-690 B.C.) [Jerusalem]. Isaiah I, in his picture of history, interpreted the advance of the Assyrian army as an instrumentality for justice in the hands of Jehovah. He contrasted reliance upon physical strength with moral stamina.

Micah (710 B.C.) [Moresheth]. The thoughts of Isaiah I were supported by the preaching of Micah, who saw man's religious duty as consisting in humility and the doing of good.

Note: The Hebrew prophets elaborated on the discussion of the evils of society, which the Babylonians and Egyptians had criticized. Our knowledge of Hebrew philosophy is more extensive, owing in part to a fuller preservation of the Hebrew records.

Assyrian Tablets (700 B.C.). We know from tablets which have been discovered that in the seventh century B.C. the rulers of Assyria had re-told the stories of the creation of the world and of the flood, stories which had come down from a much earlier time. As a result, these narrations now exist in a much longer and more detailed form than the earlier versions. The Assyrians also made collections of proverbs for the guidance of daily life.

Zoroaster (660-583 B.C) [Persia]. Zoroaster (or Zarathustra) introduced to the atmosphere of thought a fundamental emphasis which had an important influence in later times. Chiefly, he saw in all the processes of the universe a continual struggle between good and evil, truth and falsehood. His interpretation was dualistic, in terms of Ahura Mazda (God of Light) and Angra Mainyu (Bad Spirit) with their cohorts of archangels. It was apparently from contact with *Zoroastrianism* during the Exile that the Hebrews developed the idea of Satan as the great adversary of Jehovah; the Christian idea of the Devil was derived from Judaism. Zoroaster's attitude of devotion to truth and hatred of dishonesty led directly to the science and philosophy of Greece.

Book of Deuteronomy (650 B.C.). The fundamental thoughts of Hebrew prophets of the eighth century B.C. were re-echoed at the end of the seventh. Love as a motivating factor in religion affects the tone of the Law in the *Book of Deuteronomy*. In addition, the basic question is raised as to the criterion for distinguishing the true from the false prophet. Answers to this waver between personal authority (the name of Jehovah) and the empirical test (the course of history).

Zephaniah and *Habakkuk* continued the same philosophy of history as that of Isaiah I (*see* p. 8).

Jeremiah (650-585 B.C.) [Anathoth, Jerusalem]. With a note of individualism as national life came to an end in the captivity, Jeremiah declared that it shall no more be said that the fathers have eaten sour grapes and the children's teeth are set on edge; hereafter each man shall be held responsible only for his own sin, and the soul that sins shall die. And again, in spite of Jeremiah's efforts for good, the treatment he received forced him to raise the question of why the righteous suffer.

2   The Pre-Socratic Period

Reflective analysis in the form regarded as philosophy began, in a technical sense, in the Western world about 600 B.C. The Greeks were the first people who learned to think abstractly and with exactness. They were also the first successfully to use generalizations aiming at universal validity. As a consequence, they gave to the Western world the science of mathematics, which has been the basis of other sciences, and the logical analysis which pervades the intellectual disciplines of Western civilization. Among other contributions, they presented analytic and systematic treatments of the fundamental questions which had originated in earlier civilizations.

The first problem emphasized was that of *ontology,* or the nature of the basic stuff of which all things are made. Answers to this problem ran all the way from water through "the indeterminate," air, fire, and earth to immaterial number. Conviction varied between belief in one and more than one substance, irreducible in kind. Permanence and change were also subjects of controversy. The difficulty in deciding issues indicated a tendency toward *relativism.*[1]

Thales (624-550 B.C.) [Miletus]. It is customary to begin the account of western philosophy with Thales. Native to the coast of Asia Minor, he was noted as a geometrician, an economist, an astronomer, and a philosopher. In philosophy he raised the question of the nature of Ultimate Reality. What is the basic stuff of which all things are made? This, he said, is water. His method of answering the question is of prime importance. He did not appeal to tradition, in the form of either religion or poetry. Rather, he looked to experience and to what he had observed, and his answer was the result of

---

[1] The theory that there is no one absolutely true doctrine.

his own thinking. None of his writings have survived; later thinkers wrote about him and his philosophy. One of them was Aristotle, who held that the fundamental reason for Thales' view was the quantity of water that was observed in nature as well as its power and importance for life. Water, as he thought of it, was not a lifeless substance, but contained the essence of life. He was the first *hylozoist.*[2]

When Thales raised the question of the possible reduction of all reality to one substance, his method of thinking was more important than the particular answer. He supplied impetus to thinking on the basis of observed experience. He began the line of thought known as *monism* and introduced questions which have occupied philosophers and scientists for centuries.

Anaximander (611-547 B.C.) [Miletus]. The line of thought Thales suggested was carried on in the next generation by Anaximander. But Anaximander took a tremendous step when he reasoned that if we look for a substance underlying all phenomena of experience it could not be some particular form of matter like water, but would be unrestricted, unlimited, in its nature. It would, as he said, be "boundless," "infinite." In saying this he anticipated the position which is held at the present when men speak of "energy" as something which assumes various forms under different conditions, such as heat, light, magnetism, and molecular agitation. No one of these is wholly identical with energy. Each is a form, or manifestation, of energy under given conditions. But energy itself is "that which" assumes these forms and appears in these phenomena. This substance of Anaximander was not only indeterminate but also eternal, imperishable, inexhaustible, undergoing a process which includes biological evolution.

Anaximenes (588-524 B.C.) [Miletus]. The reasoning of Anaximander was too subtle for thinkers then (as it is very subtle today) and Anaximenes reverted to an empirically observable substance, air, as the Ultimate form of Reality. He believed one might as well

---

[2] Believer in the theory that all matter is alive: *hyle*–matter, *zoe*–life.

say that all things, even water, are derived from air by condensation as to say they come from water by condensation or rarefaction. In his argument, Anaximenes showed the truth of Anaximander's contention that water is not proved convincingly to be the basic Real. His thought also contains a suggestion of the reduction of qualitative change to quantitative change.

Isaiah II (*c.* 550 B.C.) [Unknown]. In Israel about this time, the author of Isaiah 40—55 continued the philosophy of history begun by earlier prophets. But he gave it a new tone by concluding that the exile of Israel had expiated the nation's sins and that it was thereby possessed of a new opportunity to serve God acceptably and live up to its ideals. The excessive suffering was interpreted as vicarious expiation, not only for Israel's sins but for the sins of other nations as well.

Pythagoras (572-497 B.C.) [Samos, Metapontum]. Anaximander had departed from the facts of the senses to find his conception of the Real. A different kind of departure occurred in the second half of the sixth century B.C. in the thinking of Pythagoras and his followers. Reports indicate that Pythagoras traveled about the then known world and finally settled in southern Italy, in the region called Magna Graecia. His work is obscured by the results attributed to him by later writers. But he seems to have founded a secret brotherhood the primary interests of which were moral and religious. He is reported to have taught a dualism of body and soul, akin to the doctrine of the mystical Orphic religious cults. To refine the soul the study of science and mathematics was undertaken, and the development of number theory was begun. The numerical relations of lengths of string and harmonious sounds given off by their vibrations were observed. The school concluded that numbers are the very essence and basis of the qualities of things and made lists of opposite attributes—odd, even, limited, unlimited, etc. The Pythagoreans formulated an astronomical theory which represented the earth and other bodies of our solar system revolving around a central fire. They also taught the kinship of men and beasts and the doctrine of transmigration of souls.

Pythagoras is credited with the discovery of the relation of the sides of a right triangle to the hypotenuse, one of the most important of mathematical theorems.[3]

Xenophanes (570-480 B.C.) [Colophon]. The notion that there is only one Ultimate Reality was stated in theological terms by Xenophanes[4] in a *didactic poem*. Apparently he was a traveling poet who noticed the different ideas of gods held by men in different areas. In Thrace men's gods were blue-eyed and red-haired; in Africa they were black and snub-nosed. This meant men were thinking of their gods as images of themselves. On this basis Xenophanes declared that if horses and oxen could form ideas of gods they would make them like fine horses and oxen. This he was sure could not be the true conception of God. He must be One and not like any particular finite being, man or animal. God must not have sense organs like men's, but "the whole of him sees, the whole of him thinks, the whole of him hears." He rules all things by the power of his mind; and he is omnipresent, not needing organs of locomotion. Xenophanes criticized the character of the gods as represented by Homer and Hesiod, who regarded them as far from ideal in their moral traits. He also expressed contempt for the popular judgments of men, who ranked outstanding athletes above men of wisdom. Having observed fossils even on mountain-sides, Xenophanes suggested a theory of evolution to account for them.

Heraclitus (533-475 B.C.) [Ephesus]. Disagreeing with the attempt to reduce all things to one permanent reality, Heraclitus thought that the fundamental characteristic of the universe was its changeableness, stating that "all things flow, nothing abides. Into the same river one cannot step twice." He believed the senses

---

[3] The Pythagorean Theorem: the square of the hypotenuse of a right triangle is equal to the sum of the squares of the other two sides.

[4] The first of the Eleatic philosophers; Xenophanes, Parmenides, and Zeno were the chief Eleatics, so-called from Elea in southern Italy where they lived.

cannot be trusted. The only permanent feature of things is the law of change to which they submit. This law Heraclitus designated by the term Logos, the rational principle which pervades the universe and keeps it in order, and pervades the thought of man when he is sane and orderly in his living. The rule of reason is the moral ideal. Thus human law is fed by one divine law. Reason is not subjective and individual. It is valid for all and is the objective bond that ties all thinking minds together. The substance that best represents the essence of the universe, its movement, is fire. Strife of opposites is the nature of all things, and harmony of opposites is what gives anything its temporary reality. As a result, the attributes of things are paradoxical; the way up and the way down are one and the same; sea water is pure for fish and impure for men.

Parmenides (*fl.* 495 B.C.) [Elea]. In the controversy over the permanent or changing character of the ultimately real, Parmenides argued for permanence. He made explicit the distinction between truth and opinion. Certain features of our thinking make it necessary, he argued, for us to hold that reality is unchanging. And we should note that thought and reality must be identical. (If it were not so we could never by thinking arrive at knowledge of the Real.) "One Thing are Thinking and Being," and in saying this Parmenides stated the basic doctrine of *idealism*. The features of thought and of reality which he noted were (1) what was afterwards called the Law of Identity ("Being doth be, and non-being is not"), (2) the Law of Contradiction ("Never I ween shalt thou learn that Being can be of what is not"), and (3) the Law of Excluded Middle ("Either there is or there is not").

The Law of Identity he interpreted as implying the unchanging, eternal character of the Real, a view which has been criticized extensively. Even now the Law of the Conservation of Energy holds that this is true quantitatively and shows the right interpretation of the meaning in Parmenides' thought.

Zeno of Elea (*c.* 490-430 B.C.) [Elea]. Zeno argued for the correctness of the position of Parmenides by showing the paradoxes implied by the opposing position. He maintained that careful analysis shows plurality and change to be appearances, not realities. Thus, if an area in space is divided into smaller and smaller parts, these finally become points and points have no content, hence they cannot be physically real; nor can the area composed of them be real. Likewise, Zeno insisted that motion is only apparent. An arrow in flight is at rest at each point in its path, and it is impossible for states of rest to add up to motion. The swift-footed Achilles in trying to overtake the notoriously slow tortoise found that he had a distance amounting to an infinite number of distances to cover, and so must fail. Objects which seem to move forward may actually be moving backward; thus, there is nothing objectively real about direction and rate of motion. Zeno originated problems which were puzzled over and not successfully handled until the development of the theory of limits and infinite series in mathematics during the seventeenth century.

Empedocles (*c.* 495-435 B.C.) [Agrigentum]. The suggestions of the Eleatic thinkers were too subtle for most minds and alternative doctrines were sought. Empedocles proposed a mediating theory, positing four irreducible substances—water, air, fire, and earth— each of which met the demands of the Eleatics for self-identity and contrast between being and non-being. At the same time the theory made intelligible Heraclitus' doctrine of change by regarding it as the mingling and separation of these elements when moved about by two forces, love and hate. The universe undergoes a cyclic process of evolution and devolution as one or the other force dominates. Empedocles held that biological evolution came about through the random combination of organs and then the elimination of those unfit for survival.

Anaxagoras (500-428 B.C.) [Clazomenae, Athens, Lampsacus]. In addition to agreeing with Empedocles in his general idea of the pluralism of realities, Anaxagoras thought the number should not be limited to four. He held that experience shows an indefinite number of kinds of substance, composed of particles which he called "seeds." For Empedocles' two forces, love and hate, he substituted one, namely Mind (Nous). Anaxagoras believed the seeds were originally mingled together throughout the universe. But Mind set all to rotating, as seen in the movement of the heavens. Thus, seeds became sorted, like to like, each finding its place, and evolved the universe. The orderliness of Nature he took to be evidence of a regulating mind (an early instance of argument from design to prove the existence of God). In reasoning that there are many kinds of seeds, he was nearer to the modern theory of chemical elements than was Empedocles. Anaxagoras was also interested in astronomy and declared that the sun was larger than Peloponnesus, that eclipses of the moon are caused by the interposition of the earth between the sun and moon, and that there are many inhabited worlds like ours. Also, he believed in biological evolution and in *panpsychism* or the omnipresence of consciousness in the universe. The theories of Anaxagoras were so unorthodox that he was accused of corrupting men by his teachings and, though he was a friend of Pericles, he decided to leave Athens.

Archelaus (5th cent. B.C.) [Athens, Miletus]. Archelaus was a pupil of Anaxagoras and has been said by some to have taught Socrates. He believed in matter in which mind was mingled, producing fire and water, whence springs life. In ethics he maintained that all judgments are matters of convention.

Philolaus (*b*. 480 B.C.) [Tarentum, Thebes]. The doctrines of Pythagoras were developed by Philolaus. His theory was expressed in terms of the limited and non-limited. He studied the properties of number (particularly the number 10) and its relation to the physical universe. The harmony of unlike elements constitutes the structure of things. Philolaus studied this harmony in the field of music. He believed that the universe has two aspects, the unchanging and the changing; the former is the dwelling of Mind. The soul is attached to the body which it leaves at death. Philolaus was also interested in physiology and medicine and is said to have been the source of much of Plato's knowledge of Pythagoreanism.

Melissus (*fl*. 440 B.C.) [Samos]. Melissus, the last important member of the Eleatic School, wrote in defense of Parmenides, arguing that Being is Perfect Unity, infinite in extent, with no rearrangement of parts, and not subject to change of feeling or to any other kind of change. Empty space, he held to be nonexistent. He lamented, too, the futility of the lives most men live, not seeking enduring wisdom.

Leucippus (*fl.* 440 B.C.) [Miletus, Abdera in Thrace]. A student of Parmenides, Leucippus did not follow his teacher's theory of monism. Instead he believed in a plurality of ultimate Reals, which he called "atoms." These material units, differing in size and shape, move in empty space (non-being). They constitute all things, even Mind, which perceives objects by way of "images" that float from things. The course of Nature is determined by "reasonable cause and necessity."

Note: By the time of Leucippus, the democratic spirit in Athens had developed so far that the right to participate in public life had been extended beyond all previous limits. Free citizens were expected to occupy themselves with the army in time of war and with the market place and the courts in time of peace. But democracy cannot live without an enlightened citizenry. In response to this need there appeared a class of traveling teachers, the Sophists, men who—according to the literal meaning of the word—were able to make people wise. They journeyed from city to city lecturing for fees, being entertained at the homes of the wealthy, and giving instruction in various subjects. Among the best-known of these Sophists were Protagoras, Gorgias, Hippias, and Prodicus—all of whom appear as characters in Plato's *Dialogues*.

Protagoras (481-411 B.C.) [Abdera, Athens]. The oldest of the Sophists was Protagoras. His specialty was civic virtue, the thing young citizens needed most to know about. This was a practical subject and practical success was his chief aim because he had lost confidence in human ability to attain absolute truth. He argued that there are always two sides to every question. The following statement was ascribed to him: "Man is the measure of all things, of things that are that they are, and of things that are not that they are not." (One possible meaning of this is the best that men can do is form honest opinions about matters but recognize that they are always personal and are based upon one's immediate sense perceptions.) Opinions are tested by the practicality they exhibit at work. Those that work are acceptable; those that fail are not. An opinion of his on such high and remote questions as the existence of the gods is: "I know not whether the gods exist or not; the question is difficult and life is short." For this idea Protagoras was accused of impiety and banished from Athens. His doctrine is an example of what is often called relativism in knowledge and ethics; it is also an expression of a form of humanism.

Gorgias (*b.* 480 B.C.) [Leontini in Sicily, Athens]. The second most noted Sophist was Gorgias. He agreed with Protagoras that man has no absolute knowledge. The best one can do is make his views as persuasive as possible. In this way, if he can win men to his opinions he can have his way in life. Regarding knowledge of the external world, Gorgias is said to have maintained that there is no evidence producible to show that anything exists. There is a gap between objects and the mind, and another gap between the mind's knowledge and the language which would express it. He believed that these gaps are unbridgeable. Therefore, each individual is shut up within the walls of his own life. Human experience plays upon the surface of things. Hence "sophistry" has come to mean the superficial treatment of any matter and the making of verbal distinctions that are of no real importance, and so forth.

Hippias (*fl.* 430 B.C.) [Elis, Athens]. Hippias was a Sophist who lectured on various subjects, including astronomy and mathematics. He is credited with discovering the curve called the quadratrix (a curve used in dividing an arc in a given ratio) in the study of the calculation of the area of a circle. In addition, he was interested in literature and music, and is said to have made collections of Greek and foreign literary works, and to have composed elegiac inscriptions and terse moral observations. He made a careful study of the text and of the episodes of Homer. He was also interested in archaeology and in politics, and he served as ambassador from

Elis to several other cities. In personality, Hippias was elegant and proud, boasted of his popularity, claimed ability to deliver an extemporary address on any subject, and was able to make all the things he wore. He charged high fees for lectures and instruction and aimed to make his pupils successful in debate, emphasizing the meanings of words and the importance of style. He also developed a system for aiding the memory. Hippias regarded Law as opposed to Nature, and a tyrant over man. Only a few fragments of his writings are extant.

Prodicus (*fl.* 430 B.C.) [Ceos, Athens]. Correct terminology was the special interest of the Sophist, Prodicus; in this way he influenced science. He taught ethics and civic affairs and served frequently as ambassador to Athens, where he made a very favorable impression. He claimed that the Sophist combined the virtues of the statesman and the philosopher. He also gave instruction in rhetoric and oratory to many wealthy young men, whom he charged large sums. Socrates said he had studied with Prodicus but could afford only a short course; however, he sent other pupils to him. In teaching rhetoric, Prodicus advocated moderate length for speeches. In ethics, he taught that the good is relative to the user, as in the case of wealth. In religion he held the opinion that the gods were derived from beneficial forces in Nature. A version of rhetorical exercise called *The Choice of Heracles* (between pleasure and noble work) has been preserved by Xenophon. Prodicus' *On Nature* has not survived.

Note: The efforts of thought before Socrates, then, ended in a multiplicity of opinions but nothing final and dependable. The basic question at this point in the history of thought was whether there is any way out of agnosticism and skepticism.

3   The Classic Period

In Socrates and his followers we meet the formulators of great philosophies which have constituted the major traditions of Western civilization. The Lesser Socratics, the Platonic Academy, the Aristotelian Lyceum, and the Hellenistic movements have their beginnings here. All later thought has to reckon with these, and a great part of it consists essentially of an elaboration or a commentary upon, or a criticism of, these movements. The questioning method of Socrates was the initial stimulus. There followed the elaboration and interpretation of his suggestions by less important followers; then the writings of Plato and the Academy; and, finally, the study of factual details by Aristotle and his school. Meanwhile, some tendencies from the Pre-Socratics continued without being absorbed entirely by the Platonists and Aristotelians.

Socrates met the relativism of the Sophists by seeking the conceptions which are common to the positions of those who disagree, thus formulating inductive definitions of the meanings of terms. He also saw in the effort to lead an intelligent existence the key to the only criterion of virtue acceptable to a rational mind. Plato presented a detailed portrayal of Socrates at work on ethical concepts, studied the nature and degrees of knowledge, attempted a description of the kind of society that would permit the leadership of the most capable, and discussed in general terms the nature of reality grasped by the process of thought. Aristotle filled out further details on the foundation laid by Plato, founded the disciplines of logic and metaphysics, elaborated individual and social ethics, and discussed fundamental features of literary criticism. The later systems centered around the attempt to find satisfaction in human living by self-control, refined enjoyment, or suspension of judgment on ultimate problems.

Socrates (469-399 B.C.) [Athens]. The influence of Socrates was felt when the Sophists were at their height. He agreed with them in so far as they insisted that man's primary interest is man. The attempt to fathom the nature of the universe before man understood himself seemed a hopeless task, and one that was hardly worth while. At least it was not to Socrates' liking.

With the Sophists he agreed that the obligation of man as the thinking animal is to ask questions about things, and exempt nothing from his questioning. "The unexamined life is not to be lived," is attributed to Socrates. However, the function of questioning is not destructive but constructive. It is destructive only in so far as rebuilding beliefs clears away the untenable. Inquiry should be for the purpose, first of all, of clarifying concepts. Without clear meanings for the terms we use no one knows what we are talking about. Such clarification is inductive; it is an attempt to find the universal principle which pervades the varied instances and cases to which terms are applied. This common core of meaning is the real meaning of a concept, its basic intention. The function of language is to communicate from individual mind to individual mind. Instability of meaning results in ambiguity. Understanding rests on univocity. Socrates was, thus, the advocate of clarity of ideas and inductive procedure. He agreed with Protagoras that man is the measure of all things, but man as the thinker in terms of universal concepts, not man as the creature of sense impressions which differ from each other as well as from the sense impressions of other persons. These concepts lie latent within the soul of man and are brought to explicit awareness by the process of questioning. This process he likened to the art of midwifery (maieutic) practiced by his mother.

Since the distinctive feature of the human animal is to think and the primary moral obligation is for man to make himself the finest specimen of manhood possible, it must follow that intelligence is the key to and the essence of virtue. To such extent that men are evil, they lack good judgment. No one would deliberately choose what would harm him. The trouble is that men do not understand what is their real good. So the situation seemed to Socrates. But claiming to have no knowledge himself, such as the Sophists professed, he went about questioning people, especially those who professed to know, in order to learn whether or not he was really right. He differed from the Sophists in that ignorance was not the end of his work, but rather the beginning. He was the perpetual student because there was always something more for him to learn, at least one more question to ask.

Thus, he became the gadfly of the Athenians, and it irritated them to find that their traditional beliefs after all were neither well-founded nor easily defensible. His position was misinterpreted, as by the comic poet Aristophanes in *Clouds,* to be the culmination of Sophistry. Taking advantage of unfavorable public opinion, a group of young politicians accused Socrates of corrupting the youth and teaching unlawful ideas about the gods. He was convicted (by a narrow margin) and, since his action was considered a capital offense, was required to drink the poison hemlock. Thus, Socrates died a martyr to the right of freedom of thought.

Democritus (460-370 B.C.) [Abdera]. The ethical philosophy of Socrates became the dominant interest of the Greek philosophers. But a divergent line, represented by Democritus, continued the interest of the pluralistic naturalists and further developed the atomistic theory of Leucippus. Democritus was the founder of the tradition in western thought which explained the universe in mechanistic terms. He agreed that atoms are inferences of thought and are too small to be seen. We live in a realm of appearances in daily life, the goal of which is to be as happy as possible.

Note: The atomistic tradition was submerged under the Socratic influence, which was continued by the Megaric, the Cynic, and the Cyrenaic groups.

Euclid (*fl.* 410 B.C.) [Megara]. The Megarics, led by Euclid (not to be confused with the geometer of a century later) held that Reality is one and is identical with the Good. It was the custom of this group to argue in defense of their position by refuting the opposite.

Antisthenes (*fl.* 406 B.C.) [Athens]. The Cynics, led by Antisthenes, emphasized the disciplining of human needs and insisted upon the severer aspects of living. Ethics, they said, is the essential part of philosophy, and the highest good is the chief concern of man. The highest good is found in virtue, and virtue is happiness. Virtue is attained by means of intelligent living and is expressed in independence of external circumstances and mastery of desires—limiting them to those that are indispensable for life. Work is the essential good and the source of satisfaction. The wise man is free from domination by custom and the acquisitions of civilization. His riches lie in this freedom.

Cratylus (5th cent. B.C.) [Athens]. Cratylus carried the Heraclitean doctrine of flux (*see* p. 13) so far that he believed one cannot enter the same river once. Acting consistently with this view, he is said to have renounced speech and merely pointed to things. He is also reported to have been Plato's teacher before Socrates.

Aristippus (*fl.* 395 B.C.) [Cyrene, Athens]. The third of the Lesser Socratic Schools, the Cyrenaic, under Aristippus taught that the feelings are the most certain facts of life; that pleasure is the good, no matter how it is induced; that immediate or sensuous pleasures are the most significant; and that the wise man lives in such a way as to secure the maximum of pleasure, which is gentle experience, since violent ones bring pain.

Plato (427-347 B.C.) [Athens]. Socrates' major influence was carried on by Plato, whose real name was Aristocles—the son of Ariston, a man of influential ancestry—who had studied the philosophy of the Pythagoreans, the Heracliteans, and the Eleatics, but whose chief association was that of seven years with Socrates. After traveling about the Mediterranean region, he returned to Athens and founded his own school (387 B.C.) in the Grove of Academus, whence it is called "the Academy."

Socrates' work and personality were Plato's chief inspirations, and in his writings (dialogues and perhaps some letters) Socrates stands as an important or central character. In the *Apology* Plato reports the defense made by Socrates before the court of Athens. Here

Socrates stands as the personification of the search for truth, the human mind asserting its right to freedom of thought, in the face of misunderstanding and opposition of special interests such as political prestige. He accepted temporary and physical defeat, confident that in the long run and in the final estimate "no evil can happen to a good man either in life or in death." In the *Euthyphro* Plato shows how shallow was the conception of piety and impiety, which was the basis of Socrates' condemnation. The firmness of the character of Socrates is presented in the *Crito*, where he resists the plea of his wealthy friend to escape from prison, to withdraw from Athens, and to live elsewhere. His sense of the obligation to remain loyal to the citizen's contract with other citizens— this contract constitutes the state—and to accept decisions against him as well as those favorable to him, leads him to remain and stand by his principles rather than to seek a brief extension of physical existence.

The type of discussions Socrates had carried on with the youth of Athens is seen in other works by Plato: the *Charmides*, a discussion of temperance or wise moderation; the *Laches*, a consideration of courage as a virtue necessary for life in peace as well as in war; and *Lysis*, a discussion of the nature of friendship and the possibility of its existence, in its best form, among any but virtuous persons.

In the *Ion* we see on the part of reciters of poetry the same lack of reflective appreciation of the nature of their work as was evident on the part of courageous generals in the *Laches*. The *Protagoras* presents a contrast between the lecture method of Protagoras and the question and answer method of Socrates, the topic under discussion being the possibility of teaching virtue. The basic suggestion is that if virtue is based upon something objective such as knowledge it can be taught, but if it rests on subjective intuition it must remain unstable in its teachableness. The *Meno* continues the discussion, with detailed attention to certain features of knowledge: the need for clear definitions, the difficulty of knowing when one has reached the true answer to a question, the necessity for an innate ability to "recall" ideas latent in the soul, the existence of degrees of knowledge, with a consequent distinction between opinion and truth. This work also shows that education is personal response to stimulating questions. Another aspect of the problem of knowledge is presented by the *Euthydemus,* which pictures the exploitation of ambiguities by the Sophists and shows the need for some kind of definite criteria for valid thinking. In the *Gorgias,* the discussion of rhetoric, as a means of gaining power, leads to the view that might makes right, but that what at first appears to be power may in the long run prove to be weakness. The *Cratylus* deals with the important instrument of communication—language. The problem of mastery over language and fulfillment of the obligation to submit to its established structure is not one easily solved. Why submit to its tyranny? Why not regard it as a product of convention and, therefore, subject to change at will? What would happen to communication if it were literally true that all things flow and that they flow at all times? The meaning of ideas must possess some lasting and social character, in order that communication may be possible.

Plato's *Symposium* presents the finite human soul as an aspiring being, longing for something it does not possess, and as a rational being, longing especially for ideal beauty and for wisdom, for an understanding of the realm of ideas. The final outcome of this is longing for immortality, which is discussed in the *Phaedo* in the setting of the last hours of the life of Socrates. Presented here are various interpretations of the nature of the soul (especially its unity and hence indissolubility) and the soul's mastery of the body in its voluntary acts. The decisive argument is that since the realm of ideas is the true homeland of the soul, and ideas are eternal, immortality, properly understood, must be a valid belief.

Life is an educative process, individual and social in character. As such it is largely the result of the individual's experience as a citizen of a state. From the state a man receives his education, which if rightly conducted fits him for his proper place in the social order. This process represents justice in its true sense. It recognizes individual differences in interests and in degrees of ability. In the ideal state, represented in the *Republic,* measures will be taken to secure for each person the best parentage possible, and an equal opportunity will be given for all to show strength and weakness. Those who show highest ability when tested will be given higher training, in which mathematics is central, until the most capable are discovered, and these will be regarded as most fit and able to direct policies of state. Because of the differing interests and capabilities among citizens, there will be three classes—the statesmen, the police and military, and the economic workers. The selective process will bring the philosophic minds to the top. They will understand the True and the Good and will be taught a truer conception of God than popular mythology gives; and they will be given noble as contrasted with ignoble conceptions of personality. The Good and the Beautiful will be one. If necessary to eliminate all favoritism, the family structure will be overruled and all children will be held in common by all parents.

The capable will ascend the ladder of degrees of knowledge and understanding till they reach the level of ideal forms. The state will be an aristocracy in the ethical, not in the economic sense, and will not sink, as actual states do, to timocracy (based on ambition), oligarchy (based on a privileged group), democracy (the incompetent average), and tyranny (arbitrary power). In the ideal society, citizens will embody in their lives and in the state the cardinal virtues of wisdom, courage, temperance, and justice, and will fulfill their destinies as immortal souls; then, passing a final judgment, they will go on to the realms of the blessed.

In the *Republic,* as in other dialogues by Plato, the principal themes are often developed through the telling of myths, tales in which the external circumstances are fabulous but which carry significant implications. The myth relieves the tendency toward over-literalness inevitable in question and answer and suggests that truth can be expressed in different forms.

The *Phaedrus* develops further the characteristic themes of the *Republic,* calling for a deep analysis and understanding of the Soul, which will enable the individual to escape superficiality in dealing with other persons and to attain mastery of truth. In literary composition, inspiration is as necessary as formal rules. The Soul is self-active, the origin of motion in all that moves, and thus an Ultimate Being. Its true home is in the realm of absolute ideas, from which it has fallen and to which a noble Soul strives to return.

Truth, as it is interpreted in Plato's *Theaetetus,* is not to be reached by sense impressions. Truth and falsehood are not to be identified by an easy intuition. A synthesis of intuition and analysis is necessary for the knowing process. This synthesis is exhibited again in the *Parmenides* where there is a severe criticism of pure and abstract rationalism, taken without reference to concrete experience. The two sides of knowledge must be taken together. Plato recognized the irreducible character of the relation of content to form, the uniqueness of "being an instance of some concept." There results, as another work, the *Sophist,* shows, a stratified conception of reality, reaching step by step from the infinite many to the ultimate one. In logic, it appears as the process of classification and definition. In the theory of reality, it allocates each aspect of experience to its proper place, allowing for relative degrees of reality and unreality, thus clarifying puzzles about the possibility of asserting what is not. In the course of the discussion Plato defines reality as the power to affect or be affected by another.

In the *Statesman* (or *Politicus*) Plato applies his newly formulated method of classification to the definition of a statesman, and returns to the suggestion of the *Republic:* the function of the legislator is to harmonize in society the various temperaments found in the citizens. The Divine Power has given man increasing responsibility for understanding and directing his own affairs. Another form of the harmonizing of elements is found in the Good as discussed in the *Philebus.* When the question is raised whether pleasure or intellect constitutes the highest good, the answer is neither alone. Both have their places, and the final good is both intelligent and pleasant. Beauty, symmetry, and truth stand together as aspects of the Good.

Plato interprets the whole concrete universe as a "moving picture of eternity" in the *Timaeus;* this is the embodiment by the Creator, in space and time, of the system of ideas which is eternal. The course of this embodiment is traced by empirical science which seeks to sum up observed facts under mathematical laws; the increasing understanding of these laws is the aim of mental activity as it evolves through time.

The *Laws* gives a less deductive description of the state than the *Republic* does. It contains a more mundane discussion of rules and regulations necessary for the conduct of society, and it makes more concessions to the ordinary human disposition, for not all men aspire after the ideal so intensely as does the philosopher. The work is a fruitful source of information about Greek customs and is full of wise observations on human life. Here again, Plato asserts that Ultimate Reality is of the nature of the Soul, the principle of life.

Thus Plato, beginning with the stimulus he found in the courageous life of Socrates, proceeded through detailed discussions of the virtues men commend to implications in the form of principles of conduct, individual and social; and through careful discussion of the meaning of knowledge, to a grasp of the nature of the concrete universe as an expression of the principles of knowledge. Consequently, he developed a complete philosophy, a picture of the nature of human personality and of the universe in which it lives.

Xenophon (*c.* 434-355 B.C.) [Athens, Persia, Elis, Corinth]. Xenophon was a talented Athenian gentleman, soldier, historian, and philosophical writer. He associated with Socrates for some time and then joined the expedition of Cyrus the Younger against his brother, Artaxerxes II (Mnemon). When Cyrus was killed in battle, Xenophon became the leader of the Greek mercenaries and led them across the mountains of Asia Minor, back to the Bosporus. He engaged in other expeditions also and never returned to Athens. In retirement near Olympia he found time to write a history, treatises on the training of horses and dogs, political treatises, and works of interest to philosophy. Among the last the most noteworthy are the *Memorabilia of Socrates,* the *Symposium,* and an

Apology for Socrates. Xenophon was not a keen philosopher, and while he preserved valued accounts of Socrates, he cannot be credited with great insight into the significance of the latter's activity. His version of the *Symposium* is thought to be influenced by the writing of Plato; the *Apology* is probably a spurious production of a later time. A work entitled *Education of Cyrus* has been said to have been written in opposition to Plato's *Republic*.

Eudoxus (408-355 B.C.) [Cnidus, Athens]. At one time a student in Plato's Academy, Eudoxus went to Egypt, to Asia Minor, back to Athens, and then to Cnidus. His work resulted from the Platonic interest in mathematics and astronomy. Eudoxus calculated the length of the year as 365 days and 6 hours and began the theory of concentric spheres to account for the motions of the planets. He also developed important theorems in geometry, using especially the "method of exhaustions," a contribution to the mathematical theory of limits.

Diogenes of Sinope (412-323 B.C.) [Sinope, Athens, Corinth]. One of the most widely known members of the Cynic School, Diogenes was noted for his application of the tenets of the school. He lived in extreme simplicity and used a tub for a house. Later he became a tutor to sons of Xeniades in Corinth. To them he taught the doctrine of self-control and avoidance of comfort because he considered pain and hunger useful in moral training.

Speusippus (*c.* 400-339 B.C.) [Athens, Syracuse]. A man of passionate temperament, Speusippus was a nephew of Plato and son of his sister Potone. He studied with Isocrates, but later became a pupil of Plato, and is supposed to have gone with him on one of his trips to Sicily. On Plato's death he became head of the Academy. Reversing the custom of Plato, he collected fees from his students. His main interest was in the theory of numbers: Reality originates in Unity and aims at the Good, both of which are independent of Mind and Reason. This Unity was not perfect in goodness, as evil also proceeded from it. He rejected Plato's theory of ideal numbers, holding only to mathematical and sensible numbers. In the theory of knowledge, Speusippus held to the interrelatedness of all things, and he attempted a classification of plants and animals. In ethics, he rejected pleasure as the highest good, yet did not believe it to be wholly bad. He wrote much, but only a fragment of *Pythagorean Numbers* has survived. His works were bought by Aristotle. Speusippus became crippled by paralysis and finally put an end to his life.

Xenocrates (396-314 B.C.) [Chalcedon, Athens]. The next head of the Academy, succeeding Speusippus was Xenocrates. He emphasized the Pythagorean doctrine of number in connection with the theory of ideas. He separated philosophy into three parts: dialectic, physics, and ethics. He recognized three classes of essences: the sensible, the intelligible, and an intermediate composed of both; these were, respectively, within the heavens, beyond the heavens, and identical with the heavens. He reasoned that the Soul is immortal, a self-moving number; happiness is the possession of one's proper individual virtue. All things are endowed with souls. In character Xenocrates was noted for his balance and integrity, which enabled him to resist all temptations to corruption and to convert Polemo from a roué to a virtuous man. On the witness stand, Xenocrates was exempted from the necessity of taking an oath. He accompanied Plato to Sicily in 361, and he went with Aristotle to Atarneus in 347. He served on three occasions as ambassador to Macedonia and later was offered citizenship, which he declined, under the Macedonians in Athens.

Aristotle (384-322 B.C.) [Stagira, Athens]. Among the students in Plato's Academy the most brilliant was Aristotle who had come from Thrace when a young man of seventeen. His father was physician at the court of Philip V of Macedonia. Aristotle was said to have been called "the reader" by Plato, and in the course of time he assisted in the instruction of the younger students. He continued for twenty years in the school, but left when Plato died and the Academy passed into the hands of Speusippus. Then he lived in Asia Minor and Mitylene; he was married and became tutor of Alexander (afterwards called "The Great") at Pella. He returned to Athens at the age of 41, where he opened his own school in the Lyceum on the eastern side of the city. There he taught until 323, the year of Alexander's death, when political opposition led to his withdrawal to Chalcis in Euboea.

Aristotle is noted for his writings on logic, physics, biology, psychology, metaphysics, ethics, politics, and literature. These works are marked by sober tone, subtle analysis, and empirical accuracy.

In logic, he produced the first textbooks ever written. They deal with some of the problems which Plato had suggested but had not considered in detail. In the *Categories,* he formulated a list of the basic ideas in terms of which thinking is carried on—substance, quantity, quality, etc. His work entitled *On Interpretation* considers the fundamental structure of the proposition, or unit of thought, and the problem of compatibility and incompatibility between propositions. In the *Prior Analytics,* Aristotle formulated the doctrine of the syllogism, or combination of two premises in order to draw a conclusion. This is the fundamental form of deduction and demonstration; but Aristotle also discusses the process of induction, by which a major premise is established, proceeding from known particulars to an as yet unknown principle. In addition, he reckoned with prevailing beliefs as premises and with difficulties in solving given problems. Intuitive reason is necessary, he said, for the grasp of ultimate principles. His *Posterior Analytics* deals with the logic of science which aims at truth and which deals with explanations, and is a field for application of the syllogism. It differs from dialectic, which deals with probable premises, and from eristic, which is concerned with success in debate. Here, Aristotle also discusses the processes of definition and classification. Another work, *Topics,* deals with argumentation on the basis of premises only probably true. In the *Sophistical Tests,* Aristotle discusses the basic fallacies into which men fall. Logic is thus concerned with the structure of thought, with the reasoning processes by which we attain truth. Centuries after Aristotle's death, these logical works came to be known collectively as the *Organon* or instrument (of science).

Aristotle stated that the *content* of thought is found first in the realm of the physical world, the world of objects in motion or undergoing change. The fundamental concepts here are those of substance, or form, and of the absence of a certain form. All the process of the physical world is reducible logically to this, the transition of substance from one form to another.

The particular "nature" of a given thing is constituted by its innate impulse to movement. Physical things are contrasted with mathematical entities in that the latter are formal only. Physical things are explained fully only when four questions about them are answered: (1) Of what matter are they made? (2) What form do they have? (3) What was their origin? and (4) Where do they lead? Replies to these questions give the material, formal, efficient, and final "causes" of concrete things. The efficient and final causes are also formal; hence, there may be a reduction to two causes—matter and form. Matter and form are relative, what is formed from one point of view being material for formulation beyond. At one extreme of the scale is prime matter without form, and at the other extreme pure form without matter. The concrete world is constituted by formed matter (the elements). There are inorganic matter, organic matter, and organisms. In addition to these, there is at times an aspect of occurrences which is irreducible. So far as we can see there is an element of chance in Nature. Nature is not ruled wholly by chance, as Empedocles had maintained, nor is it so constructed that every specific thing in it has a purpose. Nature is a realm where purpose and necessity interplay with each other.

Motion and change, Aristotle wrote, are the passage from potentiality to actuality. This is a continuous process, which involves the question of infinity. It also involves space, time, and the void. Primary bodies have their natural place, which they seek. Transformations come through the interrelation of the hot and the cold, the wet and the dry. Aristotle regards number as infinite in terms of possible addition, space as infinitely divisible though not infinitely divided. Time is infinite in both senses. Place is the inner limit of the containing body. He believed there is no void in the physical world, and one of his arguments, misunderstood by

Galileo and others, is that in a vacuum a heavy body would move no faster than a light one, for there would be no medium with which to reckon. Time is the numerable aspect of movement. There is no least instant of time as there is no least point in a line. He defined the notion of continuity as a relation in which the limits whereby entities touch each other are one. The puzzles of Zeno he solved by saying that although one cannot traverse an *infinite* space in a finite time, one *can* traverse an *infinitely divisible* space in a finite time. The motion of the physical universe is eternal, caused by a first mover which is itself unmoved and which attracts the physical world toward it.

In the process of change which occurs constantly in the physical world there are no absolute origin and cessation, only a transition of substance from one form to another. In his biological works, Aristotle held that an important change, which must be distinguished from mere alteration, is growth, a property of living things involving nutrition—or as we would say *metabolism*—and increase in size. So long as the organism can absorb more matter than is needed for the repair of waste tissue it will grow. Growth involves the mixing of the fundamental elements and is subject to the condition produced by the seasons. The course of growth is determined by inherent purpose, the action of an entelechy or essence which is fixed for each species.

There are three basic levels of life: the vegetable, with the functions of nutrition, growth, and reproduction; the animal, characterized by sensation, desire, and locomotion; and the human, with power of choice and theoretical inquiry.

Aristotle gave much attention to observing the main facts of animal life—describing structures, properties, and functionings. He dissected about fifty different animals and is especially commended for his detailed observations as to the embryology of the chicken. His view was that of the practicing physician striving to bring organs to the point of perfect functioning. Hence his interpretations are functionally teleological,[1] though the emphasis is upon apparent

---

[1] That is, interpreted with reference to the end to which they lead.

purposiveness in maintaining the species. Mechanistic details of operation, while true and important, are secondary, as in the artisan's production of an object.

In his *Psychology* he recognizes an animating principle in living things which is designated by the term "soul." This for Aristotle is a very concrete reality, manifested in various degrees by nutrition, sensation, and reason. Soul and body are closely interrelated in function, but soul is what gives unity to the functioning organism, the actualization (or entelechy) of the body. He considers in some detail the processes of nutrition and sensation, the association of the senses through common qualities, the functioning of images in consciousness, the production of movements, and the operations of thought. Reason is the capacity for grasping the formal and ideal aspects of experience. It has both active and passive aspects.

In the *Metaphysics* (Aristotle's own term was *First Philosophy*), he comes to the question of the basic characteristics of "being," the various senses in which things are real, and the fundamental principles in accordance with which things operate (logic, especially the law of freedom from contradiction). The category of substance is the most fundamental of all and is marked by the features of individuality, or combination of form and matter, and transition of potentiality into actuality. The final outcome of his thinking is the identification of metaphysics with theology. The Perfect Form is God, an essence which is not just the substance of the universe but an ideal toward which the universe "yearns" as the fulfillment of its being. But such fulfillment would be conscious realization of the meaning of this process. God then is ultimately thought, completely self-conscious, eternal, one, the highest form, and pure actuality.

The activities of man are of three kinds: theoretical (seeking knowledge), practical (regulating conduct), and productive (making things). The second, the practical, type of activity is in the field of ethics. The *Ethics* of Aristotle shows that, as the realm of Nature as a whole seems to be drawn toward some ideal, human beings also are drawn toward a highest end for man. This has a double aspect since man has an individual and a social character. What he is drawn toward in both ways is his highest well-being, the perfection of his nature or realization of his possibilities, *eudaemonia* or happiness. This is the *summum bonum*,[2] which is aimed at in all virtuous living. It is attained by the rule of reason in life, and reason counsels moderation in all things. Each specific virtue is a mean between two extremes, as courage is a mean between cowardice and foolhardiness, temperance between abstinence and overindulgence, and so on. Of course, one can not understand life perfectly nor be perfectly rational. Men are responsible beings to the extent that they can make choices and regulate their lives. Especially must they have a rational attitude toward pleasures, choosing the best and keeping them in their proper place. The highest goal of life is found in friendship, which unites the interests of persons with each other and fulfills the social demands of personality, and is perfected in the friendship of noble men. The ideal life is the life of reason, the fulfillment of human potentialities with clear understanding of life and of the universe which constitutes its setting.

In his *Politics* Aristotle shows that man by nature cannot be a pure individualist; he lives with his fellows and reaches his highest good in his relations with them; and he must understand the structure of the state of which he is a part. The state is an association rooted in the social character of man and has its origin in the simpler association known as the family. It is an organization aimed at helping man to realize his highest good—happiness. In what does eudaemonia or happiness consist? It consists in the life of contemplative leisure. This is nearest the divine and freest from external circumstances. The free man is self-reliant, but slavery is a natural thing, due to the superiority and inferiority of certain men, and can be an arrangement advantageous to both. Aristotle condemned the unlimited pursuit of wealth, beyond what is needed for living. He discussed the ideal commonwealth and the uses of

---

[2] Lat., the supreme good.

property, advocating moderation by way of education and law. The qualification for citizenship is ability to perform its functions. The acceptable forms of the state are kingship, aristocracy, and polity; the corruptions of these, respectively—tyranny, oligarchy, extreme democracy. Which form is best in a given case depends upon the character of the people. Good forms tend to deteriorate into bad ones when they do not perform their functions properly. The ideal state is the one which performs its functions to the maximum degree of effectiveness. Education should train upright citizens.

Aristotle's treatment of aesthetics is limited to rhetoric and poetry. The function of the former, as explained in the *Rhetoric,* is persuasion. For this purpose the techniques of argument are useful. The types of argument are based upon the occasions for its use— politics, declamation, and law—and must be related to the characters of speaker and audience. Attention must be given, also, to style and structure of language. In his *Poetics*, Aristotle says that poetry is fundamentally imaginative, growing out of a tendency to imitate. Its chief types are the epic and the tragic. Both must have unity, but epic has less limitation in the time of its action. Tragedy strives to arouse pity and fear in the audience who view the life of a heroic personality, pity for his past and present frailties, and fear for his future suffering; it aims to effect a purgation of these emotions. Plot, diction, and spectacle are essential elements, and must be controlled by a sense of fitness.

Before his death (at Chalcis in Euboea) Aristotle's thought ran the gamut of human interest, from logic, through the theory of Reality—of Nature, animals, and man—to the practical interests of ethics and politics, with the final touch given by the imaginative interests of literature. His influence in all these fields has been tremendous throughout the centuries. It is not surprising that Dante called him "the master of those who know."

Theophrastus (372-287 B.C.) [Lesbos, Athens]. The school of Aristotle (the Lyceum) was continued by a long succession of teachers through eight centuries. The first of these was Theophrastus. He was mainly interested in botany, though he wrote on other subjects, especially metaphysics, sensations, ethics, and literature and music. A description of a number of typical human "characters," which he wrote, is widely read.

From the time of the death of Aristotle non-Greek elements increasingly mingled with the Greek tradition. Alexander had tried by conquest to unite the known world. He had brought into closer touch with each other Greece, Egypt, Palestine, Babylonia, Persia, and even a part of India. He founded Alexandria which grew into a great city where the scholars of the time mingled. He and his successors overran Palestine and tried to Hellenize Jewish thought. From this time on, the Greek influence is evidenced in Jewish thinking, and the problem of reconciling the two traditions becomes a prominent one.

Then Rome conquered the world politically, at the same time yielding spiritually to Greek intellect. The Stoic philosophy became a technical basis for the common principles of government throughout the empire. Epicureanism was the personal philosophy of many literary minds. Probabilism became the most practicable philosophy of knowledge. Leading Roman thinkers visited the centers of philosophy in Greece and studied in the various schools. Theoretical Skepticism was professed by many. Other noble souls contented themselves with wholesome practical ethics, disregarding more subtle analysis.

Pyrrho (361-270 B.C.) [Elis]. The skeptical tendency which had been strong in the Sophists continued down through later centuries. One of the outstanding representatives of the movement was Pyrrho, who held that since sensations give only the appearance of things, there is no way to identify the things themselves. And since sensations and thoughts often disagree, there is no criterion by which to judge the truth; but appearances are sufficient for practical purposes. In ethical matters also there is no certain knowledge; men should not be too earnest in seeking to realize their ideals. Less anxiety would contribute much to their peace of mind. The wise man will suspend judgment on doubtful matters, check his curiosity, and moderate his passions. Pyrrho left no writings.

Book of Job. Some time about the second half of the fourth century B.C. the final editor of the Book of Job put it in its present form. An ancient story, represented by the prose sections in the first two chapters and the last, it raises again the question of human suffering. Job was a good man, conscious of his obligations toward God and of his responsibility for his family. He offered more sacrifices than rule required, lest his children unwittingly had sinned. He served God and his fellow men, looked after his affairs, and for a time was prosperous. Yet, in spite of all his uprightness, disaster came upon his household, a plague came upon him, and he suffered almost unbearably. Why was this?

As an explanation the hypothesis is offered that Satan was buffeting him, with the consent of Jehovah, to show the depth of his moral strength. Satan said that Job had good reason to serve Jehovah faithfully; he had not served God for naught. But Jehovah said that Job would not fail if prosperity were taken from him, or even if health were lost. According to the account, Job is sorely tried in body and mind. But he does not yield to his wife's suggestion that he curse God and die. Nor can he agree with his three friends who come to commiserate with him and who, holding to the old tradition that suffering must be punishment for sins, insist that surely at some time, even though he can not remember it, he must have done wrong. Actually, Job does not believe he has been guilty of sin warranting such punishment.

His protestation of innocence seems presumptuous to a fourth and younger friend, Elihu, who is introduced and maintains that he has an insight that has escaped older men. He believes the ways of Jehovah are too deep for men to fathom. Man cannot hope to understand the riddle of life, but he can solve his problem by trusting the wisdom of God and thereby find peace. The prose ending of the book shows Job materially more prosperous than ever, with a new family to replace the one that disaster had taken from

39

him—an unsatisfactory ending, which should have suggested satisfaction in spiritual poise in the midst of, and tested by, physical difficulty.

Epicurus (341-270 B.C.) [Samos, Athens]. A tendency of thought which continued the tradition of the Cyrenaics is to be found in the philosophy of Epicurus who started a school at Athens in 306 B.C. He wrote many works, but only a few have survived. For him the aim of philosophy was practical, and the goal of life was happiness. He made theory subordinate, an instrument for reaching the end which life seeks. According to Epicurus logic teaches that the test of truth is in sensations. Error never comes in immediate sense-perceptions, but in the judgments we make about them. We form hypotheses about the world, but these must be tested by appeal to sense experience; this conformity to sense is the test of truth.

In the field of conduct, pleasure and pain are the criteria of rightness and wrongness. What causes pleasure is good; what causes pain is bad.

The real world is a material one, as Democritus taught. It is composed of indivisible atoms, eternal in existence, differing in size, shape, and weight.

There is infinite space, and the atoms move constantly in it. They originally fell in straight lines, at the same rate of speed; but some swerved by chance and, as a consequence, there were collisions and a redistribution of the atoms. Out of this came the evolution of the universe, and plants, animals, and man. Epicurus' empirical theory of knowledge led him to conclude that gods must exist, for men have ideas of them and all ideas originate in sense perception. But the gods, too, are material and mortal beings, living in their own realm far from man. Being blessed and free from care, they do not concern themselves with men; this would be an annoyance. And man in turn does not need to concern himself about them.

Human biology and psychology are materialistic throughout. Even the soul is made of very fine, round, fiery atoms. At death the personality disintegrates; there is no immortality. Our aim should be to enjoy our existence, but this enjoyment must be of the kind that is appropriate to man. After all, man is a rational animal, not a brute beast. Mental pleasure is superior to physical, and for man the former is essential even to the latter. Pleasures are mixed with pains; moderation is necessary; subtle pleasures are less painful. The goal should be complete freedom from pain. Pleasures should not be deliberately sought, for too many desires make frustration inevitable. Virtue is necessary for happiness.

Epicurus wrote that social life evolves for the mutual advantage of individuals. Laws and institutions are the rules adopted by men for living together. There is nothing absolute about them. We follow rules for our own satisfaction. Since individual happiness is the goal of living, the wise man will participate in public life as little as possible, in order to avoid its disturbing influences and to minimize his own obligations.

Zeno of Citium (335-265 B.C.) [Citium, Athens]. The general trend of Cynic philosophy was carried on by Stoicism, which was founded by Zeno. It is reported that he was a merchant engaged in commerce, but, after having suffered shipwreck, he happened, at Athens, upon Xenophon's account of Socrates and began the study of philosophy. In time he established his own school in the *Stoa Poikile (Painted Porch)* at Athens; whence the name "Stoic."

Like Epicurus, Zeno held that ethics is the most important part of philosophy. To gain the good life men must know how to think straight and must understand the universe in which they live. Knowledge is built up inductively by generalizing sense experiences, and because of the similarity of all minds common notions are derived that are valid for all. As Heraclitus had suggested, human reason is identical in essence with a world reason that pervades the universe and keeps it in order. This is the Divine Reason, or the Logos. Conviction of knowledge comes when a feeling of finality, an irresistible impression, seizes one. The Stoics added to technical logic by discussing the hypothetical form of the syllogism.

Zeno, too, regarded the material world as the real world, but believed it is pervaded by force. Reality is designated by various terms: matter, fire, spirit, reason. All things are animated by a universal Soul. Pantheism is the true doctrine. From the World Soul all finite souls come; and they exist on different levels of perfection, from the human rational down through the animal and vegetable to the simple elements. The universe evolves through cycles, each culminating in a universal conflagration, ending one cycle and beginning the next. No souls are immortal beyond this point.

Human beings are very limited in their freedom, but the causal law of the universe goes through human beings as well as other things. As causal elements themselves, men are so far free and responsible. Man is free to determine his mental attitude toward life and what it brings him. His obligation is to live rationally and accept nature as an orderly expression of World Reason or Providence, submitting without complaint to what it brings. Zeno's own writings are fragmentary; for knowledge of his views we depend largely upon secondary sources of information.

Euhemerus (*fl.* 300 B.C.) [Messana, Macedonia]. Cyrenaic doctrine in the third century was represented by Euhemerus. He is noted for a *Sacred History* in which he interpreted the popular gods as originally heroes and conquerors and expressed the belief that religious myths are history distorted.

Strato (*fl.* 288-268 B.C.) [Lampsacus, Athens]. Head of the Lyceum after Theophrastus, Strato was called "the Physicist" because of his intense devotion to the study of nature. Actually, he excelled in every branch of learning. He wrote numerous works—on ethics, theology and metaphysics, animals, psychology, disease, logic—but they have not survived. He suffered from a lingering disease which caused him to waste away gradually and die. He insisted that Nature itself is God and explained all phenomena by the forces of heat and cold. All things have weight and are distributed in the universe according to their relative heaviness. Strato regarded time as continuous and therefore essentially different from number because the latter is discontinuous. He developed theories concerning the stars, earth, comets, and meteorological phenomena.

The activities of the soul are forms of motion, rational consciousness being its total activity. The immortality of the soul is doubtful. The ethical good is self-realization.

Arkesilaus (315-241 B.C.) [Pitane, Athens]. Leader of the Academy, Arkesilaus emphasized Plato's contention that there is no final truth in sense perception. He opposed the Stoic doctrine of the "irresistible impression" with the contention that even an "irresistible impression" sometimes proves to be false. Therefore, he concluded that the wise thing to do is to suspend judgment and not commit oneself to any belief as final. The best one can do is calculate probabilities and follow the highest. He wrote nothing.

Cleanthes (300-220 B.C.) [Assos, Athens]. Although he succeeded Zeno as head of the Stoic School, Cleanthes was not a brilliant man and added nothing to the doctrines he continued. However, he is of interest as the reputed author of *Hymn to the Most High,* which contains a line quoted by St. Paul in his discourse at Athens, recorded in Acts 17:28.

Timon (320-230 B.C.) [Phlius, Athens]. Our most direct knowledge of Pyrrho's skeptical doctrines is provided by Timon, who was a follower of Pyrrho. He wrote many works, the most noted being the *Satires* against the Greek philosophers.

Chrysippus (280-208 B.C.) [Soli, Athens]. A more creative man than Cleanthes, Chrysippus did so much to develop the Stoic School that he was called its second founder. He systematized the doctrines, argued for them, and fixed their terminology; but his writings have been received only in fragments.

Zeno of Tarsus (3rd cent. B.C.). A disciple of Chrysippus, Zeno was noted most for having raised a question about the Stoic conception of a universal conflagration.

Carneades (214-129 B.C.) [Cyrene, Athens, Rome]. In the second century B.C. lived Carneades, head of the Academy during the period when it turned to Skepticism. His teaching centers in the doctrine of probability, which was believed to be the utmost that human knowledge can attain. A man of tremendous influence, Carneades was opposed to the dogmatic claim to certainty held by some of his contemporaries, notably the Stoics, not only in theology and natural philosophy, but also in ethical standards. He left no writings.

Ecclesiastes (*c.* 3rd cent. B.C.). By an unknown author, *Ecclesiastes*—a name which is the translation of the Hebrew Koheleth—is commonly interpreted as "preacher." The author speaks of himself as a "son of David, king in Jerusalem" and, by tradition, has been taken to mean Solomon. The language used is that of the third century B.C., and the work comes possibly from various hands. Its central theme is the vanity of human existence, individual and social. As a man of wisdom, power, and wealth the author's judgments are impressive. The thought runs into Skepticism regarding ethics, immortality, and Providence. There is no great end achieved in life or in the universe. An endless round of repetition is all that is observable. There is no explanation of the world and no reliable connection between effort and outcome. Not even wisdom is finally satisfying. Man and beast pass and are forgotten. Wealth, wisdom, and work are all in vain. One should observe propriety and enjoy the moment. Soberness and patience are the best policies. Excess either of goodness or of wickedness is folly. *Ecclesiastes* belongs to a period of depression in Jewish life, and it indicates doubt about the validity of the prophetic hopes. The negative tone of the work is softened at the end and counteracted by a pious conclusion to the effect that all one can do is fulfill one's obligations and leave the outcome to God. Echoes of the Heraclitean doctrine of flux seem evident and take a form of Wisdom Literature. This work was written in the Alexandrian period of thought.

Aristobulus (181-146 B.C.) [Alexandria]. Aristobulus, a Jewish theologian, argued that Greek wisdom, even from the earliest, was derived from the Pentateuch. He regarded God as invisible and transcendent, working through His powers to affect the world.

Clitomachus (180-105 B.C.) [Carthage, Athens]. The teachings of Carneades were continued by Clitomachus.

Panaetius (180-112 B.C.) [Rhodes, Rome, Athens]. Stoicism was introduced into Roman thought by Panaetius, who is said to have taught the doctrine in a form influenced by the teachings of Plato.

He reformulated Stoicism to meet the criticisms of Carneades.

Posidonius (130-51 B.C.) [Apamea in Syria, Rhodes]. A pupil of Panaetius, Posidonius was a great traveler, a very learned man, and a follower of the Stoic School, though influenced to some extent by Plato and Aristotle. He taught a doctrine of high spirit and noble desires. Cicero was one of his pupils. Fragments of a historical work have survived to us.

Andronicus (*fl.* 70 B.C.) [Rhodes]. Andronicus, a head of the Lyceum, was noted as editor of the works of Aristotle and Theophrastus and as a writer of paraphrases and comments on Aristotle.

Titus Lucretius Carus (96-55 B.C.) [Rome]. Titus Lucretius Carus was the outstanding advocate of the philosophy of Epicurus. His poem *On Nature* is one of the chief sources of our knowledge of Epicureanism. It was published by Cicero. In content it teaches atomism, in line with Democritus and Epicurus. The universe is formed by the falling of material atoms through empty space, deviating at times from a straight line. Even the soul is material, deriving knowledge of the external world by way of images given off from bodies. The gods, too, are material beings, living untroubled somewhere in space and not disturbed in their bliss by the affairs of men. At death, Lucretius wrote, the body dissolves and all is at an end; there is no hereafter to be feared.

Cicero (106-43 B.C.) [Arpinum, Rome]. Cicero was one of the chief figures of Roman philosophy. Most of his life was centered in Rome where he was famous as a lawyer and orator and held various public offices, finally reaching the consulship; he was one of the last to hold the office before its importance was ended by the Empire.

Cicero declared that his primary interest was in philosophy, but that, because of the necessity for making a living, he was compelled to take up the practice of law and politics. When, in his late years, he was forced out of public life he withdrew to his villas, especially the one at Tusculum, and, gathering a group of friends, he discussed philosophical questions with them. He tried to be the medium of transmission of Greek culture to the Romans and had a great influence on philosophical terminology. He had studied under various philosophers, at Athens, Rhodes, in Asia Minor, and Rome. He also prided himself upon having discovered the tomb of Archimedes in Sicily and having restored it to a fitting condition.

Cicero wrote roughly in imitation of the *Dialogues* of Plato and drew freely from Plato's ideas, using the titles *Republic* and *Laws*. He translated the *Timaeus* and *Protagoras* and on a sea voyage composed a summary from memory of the logic of Aristotle. Suggestions from the Stoics also had great influence upon him. Among his works are *Tusculan Disputations, The Academics, On Ends* (Good and Evil), *On the Nature of the Gods, On Divination, On Fate, On Old Age, On Friendship,* and *On Duties.*

In his theory of knowledge Cicero was impressed with the limitations of human capacity and, with Carneades and others of his time, maintained that probability is the best that is achievable in human thinking and human principles of conduct; yet he believed that certain innate tendencies of thought and behavior are present in all men and serve as guides in living. He also thought that the common convictions of mankind in theology and ethics should be respected. "Fairness" is the keynote of ethics.

His metaphysics and theology are more Stoic than otherwise, as the result of his calculation of the most probably true system. He believed in the dignity of man, the freedom of the will, and the immortality of the soul.

In ethics Cicero combined the Stoic stern sense of duty with Plato's cardinal virtues and Aristotle's doctrine of the usefulness of honors and wealth in the service of morality.

Aenesidemus (*fl.* 80-50 B.C.) [Cnossus, Alexandria]. The doctrine of Skepticism was carried on by Aenesidemus. He formulated ten modes of argument or tropes, showing the contradictory character of experience and the impossibility of certain knowledge. He is said to have criticized especially the concept of causality and to have maintained it to be meaningless.

Quintus Sextius (*b.* 70 B.C.) [Rome]. In the second half of the first century B.C., a school begun by Quintus Sextius combined certain features of Stoicism and Pythagoreanism. His primary emphasis was upon ethics. He believed that the life of man is a constant battle against folly and that man should reckon or consider his own moral status every day.

Sotion (1st cent. B.C.) [Alexandria]. Sotion was one of the chief followers of the school founded by Quintus Sextius and was also famed as a teacher of Seneca.

The Early Christian Centuries

The beginning of what is called the Christian Era was marked by a movement new to Greeks and non-Greeks alike. To the Greeks it was "foolishness," to the Jews a "stumbling block." It claimed to be a fulfillment of the Jewish messianic hope and, at the same time, an embodiment of the Greek principle of Reason (Logos) in human personality. It centered in the personality of Jesus of Nazareth, who taught in the spirit of freedom from legal form, which had marked the prophets of Israel (in contrast to the priests), and professed not to destroy tradition but to give it new meaning.

The impression made upon the apostles is recorded in the letters and Gospels of the New Testament. The defense of the faith against the opposition of the Jews, the Skepticism of the Greeks, and the rival doctrines of Stoicism and Neo-Platonism is found in the writings of the Church Fathers. These writings culminated in the works of St. Augustine, who was a leading influence in determining the content of the beliefs of the Church. The successful advance of Christianity and the progressive formulation of its doctrines continued until the seventh century when its next formidable rival appeared in Islam.

The conquests of Alexander the Great had spread the Greek language over the eastern end of the Mediterranean area, including Judea and Egypt. An inferior kind of Greek became the language of commerce and of learning.

Philo Judaeus (*c*. 20 B.C. - 40 A.D.) [Alexandria]. An outstanding representative of this Hellenistic culture was Philo the Jew, who combined a knowledge of the literature which had been handed down from Classic Greece—including Plato, the later Pythagoreans, and the Stoics. His great problem was to reconcile the claims to truth of the Jews and of the Greeks. Giving first place to Moses, he thought that the Greeks must have derived their knowledge from the Mosaic law. He solved many apparent disagreements by adopting, on an extensive scale, the allegorical interpretation of the Scripture.

He regarded God as transcending human description, except in the very general terms that He contains all perfection and pervades all things with His reality. Philo believed God becomes partly intelligible to men by way of the Logos or Rational Principle referred to by the Greeks. He calls this Logos the first-born son of God, the highest archangel, and the high priest. It is also the spirit of wisdom, the creative word of God by which all things were formed out of chaotic matter. Man is a twofold being, spiritual soul and material body. His ideal should be to escape from the body and its evil influences and to rise again to God. This the wise man strives to do, and he succeeds in some degree with divine help. Typical of Philo's works are the essays *On The Creation of the World* and *Allegorical Interpretation of Genesis.*

Jesus (*c.* 5 B.C. - 29 A.D.) [Nazareth, Jerusalem]. The Christian movement began not as a philosophical doctrine but as a practical way of living and was based upon an intuitive belief in the character of God as a benevolent ruler of the universe, expressing himself by incarnation in the human form of Jesus. The Gospels relate that Jesus, after a few years of teaching the doctrine of love of God and the obligation of kindliness on the part of man toward man, suffered crucifixion through the intrigue of the traditional Jewish leaders. The latter accused him of starting a seditious movement against Rome, thus calling him to the attention of the Roman Procurator and bringing about his death. But according to Christian belief he was raised from the dead and, after an interval of a little over a month, was taken on high to remain until a final judgment of the world should occur.

The ethical teachings of Jesus centered in an attitude of sympathy for one's fellow men. He summed up the whole law in the two quotations from Jewish thought: "Thou shalt love the Lord thy

God with all thy heart and soul and mind; and thy neighbor as thyself" and "The true satisfaction of life is not to be found in ambition and material possessions; the kingdom of heaven is within you."[1] Jesus sided with the prophets rather than with the priestly tradition, emphasizing the spirit more than the letter of religion.

Paul (?-64 A.D.) [Tarsus, Jerusalem, Rome]. The Christian movement was at first opposed violently by Saul of Tarsus, a Jewish Roman citizen. But after a transforming experience near Damascus he, in time, became the most ardent advocate and leader of the Christian movement and, as such, changed his name to Paul. He traveled through Palestine, Asia Minor, Greece, and finally to Rome, preaching the doctrine. In Rome, the tradition of the Church tells us, he was beheaded and was buried just outside the wall of the city. Meanwhile, Peter had also gone to Rome, had met death as a martyr, and had been buried where the cathedral of St. Peter now stands.

The most fundamental point of Paul's teaching was the substitution of a belief in salvation by faith in Jesus for salvation by obedience to the Jewish law. He, as Jesus had, emphasized the spirit more than the letter of religion and taught that those who established a right relation with God would automatically do good to their fellow men. Paul instructed that the Jewish religion and others were preliminary stages toward a universal doctrine which would contain the truth and ideals that all men naturally seek. He also developed an interpretation of history to the effect that the truth which had been presented to the Jews, and had been rejected by them, had passed to the gentiles. But Paul foretold a time when the two would come together in the end as a common truth, valid for all. As an organizer of churches, he gave many instructions for the details of conduct. The significance of these was greater within the larger framework of the movement. His letters to the Corinthians, to the Galatians, and to the Romans are central works.

---

[1] Luke 12:15; 17:21.

Seneca (3 B.C. - 65 A.D.) [Córdoba, Rome]. Contemporary with Paul was L. Annaeus Seneca, who studied Stoic philosophy at Rome and became an eminent lawyer. For a time he was banished to Corsica, by the Emperor Caligula, but he was recalled to become the tutor of the youth who later became Emperor and was called Nero. Personal enemies aroused the jealousy of the Emperor, and because of this Seneca committed suicide about a year after Paul had been beheaded. Seneca left many essays on practical ethics in the spirit of Stoicism, on such themes as *Wrath, The Brevity of Life, Mercy,* and *The Happy Life.* He also wrote a popular work on astronomy and a number of tragedies in imitation of the Greeks.

Barnabas (?-c. 75) [Cyprus, Jerusalem, Antioch]. Barnabas, "Son of Exhortation" was the name given Joseph. He was a member of the Church at Jerusalem and was related to Mary the mother of John Mark, whose house in Jerusalem was a gathering place for Christians. Barnabas sold his property and contributed the proceeds to the communal life of the Christians; he has been noted as a good man and effective preacher. He sponsored Paul when the Church at Jerusalem feared to accept him. With Paul, he took relief to those suffering from famine in Jerusalem; then he went with him on the first missionary journey into southeastern Asia Minor. He supported Mark when Paul disapproved of the fact that Mark left the missionary group at Pamphylia on the first journey; at first he sided with Peter in the dispute with Paul over the need for Gentile Christians to accept the Mosaic law, but later he supported Paul. Barnabas' prominence in the early Church caused many works to be ascribed to him, among which are: *Epistle to the Hebrews, Epistle of Barnabas,* and a *Gospel;* these ascriptions are not commonly accepted as authentic.

Pliny the Elder (23?-79) [Como, Germany, Spain, Rome]. Gaius Plinius Secundus, or Pliny, was well-educated in Rome, served as a soldier and traveled widely in Germany, and then devoted himself to study and writing on oratory and grammar for the guidance of his adopted nephew. In addition he studied law and wrote *Training of a Knight* and essays on German and Roman history. His *Natural History* is the only one of his numerous writings that has survived. It includes astronomy, geography, zoölogy, botany, anthropology, etc., with digressions on human institutions, inventions, fine arts, and his own philosophic creed of Pantheism in which he rejected belief in immortality. Pliny is not too discriminating in what he accepts, and his meaning is not always clear, though the work is a source of information on many topics. He leaned heavily on Aristotle in his thinking. He became a personal friend of the Emperor Vespasian. Pliny was in command of the fleet when Vesuvius erupted and overwhelmed Herculaneum and Pompeii. His interest aroused, he landed to observe the occurrence and was suffocated by the vapors of the eruption.

Gospels. The growth of Christian literature produced the biographies of Jesus—the Four Gospels according to Mark, Matthew, Luke, and John. The Gospel according to Mark, which is supposedly based on Peter's story and shows close contact with both the Romans and the Jews, presents Jesus as the Great Martyr; Matthew's Gospel describes Jesus as the fulfillment of the Jewish messianic hope; the Gospel of Luke speaks of him as the Universal Saviour; John's Gospel points out Jesus as the incarnation of the Principle of Reason in the universe (the Logos of the Greeks), using phrases of the kind employed by Philo.

Plutarch (46-125) [Chaeronea, Athens, Rome]. A teacher and lecturer on philosophy, Plutarch was commemorated by his fellow citizens for his upright character. He is noted for his *Parallel Lives* of famous Greeks and Romans and for essays on many subjects, including education, successful living, natural history, archaeology, and religion.

Clement (*fl.* 95) [Rome]. One of the Apostolic Fathers, Clement was the first of fourteen bishops of Rome having this name. He was identified by Origen with the "fellow laborer" mentioned by St. Paul in his letter to the Philippians 4:13, though the identification is not well established. Two letters ascribed to Clement have come down to us, but only the first is regarded as authentic. Written about 95 A.D., and directed to the Church at Corinth, it deals with unsettled conditions within the Church—jealousies, strife, and disorder. It cites instances of repentance and obedience from the Old Testament and of humility on the part of great men, together with injunctions toward peace, love, and good organization in the Church.

Epictetus (60-117) [Hierapolis, Rome, Nicopolis]. Epictetus was born a slave but became a freedman and expounded the Stoic doctrine in his *Discourses.* He taught the recognition of the course of Nature as the will of God, recommended the acceptance of that which is not within man's power—holding that the human will is the one thing under man's control, whereby he can determine the attitude he takes towards the vicissitudes of life. His outlook should be cosmopolitan, that is, he should view all men as if they had similar capacities and similar problems and, therefore, as if they were essentially equal.

The first half of the second century was the sub-apostolic period, i.e., the time of those who had known the apostles personally, but not Jesus himself. It was a period when the new Christian movement was competing with the older doctrines (Greek philosophy, the mystery religions, and the Jewish tradition) and defending its faith.

Ignatius (*d.* 111) [Antioch, Rome]. Among the important men of his time was Ignatius, who in his letters urged the unity of the Church through obedience to the bishop and other authorities and warned against preachers of heresy. He died a willing martyr in the Colosseum at Rome. Several of his letters have come down to us.

Polycarp (69-155) [Smyrna]. A letter that has survived relates the beliefs of Polycarp, which were similar to those of Ignatius, and also speaks of the apostolic succession, i.e., continuously passing on the spiritual power and the authority to each generation by actual hand to hand contact. Polycarp, like Ignatius, died a martyr's death.

Papias (*fl.* 140) [Hierapolis]. A companion of Polycarp, Papias is referred to as a preserver of tradition. He wrote an exposition of the Lord's Oracles which was quoted extensively by later **writers.**

He tells us that the original source of the Gospel of Matthew was a collection of the sayings of Jesus, made after the practice of the time, in the Hebrew language. The fact that all our Gospel manuscripts are in Greek suggests that they are, for the most part, later compositions based upon earlier documents which have not survived. The fragment of papyrus which was discovered at Oxyrhynchus, Egypt, near the end of the nineteenth century—containing a page of sayings of Jesus, in Aramaic—may be a remnant of such an earlier work.

Nicomachus (*fl.* 130) [Gerasa]. The Neo-Pythagorean philosopher Nicomachus wrote *Introduction to Arithmetic,* which was frequently used and commented upon by later writers. He also wrote a work on the Pythagorean theory of music, *Enchiridion Harmonikes.*

Marcion (*fl.* 140) [Sinope, Rome]. A wealthy shipowner, Marcion was converted to Christianity. He felt a great contrast between the God of the Old Testament and that of the New Testament and maintained they were not the same. His interpretation of Jesus was Docetic,[2] i.e., Jesus only *seemed* to suffer in the crucifixion. He regarded Paul as the foremost interpreter of Christian doctrine and rejected those New Testament books which did not seem to agree with his own views. He set up his own church, based on democratic tenets, and regarded the ascetic life and celibacy as the ideal existence. He also modified the ritual and allowed repeated baptisms. A work entitled *Antitheses* set forth his doctrines. The Church did not accept his views.

Flavius Justinus (105-165) [Nablus, Rome]. Called Martyr and a student of the philosophy of Plato, Aristotle, and the Stoics, Justin held that a rational power, the Logos, is produced by God and disseminated through all men. They have thereby an innate consciousness of God. All men who live according to this Logos are Christians regardless of where or when they live, even though they be called atheists. He thought the philosophers of Greece must

---

[2] *Docetae* were those who believed that the body of Christ was not material, but was a phantom (appearance) of celestial substance.

have read the writings of Moses and the prophets. But he maintained that a special revelation came through Jesus as Christ and that human immortality is a gift from God. He believed that there will be a first resurrection and a reign of Christ for 1000 years and, later, a general resurrection. His chief work is his *Apology*.

Numenius (*fl.* 160) [Apamea]. Numenius was an eclectic Platonist, who was influenced also by Pythagoras. He called Plato a "Moses speaking Attic Greek." In his theology he distinguished three levels of divinity: the Principle of Being, the Principle of Generation, and the World. He believed that the soul existed before this life and became involved in the body because of its guilt. Numenius wrote a work entitled *Differences among the Various Academics*.

Marcus Aurelius (121-180) [Rome]. Marcus Aurelius, a ruler of the Empire, found relief from the cares of State in Stoic doctrines. He left us *Meditations,* a collection of essays which gives a series of maxims for maintaining peace of mind through belief in a rational world order directed by Providence, and for being unafraid of death which is a natural occurrence. He thought that one must bear in mind the kinship of man with God and free one's interests from concern with circumstances, resign oneself to the will of God, and love all mankind. Aurelius endowed chairs of philosophy in the four schools in Athens; he opposed the theological teachings of Christianity.

Lucian (*c.* 125-200) [Samosata, Athens]. In a work entitled *Dream,* Lucian tells that his parents intended him to be a sculptor. But by a careless stroke he spoiled a slab of marble and because his teacher, who was his uncle, cudgeled him, ran back to his home. In the night two beautiful women appeared to him, representing literature and handicraft, respectively, and appealed to him to follow one field or the other. He decided in favor of literature, and his success therein was publicized as an example of what a poor boy could achieve. He traveled throughout Greece and the Roman Empire as a popular lecturer. He wrote rhetorical pieces, literary criticism, biography, romances, and the *Satirical Dialogues.*

which are the most mature and characteristic of his works. His early writing was so light in tone as to appear trifling. Later, he developed more depth, but still there remained a sarcastic and even cynical tone, directed against the shams of life, the superstitions of traditional religion, the pretensions of the philosophers, historians, and litterateurs of the day. Lucian was noted for his brilliance in expression but also displayed a degree of hardness in attitude.

Tatian (2nd cent.) [Syria, Rome]. Tatian, a pupil of Justin, was a teacher of philosophy and rhetoric who became a strong opponent of heathen culture. Eventually he became one of the so-called Gnostics,[3] who were frequently attacked by early Church Fathers. He interpreted God as the World Reason, revealing itself and working creatively through the Logos. Man consists of body, soul, and spirit, is possessed of freedom, and is corrupted by sin. His chief works are *Address to the Greeks* and *Diatessaron*, which is a combination of the Four Gospels into one, for a while used extensively in the early churches.

Galen (130-200) [Pergamum, Rome, Sicily]. A very learned man and an eclectic philosopher, Galen studied in all the important schools, but was most influenced by Aristotle. He traveled widely and gave lectures and demonstrations. He was a strong critic of almost all the contemporary doctrines and, consequently, gained much ill will. He wrote commentaries on Plato and Aristotle and is credited with recognizing in *On the Number of Syllogisms* the fourth figure of the syllogism as independent of the first. His medical work, which was marked by accuracy of observation in anatomy and physiology, was based upon dissection of animal organisms. In these sciences, his theories were dominant until the seventeenth century.

Irenaeus (*c.* 130-202) [Asia Minor, Rome, Lyons]. Inspired by Polycarp's preaching, Irenaeus became Bishop of Lyons and one of the leading Fathers of the Greco-French church in southern France.

---

[3] Believers of the theory that salvation comes through possession of a superhuman knowledge.

He was an influential preacher, and his writings give valuable information concerning doctrine. He expounded the beliefs of various sects, especially those of the Valentinian Gnostics (who interpreted the universe in terms of wisdom embodied in a system of eons), but opposed Gnosticism as such. He attempted to reconcile dissident sects with the Church and went to Rome in behalf of the Montanists (a group which resisted the tendency of the Church to merge its spiritual functions with those of a temporal and a secular nature). Irenaeus emphasized the Gospel of John, reinterpreting the divine Logos as the "voice" of God speaking to man. His interpretation of Catholic doctrine emphasized the unity of faith, the grace of truth, the apostolic succession, and the exposition of the Bible by the Church. Later, he had great influence, especially in the Greek Church. An unverified statement from the sixth century says that he suffered martyrdom. Irenaeus wrote *Against Heresies,* which exists in fragments in Greek and in a Latin translation; he also left the earliest catechism in existence, known only in an Armenian translation.

Sextus Empiricus [Rome?]. Toward the end of the second century a highly important set of writings connected with the name of Sextus Empiricus was produced. Unfortunately, we know nothing of his personal life. There are no external accounts of him and no internal references sufficient to indicate where he lived, though Rome seems the probable place. The designation "Empiricus" indicates that he was a physician. He wrote in Greek, and his writings are our main source of knowledge about the skeptical movement. In *Outlines of Pyrrhonism,* he states the tenets of Skepticism and the reasons for them. In comparing his position with those of other schools, Sextus Empiricus quotes at length from many writings which would otherwise have been lost. Thus, his work has been one of the chief sources of first-hand information about them. He became involved in the question of the criterion of truth and strongly influenced many of the most basic problems in the theory of knowledge and in logic. His writings give very penetrating criticisms of the ideas of God, cause, motion, goodness, and other conceptions. In *Against the Logicians* and *Against the Ethicists,* he canvasses the whole field again and again.

Clement of Alexandria (*d.* 216) [Athens, Alexandria]. Christian thinkers in the second and third centuries continued to defend their faith against the traditional beliefs of Greece and Rome and to clarify the doctrine of the Church, which was being more thoroughly organized. One of the most conspicuous names is that of Clement of Alexandria. He was a conscientious student of Greek literature (especially philosophy) and of the Bible, and when converted to Christianity he attempted to do for the reconciliation of Greek and Christian thought what Philo (*see* p. 48) had attempted for Judaism and Greek philosophy. He became head of the Catechetical School[4] at Alexandria. His *Miscellanies* is one of our important sources of knowledge about the early Greek philosophers. Clement regarded Christianity as a system of philosophy, which had advanced beyond the Greeks, and for which the Greeks had been a preparation (through the Logos which enlightened all men in some degree). He judged that in the course of personal growth one develops through faith and love to knowledge. Clement emphasized that "neither is knowledge without faith, nor faith without knowledge."

Tertullian (*c.* 160-230) [Carthage, Rome]. Well-educated in Greek literature (especially Plato) and Latin, and possessing a legal education which influenced his attitudes, Tertullian was converted to Christianity and studied the Bible and the Church Fathers. He had such authority that he has been called the creator of Christian Latin literature; his writings mark the point of change from the use of Greek to the use of Latin as the chief language of the Church Fathers. It was in *On the Flesh of Christ* that he used the famous thought "it is certain because it is impossible." He thereby put faith above reason. Late in life he became a Montanist and separated himself from the orthodox church. The Montanists reacted against the secularizing of the Church. It was at this time

---

[4] Organized for instruction in the rudimentary doctrines of Christianity.

(200 A.D.) that the organization and fundamental forms of worship of the Catholic Church became definitely established.

Alexander of Aphrodisias (*fl.* 200) [Aphrodisias, Athens]. Head of the Lyceum, Alexander was also the most outstanding commentator on the works of Aristotle, especially on the *Metaphysics.* As a consequence, he was called "Exegete" or "Expounder." His works had great influence on later interpreters; they were translated into Latin and most of them have been preserved. He also wrote treatises of his own: especially *On Fate,* against the Stoic doctrine of necessity; and *On the Soul,* against immortality of the entire soul, identifying the active intellect with God. He attempted to restore the doctrines of Aristotle to their original form, free from the accretions of Neo-Platonism.

Note: The third century A.D. was marked also by the culmination of a new interest in the study of Plato, an interest centering in those aspects of his teaching which emphasized esthetic experience and suggested a mystical grasp of reality.

Ammonius Saccas (170-241) [Alexandria]. Because he was said to have been a Christian porter originally this philosopher was called Ammonius Saccas. He was self-taught in philosophy and is credited with being the formulator of the Neo-Platonic doctrine which became a kind of mystical religion and a strong rival and opponent of Christianity. He wrote nothing, but depended upon oral teaching to establish his doctrine.

Diogenes Laërtius (3rd cent.). In his book *Concerning the Lives and Opinions of Eminent Philosophers,* Diogenes Laërtius provides information about the lives and personalities of philosophers and summaries of their views. Though not a scholarly work, it is one of the sources always considered; it is our only source of knowledge about some ancient thinkers.

Origen (185-254) [Alexandria, Caesarea, Tyre]. Origen was the most brilliant pupil of Clement, whom he succeeded as head of the Catechetical School. Origen studied Plato and the Stoics, worked under the Neo-Platonists, and also became acquainted with Hebrew writings. His greatest activity was in the textual criticism of the Scriptures. He published a *Hexapla* of the Old Testament (an edition with six versions in parallel columns). He wrote many commentaries. One of his works, *Against Celsus,* is a significant presentation of his views opposing Gnosticism. Another, *Fundamental Doctrines,* undertakes to systematize the beliefs of the Church. Origen advocated the attainment of peace and superiority to all travails through contemplation and self-knowledge. In his interpretations of Scripture he emphasized the ideas involved rather than the historical details. He placed great emphasis upon the Logos doctrine in interpreting the personality of Jesus as the Christ. Various points in his teachings came into disfavor with the Church later on, and his influence and high position waned accordingly.

Sabellius (*fl.* 220) [Lybia, Rome]. The leader of the *Modalists*[5] was Sabellius. This group believed in the unity of God, regarding the three Persons of the Trinity as three aspects of the same Being which manifest themselves successively as Creator, Redeemer, and Life-giver. The doctrine implied *patripassionism,* i.e., that the Father suffered crucifixion through his identity with the Son. The theory was declared to be heresy; opposition to it crystallized in *Trinitarianism.*[6] None of Sabellius' works are known.

Cyprian (*c.* 200-258) [Carthage]. As well as being an outstanding leader in the Church of Africa, Cyprian studied law and taught rhetoric at Carthage. He was a wealthy man, converted to Christianity, who gave much of his fortune to the poor, devoted his time to study, and was made bishop in 248. It was a troublous time. Cyprian tried to establish strict discipline, but met with strong opposition. His later life was marked by a struggle to maintain a balance between the faction that supported leniency and the faction that advocated severity for those who had lapsed in faithfulness during the time of persecution. Then he was censured for his op-

---

[5] Believers that Father, Son, and Holy Spirit were three modes of appearance of the one God.

[6] The belief that God is one substance, but three persons individually; the ultimate mystery.

position to Rome over the acceptability of baptism by heretics, and he maintained that the Bishop of Rome did not have judicial authority over other bishops. He suffered martyrdom by the sword under Emperor Valerian. Cyprian's best known work is *Unity of the Catholic Church,* which he based on the Universal Church, not the Roman episcopate. He emphasized the importance of infant baptism and of penance; he believed that there is no salvation outside the Church.

Plotinus (205-270) [Lycopolis, Alexandria, Rome]. The great pupil of Ammonius, Plotinus was also an organizer of the ideas of Neo-Platonism. His teaching is in many respects akin to that of Philo, except that it did not emphasize Jewish tradition. For Plotinus, also, God is the Ultimate Reality, a spirit so lofty that He is beyond all finite description. The nearest approach is to speak of Him as One, the Infinite Cause from which all finite things emanate. He is beyond all thought, all goodness, all beauty—as we know things. The Universe exists as an overflow from the superabundance of His reality, as water flows from a spring without diminishing the supply.

There is a scale of reality, leading from God down to matter. Matter is negative, relatively unreal, phenomenal only, and marked by imperfection and evil. The chief steps down from God are Mind (Nous), soul (life), and matter. In thought, distinctions are begun; this plurality continues increasingly down to material beings. The human soul is part of the World Soul; it is in part Mind, in part sensory being, and is distracted by affinities in both directions. The fall of man is the descent into a sensory being.

Plotinus developed details of psychological theory, dealing with sensation, imagination, memory, and thought. This last brings knowledge of ideas, the spiritual, and the divine. He also had a theory of beauty, which reveals the spiritual essence of things shining through in splendor. In statements of later Neo-Platonists ideas became Gods, constituting a form of polytheism.

Salvation consists in communion with and reuniting with God. It comes partly through turning attention within, the practice of unselfishness, and learning to think in general terms, which helps the soul toward this mystic union. Social life also increases this unselfishness. But the final step comes only in a mystical experience which is very rare, and which Plotinus himself had attained only three or four times in his life. His view of society was based on Plato's *Republic*.

The doctrine in Plotinus' *Enneads* (gathered together by Porphyry) was for many years a strong rival of Christianity in the Roman Empire.

Amelius Gentilianus (*fl.* 250) [Etruria, Apamea]. Plotinus' lectures were recorded by Amelius Gentilianus in a hundred books along with his own interpretations, which emphasized the unity of all souls in the World Soul. In opposition to the interpretations of Porphyry, he wrote on the differences between Plotinus and Numenius, gathering together the works of Numenius. He also wrote commentaries on some of the works of Plato. None of his writings has survived.

Mani (215-276) [Ctesiphon, China, India]. A doctrine combining elements from Persian and Christian doctrines was developed by Mani. He represented the universe as the scene of conflict between light and darkness, good and evil. This struggle began before the appearance of man, but continued throughout human history. The light works through the illumination of great leaders like Buddha and Zoroaster. Jesus in his crucifixion was a symbol of salvation. Final salvation comes through an ascetic life which withdraws from contact with matter. Mani died a martyr, being flayed and crucified as a result of the opposition of the Magi. The doctrine of Manichaeism became widespread in Asia and Europe, exercising an influence down to the Reformation. Fragments of Manichaean documents in Persian, Turkish, and Chinese have been found in Central Asia.

Porphyry (233-304) [Tyre]. The writings of Plotinus were edited by Porphyry, resulting in their present form. Porphyry also continued the teachings of Neo-Platonism, adding some thoughts of his own in favor of asceticism and in opposition to magic and demon worship. His later fame came through *Introduction to the Categories* (an introduction to the *Logic* of Aristotle) which included a statement about universals that became the topic of a lengthy controversy during the Middle Ages. "Porphyry's Tree" is a classificatory scheme of types of Being, from the most comprehensive or universal to the individual.

Hermes Trismegistus (Thrice-great Hermes). The name *Hermes Trismegistus* is applied by certain Greeks to the Egyptian God Thoth. He is reputed to be the inventor of magic and alchemy, the originator of Egyptian culture, the patron of literature, and the scribe of the gods. According to Clement of Alexandria, he composed forty-two "Hermetic" books on a variety of subjects, ritual and otherwise. In the third century particularly, the name was prefixed to a collection of writings based upon Oriental, Stoic, and popular Greek conceptions. Their tone was Mystical and Gnostic, representing various systems. Together they comprise the *Corpus Hermeticum.* Many similar works now lost are slightly known through quotation by various authors. A few were translated into Latin or Arabic. This doctrine presented the idea that God is infinite, incomprehensible, nameless, and above all Being and the Ground of Reason, which are created by Him; capable of being known only as one becomes identical with Him. The Hermetic principle is akin in some respects to Neo-Platonism.

Arnobius (*fl.* 300) [Numidia, Sicca]. Arnobius, a professor of rhetoric, wrote *Against the Nations,* which is of interest because it shows the type of arguments used for converting the heathen. It attempted to answer the complaint that the calamities and disasters of the time were due to the impiety of the Christians. Arnobius exhibited little knowledge of the Bible, seemed to know only the life of Christ, and never quoted the New Testament directly.

Lactantius (260-340) [Sicca, Nicomedia, Treves]. Although he was of Italian descent, Lactantius studied rhetoric in Africa under Arnobius and then taught it in Nicomedia. The Emperor Constantine invited him to come to Gaul to tutor his son. His principal work consisted of seven books entitled *Divine Institutions;* in the first three he criticized paganism, and in the last four he maintained the necessity of Christianity for true wisdom and virtue. He had Manichaeist tendencies which were not approved by the Church. He was noted for his fine Latin style, was called the Christian Cicero, and was a great favorite in the Middle Ages.

Eusebius (260-340) [Caesarea]. Disagreement over the interpretation of the personality of Jesus led the Emperor Constantine, who had espoused Christianity in 313, to call a general council of the Church officers at Nicaea, in Asia Minor, in 325 A.D. A central point at issue at the council was the status of Jesus in the Trinity. The Secretary of the Council of Nicaea, Eusebius, made the introductory address. His *History of the Christian Church,* completed about the time of the council, is one of the most important documents of early Church history and preserves accounts of many persons and events not otherwise known. His *Praeparatio Evangelica* evaluates the writings of Greeks and Hebrews (in favor of the latter) before Christianity. The *Demonstratio Evangelica* justifies the Christians for going beyond the Jews in new principles and practices. Eusebius also wrote a *Chronicle* of universal history with comparative tables of chronology and used the allegorical method of interpreting Scripture.

Jamblichus (270-330) [Syria, Rome]. A pupil of Porphyry and continuer of the Mystical doctrines of Neo-Platonism, Jamblichus also developed a defense of polytheism, with a hierarchy of super-terrestrial (celestial, subcelestial, and natural) gods, besides angels, demons, and heroes. He wrote *On the Pythagorean Way of Life* for the purpose of introducing a system of worship of Pythagoras. He was also interested in numbers as symbols of hidden truths and relations.

Chalcidius (*fl.* 315) [Rome?]. A part of Plato's *Timaeus* was made available by Chalcidius in a Latin translation, accompanied by a *Commentary,* and thus helped to bring some direct knowledge of Plato's thought to the Western world. Chalcidius was probably a Christian philosopher. He was called a "very illustrious man."

He rated Plato very high, regarding him as a standard authority and placed Aristotle next. He was an eclectic Platonist, cited dialogues other than the *Timaeus,* but mingled Christian ideals with Platonic; he was influenced also by Stoicism and Neo-Platonism, as well as Jewish and Peripatetic thought as transmitted by Posidonius. His translation of Plato is not exact.

Arius (280-336) [Alexandria]. Presbyter of his city, Arius held that the son was subordinate to the Father in the Trinity; he was of like nature (*homoiousios*), but not identical (*homoousios*). Arius maintained strict monotheism rather than Trinitarianism. Arianism, represented by his *Deposition,* was declared heresy at Nicaea and again at the Council of Constantinople in 381, but it continued to be advocated in various quarters.

Athanasius (298-373) [Alexandria]. The Trinitarian point of view was supported at Nicaea by the patriarch of the city, Athanasius. He held that the Son is equal to the Father, not inferior. This was fundamental to Trinitarian doctrine, that accepted by the Church. Athanasius' life was one of controversy, including five periods of exile. His *Incarnation of the Word of God* was an important work written early in his lifetime.

Apollinaris the Younger (310-390) [Laodicea]. When the Emperor Julian forbade the teaching of the classics, Apollinaris wrote the content of the Old Testament in the form of the poetry of Homer and Pindar and wrote the New Testament as Platonic dialogues. Apollinaris held that Christ was wholly Logos and had no human soul. Although this view was condemned, he had many followers. A volume, *Paraphrase of the Psalms,* is in existence.

Aphraates (4th cent.) [Edessa]. Aphraates composed a number of expositions of Christian doctrine in Syriac, arranged acrostically in his *Homilies* (337-345). His quotations from Tatian's *Diatessaron* give us our most extensive knowledge of this work. In general, his views are similar to those of the Greek Church. According to some reports he died a martyr.

Victorinus (*fl.* 350) [Africa, Rome]. Known chiefly as a grammarian, Victorinus taught rhetoric at Rome, and in his late years became a Christian. He taught Jerome, and his translations of Plotinus and other Neo-Platonists were used by Augustine. He also wrote commentaries on Pauline Epistles and a treatise against the Arians and the Manichaeans. He closed his school when Emperor Julian forbade Christians to lecture on polite literature. Later, he was commemorated by a statue in the Forum of Trajan.

Julian (331-363) [Milan, Paris, Constantinople]. The Roman Emperor Julian, who had in his youth been subjected to a monastic education, revolted against it (preferring Greek literature and philosophy) and avowed himself a pagan (361), but promulgated an edict of toleration. However, he chose most of his officers from those who followed the old Greek religion; he required the Christians to contribute to the rebuilding of the pagan temples. He wrote a book, *Against the Christians,* all copies of which Theodosius II ordered destroyed.

Ambrose (*c.* 340-397) [Trier, Rome, Milan]. The patron saint of Milan, Ambrose was educated at Rome, studied law, entered the civil service, and became an excellent administrator. Called to be bishop in 374 while still a catechumen, he hesitated but finally accepted. He was gentle and wise and was loved by the people, but he was severe toward all transgressors. He was strongly influenced by the Greek theologians and emphasized the ascetic life. Modifications in the Church's ritual, which are still retained at Milan, were made by Ambrose. He opposed efforts to introduce Arian (*see* p. 65) worship into the churches. Also, he was a friend of Monica, mother of Augustine, and was successful in winning Augustine to the Church. He wrote commentaries on the early Old Testament narratives, Psalms, and the Gospel of Luke; he wrote treatises *On Repentance, On the Holy Spirit,* and *On the Christian Faith;* he also wrote several hymns. The Ambrosian Library in Milan was named after him.

Jerome (340-420) [Strido, Rome, Bethlehem]. The great linguistic scholar of his day, Jerome was interested also in biblical archaeology and in the Church Fathers. He wrote commentaries on the Scripture and was commissioned by Pope Damasus to re-translate the Bible into Latin. His work became the basis of the Vulgate Version used in the Roman Catholic church. He established the distinction between canonical[7] and apocryphal[8] books. A bitter spirit often marked his controversial writings.

Jovinian (*fl.* 388) [Milan, Rome, Boa]. A noted heretic, Jovinian opposed Monasticism, excessive fasting, and celibacy, though he himself was unmarried. He maintained that Mary was not a virgin after bearing Jesus, also that divine blessing does not depend upon good works, and that a true Christian can not sin wilfully. The opinions he advocated at Milan were opposed by Ambrose, Jerome, and Augustine. He went to Rome, where he and his followers were excommunicated, and the Emperor Honorius enacted laws against the Jovinians. In spite of his banishment to the Island of Boa off Illyria, his ideas spread, and a number of nuns married. No writings have been handed down from him; our knowledge rests on Jerome's treatise against him.

Donatus (4th cent.) [Casae Nigrae]. When a bishop in North Africa, Donatus and his followers (Donatists) maintained that the sacraments were invalid when administered by unworthy persons and that known sinners should be denied Church membership. This position was later opposed by Augustine and rejected by the Church. Donatus' writings have been lost.

Plutarch of Athens (350-430). The Neo-Platonic doctrine was taught in the Academy by Plutarch. He believed that Aristotle should be studied before Plato and that points of agreement should be emphasized. He wrote an important commentary on Aristotle's *Psychology* in which he held that souls do not perish with the cessation of sensation. Plutarch also believed in the effectiveness of theurgic rites (magic, supposed to rest on divine power).

Macrobius (*fl.* 395-423). Little is known of the details of Macrobius' life except that he was Greek. He is credited with two works: *A Commentary on Scipio's Dream,* and *Saturnalia.* The former is

---

[7] Books accepted as genuine and inspired.
[8] Books of doubtful ("hidden") authorship and authority.

based on a passage from Cicero's *De Republica,* dealing with the immortality of the soul; it was read a great deal in the Middle Ages. *Saturnalia* is a dialogue which gives valuable observations on history, mythology, grammar, and literary criticism. Macrobius traced all forms of worship to that of the sun. His quotations are valuable sources of information about earlier writers.

Note: The period of Church history from 100 A.D. to 400 A.D. is commonly called the Patristic Period, that is, the period of the Church Fathers. It reached its culmination in the personality and work of St. Augustine.

Aurelius Augustinus (354-430) [Tagaste, Rome, Milan, Hippo]. Born Aurelius Augustinus near Carthage—of a Christian mother, Monica, and a Roman father, Patricius, who became a Christian late in life—he was afterwards called St. Augustine. He was educated in the Latin and Greek classics; thereafter he took up Manichaeism, then Neo-Platonism. He went to Rome to establish a private school and afterwards to Milan. Here, influenced by the preaching of Ambrose, he became a Christian. At this point, he returned to Africa, was made Bishop of Hippo, and became perhaps the most vigorous mind of the Middle Ages, doing much to formulate the most widely accepted interpretation of the doctrines of the Church.

Among the writings Augustine produced just before becoming Christian are dialogues modeled on Cicero's *Tusculan Disputations,* and given the titles *Against the Academics, On the Happy Life,* and *On Order.* In *Against the Academics,* reflecting upon the theory that probability is all that we have in human knowledge, he arrived at the conviction that degrees of probability can be measured only if there is an absolute standard by which to measure them. He sought this absolute standard.

From the early days of his Christian life came the *Soliloquies,* in which he examined his own state of mind and sought for the basis of certainty. Here, he made the famous statement that the one thing most certain was his own uncertain state of mind.

The human mind gains knowledge by two methods: first, by proceeding inductively from sense data to the causes of things, moving progressively toward a First Cause of all; second, by looking reflectively within and studying one's inner processes. Things are real when they participate in form and number, unity and order. Knowledge of an external world comes only through activity of the soul; knowledge is possible only because of a divine light illuminating the soul.

All judgments, by making comparisons of one thing with another, imply an absolute standard. This absolute standard is the mind of God, the source of all enlightenment, virtue, and beauty. Augustine believed as Plotinus had declared that God transcends human comprehension; hence our knowledge of Him is more negative than positive.

The universe is not an emanation from God, but a creation out of nothing. All things were created instantaneously, but not in their full reality. Only in time are the potentialities fully actualized. Time itself was created; there was no time before creation.

Evil is involved in the universe as a negative element. According to Augustine, lack of knowledge, of power, and of beauty constitutes evil. It has its place in the structure of things and therefore contributes to the final goodness of the universe.

In his interpretation of human existence Augustine held that the first man was created with free will, able to choose between right and wrong. But the consequence of his evil choice has passed down through the race so that man has become ever more deeply involved in sin; it has now become original to his nature. By Divine Grace the will of man can be made free to know the truth and serve the good again. Some persons are predestined to salvation by the grace of God. Without this choice of some men for salvation all men would be lost through their sinfulness. He thought that only by this Divine Grace could someone like himself, who had been sinful in his youth, be changed to a servant of God. (When Augustine looked back upon his own life before his conversion, and reviewed it in his *Confessions,* he judged himself to have been very sinful. Probably his conduct had not been worse than that of most other young men of his time.)

69

After becoming an official of the Church Augustine participated in controversies over questions of policy and interpretation. Against the views of the Donatists (*see* p. 67), he advocated the acceptance of those persons who returned to the Church after lapsing on account of persecution. Opposing the opinions of the Pelagians (followers of Pelagius, *see* below) he insisted upon a limited degree of individual freedom and responsibility.

Augustine discussed the Trinity by means of an analogy with the three fundamental phases of personality—knowing, willing, and feeling—although ultimately he believed it to be a mystery beyond human comprehension. God is the perfection of knowledge, power, and good will. His attributes are omniscience, omnipotence, and supreme kindliness.

The assembly of those who are saved both in this world and beyond constitutes the *city of God,* which is contrasted with the *city of the world.* The terrestrial city is concerned with the maintenance of man's material existence. The city of God is concerned with his spiritual destiny. Man's loyalty is twofold and often involves him in conflicts. There was, even at the time of Augustine, a conflict between the acceptance of the traditional gods of Rome and of the God of Christianity. He was sure the city of God ought to and finally would dominate all things. He believed that men must ally themselves with it because of its holiness, unity, apostolicity, and catholicity. His doctrine became the theoretical basis of the papacy's claim to authority.

Pelagius (*c.* 360-420) [Britain, Rome, Africa, Palestine, Lydda]. From Scotland or Ireland Pelagius journeyed to Rome, where he criticized the low standard of morality which was prevalent. He argued his interpretation by showing the powers of human nature and attacked his opponents' contention of human weakness. He insisted that Augustine's doctrine of total depravity and bondage of the will undermined all human effort. He held that obligation implies ability. His own religious life had been free from intense internal struggle. Withdrawing to Africa, then to Palestine, Pelagius lived quietly for a while until summoned before Bishop John of

Jerusalem on the charge that he believed that man could be without sin with the help of God; but the prosecution broke down. Pelagius held that the will is free at each moment regardless of previous conduct. He rejected the doctrine of original sin and the theory that all men were injured by the sin of Adam. He embraced the idea that freedom is the possession of the heathen as well as the Christian; that man can keep perfectly whatever law he knows. Pelagius also thought that grace can aid man after he has made his initial decision. This view was counter to that of the Church. He wrote *On the Trinity, On Free Will,* and *Commentary on Paul's Epistles.*

Hypatia (365-415) [Alexandria]. Hypatia, daughter of a noted mathematician, was a famous woman teacher of Neo-Platonism. She was well-known for her beauty, character, and intellectual acumen, and attracted many students. The ill will of the Christians was aroused against her, and they have been said to have seized her in her carriage, dragged her to a church, stripped, murdered, dismembered, and burnt her. She is said to have written commentaries on the *Arithmetic* of Diophantus and the *Conics* of Apollonius.

Martianus Capella (*fl.* 430) [Madaura, Carthage]. An encyclopedia called *Satyricon* was written by Martianus Capella and was much used in the Middle Ages. It formulated the sevenfold classification of the liberal arts: the trivium—grammar, rhetoric, logic; and the quadrivium—arithmetic, geometry, astronomy, and music. He theorized that the solar system is heliocentric.[9]

Nestorius (*fl.* 428) [Germanica, Antioch, Constantinople]. The patriarch of Constantinople, Nestorius opposed the use of the phrase "Mother of God" in reference to Mary. He held that there were two natures in Christ; that Mary possessed only one, the human, and the Holy Spirit possessed the other. She was mother of the human, not the divine, nature in Jesus. This became a topic of debate and was declared heresy at the Council of Ephesus in 431. Yet the belief spread, and Nestorian churches developed through Armenia, into Persia, and beyond. *The Bazaar of Heraclides* is

---

[9] The sun is a center, and the solar system revolves around it.

71

Nestorius' defense of his interpretation of Jesus' personality.

Proclus (411-485) [Constantinople, Athens]. Proclus was the last important teacher of Neo-Platonic philosophy at Athens. He wrote commentaries on Plato and attempted a systemization of Neo-Platonic teachings, exaggerating some of their features; he also wrote *On Providence,* and *Fate,* and the *Existence of Evil,* and works on astronomy and mathematics.

John Stobaeus (5th cent.) [Stobi]. John Stobaeus made a collection of extracts for the instruction of his son. These selections have come down to us under two headings: *Ecologues* (physical and moral extracts), and *Florilegium* or *Anthology.* Though sometimes confused in classification, this collection is very valuable and preserves parts of the original writings of five hundred early philosophers.

Pseudo-Dionysius the Areopagite (5th cent.) In the fifth century appeared a set of works ascribed to *Dionysius the Areopagite,* who was converted by Paul's teachings in Athens. The writings are strongly influenced by Neo-Platonic teachings and include the *Celestial* and *Ecclesiastical Hierarchy, Concerning Divine Names,* and *Concerning Mystical Theology;* they also include ten letters to men of the Apostolic Age. The works combine Neo-Platonism and Christianity into one system, developing a series of mediators between God and man and a hierarchy of officers and laymen in the Church. They also discuss the attitudes of God and the function of symbols. These writings had great influence upon later theologians, artists, and literary minds.

Dionysius Exiguus (6th cent.) [Scythia, Rome]. The canons and decrees of the Church councils, and decretals of the popes were collected by Dionysius Exiguus, who thus had great influence on Canon law in the West. He was also an astronomer and mathematician and introduced the reckoning of time according to the Christian Era, a method which has been used since.

Boethius (480-524) [Rome, Pavia]. A statesman and a philosopher, Boethius became consul in Rome under Theodoric. His upright character and just administration aroused ill will, and he was accused of designs against the Emperor. While in prison he composed his best-known work, *The Consolations of Philosophy*—partly in prose, partly in poetry—representing a dialogue between himself and a personified form of philosophy, and dealing with God, Fortune, Evil, and Freedom. It was translated into many languages and has been read widely. In addition, Boethius translated much of Aristotle's *Logic,* wrote commentaries on the writings of Porphyry and Cicero, and worked on his own logical doctrines, as well as on arithmetic and music. All these writings were very influential in the schools. Several theological treatises also are ascribed to him. Though innocent of the accusations against him, Boethius was eventually put to death.

Cassiodorus (*c.* 490-580) [Scylaceum]. The Roman historian whose writings afford much of the existing information about the Kingdom of the Goths, in Italy, is Cassiodorus. He was of noble family, held high offices, and became Secretary to Theodoric the Ostrogoth, after whose death he became chief minister to the queen. He wrote a *History of the Goths,* which is known only through an epitome. A collection of state papers entitled *Various Letters,* which he wrote as Secretary, throws much light on the affairs of the Church, the condition of the people, and the administrative system of the kingdom. He was the most outstanding scholar of his day. Late in life he founded a monastery near his birthplace and spent the rest of his life in study. (The monks were required to spend their time in meditation, study, copying of manuscripts, and translation into Latin of Greek works, among which was *The Antiquities* of Josephus. Their studies included both sacred and secular learning.) The writings of Cassiodorus included an essay *On the Soul,* an encyclopedia of arts and letters, and commentaries and notes on the Psalms, Paul's letters, the Acts, and the Apocalypse.

Damascius (*fl.* 529) [Damascus, Alexandria, Athens]. The last head of the Academy was Damascius. When it was closed by Justinian, he went, with six colleagues, to the Persian court of Chosroes, but in 533 he returned with his companions. He was a follower of the Neo-Platonic tradition. His chief work was *Difficulties and Solutions of First Principles.*

73

Simplicius (*fl.* 529) [Cilicia, Athens]. Simplicius was teaching at Athens when the schools of philosophy were closed by Justinian in 529. With Damascius he took refuge for a while at the court of Persia and later went to Alexandria. He is noted chiefly as a commentator on Aristotle and earlier philosophers.

Evagrius (*c.* 536-600) [Epiphania, Antioch]. The legal adviser to Gregory of Antioch was Evagrius, who is noted chiefly for his *Ecclesiastical History* covering the period from 431 to 593. This work gives many valuable excerpts from original documents and throws light on the history of dogma.

Gregory of Tours (538-594) [Clermont-Ferrand, Tours]. While Bishop of Tours, Gregory showed himself a firm administrator in both ecclesiastical and secular affairs. He wrote various works, such as *On Miracles* and biographies of the Church dignitaries, but the most important was his *History of the Franks*.

Gregory the Great (540-604) [Rome, Constantinople]. Although prefect of Rome, Gregory was so attracted to the religious life that he resigned his position, founded a number of monasteries, and became a monk. After a diplomatic period in Constantinople he returned to Rome, where he wrote lectures on the books of the Bible. He set out as a missionary to England, but was recalled and later was elected Pope. He was a great administrator, increased the authority of the See of Rome, and made the Papacy a temporal power. He also sent missionaries to England. Gregory revised the liturgy of the mass and is credited with the revision of Church music. He also clarified the doctrines of angelology, purgatory, the Eucharist, and relics. His *Moralia* was widely used.

Isidore (570-636) [Seville]. The seventh century was the time of Isidore, who was Archbishop of Seville, Spain. He was prominent in Church councils, but his fame rests chiefly on his voluminous works. His *Twenty Books of Origins or Etymologies,* which preserves much of the past knowledge of the Greeks and Romans, was widely used by schoolmen. He also wrote biographies, a work on physical philosophy, and *Catholic Faith.*

Maximus the Confessor (*c.* 580-662) [Constantinople, Scutari, Thrace, Colchis]. Although he had served as Secretary under Emperor Heraclius for twenty years, Maximus entered a monastery at Scutari and became its abbot. He was an advocate of orthodoxy against Monothelitism (the doctrine that there was only one will in the personality of Christ, not two). For his opposition to the Monothelite doctrine he was banished to Thrace. After seven years he was recalled and commanded to accept Monothelitism; when he refused, his tongue was cut out and his right hand cut off; then he was banished to Colchis, where he died in 662. Later he was canonized as a saint. His writings consisted of exegeses, comments on the Church Fathers and on the doctrines and controversies of the Church, and ethical and ascetic treatises.

6   From Mohammed to Anselm and Aquinas

A new influence in the thought and the history of Africa, Europe, and Asia came with the rise of Islam in the first half of the seventh century and with its spread during the two following centuries. The Church continued to teach and to send missionaries into Northern Europe as far as the British Isles. The growth of the schools occurred in this period, leading on the one hand to heretical questioning, and, on the other, to analysis, clarification, and formulation of the details of doctrine. Powerful leaders in the Church strengthened its organization and policies. But Semitic minds, Arabic and Jewish, were increasingly active. They studied Aristotle especially, increased his influence in the atmosphere of thought, and were also in closer touch with Persian and Indian thought than were Christian minds. The Church's initial opposition to this influence soon gave way, and it was used in the service of Christian theory which led to the great summations of Alexander, Albert, and Thomas. Meanwhile, there was a revival of interest in Mysticism, the religious technique which makes the individual conscious of the presence of God without the mediation of an organization.

Mohammed (570-632) [Mecca, Medina]. In the seventh century lived Mohammed, who came from a religious family and spent his early life in commerce. He made a number of caravan trips to Syria and Palestine, where he met with Jews and Christians. He was dissatisfied with the moral conditions of his people and, at the age of forty, felt called to preach a new doctrine—of one absolute God, Ruler, and Judge of the world. He denounced idolatry and infanticide. For a long time he had little success and, in 622, fled from Mecca to Yathrib, later called Medina (The City). There he had increasing success. Adding military power to preaching, Mohammed reorganized his ideas and began to seek extension of his power to surrounding countries. His teachings were assembled, after his death, into the Koran. It includes material from Arabic traditions, Jewish doctrines, and the Christian New Testament, all of which he restated in a new form. Its chief doctrines expound beliefs in Allah, angels, the prophets of Allah, the Koran, divine decrees, and a final judgment. The duties of the followers are: repetition of the simple creed, prayer five times a day, almsgiving to other Moslems, fasting, and a pilgrimage to Mecca. The Koran advocates also abstention from wine, music, and pork, and commends labor and poverty.

Severus Sebokht (*fl.* 650) [Mesopotamia]. As a bishop in Mesopotamia, Severus Sebokht made the first reference to Hindu numerals. He spoke of nine signs in a manuscript a fragment of which is now in Paris; apparently, the symbol for zero was not known to him.

Aldhelm (*c.* 640-709) [Malmesbury, Canterbury, Sherborne]. One of the most learned men of his day, Aldhelm knew Latin, Greek, and some Hebrew. He was the first Englishman to write Latin as well as Anglo-Saxon poetry. He was noted for a number of riddles, and he set some of his poetry to music. His *In Praise of Virginity* is also well-known.

Bede the Venerable (672-735) [Jarrow]. An English historian and theologian, Bede spent most of his life at the monastery at Jarrow. He worked on grammar, natural phenomena, and chronology, especially the determination of the date of Easter. He wrote various historical works; by his *Ecclesiastical History of the English Nation* he earned the title of Father of English History. He wrote Biblical commentaries, based upon the Latin Fathers, making use, for the most part, of allegorical interpretations.

John of Damascus (700-754) [Damascus, Jerusalem, Constantinople]. The author of the standard textbook of theology in the Eastern Church was John of Damascus. He defended the worship of images in the Church, in opposition to the Emperor's order. His last years were spent in a monastery near the Dead Sea. He wrote a work entitled *Fountain of Knowledge* in which he expounded

Aristotle's logic and theory of reality, discussed various heresies, and systematized the orthodox faith, thereby developing the theology of the Greek Church. The work was very influential in later thought in the West as well as in the East.

Paul the Deacon (*c*. 720-799) [Pavia, Monte Cassino]. Paul was well-educated in Latin and knew some Greek. He wrote histories, homilies, poems, and a commentary on the Benedictine rule. Part of his life was spent at the court of Charlemagne.

Alcuin (735-804) [York, Tours]. Alcuin went to the court of Charlemagne in 781 and taught for eight years at the palace school, which was one of those he established in connection with cathedrals and monasteries. Then he founded a new school at Tours which became more famous than the palace school. Alcuin was influenced by Augustine. He wrote a book on grammar and logic and a work entitled *Essence of the Soul*. His chief importance is as a teacher rather than as a creative thinker.

Rhabanus Maurus (784-856) [Mainz, Fulda, Tours]. A prominent master in the schools, Rhabanus Maurus studied under Alcuin at Tours and introduced the learning of the times to Germany. He wrote an encyclopedic work, *On the Universe;* his only points of originality were in chronology and grammar.

Paschasius Radbertus (786-*c*. 860) [Soissons, Corbie]. After much controversy Paschasius Radbertus was credited with bringing to an authoritative exposition—in accordance with the doctrines of Ambrose, Augustine, and Chrysostom—the interpretation of transubstantiation (Real Presence) which has been accepted by the Church. This interpretation is found in *The Body and Blood of the Lord* (831). He made a distinction between what appears to the senses and what faith teaches. He also wrote a life of Abbot Adelard; a treatise, *On Faith, Hope and Charity; Commentary on Matthew;* and expositions of Psalms and Lamentations.

Al-Kindi (800-870) [Basra, Bagdad]. Al-Kindi was the first great Arabic philosopher and a follower of Aristotle, though influenced also by Neo-Platonism. He regarded mathematics as the basis of science, but wrote also on music, physics, medicine, and psychology.

Al-Kindi was the first of the Arabian encyclopedists. His doctrines were opposed by the Arabian traditionalists. One of his important works is *Theology of Aristotle.*

Gottschalk (*c.* 808-868) [Fulda, Soissons, Mainz]. The son of a Saxon count, Gottschalk was placed by his parents at an early age in a monastery at Fulda. Later he tried to secure a release from his vows but was prevented by the Abbot Rhabanus Maurus. Gottschalk moved to the monastery of Orbais, near Soissons, devoted himself to the study of the writings of St. Augustine, and became a strong believer in absolute predestination—to sin and to condemnation as well as to salvation, implying no freedom or responsibility. He traveled to Italy and Dalmatia, where his views spread with considerable success. Rhabanus accused him of neglecting the distinction between foreknowledge and foreordination. Gottschalk started a controversy in which a number of outstanding figures participated, some on his side. At a synod at Mainz, he was convicted of heresy and condemned to be whipped and imprisoned. At Quierzy he was condemned as a despiser of authority and as a disturber of the peace of the Church, and he was unfrocked. He spent the last twenty years of his life in the monastery at Hautvilliers, near Reims, though influential friends continued their futile efforts on his behalf. Only two professions of faith and some poems have survived from Gottschalk's writings.

John Scotus Erigena (810-877)[Ireland, Paris]. Following Gottschalk, the next outstanding personality in western philosophy is John Scotus Erigena, generally regarded as the first great philosopher of the Christian Middle Ages. He translated the Neo-Platonic mystical work supposed to have been written by Dionysius the Areopagite at the time of St. Paul, and that work had great influence upon his ideas. His most important writing was *On the Division of Nature.* John Scotus Erigena held that philosophy and religion are really the same, the functions of philosophy being to divide, define, demonstrate, and analyze. That which can not be known does not exist for us. Nature is the designation of the totality of things, ranging from the purely creative but uncreated (that is, God) through the creative and created (the Logos or the realm of types of things) to the realm of phenomena which are created but do not create anything. Beyond this is the uncreated which is God, as the end to which all things finally return. The tone of this philosopher's work was so pantheistic that it was condemned in the thirteenth and sixteenth centuries, but it has been widely read and has influenced many thinkers.

Photius (820-891) [Constantinople]. During a troubled and controversial life, Photius helped to carry on the tradition of classical philosophy. In his *Myriobiblion* and *Lexicon* he preserved extracts and abridgments of many writers which would have been unknown otherwise.

Eric of Auxerre (*c.* 837-881) [Auxerre, Fulda, Ferrieres]. Eric of Auxerre studied at St. Germain of Auxerre, then at Fulda and Ferrieres, under disciples of Rhabanus Maurus. Returning to Auxerre he became master of the school, and under his direction it became one of the outstanding schools of France. To works of Aristotle, Porphyry, and Boethius, Eric added running commentaries dealing mostly with dialectical and logical problems. He followed the tradition of Aristotle and Boethius in thinking that letters constitute meaningful words, words express concepts, and concepts reflect objects. He departed from true realism in the interpretation of universals, leaning toward nominalism. Eric was influenced by the thought of Erigena. He also wrote a poem on the life of St. Germain.

Remi of Auxerre (841-908) [Auxerre, Reims, Paris]. Concerning himself chiefly with the question of the locus of ideas, Remi came to the conclusion that they exist in the mind of God. He tried to reconcile the theory of Erigena with the views of its opponents. One of Remi's more important works is *Interpretations of the Psalms*.

Al-Farabi (870-950) [Bagdad, Damascus]. An Arabian philosopher, al-Farabi was called "The Second Aristotle," although he was influenced by Neo-Platonism. He carried on the encyclopedic tradition of al-Kindi. Al-Farabi recognized the non-existential character of essences and argued the necessity of a Creator. Corporeal beings arise as images of the World Soul. His commentaries helped to introduce Aristotle to the Arabs.

Saadia ben Joseph (892-942) [Egypt, Babylonia]. Although he is regarded as the outstanding figure in the literary and the political history of early medieval Judaism, Saadia ben Joseph wrote at a time when thought was at a low ebb. He was a champion of the orthodox school, defending the traditional calendar and festival dates. In the midst of controversy he was made Gaon of Sura, then deposed, and later reinstated. Most of his works were written in Arabic; some were commentarial, some polemic, some philosophical, dealing with rational foundations of faith and influenced by Aristotle. One of his important works was *Book of Beliefs and Convictions.*

Suidas (*fl.* 950) [Constantinople?]. Suidas represents the tradition of classical learning in the tenth century, as contained in his *Lexicon,* a combined dictionary and encyclopedia of scriptural and pagan subjects.

Gerbert (940-1003) [Aurillac, Reims, Rome]. Gerbert became Pope Sylvester II. He is credited with helping to extend the use of Arabic numerals in Europe and was also interested in astronomy. While master of the school at Reims, he developed a curriculum which directed attention to the study of nature. In a reported discussion with Otric, most famous of the Germans, he employed methods of analysis and an organization of knowledge which were developed further in the scholastic period. These methods are illustrated in his *Booklet on the Rational and the Use of Reason.*

Avicenna (980-1037) [Bokhara, Ispahan]. The Arabian philosopher Avicenna (also known as ibn-Sina) was a student of Neo-Platonism and Aristotle, as well as of medicine. He was especially interested in metaphysics, in which he combined the features of the two philosophies. He believed reality extends from a Supreme Intelligence to matter, whose existence is negative. His theories of the status of universals (moderate realism) and of the nature of the soul (Aristotelianism) were often quoted by the Scholastics.

Translated into Latin, his works stimulated the revival of interest in Aristotle and his philosophy in the twelfth and thirteenth centuries. Avicenna was sometimes called "The Third Aristotle." His *Healing* contained doctrines which influenced the development of medieval philosophy.

Berenger (999-1088) [Tours, Chartres]. A very popular teacher of logic and metaphysics, Berenger was influenced a great deal by Augustine. His doubts about transubstantiation were regarded as heresy, and he was excommunicated and imprisoned. He signed a retraction after much discussion and passed his last years in retirement.

Bahya ben Joseph ibn Paqudah (*fl.* 1040) [Saragossa]. The Jewish philosopher Bahya was the author of *Duties of the Heart,* a work very influential in the Middle Ages. He meant to make the Law a part of the inner life of man. He taught the unity of God and urged gratitude and love toward God for His creation of the world.

Peter Damian (*c.* 1002-1072) [Ravenna, Fonte Avellana, Ostia, Faenza]. As a result of harsh treatment by his family in his early years, Peter Damian adopted a life of extreme asceticism. Later he was well-known as a teacher and superior in the hermitage of Fonte Avellana, where he was noted for his wise rule; he founded several sub-hermitages. He wrote vigorously his opinions on the course of Church affairs. His *Liber Gomorrhianus* (*Book of Gomorrha*) denounced the vices of the clergy; in addition to written opposition, he joined the movement for reform under Hildebrand and strongly opposed simony and clerical marriage. Damian was a frequent legate and mediator and was counselor to several popes. In 1057 he was made Cardinal Bishop of Ostia against his will. He presided over a council at Milan in 1059 and also assisted Alexander II in his struggle with Honorius II, who was anti-pope. Peter Damian was papal legate to Germany in 1069 and persuaded Emperor Henry IV to abandon his plan to divorce Bertha.

Lanfranc (1005-1089) [Pavia, Caen, Canterbury]. Lanfranc opposed Berenger in the controversy over the Real Presence in the mass. His view of transubstantiation was set forth in *De Corpore et Sanguine Domini* (*On the Body and Blood of the Lord*). Born of a noble family, he was educated for the law and became famous as a teacher of law in France. He was a pioneer in the renaissance of Roman law and drew students from all Europe. He became prior of Bec where he taught logic and dogmatic theology. He had political as well as religious influence, and he was not always averse to the use of forged documents. He separated the ecclesiastical and the secular courts, favored the independence of the English Church, and secured the succession for William Rufus. He elevated clerical discipline and education, and his authority made the school at Bec famous. He was later appointed prior of the Abbey of St. Stephen at Caen and, in 1070, was made Archbishop of Canterbury, England. Through Lanfranc the Church of England imbibed a strong Norman influence; he acted as Regent in the absence of William of Normandy.

Constantine the African (*c.* 1015-1087) [Carthage, Salerno, Monte Cassino]. Translations of the physical science of the Arabians, which began to spread into Europe in the twelfth century, were made by Constantine. Early in his life he began the study of medicine and traveled as far as the East. He studied Arabic and supported the translation of Greek and Arabian medical works. Jealousy of him at Carthage led him to accept a position at Salerno. He attracted much attention but after a few years became a monk at Monte Cassino. His chief work was *Liber Pantegni* (*Book of all the Arts*), a translation of a work by Ali Ben el-Abbas. Constantine's original works have become badly mingled with works later ascribed to him.

Solomon ibn-Gabirol (Avicebron) (1020-1070) [Málaga]. Solomon ibn-Gabirol was the first of the important Jewish philosophers in Spain and was also a noted poet. His principal work, *The Fountain of Life,* influenced the Scholastics. He blended Judaism with Neo-Platonism and Aristotelianism, teaching the importance of contemplation and effort toward union with God. Avicebron believed in the pre-existence of the soul and thought knowledge was a kind of reminiscence. All finite things, whether terrestrial or celestial, have their own type of matter and form. The divine will mediates between God and the world.

Anselm (1033-1109) [Aosta, Bec, Canterbury]. One of the most famous of the medieval philosophers is Anselm. He is noted chiefly for his discussion of the proof of the existence of God. Augustine, who was the favorite author of Anselm, had interpreted God as the supreme member in a scale of terms reaching to infinity. But this left open the question of whether such a last term was merely an idea or referred to a real being which corresponded to it. Anselm, in his *Proslogium,* argued that the Being than whom no greater can be thought must exist, by definition, for an unrealized idea is not so great as a realized one. This is called the ontological argument for the existence of God. It was criticized by Gaunilon, a monk contemporary with Anselm, and has been criticized since, e.g., by St. Thomas and Kant, for a definition, logically, has no "existential" import. This has been restated by later thinkers.

In his theory of knowledge, Anselm is called a realist; that is, he held that a general idea in the human mind refers to something general which is beyond the human, and which is as real as something individual. Such an idea is not a mere *impulse* of the voice, not a mere *name* which names nothing.

Anselm held that revelation lays a basis for reason and that one must accept the beliefs of the Church before one can undertake to understand them. This puts orthodoxy prior to inquiry. His essay *On Truth,* is the first consideration of this question, apparently, for centuries. The popular conviction that the Church had the truth, evidently made the consideration of the question seem unnecessary. Given faith as the basis, Anselm assigned to pure reason an unlimited power of demonstration, as in the ontological argument. All articles of faith, once adopted, can be proven by logic alone. Thus, he tried to make intelligible the notions of the Omniscience of God, the Trinity, the Incarnation, and the freedom of the human will—maintaining that freedom is not foreign to rational living.

Manegold of Lautenbach (*fl*. 1084 - *c*. 1103) [Lautenbach, Rottenbuch, Marbach]. Manegold wandered through Germany and France teaching his doctrines and then became an Augustinian monk, later advancing to high rank in his order. He was influenced by the thought of Peter Damian, opposed the use of dialectic, and held that theology is not subject to logic. Logic can not produce certitude on any question; certitude rests on revelation as found in the Scriptures. The literal study of Scripture is basic. Authority is final on such questions as the belief in the Virgin Birth of Jesus, the Resurrection, etc., though there are contradictions between Catholic doctrine and the ancient philosophers. Most philosophy is superfluous. The differences among philosophers he declared to be due to the influence of the devil. He advocated return to the earliest forms of monasticism and exerted great influence in reforms in accordance with the principles of Gregory VII. Manegold incurred the disfavor of Henry IV of Germany, who imprisoned him for a time. In social theory, he maintained that loyalty to the king was based upon a social contract, by which the king also was bound. One of his most noted writings was *Against Wolfhelm* in which he rested on Macrobius' *Commentary on the Dream of Scipio*.

Odo of Tournai (1050-1113) [Orleans, Tournai, Cambrai, Anchin]. Odo won a great reputation as a teacher at Tournai. He became a monk and later was abbot of St. Martin's in Tournai. He was made Bishop of Cambrai, but declined investiture from Emperor Henry IV. The latter's son Henry V restored the see to Odo in 1106. Odo worked hard for his diocese, but was exiled in 1110 because he had not received the cross and ring from the Emperor. He was captivated by Plato's *Timaeus* and engaged in controversy with the anti-realists. In *De Peccato Originali* (*On Original Sin*), he applied the doctrine of realism and supported Traducianism, i.e., he believed that new souls are not new substances but new properties and accidents to the "human species." There was also a suggestion of Mysticism in his doctrine. Odo died at Anchin. Unfortunately, most of his works were lost.

Roscelin (1050-1120) [Compiegne, Tours]. The traditional opponent of Anselm's realism in the interpretation of universals was
Roscelin of Brittany, who was also for a time teacher of Abelard.
Noted as an interpreter of Aristotle, Roscelin had many followers, and was called the New Founder of the Lyceum. He wrote
no treatises, but merely expounded his position orally. We know
his doctrines only through those who opposed him and they have
represented him as adhering to nominalism, i.e., he thought that
universals are merely words. This led him to state that the relation of whole and part is the result of mental analysis and that
the doctrine of the unity of the Trinity is unreal. Tri-theism
replaced Trinitarianism (*see* p. 60). His theory of knowledge also
implied sense-empiricism. Roscelin's views are reported to have
been condemned at Soissons and at Reims, he retracted them on
both occasions, but continued to teach. His doctrines brought
suspicion upon the use of dialectic in discussion.

Al-Ghazali (1058-1111) [Tus, Bagdad]. An Arabian who began
as a philosopher, al-Ghazali later rebelled against the disagreements
of philosophers and resorted to an ascetic theology and Mysticism.
He wandered from city to city and finally back to Tus, where he
died. His chief work was *Destruction of the Philosophers*.

William of Champeaux (1070-1121) [Paris]. An outstanding defender of realism in the interpretation of universals, William of
Champeaux was also a teacher of Abelard, and he became involved
in a controversy with his pupil, who overcame him in the discussion.
Later, he began the mystical movement associated with the monastery of St. Victor, in Paris. A fragmentary work *De Essentia et
Substantia Dei* (*On the Essence and Substance of God*) presents
his position.

Adelard of Bath (12th cent.) [Bath, Tours, Laon]. Born in England, Adelard traveled and studied on the Continent, in North
Africa, and Asia Minor, and became acquainted with Arabian
learning. On returning to England he translated Euclid's *Elements*
into Latin, and this became a textbook in the schools. His chief
contribution to philosophy was his discussion of the theory of in-

difference in a work *De Eodem et Diverso* (*On the Same and the Different*), written as a dialogue between himself and a nephew. It was an allegory in which worldliness and philosophy attempt to win the soul of man. He also wrote on astronomy, on the abacus, and on medicine.

Peter Abelard (1079-1142) [Melun, Paris, Cluny]. The outstanding figure of the first half of the twelfth century was Peter Abelard. He studied under Roscelin and was an unusually popular teacher, but he had a rebellious disposition and was constantly getting into difficulties. His love affair and marriage to Eloise are famous. Finally, he became a Benedictine monk and Eloise became a nun. He told his story in his autobiography *History of Calamities*.

Peter Abelard confirmed the method of dialectic, presenting both sides of the theses of theology as expressed in the opinions of the Church Fathers. This is his method in *Sic et Non* (*Yes and No*).

He does not make an explicit statement of conceptualism, a position opposed to both extreme realism and extreme nominalism in connection with the problem of universals, but his theory implies this throughout. A conceptualistic view regards universals as objective to man but not to the mind of God, as in Abelard's *Summa Dialecticae* (*Summary of Dialectic*).

He maintained that faith must meet the demands of reason in order to claim acceptance. This led him to identify theology with philosophy and to minimize the appeal to authority, a procedure which offended the Church.

In his metaphysics, Abelard held that God created everything from an inner necessity of his own being. Consequently, this must be the best world possible, because of the supreme goodness of God.

Peter Abelard reasoned that the freedom of man lies in his judgment; the moral quality of an act lies not in the act itself, but in its intention.

Bernard of Chartres (*fl.* 1119). Bernard of Chartres was called the leading Platonist of his time. He was an extreme realist in his interpretation of universals; God, ideas, and matter are the ultimate realities. His principal work was *On the Exposition of Porphyry*.

Gilbert de La Porrée (1070-1154) [Poitiers, Chartres, Paris]. A pupil of Bernard of Chartres, Gilbert was a representative of that school. Here, he taught for twenty years, before lecturing at Paris on dialectic and theology, and returned as bishop in 1142. His thinking was marked by an eclectic tendency which attempted to unite Platonism and Aristotelianism. On the basis of his doctrine of universals Gilbert is often classed with the ultra-realists, but he insisted that the mind abstracts universals from individual things and makes them universal. In some discussions he considered the unity of the universal to be based upon similarity of essences, which is not ultra-realistic doctrine. In his interpretation of the metaphysical status of universals he considered that they *subsist,* while the particular instances of them which occur exist *substantially;* e.g., "unity" is a subsistent distinct from anything which is "one." In theology he harbored views which were suspected of heresy and were tried at a council at Paris in 1147. But the council was unable to arrive at a decision; at a second session at Reims the following year a decision was still lacking. Gilbert's greatest work was *On Six Principles,* a treatise on six of Aristotle's categories. It had great influence on Albert and Thomas, as well as other philosophers.

Theodoric of Chartres (*fl.* 1121-1150) [Chartres, Paris]. After he was master of the school at Chartres, Theodoric taught at Paris and then returned to Chartres. In his studies he gave more attention to Platonism than to Aristotelianism and favored Platonic realism. Following Neo-Platonism he identified unity with divinity and divinity with reality. Thus his system tended toward Pantheism. He escaped explicit Pantheism through a distinction between the formal essence in each creature, which is divine, and the individual essence, which is unique for each created being. Theodoric undertook also to show in his book *On the Work of the Six Days* that the Mosaic and the Neo-Platonic accounts of creation agreed. He regarded Moses as an eminent philosopher. Theodoric was a diligent student of the classics and was interested in the *Planisphere* of Ptolemy, which he knew in a Latin translation from the Arabians of Toulouse.

William of Conches (*fl.* 1122) [Paris]. A pupil of Bernard of Chartres, William of Conches taught Platonic realism at Paris. In his theology his identification of the Holy Ghost with the World Soul suggested Pantheism. Upon being warned about this point he abandoned theology and gave his attention to the study of Nature. He was one of the first to become acquainted with the physical science of the Arabians through the translations of Constantine the African. There is great uncertainty about the authenticity of writings ascribed to him, which seem to include running commentaries on the *Timaeus* of Plato, *On Boethius,* and a treatise *On Philosophy.* William of Conches' studies were centered chiefly in cosmology and psychology. In the former he was an atomist; in the latter he emphasized the physiological aspects and asserted the localization of function in the brain.

Judah ha-Levi (1085-1140) [Toledo, Palestine]. One of the greatest Hebrew poets, Judah ha-Levi was also an anti-rationalist. His chief work, *The Book of the Khazars,* was a dialogue in defense of Judaism, attempting to show the superiority of revealed religion to reasoned truth. He pointed out the dependence of Christianity and Islam upon Judaism; he regarded the Jews as possessed of a unique religious sense and Palestine as an unequalled region.

Abraham ben Ezra (1093-1167) [Spain, Italy, Provence]. Hebrew commentaries, especially on the Pentateuch, and short philosophical treatises were written by Abraham ben Ezra. He dealt with the problem of knowledge and the conception of the universe, being influenced by Neo-Platonism and the thinking of Avicebron (ibn-Gabirol).

Hugh of St. Victor (1096-1141) [Hartigam, Paris]. Hugh of St. Victor was a member of the orthodox Mystics who supported direct spiritual grasp of the highest truth and reality in contrast to the later analytic method of Scholasticism. He maintained that the Church possesses the criterion for truth of insight, that God is above all reality and includes it within Himself. In addition, he insisted that God is reason, wisdom, and love; man is destined for participation in the divine blessedness. To the inner vision of God, the soul rises above intellect to ecstasy. He stated that the soul is an immortal animating substance. Hugh's greatest work is *On the Sacraments.*

Peter the Lombard (1100-1160) [Novara, Bologna, Paris]. *The Four Books of Sentences* proved Peter to be a very influential person. This is a collection of the opinions of the Fathers on Catholic doctrine. It became a basic textbook for the schools and received a great deal of comment.

Abraham ben David (1110-1180) [Toledo]. Abraham ben David was a Jewish historian and philosopher with Aristotelian leanings. He wrote *Exalted Faith* which dealt with the principles of philosophy, religion, and ethics.

Gerard of Cremona (1114-1187) [Cremona, Toledo]. One of the first, and among the most famous, translators of Arabic documents into Latin was Gerard of Cremona. These translations included works of Aristotle, *Commentary* by Themistius, *Almagest* by Ptolemy, the writings of several Arabians—al-Kindi, al-Farabi, al-Hazen—and also works of Euclid, Hippocrates, and Galen. Gerard was a member of the College of Translators founded by Bishop Raymond of Toledo.

John of Salisbury (1115-1180) [Salisbury, Canterbury, Chartres]. A student of Abelard and others, John of Salisbury became secretary to the Archbishop of Canterbury and was present at the assassination of Thomas à Becket. Later, he was Bishop of Chartres. His *Policraticus* (*Of City Government*) was a description of an ideal state analogous to Plato's *Republic,* with the clergy at the head. In his *Metalogicus* (*Beyond Logic*), John combined Augustinian and Aristotelian philosophy, dealing with the fundamental problems of knowledge, including substance and movement. He was opposed to abstract speculation which was not applicable to concrete living. The writings of John of Salisbury are important sources of information on much of the thought of the Middle Ages.

Richard of St. Victor (*fl.* 1162-1173) [Scotland, Paris]. Richard was a pupil of Hugh and succeeded him as prior of St. Victor. In his thought, he emphasized Mysticism and opposed secular learning. He declared the latter to be nothing but error and vanity. All truth not confirmed by scriptural authority was suspect. Ultimate Truth is partly above reason, partly contrary to reason. Richard said that many of the master workmen in the shop of Aristotle will learn to be common workers in that of the Saviour. He wrote several treatises on Mystical experience, including, for example, one on the preparation of the soul for contemplation, and indicated six steps of progress: (1) contemplation of visible and tangible objects, (2) study of the works of Nature and Art, (3) study of character, (4) study of souls and spirits, (5) entrance to the realm of the mystical, and (6) ecstasy. Platonism, from Plotinus and Pseudo-Dionysius to Anselm, influenced his thinking. He was regarded by Dante as one of the greatest teachers in the Church. Richard's outstanding work was *On the Trinity*.

Averroes (ibn Ruschd) (1126-1198) [Cordoba, Seville, Morocco]. The representative of Arabian scholarship in the twelfth century, Averroes (ibn Ruschd) was interested in medicine, astronomy, and politics, as well as in philosophy. He was regarded as the greatest of the commentators on Aristotle and discussed his *Logic, Metaphysics,* and *Psychology*. He held numerous important posts and was judge for a while at Seville and physician to the Calif. He met with opposition because of the independence of his thinking, but his teachings were highly regarded in later times by the Scholastics. In answer to al-Ghazali he wrote a *Destruction of Destruction*. Averroes regarded religion as an allegorical world-view for the common man, beyond which the philosopher seeks the deeper truth. Through all men runs a common human intelligence or Active Intellect. The soul is immortal only in so far as it reflects the universal Active Intellect, the Divine Reason. Averroes made a distinction between believing by reason in the unity of the intellect and by faith in its plurality. This became the basis of his followers' mistaken position—that what is true in philosophy may be false in theology, and vice versa—the doctrine of the "twofold truth."

Alan (1128-1203) [Lille, Paris, Citeaux]. The thought of Alan was influenced chiefly by Aristotle and Boethius. His *On the Theory of the Catholic Faith* follows a deductive-mathematical method, based on definitions, postulates, and axioms. In a didactic poem, *Anti-Claudian,* he gave a summary of contemporary knowledge. In the *Laments of Nature,* he recorded his philosophy of nature. God he regarded as a Unit or Monad, working in things, as the cause of their form and matter.

Maimonides (1135-1204) [Cordoba, Fez, Cairo]. Jewish thought reached one of its highest points in the work of Moses Maimonides, the greatest of the Jewish students of Aristotle. In his *Guide for the Perplexed,* he attempted to combine the two sources of wisdom, the Bible and Aristotle. Where the two lines of thought disagree, he inclined toward the Jewish. Thus he accepted the idea that the world is only possibly, not necessarily, eternal; and just souls, only, acquire immortality. He believed that reason needed supplementation by religion. Anthropomorphic descriptions of God he regarded as figurative; according to him God is really beyond description.

Joachim of Floris (*c.* 1145-1202) [Celico, Casamari, Corazzo]. An Italian and classed as a Mystic or Pantheist, Joachim traveled widely and then became a Cistercian monk at Casamari. He served in various capacities and established an abbey, San Giovanni in Fiore, under his own rule. He wrote against the opponents of the Christian faith, but his own views were not entirely approved by the Church, especially a criticism of Peter Lombard's theory of the Trinity. Joachim divided history into three periods: the past, or the Age of the Father, or the Law; the present, or the Age of the Son, or the Gospel; and the future, or the Age of the Spirit, or the age of contemplation, of monasticism directed wholly to ecstasy. He believed that the Church of Peter will be purified, though not abolished, that the hierarchy will efface itself, and that the entire world will become a vast monastery. His ideas spread widely in Italy and France. A council at Arles in 1260 condemned his writings. One of his works, *Commentary on the Apocalypse,* was very influential; in it he extolled the Franciscans and criticized the Papacy. Dante revered him highly.

Amalric of Bena (*d.* 1204) [Chartres, Paris]. As a result of the influence of John Scotus Erigena and the Pantheism of Chartres, Amalric taught, at Paris, a pantheistic philosophy and theology, mingled with theosophic rationalism. He held that God is immanent in all things, for all rest on the Divine. Every man as well as Christ is an apparition of God, a member of Christ. He who remains in the love of God can not sin. Amalric maintained that God was revealed in three revelations: in Abraham in the epoch of the Father, in Christ in the epoch of the Son, in Amalric and his disciples in the epoch of the Holy Ghost. This doctrine led some of his followers to indulge in excesses. Amalric was a subtle dialectician and lectured also on the philosophy of Aristotle. He was called to account by the Church and retracted, but this did not prevent the spread of his ideas. Although he appealed to the pope, the condemnation was ratified. His death was said to have been caused by his humiliation. In 1209 twelve of his followers were burned at Paris, and Amalric's body was exhumed and was burned.

Robert Grosseteste (also Greathead, Robert of Lincoln) (*c.* 1175-1253) [Suffolk, Oxford, Paris, Lincoln]. One of the most learned men of the Middle Ages was Robert Grosseteste. He studied at Oxford and Paris, and his knowledge included Latin, Greek, French, and Hebrew, as well as mathematics, medicine, music, science, and Scripture. He was the first rector of the Franciscan school at Oxford and, in 1235, was elected Bishop of Lincoln. He undertook a vigorous program to reform abuses in his diocese. He was a man of very strong character, but undiplomatic and controversial, and became involved in many disputes. He clashed even with the pope by refusing to induct into office the pope's appointees if he did not approve of them. Where the rights of the national church conflicted with the claims of Rome he stood with his own countrymen. He accused the papal curia of being the cause of the evils of the Church. Only his great influence prevented his being disciplined. He was familiar with the Neo-Platonic materials of the Arabians and the translations of Aristotle. Grosseteste wrote commentaries on Aristotle and translated works of Aristotle and others; he also sought to reconcile Augustine and Aristotle.

William of Auvergne (*fl.* 1220-1249) [Aurillac, Paris]. A student at Paris, William of Auvergne later taught in the faculty of arts and in the faculty of theology. He was made Bishop of Paris in 1228, but continued an active interest in the university. His work was the first stage in the trend toward the use of Aristotle's philosophy as a basis for the exposition of Christian doctrine, in opposition to the prevailing Augustinian tradition. The existing text of Aristotle was full of errors and perversions introduced by the Arabian commentators. William rescued Aristotle from the Arabians and prepared the way for Alexander of Hales, Albert the Great, and Thomas Aquinas, though his range of thought was not so wide as theirs. William considered especially the Manichean heresy and opposed the Arabic doctrine of the eternity of the world. He identified the intelligible world of Platonic ideas with the Son of God. He wrote books on many subjects, including *On the Trinity, On the Universe,* and *On the Immortality of the Soul.*

Bartholomew the Englishman (*fl.* 1224-1231) [England, Paris, Magdeburg]. Although English by birth, Bartholomew entered the Order of St. Francis and became professor of theology at the University of Paris. He continued there until 1231, when he was sent to Magdeburg. He was succeeded at Paris by Alexander of Hales. Bartholomew was the author of *On the Properties of Things,* an encyclopedia of the sciences of the time, from theology and philosophy to botany and mineralogy. It was the first of the important encyclopedias of the Middle Ages and contained the works of Greek, Arabian, and Jewish naturalists and medieval writers, which had been translated recently into Latin. Bartholomew's work enjoyed great popularity and was translated into French, Belgian, English, and Spanish, so that it was accessible to the laity. Though his work is not scientific, it is a valuable source of information.

Alexander of Hales (*c.* 1180-1245) [Gloucester, Paris]. With the assistance of his students, Alexander of Hales wrote a *Summa Uni-*

versae Theologiae, the first after the ban had been removed from the reading of all of Aristotle's works. He attempted the reconciliation of Augustine, Aristotle, and the Arabians. The method of presentation which he employed offers a proposition, considers objections to it, and then replies to the objections. He also outlined the plan of discussing the nature of God, of Man, and of the God-Man.

He was impressed with Anselm's ontological argument and held that a potential knowledge of the existence of God is impressed on the nature of man, but that man cannot fathom the essence of God. According to Alexander's ideas, God is pure activity without matter and form, but the universal matter is different from that believed in by Avicebron; it is partly spiritual. Universals at first exist before things, in the mind of God, which is constituted by the Platonic intelligible world; then universals exist in things. He maintained that the soul is the form of the body, but is composed of a spiritual matter. It has capacities for knowing the external world, created spiritual substances, and first principles. Knowledge of the super-sensible is achieved through divine illumination in the soul.

Alexander of Hales had great influence upon Albert the Great, Thomas Aquinas, and Bonaventure.

David of Dinant (13th cent.) [Belgium?, Rome?, Paris?]. A representative of the pantheistic movement at the end of the twelfth century was David of Dinant. He studied the philosophy of Erigena and was influenced by Arabian thought. Other writers report that he identified God with primal matter, bringing his Pantheism into line with the materialistic tendency of the time. The Ultimate Real he divided into three categories: separate substances, souls, and bodies; but these are one in essence, and God is the first indivisible among eternal substances. His views were regarded as based upon the *Physics* and *Metaphysics* of Aristotle. David's views were condemned by the Church and his writings proscribed. Hence he is known only through the writings of Albert the Great and Thomas.

Adam Marsh (?-1258) [Somerset, Wearmouth, Oxford]. Adam Marsh was a Franciscan (Friars Minor) who was educated at

Oxford and who succeeded Robert Grosseteste as lecturer at its Franciscan house. He was acquainted personally with many of the most distinguished men of the time. His main interest was reform, which he wished to accomplish by peaceful means. He influenced the organization of studies at Oxford and was known throughout Europe as "Doctor Illustris." Roger Bacon expressed high regard for Adam Marsh and mentioned him with Grosseteste as "the greatest clerks in the world." Marsh wrote commentaries on Scripture, Dionysius the Areopagite, and other topics.

Albert the Great (1193-1280) [Lauingen, Swabia, Padua, Cologne, Paris]. Reputed to have almost superhuman knowledge, Albert the Great wrote vast and numerous works, including commentaries on Aristotle's writings and philosophical and theological treatises. In his day, he was also an authority on the physical and biological sciences. He taught logic and interpreted universals from the point of view of moderate realism. In metaphysics he emphasized the cosmological proof, in preference to the ontological, of the existence of God (as First Cause). He followed Augustine's theory of the creation of the world out of nothing and denied that it is the best possible world. Albert's interpretation of the nature of the soul is essentially Aristotelian, but he disagreed with the Arabian interpretation of the identity of the intellect in all men.

He encouraged scientific investigation, drew information from Arabian and Jewish commentators on Aristotle, and did not hesitate to disagree with Aristotle when his own observations seemed to warrant it. He was the originator of the idea of the affinity of chemical elements; he believed in the possibility of transmutation of elements, but not by the philosopher's stone; and he carried on significant experiments in botany and zoölogy. Also he acknowledged the debt that Christian thought owes to Platonism. A specimen of Albert's thought may be seen in his *Summa Theologiae*.

Roger Bacon (1214-1294?) [Ilchester, Oxford, Paris]. Roger Bacon was a notable figure of the second half of the thirteenth century. His varied interests touched on the following fields: linguistics, mathematics, and physical science.

He thought that Christians should go back to the Hebrew and Greek to read the Scriptures and regarded Aristotle very highly, but not the commentators upon him. He advocated the use of observation and experiment in science. He belittled the use of deductive reasoning and referred to the use of the telescope in astronomy; he declared that the Milky Way is made of many stars. In addition, he suggested the possibility of locomotives, flying machines, suspension bridges, and circumnavigation of the globe. *Opus Maius* was Roger Bacon's chief work. He got into difficulty repeatedly with his superiors for attacks on his contemporaries and for insubordination; he was imprisoned twice and died in obscurity.

William of Moerbeke (1215-1286) [Moerbeke, Viterbo, Lyons, Corinth]. A Belgian Dominican, William of Moerbeke was one of the most distinguished men of letters of the thirteenth century. He was a friend of Thomas Aquinas and of the mathematicians and natural scientists of his day. He was Archbishop of Corinth in the years 1277-1286. At the request of Thomas Aquinas, William undertook to translate the works of Aristotle into Latin. He was the first translator of the *Politics* (1260) and also translated other works, including those of Proclus. These translations, though verbally literal, are valuable and became classics in the fourteenth century. William also translated mathematical treatises, commentaries on Aristotle's works, and a treatise of Ptolemy. William's works were used to support the Neo-Platonic interest of the thirteenth century; his contemporaries dedicated books to him.

John of Fidanza (St. Bonaventure) (1221-1274) [Bagnora, Paris]. A student of Alexander of Hales, John of Fidanza, later known as St. Bonaventure, became a Franciscan, but was also a close friend of Thomas Aquinas, a Dominican. Their friendship was unaffected by the rivalries of the two orders. Bonaventure's works were *Itinerarium Mentis in Deum* (*Journey of the Mind to God*) and *De Reductione Artium ad Theologiam* (*On the Reduction of the Arts to Theology*).

His philosophy was a combination of Platonic and Aristotelian elements, with an emphasis upon the Mysticism in Plato. Bonaventure accepted those of Aristotle's views which were consistent with revelation and tradition. He distinguished between theology and philosophy, the former dealing with supernatural truth, the latter with natural truth, and he attached importance to both the emotional and the volitional sides of theology.

All finite beings he regarded as composed of form and matter, actuality and potentiality; there is no form without matter. A substance contains a plurality of forms, and individuality is effected by both form and matter. Created substances become what they are by virtue of both potencies in the matter and seminal principles involved in it. Bonaventure maintained that all knowledge comes by illumination, of which there are four aspects—that which lies in the external object through its capacity for being known; that which comes from the activity of the sense organ; that which depends upon the capacity of reason to generalize; and that which by divine grace brings the interpretations of reason into identity with the mind of God and thus gives certainty. He thought that in nature we find a trace of God, in ourselves an image of God, and that in Mystical ecstasy the soul is united with God. We rise from a knowledge of creatures to a knowledge of God, the Cause and Creator of nature. He reasoned that at the beginning the mind is a blank tablet, receiving impressions through the senses. Some general ideas are derived by means of the activity of the intellect, some are infused by God. Bonaventure reasoned that knowledge of the soul and of God is independent of sense; God is the prime object of knowledge.

Thomas Aquinas (1225-1274) [Roccasecca, Cologne, Paris, Rome]. In many respects, the most influential figure in the thirteenth century was Thomas Aquinas. Born of noble family, he joined the Dominican order against the wishes of his family; he studied at Naples and then under Albert the Great at Cologne and Paris. He was underestimated by his fellow students because of his quiet manner, but great things were predicted of him by his teacher. He became a famous teacher himself and lectured in numerous centers of learning. Among his works are commentaries on Aristotle, the

Scriptures, the Books of Sentences, the treatises of Boethius, and others; but his greatest works are *Summa Contra Gentiles* and *Summa Theologiae.*

In Thomas' theory of knowledge the essential point is that there are levels, especially two—that which deals with facts of nature, and which reason is competent to deal with; and that which deals with truth beyond nature, and which must be revealed to faith, e.g., the mysteries of the Christian doctrine. These two are not opposed to each other, but faith must set in where reason reaches its limit.

According to the writings of Thomas Aquinas, the process of reasoning is fundamentally inductive, beginning with the data presented by sense and passing to ever larger generalizations into science and philosophy. Science is knowledge of facts by way of general principles. Philosophy is knowledge of ultimate things by way of reason. Theology has two divisions: (1) natural, which can be understood by reason, and (2) revealed, which must come through faith which reaches beyond reason. Universals exist *before* things in the mind of God, *in* things in the natural world, and *after* things in the mind of man. Knowledge is attained when human ideas exactly fit their objects as the impression on wax fits the object which imprinted it.

Man is a being composed of soul and body, the two being essentially one as form and matter are one in a concrete thing. Thomas concurred with Aristotle's belief that the soul is the "form" of the body and is incomplete without it. Thomas believed that at death the soul survives the body, but it must remain in an incomplete state until the resurrection when it will be re-embodied. The soul is the principle of life and functions through different faculties—the locomotive, the nutritive, the sensitive, the appetitive, and the intellectual. Being immaterial, it is immortal. Since the process of knowledge is fundamentally inductive, there is nothing in the intellect which was not first present in sense.

Thomas maintained that in metaphysics the most universal notion is being. This ranges all the way from God, the highest form, to matter, the lowest form. It covers both actuality and potentiality and is interpreted by the four Aristotelian causes: formal, material, efficient, and final. He thought material embodiment is what distinguishes one individual from another. The world was created out of nothing, as were space and time, though Thomas, in a concession to Aristotle, admits that the eternity of the world is conceivable. The existence of God can be proved by way of the concepts of an Original Mover, a First Cause, a Necessary Being, and a Highest Perfection. Thomas rejected Anselm's ontological argument, yet insisted that existence is implied analytically in the conception of God.

The highest good is the happiness which comes from the knowledge and the love of God. Thomas stated that this can be begun in this life but not completed here. Virtue consists of living in a way directed toward this end and expresses itself in the theological virtues of faith, hope, and charity, and in the cardinal virtues of prudence, courage, temperance, and justice. Health, possessions, and friends are essential means to happiness.

Since man is by nature a social animal, he inevitably lives in social groups. The rules for living together are formulated in the laws of the State, the aim of which is to maintain conditions for the highest welfare of men. He explained that the will of the people counteracts tendencies to tyranny. Although monarchy is most "in accord with nature," he believed an acceptable form is that which performs well the functions of the State, including the education of the citizens and the maintenance of freedom from economic want.

To support his doctrines, Thomas Aquinas drew from Greek, Jewish, and Arabian thinkers as well as from the Christian tradition.

Witelo (1225-?) [Silesia, Padua, Viterbo]. Witelo's interest in science led him to Padua, where he studied philosophy, mathematics, and natural science. Here, he became the friend of William of Moerbeke, to whom he dedicated his *Perspectives*. He treated in detail the phenomena of optics, including its geometrical aspects, the propagation of light, the structure of the eye, illusions, mirrors, and the refraction of light passing from one medium to another. His work greatly influenced the history of science. He made use of Greek and Arabic sources in Latin translations but added his own original contributions. In psychology, his thought was independent of theological traditions. Witelo's theory of reality was Neo-Platonic in trend He divided the Real into two orders, the intelligible and the corporeal, and connected them by the bond of causality. All things are derived from the Being of God, their intelligibility from His, and their life from His life. Other facts concerning Witelo's life and death are uncertain.

Peter of Spain (1225-1277) [Lisbon, Rome?, Viterbo]. Peter of Spain first studied at the cathedral school of Lisbon, and then he entered the University of Paris where he attended the lectures of Albert the Great on the works of Aristotle—especially those on the *Physics* and the *Metaphysics*. He also studied theology and medicine. In 1247 he became a professor of medicine at the University of Siena where he wrote his *Summary of Logic,* which was the favorite textbook in logic for nearly three centuries and was translated into various languages. Peter also brought together into one volume a collection of medical prescriptions. In 1272 he was appointed physician in ordinary to Pope Gregory X, then was made Archbishop of Braga, and in 1273 became Cardinal Bishop of Tusculum. In 1276 he was elected pope and took the name of John XXI. He was deeply involved in political issues, but he found time for scientific study and concern with the doctrines taught at Paris.

John's death was caused by the collapse of an apartment which had been added to the papal palace at Viterbo so that he might have quiet for study.

Siger of Brabant (*fl.* 1266-1283?) [Paris, Orvieto]. Siger was the leader of Latin Averroism, which was popular in the middle and late thirteenth century, and was mentioned by Dante in the *Commedia.* Thomas Aquinas expressly opposed Siger's doctrines. Siger led the opposition to his Scholastic masters, Albert and Thomas, though condemned in 1270. His principal work was *On the Intel-*

lective Soul. It called forth Thomas' treatise *On the Unity of the Intellect.* Among Siger's teachings were: cosmic and psychic determinism, and control by celestial phenomena of events on our globe and of human destiny. He reasoned that civilization and religions, including Christianity, are subject to eternal reversibility. Men are mortal, but the race is immortal. Man is not a free agent. There is one intellectual spirit which is united temporarily with each human organism to carry on the process of thought. He appealed to the theory of twofold truth in theology and philosophy to justify his claim still to be Catholic.

In 1277 a second condemnation ended his teaching. He appealed this decision to the Roman Court, but was assassinated by his secretary.

Raymond Lully (1234-1315) [Majorca, Aragon, Tunis]. Converted from a dissipated life, Raymond Lully was dominated by the idea of converting the Moors to Christianity; he traveled about Europe seeking support for his project. His chief work was his *Ars Magna* (*Great Art*), a study of the ultimate principles presupposed in all logic and metaphysics, in which the elements of thought are represented by letters and geometrical figures to show their valid combinations. He invented a logical machine by which he hoped to demonstrate truth. He wrote a novel describing a Utopia in the tradition of Plato, and he was also a poet of high ability. At Tunis he was stoned by the Muslims and died of the wounds.

John Peckham (1240?-1292) [Sussex, Paris, Oxford, Rome, Canterbury]. Following his education at Lewes and Paris, John Peckham entered the Order of Friars Minor (Franciscan). He taught at Oxford, became Provincial of England, and later was called to Rome as lector of the sacred palace. In 1279 he was elected Archbishop of Canterbury. He visited every part of his province, uprooting abuses. His zeal subjected him to complaints, some of which were upheld in Rome. However, he renewed the condemnation of certain errors of Averroism. John Peckham was marked by complete adherence to principle and by his activities in behalf of the poor; he was sincere and humble and was admired by his contemporaries; he defended his order staunchly against its enemies. His writings include letters, poems, and a work entitled *Life of St. Anthony of Padua.*

Matthew of Aquasparta (*c.* 1240-1302) [Aquasparta, Paris, Bologna, Rome]. Matthew entered the Franciscan Order at Todi, studied at Paris, and taught at Bologna. He was John Peckham's successor as teacher of theology to the papal curia. In 1287 he was elected general of the Franciscan Order and reorganized the studies pursued in this organization. In 1288 he became a cardinal. Matthew was a faithful disciple of Bonaventure and developed his doctrine. He was a member of the older Franciscan school, preferring Augustinianism to the Aristotelianism of Thomas Aquinas. His principal work was *Quaestiones Disputatae* (*Disputed Questions*). He also wrote many other works, among them *The Excellence of Scripture, Procession of the Holy Spirit,* and *On Human Knowledge.* Matthew was sent as papal legate to Florence to make peace between the Guelphs (black) and the Ghibellines (white), but without success. Dante, a Ghibelline, speaks strongly against him in the *Paradiso.*

Peter John Olivi (*c.* 1248-1298) [Serignan, Rome, Narbonne]. Olivi entered the Friars Minor at Beziers and later studied at Paris. He became leader of the rigorists in applying the rule of the order. At Strasbourg in 1282 he was accused of heresy and his writings were confiscated. Thereafter he defended himself successfully, and Matthew of Aquasparta sent him as lector to Santa Croce in Florence. But sentiment was still divided over him. His friends venerated him as a saint, but the General Chapter of Lyons ordered his writings burnt as heretical (1299). The feeling against him has been judged by some to be due to his extreme rigorism. He wrote speculative treatises (especially *Quaestiones*), and exegetical works on the books of the Bible. Opponents criticized his views regarding the moment of transfixing of the Lord's body with the lance, the manner of union of soul and body, and infant baptism. In 1318 his tomb was destroyed.

Dietrich (Theodoric) of Freiberg (*c.* 1250-?) [Freiberg, Paris, Toulouse]. Dietrich was a Scholastic Mystic. He was Provincial for Germany 1293-1296 and, in 1297, was master of theology at Paris. He wrote numerous works on optics, natural philosophy, psychology, metaphysics, epistemology, theology, and other subjects. He formulated the theory that the rainbow is formed by the diffraction and reflection of sunlight by raindrops. He emphasized the importance of experimentation in natural science. His philosophy was primarily in agreement with that of Thomas, but he was influenced as well by Augustine and Proclus in his theory of knowledge and his psychology. In ontology, he maintained no real distinction between the existence of a thing and its essence, nor (in his view of creation) between emanation and reversion. Dietrich exercised strong influence over Eckhart and Tauler and was noted as a preacher. *De Esse et Essentia* (*On Being and Essence*) was one of his important works.

Peter of Abano (1257-1315) [Abano, Constantinople, Paris, Padua]. Peter of Abano studied and traveled widely. For twenty years he lived in Constantinople, where he acquired a thorough knowledge of Greek. Later, he went to Paris where his chief ideas began to take form. In 1307 he was appointed to the chair of medicine and natural science, and perhaps mathematics, at the University of Padua, a position which he held until his death. He is reported to have explained the resurrection of Jesus and later accounts of the resurrection of saints by the hypothesis of only apparent death. He was a compiler rather than a translator, introducing Aristotle's *Problems* to the Western world and writing *Conciliator of the Differences of Philosophers, Especially the Medical*. Peter also wrote *Handbook on Astronomy,* a work on astrology rather than astronomy, which has not survived. His position on Averroism is undetermined.

Johannes (Meister) Eckhart (1260-1327) [Hochheim, Paris, Cologne]. A Dominican, Meister Eckhart became Provincial for Saxony and Vicar General for Bohemia. In his *Opus Tripartitum* he colored the Aristotelianism of Thomas with the Mysticism of

Pseudo-Dionysius. He asserted that the Divine Essence and Existence are one and that all things exist in identity with God. The Divine Existence is especially manifest in the human soul, whose end is union with God. Preaching in the vernacular Johannes Eckhart began the philosophical German language. He was tried for heresy and abjured his errors. A portion of his views were officially condemned.

The Transition to Modern Philosophy

The ascendancy of the Church was never complete. There had always been heresy. In the fourteenth, fifteenth, and sixteenth centuries there were outstanding men who did not agree with Thomas Aquinas in his emphasis upon reason as superior to the will. The nominalistic view also sprang up once more. Among Jewish thinkers there was criticism of traditional thought. Mysticism had several outstanding followers, who protested against intellectualism. The demand was being made that the Christian Scriptures be translated into the vernacular so that they would be directly accessible to the common man. There was a reawakened interest in the more humane dialogues of Plato, like the *Phaedrus* and *Symposium,* as against the dominant medieval concern with the *Timaeus.* There was a new interest in Aristotle for his own sake without reference to the use of his doctrines by the Church. Machiavelli asserted the rights of the state as an organization independent of the Church, and Luther challenged the authorities to debate the rightness of some of their practices, especially with regard to the sale of indulgences. Interest in natural science was strong, and the Copernican theory in astronomy became influential. In politics, opposition to the power of the numerous independent feudal lords began to show itself.

John Duns Scotus (*c.* 1270-1308) [Scotland, Oxford, Paris, Cologne]. The most outstanding figure at the beginning of the fourteenth century was John Duns Scotus. Noted for his critical ability and influenced by Augustine, Anselm, and the Arabians, Scotus partly agreed and partly disagreed with Thomas Aquinas. He emphasized the priority of will in man and God, whereas Thomas had maintained the priority of reason. Consequently, Scotus ranked theology above philosophy and approached the position of the double nature of truth, though he held that there is no inherent conflict between faith and reason. The two supplement each other; yet reason cannot explain the mysteries of faith, nor can it demonstrate the divine nature and purpose, the predestination, or the immortality of the soul. Only faith through revelation can give certainty. Theology is practical, not theoretical, in its aim. Scotus' view of universals was that of a moderate realism. In his theory of reality he held that there are subtle distinctions in types of form and matter, and on the question of the principle of individuation he maintained that there is a factor distinct from both form and matter. There is a specific difference distinguishing species from each other and a difference distinguishing individuals. In ethics, Scotus believed that the commandments which concern our life and relations with each other are necessary merely because God prescribes them. His *Opus Oxoniense* (*Oxford Work*) was composed about 1305-1306 while he was at Oxford.

Marsilius of Padua (1270?-1342) [Padua, Paris]. Though only a layman, Marsilius was a physician, a theologian, and a canon of Padua. He served in the army of the Emperor, then went to Paris to complete his study of medicine, and became rector of the University in 1313. He supported Louis of Bavaria after Pope John XXII had excommunicated Louis as a supporter of heretics. With John of Jandun, Marsilius composed *Defensor Pacis* (*Defender of Peace*), in 1324 and presented it to Louis. This asserted that though God is the ultimate source of all power, it comes immediately from the people. Law is the expression of the will of the people, not of the prince. By majority vote the people can enact, interpret, modify, and revoke. The work further maintained that the Church has no visible head (it being uncertain whether Peter ever came to Rome) and that Peter had been given no more power than the other apostles. The pope calls the ecumenical councils, but is subject to them. The Church can do nothing without the authorization of the State. These doctrines were condemned by the pope, but they were translated into various languages and were one of the bases of the Reformation.

Nicholas of Autrecourt (*fl.* 1320-1347) [Autrecourt, Paris, Metz]. While studying in Paris, Nicholas of Autrecourt adopted a thoroughly skeptical position. As Aristotle had shown, all knowledge rests on the principle of contradiction, but there is no proof of the validity of this principle. Our inner experience or consciousness gives awareness of our own acts, but no proof of the existence of the soul, nor of the existence of the outer world. Nicholas rejected the analytic necessity of any causal connection between phenomena. No one has been able to produce evidence of the existence of substances distinct from the sense qualities, either through intuition (which would be possessed by all men) or by deductive inference, because from one existence another can not be inferred. Yet Nicholas held an atomistic theory of cosmology and maintained a doctrine of the perfection of the total universe; he accepted the dependence of all things on God. On account of his doctrine, he was dismissed from his lectureship and was called before the Court at Avignon. Nicholas was required to burn his letters and his chief work *Exigit Ordo Executionis* (*The Order of Execution Demands*), and to recant.

William of Ockham (1280-1349) [Ockham, Oxford, Paris]. Regarded usually as an advocate of nominalism, William of Ockham's nominalism is not of an extreme form; rather it is a variety of conceptualism known as *terminism*. He regarded the universal as an intention of the mind; and held that the objects of science are propositions rather than things. Only the "term" as it exists in the mind has universality. Knowledge of individual things must be intuitive, and in understanding things one must not employ a plurality of concepts beyond necessity. This is "Ockham's Razor," which cuts off superfluous entities. The limitation of human reason led William to conclude that the proofs of the existence of God are unconvincing and that the principles of morality can not be shown to be necessary. Both are matters of faith. The conclusions which others later drew from his philosophy went beyond his own position. William was in continuous conflict with Pope John XXII and wrote much in opposition to the temporal power of the pope. His *Commentary on the Books of Sentences* is outstanding.

Levi ben Gerson (1288-1344) [Bagnols, Avignon, Orange]. Levi ben Gerson, a Jewish philosopher, was a noted commentator on the writings of Averroes. He was also the author of *War of the Lord,* which contained a summary of Arabian astronomy. He criticized the syncretism[1] of Aristotelianism and Jewish orthodoxy and wrote a *Commentary on the Pentateuch.* He regarded intellectuality as a condition of immortality and taught that God's knowledge is general, not particular.

John of Jandun (*c.* 1300-?) [Paris]. John of Jandun was graduated from the University of Paris, and became a philosopher, theologian, and writer on politics. He collaborated with Marsilius of Padua in writing the *Defender of Peace* (1324) against Pope John XXII. For this the authors were condemned. Works ascribed to John include commentaries on Aristotle's works, commentaries on Peter Lombard's *Sentences,* and *Question.* The latter work favors Averroes' views on the substance of the world and maintains the theory of twofold truth in theology and philosophy, stating, for example, that the eternity of the world is true in philosophy and that creation is true in theology. With Averroes, John asserted that there is only one universal intellect which pervades all human minds. The individual soul is not immortal, nor is the will free. According to John of Jandun, Averroes rates higher than Thomas.

John Buridan (1300-1359) [Béthune, Paris]. A follower of the nominalism of Ockham, John Buridan was famous for an extensive work entitled *Compendium of Logic* and for commentaries on the various works of Aristotle, especially the *Ethics* and the *Physics.* His concern with the problem of freedom led to the well-known story ascribed to him (apparently incorrectly) of the ass which starved to death when placed midway between two bales of hay because there was no factor to turn him to one or the other.

---

[1] The attempt to fuse two (or more) sets of ideas which were originally different.

John Tauler (1300-1361) [Strasbourg, Cologne, Basel]. One of the most noted followers of Eckhart was John Tauler. He was interested especially in the ethical and religious aspects of Mysticism and concentrated attention upon his own consciousness in his attempt to grasp the immanence of God. He was noted for his collection of essays entitled *Sermons*.

Nicholas of Oresme (?-1382) [Lisieux, Paris, Rouen]. Nicholas of Oresme studied at Paris and later became Bishop of Lisieux. He criticized ecclesiastical disorders of the time and wrote a work on Christology. However, he is better known for his works in mathematics, physics, and economics. He used rectangular co-ordinates in three dimensions to represent the properties of geometric figures. Nicholas wrote a work on astronomy (*Treatise on the Sphere*, 1377) and a commentary on the heavens and the earth, reasoning that belief in the movement of the earth was an application of simplicity in theory and answered objections based on texts of Scripture. He formulated a law of falling bodies. His views on economics are found in translations and also in *Commentary on the Ethics, Politics, and Economics of Aristotle*, and *Treatise of Coins*.

John Wycliffe (1320-1384) [Yorkshire, Oxford, Lutterworth]. As well as being a popular lecturer at Oxford, John Wycliffe became the King's Chaplain and defended the government's right to deprive unrighteous clergy of their property. He rejected transubstantiation as taught by the Church and criticized the tolerance of social conditions. His *Trialogus* (*c*. 1384) summed up his beliefs. He was repeatedly called before the Church to account for his teachings. Wycliffe subordinated tradition to the right of the individual to formulate his judgments on the basis of Scripture and reason, and to associate with others on this basis. The divine law is found in conscience. Wycliffe maintained England's right to self-preservation and denied the papacy, as a spiritual power, the right of sovereignty over an independent country. He held that "Peter's pence" was charity and not subject to demand as papal taxation. When the nation needed the money, the pence could be withheld. He undertook the translation of the Bible into English and spread it among the common people by way of "poor priests," young men not in clerical orders. Wycliffe died of heart disease, but his body was exhumed—after formal condemnation at the Council of Constance in 1415—in accordance with the decree of the Council, and was burned.

Hasdai Crescas (1340-1410) [Barcelona]. A Jewish philosopher, Hasdai Crescas wrote *Light of the Lord,* which influenced Spinoza's thinking. The work dealt with the predicables, creation, and free will and opposed the influence of Aristotle. He wrote also *Refutation of the Cardinal Principles of the Christians.*

John Gerson (1364-1429) [Gerson, Paris, Lyons]. A representative of an orthodox mystical movement which opposed both Scotus and Ockham, John Gerson accepted only the kind of philosophy which was touched with piety. His chief work was *Speculative Mystic Philosophy* (1403). He was for a time Chancellor of the University of Paris and was also involved in the papal schism and the choice of a new pope, Alexander V.

John Huss (c. 1370-1415) [Husinetz, Prague]. John Huss, rector of the university and a follower of Wycliffe, preached his ideas at Prague. As a result, he and his followers were excommunicated. He criticized the corruption of the Church and, in particular, the practice of selling indulgences. Huss was invited to the Council of Constance, where he was arrested and accused of heresy. He was condemned and burned at the stake, and his ashes were thrown into the Rhine. The charges against him were based chiefly upon his work, *On the Church* (1413).

Pierre d'Ailly (1350-1425) [Compiegne, Paris]. As a defender of the nominalism of Ockham, Pierre d'Ailly maintained the greater certainty of the self as compared with the external world; he asserted also the indemonstrability of the existence of God, a belief which is accepted on the basis of faith. He became master of the University of Paris and was made Cardinal in 1411. He was a many-sided thinker and writer and took active part in the problem of the papal schism. His writings on geography influenced Columbus and Americus Vespucius. He wrote *Tractate* and *Sermons.*

Marsilius of Inghen (1362-1392) [Inghen, Paris, Heidelberg]. Though influenced by Thomas Aquinas, Marsilius of Inghen wrote in defense of the doctrine of Ockham; he also wrote on theology and physics. A very successful teacher, he became rector of the University of Paris and, in about 1383, went to Heidelberg as rector of the university, which had been founded there twenty-three years before. He wrote *Questions Concerning Four Books of Sentences.*

Raymond of Sabunde (?-1432) [Barcelona, Toulouse]. Raymond of Sabunde took a position midway between Scholasticism and Mysticism. He believed that religious revelation and the revelation of God in nature are two "books" given us by God. Every creature is, as it were, a "letter" written by the "finger" of God. The basis of all knowledge is awareness of self. He believed that the self is the surest datum. The proof of the existence of God is based on the necessity for a highest judge and remunerator. The highest good is growth in God who is almighty and who will never choose what is unbefitting Himself. Raymond wrote *Natural Theology* (*c.* 1432).

Joseph Albo (c. 1380-1440) [Aragon, Tortosa]. Joseph Albo, a Spanish Jew, was a pupil of Hasdai Crescas. Albo was also an active participant in theological discussion and wrote *Principles,* which included his views on the existence of God, revelation, and retribution. This work had wide influence.

Thomas à Kempis (1380-1471) [Kempen, Deventer]. The author of *Imitation of Christ* was Thomas à Kempis. This book has been read widely as an aid to devotion and is said to have been translated into more languages than any other book except the Bible. Thomas à Kempis led a quiet, contemplative existence in an Augustinian monastery and wrote numerous tracts on monastic life.

Nicholas of Cusa (1401-1464) [Kues, Padua, Liége, Todi]. Because he was interested in reform in the Church, the Catholic Cardinal Nicholas of Cusa broke away from Scholasticism and taught that God can be apprehended only by intuition, not by intellect. As a student of astronomy, he taught the revolution of the earth around the sun and the existence of many worlds. Also he declared the *Donation of Constantine* to be a forgery; this document professed to give the Church temporal sovereignty over Rome and all western regions. He believed that man's wisdom lies in admitting his ignorance. God is the reality in which all things participate and in which all contradictions are transcended. Nicholas' best-known work is *De Docta Ignorantia* (*On Learned Ignorance,* 1440).

Gabriel Biel (1403-1495) [Speyer, Mainz, Tübingen]. Biel composed *Epitome and Collection from Ockham on the Four Books of Sentences* (a collection of opinions), in which he expounded and defended the teachings of Ockham. He also wrote a significant work on economics, *On the Power and Use of Money.*

Marsilio Ficino (1433-1499) [Figline, Florence, Careggi]. At the end of the fifteenth century an attempt was made at Florence to establish a society based upon Plato's Academy. Marsilio Ficino's family intended that he study medicine, but he was befriended by Cosimo de Medici and became a priest, spending most of his life in Florence where Cosimo had set up his Platonic Academy. He translated Plato's *Dialogues,* and some writings of Porphyry, Proclus, Pseudo-Dionysius the Areopagite, and Plotinus. (This direct return to the writings of Plato was a characteristic of the age.) Ficino's most important original work was *Theologia Platonica* (*Platonic Theology,* 1474). He was interested in the humanism of the day, but sought its goal by way of Plato. He endeavored to show the harmony of Plato and Christian faith, citing Augustine as his precedent. He stated that Plato was inspired and must be studied in order to render Christianity rational and acceptable to the skeptical. Both philosophy and religion are manifestations of the spiritual life. Each needs the other in order to attain the *summum bonum.* The highest good is not dependent upon the Church, but upon an impulse universal to man. Ficino also drew ideas from Aristotle and from the Scholastics.

He maintained that all souls by an inner urge seek truth and goodness, i.e., God. This is an *appetitus naturalis;* each being seeks its own natural end. There is a highest being for each species from which its essence is derived. Ficino reasoned that there are levels of being, of which God is the Perfect One, the source of all, and in whom all oppositions are overcome. The individual soul stands in a position intermediate between God and its body and must have a body. The soul can not fully attain its goal here; so there must be a hereafter; and a resurrection of the body is necessary.

Isaac ben Jehudah Abarbanel (1437-1508) [Lisbon, Spain, Naples, Venice]. Abarbanel was a Jewish scholar and statesman, successful as a merchant, who suffered under the banishment of Jews from Portugal, Spain, and Naples. He was noted for his biblical exegesis and commentaries on the thoughts of Maimonides. He was also influenced by Crescas.

Leonardo da Vinci (1452-1519) [Vinci, Florence, Milan]. As artist, engineer, scholar, Leonardo da Vinci left over 5,000 pages of manuscript, containing undeveloped and unorganized suggestions, observations, and sketches. He enunciated basic principles and discoveries, including heliocentric astronomy and Galilean mechanics. He held that mathematical investigation and technique must replace traditional speculation. He emphasized the union of scientific thought and practical activity. Experience and experiment are the bases of science. Yet the senses yield only raw material that must be worked into rational knowledge. Reflective reason is outside the senses. Certainty comes only with mathematical formulation, and the culmination of mathematics is mechanics, drawing conclusions from cause to effect and vice versa. Da Vinci's artistic productions include religious paintings, especially "The Last Supper" (at Milan). He applied his knowledge to the study of geology, botany, anatomy, aviation, and other fields.

John Pico of Mirandola (1463-1494) [Padua, Paris, Florence]. In receiving a thorough classical education John Pico studied Hebrew and Arabic, and also read the Scholastics. He was acquainted with the vernacular poetry and the literature of Italy and had a number of friends among the humanists, including Ficino. Later he became acquainted with Savonarola, the critic of the Church. Pico's basic conviction was that man has freedom to choose a way of life from among endless possibilities and to rise to higher levels. He opposed astrology on the ground that it subjects man to forces above him. He also got into difficulties with the Church about his ideas, which are indicated in his *Oration on the Dignity of Man* (1486). The latter was an introduction to an intended disputation of over 900 theses, proposed at Rome (1487), which the pope prohibited. An *Apologia* in defense of some of the disapproved theses follows the *Oration*. John Pico's wide studies had led him to the conviction that there is a basic unity pervading all philosophy; he was interested in bringing this unity to light and in adding Platonism to the strong Aristotelianism of the time.

Agostino Nifo (1473-1546) [Sessa?, Padua]. Nifo was a representative of Averroism. He wrote commentaries on works of Aristotle and a treatise entitled *On the Intellect and Demons* (1492), in which he maintained that there are no immortal beings besides the intelligences of the spheres and the single intellect of men. He was commissioned to refute Pomponazzi's theory of immortality and to appeal to Thomas Aquinas' interpretation of Aristotle against that of Alexander of Aphrodisias. Ostensibly he did so, but in reality his sympathies were the other way. He joined a movement against Ptolemaic astronomy and edited the works of Averroes. In ethics, Nifo advocated the wise enjoyment of the artistic life.

Desiderius Erasmus (1466-1536) [Rotterdam, Paris, London, Basel]. Erasmus was the most outstanding of the humanists. He became an Augustinian reluctantly, because he preferred literary study to the life of the Church. He was seriously interested in theology, but he opposed what he regarded as the obsolete customs and modes of thought of the Middle Ages and advocated a return to a simple Christianity free from ecclesiastical ceremonial. His *Encomium Moriae* (*Praise of Folly,* 1509)—written with a play on the name of Sir Thomas More, whose close friend he was—was a biting satire on the weaknesses of all classes of men; it became one of his most popular works. Perhaps his greatest contribution to scholarship was an edition of the New Testament (*New Testament in Greek,* 1516) with a Latin translation which revealed many inaccuracies in the Vulgate version used by the Church. He remained aloof in the controversies which involved Luther, refusing to take sides, since he had friends in both camps. He was the embodiment of cool common sense and of faith in liberal studies and freedom of thought. Among his works were editions of the Greek and Latin Classics and the writings of the Church Fathers, published while he was at Basel. By means of his own writings he made Latin a living language.

Niccolo Machiavelli (1469-1527) [Florence]. Machiavelli was a statesman who placed the state at the center of human living and made even the moral and religious life dependent upon it because he was disillusioned by the corruption of the Church. In 1513 he set forth his position in his two best known works, *The Prince* and *The Discourses of Livy.* He studied the classic Roman historians and aimed to revive the Roman state. A thoroughgoing realist, he made an exhaustive study of the measures requisite for maintaining the power of the State. His great importance for modern political philosophy is attributed to his secular approach and his keen analysis of the nature of political problems and techniques.

Pietro Pomponazzi (1462-1525) [Mantua, Padua, Bologna]. Pomponazzi was both a doctor of medicine and a professor of philosophy. At Bologna (in 1516) he wrote *Immortality of the Soul* in which he disagreed with the current Thomistic and Averroistic interpretations of Aristotle's view on immortality. He defended the dignity of the individual and gave the soul a naturalistic interpretation, but regarded belief in immortality as a matter of faith. Above all, he maintained that belief in immortality is not a postulate or basis of moral conduct.

Sir Thomas More (1478-1535) [London]. Thomas More was educated at Oxford and the Inns of Court. He was a friend of Erasmus and was an outstanding representative of Renaissance humanism. He lectured on Augustine's *City of God* and, in 1516, published *Utopia,* which was both a description of an ideal commonwealth, and a satire upon the society of his day. *Utopia* advocated the willing subordination of the individual to the commonwealth, the community ownership of goods, national education, and employment for all. Magistrates were elective, and the glories of war were renounced. More became Lord Chancellor, but as a very devout Catholic he refused to recognize Henry VIII as head of the English Church; as a result, he was imprisoned and beheaded. He was canonized in 1935.

Huldreich Zwingli (1484-1531) [Wildhaus, Glarus, Zurich, Berne, Kappel]. Zwingli was a student of the classics and of the Greek New Testament, a humanist, and a friend of Erasmus. His thinking was theocentric and he regarded God as all-pervading. He accepted Augustine's doctrine of original sin. He supported a doctrine of election, as an expression of divine goodness and rational will, and a doctrine of atonement by substitution. The sacraments were to him symbols rather than conveyers of Divine Grace; thus he differed from Luther in his interpretation of the Lord's Supper as a commemorative service. His *Commentary on the True and False Religion* was published in 1525. Zwingli died at Kappel in a battle of the civil war which his views had incited between the Catholic and the Protestant cantons of Switzerland. While carrying the banner as chaplain he was struck down, then killed, and his corpse was quartered and burned.

Martin Luther (1483-1546) [Eisleben, Wittenberg, Worms]. Although he intended at first to study law, Martin Luther became an Augustinian friar. He lectured successfully at the University of Wittenberg, where, on October 31, 1517, he posted his request for discussion of 95 theses regarding the beliefs and practices of the Church. As the result of the study of St. Paul's Epistles, he became convinced that salvation is through faith alone, not through works or ritual. He objected to the Church's practices in connection with indulgences. Discussion led to further differences of opinion, and Luther's side was taken up by the German princes and electors. Confined by friends in Wartburg Castle, he translated the Bible into German and planned reorganization of the work of the Church. Luther's view of Scholasticism was derived from Gabriel Biel. He rejected Scholasticism and the Aristotelian tradition in favor of

Mysticism, because he distrusted the effectiveness of reason.

In connection with his earlier belief in salvation through faith alone, he found the revealed Word of God in the Bible and was not averse to the possibility of a twofold truth. His conviction was that salvation is by the free grace of God without institutional sanctions, and he accepted only the sacraments of baptism and communion, which he interpreted as not involving transubstantiation. While he believed in free will, he also believed Omniscient Providence knows the choices men will make. The work entitled *Confession of Augsburg* (1530) summed up Luther's doctrine.

Paracelsus (Theophrastus Bombast von Hohenheim) (1493-1541) [Einsiedeln, Strasbourg, Basel, Salzburg]. Paracelsus was a physician who believed that medicine should be concerned with the entire welfare of humanity. He was a man of very varied interests and lectured for a time at the University of Basel. He delivered his lectures in German, and he rejected the authority of Galen and Avicenna. He advocated simplicity in practical affairs, observation of Nature, knowledge of physical science, and investigation of phenomena which later became the subject matter of chemistry; but he was not convincing because he did not follow his own theories in detail. He made certain deductions from Neo-Platonic metaphysics and from theology which indicated the complex unity of the personality and its connection with the whole universe as a background. But his specific contribution to medical science was slight. He published a work entitled *Surgery*, (*Chirurgia Magna*).

Sebastian Franck (1500-1545) [Donauwörth, Strasbourg, Esslingen, Ulm]. Franck was a pantheistic, spiritualistic preacher who went from place to place in brief pastorates. He married before he was appointed to Strasbourg. Because of his violent attacks on both spiritual and secular powers in *Chronica,* he was dismissed from Strasbourg in 1531. During the succeeding years he was a soapmaker and printer. In his *Paradoxes* (1534), he propounded his pantheistic and spiritualistic views in opposition to all religious systems. He went to Basel where he continued to publish his views in popular writings which were widely read. Franck was disclaimed by Lutherans, Zwinglians, and Anabaptists; he stood for religious tolerance, and his ideas continued to carry weight, especially in Holland. He taught his students to exercise complete freedom of judgment apart from all theological dogma.

John Calvin (1509-1564) [Noyon, Paris, Basel, Strasbourg, Geneva]. Calvin was a student of theology, law and languages. He became a partisan of the Reformation and, in 1536, wrote his *Institutes of the Christian Religion*. He was a professor of theology at Strasbourg, whence he went as a delegate to the Diet at Worms. He prepared a catechism and liturgy, introduced congregational singing, and was of prime importance in organizing Protestantism. The rigor with which he applied his principles gave rise to opposition. Calvin stood for the absolute sovereignty of God in history and in life and for the complete dependence of man upon God's will. Man has freedom to yield to this will, but the conditions of his salvation are determined by God; and salvation comes through the working of the grace of God, before whom all believers are equal.

Petrus Ramus (1515-1572) [Cuth, Paris, Heidelberg]. An opponent of Aristotelianism, Ramus sought to free logic from the subtlety of the Scholastics. He believed that logic is the art of rational discourse. Its first part is the search for the grounds on which a question is to be answered; its second deals with the judgment, in three stages: syllogism, method and system, rising to ideas and God. In 1543 he published his *Aristotelicae Animadversationes (Observations on Aristotle)*.

Girolamo Cardano (1501-1576) [Milan, Pavia, Rome]. In his time, Girolamo Cardano was a noted mathematician, philosopher, and physician. His basic conception was hylozoistic naturalism, based on the continual transformation of one thing into another, indicating an original matter infinite in extent and filling all space, leaving no vacuum. A World Soul must be assumed to account for the production and movement of things. Love and hate penetrate all. Light and warmth are the phenomenal forms of the World Soul. Opposed to the light from heaven is the earth which is damp and cold, separating into earth, water, and air. Out of these develop all things, including metals and life. Each species has its own significance, which is to be studied by science. Cardano reasoned that the end of man is to know God and to mediate between the divine and the mortal. The rational soul is immortal and when permeated with light is inseparable from God. True wisdom is gained by union with God and by mathematics, as God has subjected the world to mathematical law. Men form states because of the weaknesses of individuals. Laws must be strong and unified under religion. Cardano's chief works were *On Subtlety* (1552) and *On the Variety of Things* (1556).

Bernardino Telesio (1508-1588) [Cosenza, Padua, Rome, Naples]. Another representative of the independent spirit of his time was Telesio. He studied mathematics and natural science, departed from the Aristotelian tradition, and founded an Academy of Science at Naples. About 1570 he wrote his most important work, *On Nature According to Its Own Principles*. He was influenced by the Pre-Socratics and the Stoics and regarded all reality as reducible to the hot and the cold and to matter. These accounted for such things as movement, rest, expansion, and contraction. In theory he was a strong empiricist, but his cosmology was panpsychist. Life and consciousness result from the principle of warmth, to which God has added the soul. The aim of all things is self-preservation; what contributes to this is good, what opposes it is evil.

Fausto Sozzini (1539-1604) [Siena, Geneva, Transylvania, Poland]. Sozzini, a vigorous theological disputant, was opposed by both Catholics and Protestants because he maintained a Unitarian position. He thought that no doctrine contrary to reason or moral progress should be accepted. In addition, he asserted that Christ was superhuman but that tradition had placed unwarranted interpretations upon Him. Opposition to Sozzini became so great that he spent his last years in retirement. But, in spite of this feeling, his writings, especially *De Jesu Christo Servatore* (*On Jesus Christ the Saviour,* 1578), had great influence on Unitarian thinking.

Michel de Montaigne (1533-1592) [Perigord, Bordeaux]. Montaigne is noted for his *Essays* (1580), literary expressions of an independent, critical attitude toward human existence, written as a result of a life spent largely in public office. He possessed an air of detachment which perpetuated the skeptical tradition of the ancients. At times Montaigne seemed to fall back upon a supernatural faith, though he was never an ardent defender of tradition. For the most part his position is one of common sense naturalism, which does not allow itself to be disturbed by anything.

Giordano Bruno (1548-1600) [Nola, Venice, Rome]. The figure that attracted most attention at this time was Giordano Bruno. He became a Dominican, but was later dissatisfied with the Dominicans' teachings. He cast aside their garb, wandered about Europe, and is reported to have joined the Reformed Church, only to find this unsatisfactory. He was arrested by the Inquisition at Venice and was brought to Rome, where, after imprisonment for seven years, he was burned at the stake.

He opposed Aristotelian logic and cosmology and was influenced largely by Nicolas of Cusa. Bruno embraced a pantheistic doctrine, identifying God and Nature, the active and the passive sides of reality. Each is infinite, he insisted, and there could not be two infinites, for they would limit each other. God is all Being, and the universe is his manifestation. He is the Soul of the Universe, the Monad of monads. Man is an emanation from God and returns to Him. The Copernican doctrine which had been published in 1453, ninety-five years before Bruno's birth, convinced him that the universe is one, the stars being suns like our own, centers of many solar systems. A typical work is *Concerning the Cause, the Principle and the One* (1584).

Jacob Zabarella (1532-1589) [Padua]. Zabarella was the most outstanding Aristotelian of the school at Padua, sometimes classed with Averroes, sometimes with the Alexandrists. Though he accepted the authority of the Church, his interpretations of Aristotle were not always in line with Christian doctrine. He believed in an original matter infinite in extent and eternal in existence. The heavens themselves are the independent source of all things, and the proofs of the existence of an independent God are all inadequate.

Similarly, he thought, the soul of man is simply the unity of the body. Human knowledge can free itself from the material and sensory only far enough to make generalizations. The First Mover flows into the soul of man and makes knowledge possible. Zabarella left immortality undetermined. Knowledge has two levels, natural objects and the elaborations which result from reflection. It is with the latter that logic deals; the sciences are applied logic, working in two directions between cause and effect. A work typical of Zabarella is *De Rebus Naturalibus* (*On Nature,* 1589).

Valentine Weigel (1533-1588) [Naundorf, Zschappen]. Weigel studied at Leipzig and Wittenberg, became a pastor, and acquired repute as a preacher, pastor, and administrator. His doctrines were suspected by churchmen, but he was able to clear himself. It became evident only after his death that he was at variance with the doctrines of the Church. His most important work was *Dialogue on Christianity.* He expressed contempt for all books and depended upon "inner light," but acknowledged dependence upon Plato, Pseudo-Dionysius the Areopagite, Thomas à Kempis, Eckhart, and especially *Theologia Germanica.* He connected philosophy with theology, clearly presenting an idealistic doctrine. He reasoned that there is space only within the universe; hence heaven and hell are not places. The activity of the human spirit generates all knowledge. When this inner light is joined by the indwelling spirit of God, supernatural knowledge results. Salvation results from the ascendancy of the principle akin to God over the worldly element alien to Him. To Weigel, the historical aspects of Christianity were subordinate.

Francisco Patrizzi (Patricius) (1529-1597) [Dalmatia, Padua, Ferrara, Rome]. Francisco Patrizzi wrote his chief work, *A New Philosophy,* while in Ferrara. It showed the influence of Neo-Platonism in that he interpreted the universe as a reflection of the Supreme Light, grounded in an Ultimate One, pervaded by a World Soul, and rendered orderly by these ultimate principles. From the Ultimate One flows all plurality; but through the force of Love the world of plurality will be re-united with the One. According to

Patrizzi, the spiritual and the corporeal are opposed to each other, as activity against passivity. The corporeal world acts only because there is a spiritual principle in it, but how these are united is a riddle. The soul and light are mediators between them. Matter possesses also the properties of extension and resistance. Our knowledge of pure space is more exact than that of physical things. Patrizzi hoped by his philosophy to reconcile science and Christian faith, and even to win heretics back to the Church, especially the German Protestants.

Francisco Suarez (1548-1617) [Granada, Rome, Salamanca, Lisbon]. Suarez was a very learned Jesuit, who followed in the tradition of Christian Aristotelianism. His *Disputationes Metaphysicae (Metaphysical Disputations,* 1597) offers a complete exposition of his philosophy. He showed mediatizing tendencies in a system called *congruism.*[2] He regarded theology as superior to philosophy and resting on divine revelation. Suarez' treatise on law opposed the divine right of kings and was regarded highly by Grotius. He also wrote a treatise against Anglicanism.

---

[2] The doctrine that divine grace is given when conditions are favorable for receiving it.

The thought of the Renaissance period was gradually assimilated into early modern philosophical thinking. There was no sharp division; the roots of the later period extended from the earlier one. In fact, much of what was afterwards called "modern" thought is a rediscovery of ancient theories, with a better appreciation of their aim and meaning. The influence of the medieval is felt strongly in many ways today, and the modes of thought formulated in the ancient world are still at work.

The seventeenth century was the time of the florescence of British empiricism and Continental rationalism. From Francis Bacon, on the one hand, and Descartes, on the other, ran two streams of emphasis in thought which were merged by Kant in the next century. Mysticism in religion was still a basis for philosophical thought, though rational study of comparative religion, culminating in the doctrine of rational or natural religion, was equally fundamental. The philosophy of the ideal society was continually studied, and suggestions regarding international relations were proposed. Obedience to the voice of conscience was strictly advocated. New aspects of natural science were incorporated into philosophy. Aristotelian logic was re-formulated, and the problem of knowledge was made a central concern. In addition, metaphysical questions received a large share of discussion. The period was indeed intellectually active and laid the foundation for many later developments.

Pierre Charron (1541-1603) [Paris, Bordeaux]. At first Charron studied law, but, dissatisfied with this profession, he began the study of theology and eventually became a priest. In his personality a lively temperament and a longing for seclusion and peace were in conflict. Perhaps as a result of this personal phenomenon, he reasoned that all men possess a double character, using the world on the one hand as an instrument for their ends, and on the other hand regarding it as something strange and foreign. He defended the Church and its beliefs, yet yielded to a skeptical attitude toward knowledge of the world. This is the essence of the wisdom he presented in his chief work *De la Sagesse* (*On Wisdom, c.* 1601): Man must begin with an understanding of himself, then live in accord with nature, and follow the cardinal virtues—prudence, justice, power, and temperance. The traits of men are vanity, frailty, inconstancy, and misery. Man differs from animals only in degree, and he pays particular penalties for the difference. Certainty is impossible; only the will can provide mastery of emotions and freedom of spirit and judgment. This is the spark of the divine spirit within man, which gives him his true worth.

Jacob Boehme (1575-1621) [Altseidenberg]. Jacob Boehme, who wrote a number of works, made his living as a cobbler and wrote in German, the only language he knew. His chief work was *Aurora* (*The Rising Dawn,* 1612), in which a mystical doctrine presented God as the abyss from which all things come and into which they return. All occurrences acquire significance through opposition, without which no progress would occur. The world is a manifestation of God who is both transcendent and immanent.

Boehme was especially concerned with the problem of evil and attributed it to a dual structure in the nature of God Himself. Everything is known through contrast with its opposite. Hence without evil God could not manifest his goodness, knowledge, life, and movement. God's nature contains seven primordial qualities, three representing phases of love, three representing phases of anger, and one representing fire (the principle of life). The Divine Nature in its first stage of development is the Father. He looked into Himself, formed the image of Himself, and this is the Son. The procession of this vision from the original nature of God is the Holy Ghost. Lucifer became enamored of the anger qualities of God and refused to advance from darkness to light, and therefore he fell, an event which resulted in the creation of the material world. Boehme believed that heaven and hell are on earth. He who renounces evil and develops from darkness to light, is already in heaven; he who clings to evil is already in hell.

Francis Bacon (1561-1626) [London, Cambridge, Paris]. Prominent in English life during his time, and finally made Lord Chancellor, Francis Bacon attempted to express the spirit of the age in his *Novum Organum* (1620). He intended to present in this work an inductive logic in contrast with the deductive which Aristotle had developed and which Bacon understood the Church to be using to support its doctrines. He proposed to organize investigation and to have many observers who would gather data, make limited summations, then pass them on to higher centers for larger generalizations. This was to be used for the furtherance of human happiness.

An essential feature was the formulation of methods for establishing causal connections. Exceptional cases were to be carefully noted and hasty generalizations avoided. Bacon thought that men's minds must be cleared of idols involuntarily worshipped—prejudices due to the interest of the individual (idols of the cave), the customs of the human race (idols of the tribe), the use of words (idols of the market place), and the influence of great names (idols of the theater). He believed experimental methods should be encouraged. In theology, he recommended a distinction between natural and revealed religion. The former could be studied as other fields of human knowledge are studied, but the latter, resting on a source beyond the tests of science and philosophy, must be left to those to whom such knowledge is granted. The observer, he thought, should keep his own personality in subjection and let Nature write her record without individual interference. But on the whole, he advocated "a marriage between the empirical and the rational."

Bacon has been criticized for having done too little of concrete value in the way of experiment; still, he died a martyr to this method, catching a fatal cold when testing the efficacy of refrigerating a fowl with snow.

Tommaso Campanella (1568-1639) [Calabria, Naples, Paris]. Campanella was another representative of the tendency of his time to emphasize empirical science and to examine the conditions of human knowledge. He considered the inner sense to be the basis of whatever validity there is in our knowledge of the external world. The inner sense is the basis of assurance of one's own existence and of the analysis of one's own experience. Proceeding from the sense of limitation of one's powers of knowing and acting, one arrives finally at the conception of a Being with infinite attributes, or God. The dread that all finite beings show toward annihilation indicates a desire on the part of all to return to God. This is the natural root of religion. In his *City of the Sun* (1623), Campanella outlined the structure of an ideal government, originating in a Divine Source, being transmitted through a representative on earth, like the pope, to a world-monarchy and on to subordinate units of government.

Lord Edward Herbert (1583-1648) [Cherbury, Eyton, Oxford, London]. Another symptom of the spirit of the early modern period is the deistic movement which took its start from the thought of Lord Edward Herbert of Cherbury. He was a soldier and a diplomat as well as a philosopher of religion, and he made an attempt to deal with the phenomena of religion on a natural rather than a supernatural basis. In an essay on *Truth* (1624), chiefly the truth of religion, Herbert maintained that there is a universal natural religion which characterizes all mankind and centers in the recognition of man's relation to God and to his fellow man. Out of this natural religion have come all the special forms of "revealed" religion by way of the interpretations and arrangements of priests and rulers. The true religion is a religion of reason, universal in its validity and based not on special authority, but on the inner nature of man. As such it appeals not to the unusual or miraculous, but to the common experiences of men. He believed that even the central and most valid part of Christianity is to be found in the ethical rather than the metaphysical aspect of it.

Hugo Grotius (1583-1645) [Delft, Leiden, Paris, Rostock]. A man with a wide range of interests, Hugo Grotius was a student of the classics, a commentator on the Scriptures, and a participant in public life. He is best known for his work *On the Law of War and Peace* (1625) in which he rested jurisprudence upon human nature and its needs. What reason deduces from these needs is basic law and is independent of particular periods of history or particular geographical locations. For content he reverted to the practices of Roman Law, as generalized in the customs of various peoples concerned and as interpreted under Stoic doctrine. This gave a basis to international law. One of Grotius' fundamental tenets was freedom of the seas.

Galileo Galilei (1564-1642) [Pisa, Vallombrosa, Florence, Padua]. Galileo was educated at Vallombrosa and Padua, where he studied classical languages, logic, and science, but was displeased with the science he was taught. His natural ability expressed itself in music, painting, and mechanical invention. His observation of a lamp swinging in the cathedral at Pisa led him to formulate the Law of the Isochronism of a Pendulum. Soon after this he invented a hydrostatic balance, wrote on the center of gravity of solids, and established fundamental laws of dynamics. A report about the telescope led him to construct one of his own and improve it until instruments which he had perfected and had produced were in demand throughout Europe. With this telescope he showed the mountains on the moon, discovered the satellites of Jupiter, and concluded that the Milky Way is composed of stars. He also observed the form of Saturn, the phases of Venus, and the spots on the sun. His discoveries led to questions regarding consistency with Scripture, and he was admonished to avoid theological discussion. He promised to do this and accordingly remained silent for several years. But in 1632 his *Dialogue on the Two Greatest Systems of the Universe* was published. Here, he compared the Copernican theory with the Ptolemaic theory of astronomy. He was called to Rome and examined by the Inquisition, required to recant, and incarcerated for a short time. Galileo spent his last years working in seclusion near Florence.

The philosophical significance of his work lies in the detailed confirmation of the mathematical structure and operation of the physical world and in the impetus he gave to the scientific interpretation of the universe, independent of theological views. His work emphasized the importance of appeal to the observation of nature instead of the importance of appeal to the Aristotelian tradition. Moreover, he defined the meaning of cause and effect and recognized force as an important factor in physics. His method was the fitting of mathematical formulas to empirical observation. Also, he stated the subjectivity of sense impressions.

Cornelius Jansen (1585-1638) [Acquoi, Louvain, Paris, Ypres]. Jansen supported the Augustinians in a struggle against the Jesuits, whom he accused of granting absolution without sufficient regard for the disposition of penitents. He maintained that the utter corruption of human nature made man helpless, without free will, and completely dependent upon the grace of God for salvation. He and his followers (the Jansenists) were noted for their severity and moral rigorism. Jansen was interested in a plan to make Belgium an independent Catholic republic analogous to Protestant Holland. The Church disapproved his doctrines and consequently his writings. His great work *Augustinus,* finished just before his death, was published posthumously (1640).

René Descartes (1596-1650) [La Haye, Paris, Neuburg, Holland, Stockholm]. Descartes was interested especially in establishing human knowledge on the firmest possible foundation. But he had noticed that throughout the centuries all the impressions of sense had been doubted by Skeptics. This made him wonder whether or not there was any way to reach certainty. He had studied mathematics, with notable success, and had united co-ordinate geometry and algebra, constituting analytic geometry. Therefore, he revived the mathematical ideal of the Platonic school as a model for philosophy.

However, mathematics is formal and non-existential, and natural science is concerned with existing facts and entities. Descartes sought a way to escape from the objections of the Skeptics. This he found in the Greek suggestion "Know thyself," and in the inward reflection supported by both Augustine and Campanella.

He formulated his classic phrase "cogito, ergo sum" ("I think, therefore I am") as given in his *Discourse on Method* (1637) and elsewhere, e.g., *Meditations* (1641) and *Principles of Philosophy* (1644). Even his doubting was evidence of his own individual existence. Here was the absolute beginning for all thought. Truth is to be reached by following out the implications of one's own experience of inner certitude. This inner sense of certitude was a reply to Bacon's suggestion that the observer eliminate himself from experience; according to Descartes, this is impossible. The argument is also a revival of Socrates' view that all knowledge comes ultimately from within.

After having established the certainty of his individual self, Descartes found it necessary to justify his belief in anything beyond himself. He asked himself how he knows the course of experience is not just his own dream. He thought this problem is solved by the consideration that if there were no material world, God would be allowing men to live continually with a false belief. This would be equivalent to deceiving men, which is counter to the character of God, for, as the thought of the centuries has held, God is the Perfect Being. This consideration presupposes the existence of God; and this is proved by the fact that we have the idea of perfection, which we, as imperfect beings, could not have originated, for this would be deriving an effect greater than its cause, a situation impossible in the light of the operation of causality. Descartes adds the consideration, derived from medieval thought, that the idea of God as a Perfect Being necessarily implies the idea of his existence, just as from the idea of a triangle it follows that the sum of its interior angles is two right angles. Upon the existence of God rests the validity of the existence of the realm of ideas. The idea of God must be innate in man, planted there by a cause adequate to the conception. All ideas are either adventitious, factitious, or innate. Only the last accounts for God. Error is due to the interference of the will with the spontaneous operation of ideas. The criteria of truth are clearness and distinctness, which really refer to the internal structure of ideas and their relations to other ideas.

Having justified the belief in the existence of spirit and matter, Descartes took up the urgent question of their interaction. They seem evidently to interact in the case of the human being, for our sense impressions are induced by the material world, and by deliberation our ideas seem to determine in some degree the movements of our material bodies. But it is impossible to say how the tangible and the intangible types of reality can influence each other. In fact, Descartes concluded that the interaction is a miracle effected only by the omnipotence of God. The point at which it is effected in the organism is the pineal gland within the brain, a structure that is not duplicated like the hemispheres of the cortex.

Descartes reasoned further that the soul has active and passive phases, the active being the processes of knowledge and volition, the passive being the states of sensation and emotion. The function of emotion is to incite the soul to certain volitions, though these can sometimes be aroused by thought. Conflicts between appetite and will result from simultaneous opposing tendencies to movement in the pineal gland. Following virtue will give the soul the inner strength which will make external troubles ineffectual.

Animals which were regarded as not having souls, he concluded, were *automata,* elaborate mechanisms which behave as they do because of their complex structures, but which are not really conscious.

Descartes established a dualistic separation of the realm of mind from the realm of matter and interpreted the latter so that he profoundly influenced the philosophy of modern science. His definitive expression of mechanism, which revived the approach of the ancient materialists and added the language of mathematics as the key to material nature, came to be known as the "Cartesian Revolution." He conceived the material world in terms of extension, divisibility, figure and motion; he stated that the infinitude of mathematical figures is sufficient to explain the infinite diversity of things. Matter is inert, receiving its motion originally from the First Cause, God, but subsequently acting solely in accordance with the laws of motion, and evolving the universe from an originally homogeneous mass. In his *Dioptrics,* Descartes applied his theories to the phenomena of vision.

Kenelm Digby (1603-1665) [Gayhurst, Oxford, Paris, Florence]. A naval commander and diplomatist as well as a philosopher, Kenelm Digby engaged in a private adventure which involved capturing several Flemish and Spanish ships off Gibraltar. This conduct was the subject of complaint by the Venetians and was disavowed by the English government. In his philosophy, Digby attempted to unite Aristotelianism, mechanism, and idealism. In religious conviction he wavered between Catholicism and Protestantism. He spent much time in Paris in the company of the learned. In 1644 he published the treatises *On the Nature of Bodies* and *On the Nature of the Soul.* He dealt with the corpuscular theory, making a sharp distinction between substance and quantity. Substance is the essence of a thing. Quantity is the interpretation of an object from the standpoint of size and, therefore, of extension and divisibility. Knowledge results from the occurrence of immaterial entities corresponding to external objects. Connected with the subjective contents are the processes of judgment and inference. All knowledge depends upon the unifying capacity of the soul. Digby believed this activity to be so unique that there is nothing in the intellect which is in the senses.

Benjamin Whichcote (1609-1683) [Shropshire, Cambridge, London]. Whichcote was provost of King's College and then Vice Chancellor of Cambridge. Cromwell consulted him about granting tolerance to the Jews. His puritan views cost him the provostship in 1660, but, complying with the Act of Uniformity, he was given the parish of St. Anne's, Blackfriars. He lectured on Sunday afternoons at Trinity College (1636-1656) and his reputation rested chiefly on his discourses, in which he sought to turn men from argumentation to the moral and spiritual realities that lie at the basis of religion, i.e., from words to realities and to reasons. He recognized two sources of enlightenment for man—reason and Scripture—both of which should be used. Christianity does not reject what is good in man, but rather completes and interprets it. Whichcote was the founder of Cambridge Platonism and a leading figure in the movement.

Pierre Gassendi (1592-1655) [Provence, Aix, Digne, Paris]. Gassendi revived the atomistic theory of Epicurus and combined it with theism. He objected to Descartes' theory of doubt and insisted that it is not merely from thought but from all of man's activity that the existence of the self can be inferred. The atoms were created by God out of nothing and were given an indestructible impulse toward movement. Organisms develop out of atoms with feelings. The order of nature comes from God. Science is concerned with secondary causes. The rational soul is immaterial. Gassendi reasoned that thought and volition are free. Knowledge results from sensation. The goal of life is happiness, which is attainable only through virtue. His book, *The Philosophy of Epicurus,* was published in 1649.

Thomas Hobbes (1588-1679) [Malmesbury, Oxford, Paris]. From the views suggested by Bacon, with whom he had been associated personally for a time, Thomas Hobbes drew a materialistic conclusion. He professed nominalism and analyzed mind as composed of sensory contents. Reality is individual and corporeal. He denied spiritual substance, yet he held that the appearances we experience are not identical with the material bodies that produce them. He thought of man fundamentally as a kind of mechanism; he even thought of the State as matter in motion.

Against this background, Hobbes developed in *Leviathan* (1651) a theory of the State, beginning with the assumption that men are by nature self-seeking and hostile toward each other. Yet finding constant hostility intolerable, they form a contract and turn over the enforcement of it to a sovereign power, to which men are thereafter irrevocably bound to be loyal in all circumstances. The State which is subject to rejection is no State at all but only disguised chaos. The purpose of the *Leviathan* was to expound the basis of human government; in the course of his discussion Hobbes raised many detailed questions about the books of the Bible. In this way he participated in the development of critical Bible study.

Despite his professed interest in the subject of the Christian Commonwealth, the underlying naturalism in his theory of man and society aroused great hostility during and after his time.

James Harrington (1611-1677) [Upton, Oxford, Isle of Wight, London]. James Harrington was a soldier, diplomat, and political philosopher. His ideas were fundamentally republican though he was for a time in the suite of Charles I. He did not take active part in the civil war, and after Charles's death he wrote *Oceana* (1656), which he dedicated to Cromwell. In this work he attempted to describe an ideal constitution, suited to England, under a law-giver like Cromwell. He selected property, especially in land, as the basic determiner of power. But he thought that executive power should not be in the same man or group for a great length of time. Landholding should be limited to an income of £3000 ($15,000). Voting by ballot should be used by the people in accepting laws passed by the senate; and magistrates and legislators should be rotated. The work became the subject of much controversy. After Cromwell's death, Harrington and some of his associates formed a club, the Rota, to try to put these policies into practice, but without success. He was arrested by order of Charles II and imprisoned in the Tower of London, but later released.

Blaise Pascal (1623-1662) [Clermont-Ferrand, Port Royal, Paris]. Pascal was a precocious youth, who formulated important mathematical theorems even in his teens. Later he joined the Jansenists at Port-Royal and led an ascetic life. His *Provincial Letters* (1656-1657) were directed against the Jesuits' doctrine—an opinion favoring liberty may be followed rather than strict law if the opinion commends itself to judicious minds or is supported by sound authority (probabilism). His letters were widely read.

Pascal maintained that man stands in a mid-position between Skepticism and dogmatism, misery and happiness. Man has certain immediate insights; e.g., he knows that there are such things as space, time, movement, number, and truth. Pascal wrote that sense and reason deceive each other. Then feeling functions, bringing satisfaction. Religious feeling is independent of understanding.

In it alone is there peace. Pascal asserted that the belief in God is a wager on which one can lose nothing.

Robert Boyle (1627-1691) [Lismore Castle, Eton, Florence, London, Oxford]. Robert Boyle studied the work of Galileo, and then he dedicated his life to scientific research, later becoming a member of the "Invisible College," which was incorporated as The Royal Society of London. He regarded matter as having purely mechanical properties. His investigations of the properties of air led to the law of the relation of the volume of a gas to the pressure upon it. He embodied the spirit of Bacon's *Novum Organum* though he claimed independence of all teachers. He also attempted to effect the transmutation of metals. Chemistry was his favorite study, but many of his discoveries were in physics. In *The Skeptical Chymist* (1661), he criticized current theories and advocated the view that matter is composed of corpuscles which in different arrangements constitute various substances. He studied the chemistry of combustion and of respiration, but was averse to undertaking anatomical dissections. He was also interested in the study of the Scriptures and studied Hebrew, Greek, and Syriac. Through the provisions of his will, he established the Boyle Lectures on the defense of Christianity against rivals; and he excluded discussion of the controversies between Christians. He supported missions to India and had a Gaelic translation of the Bible made at his own expense.

Joseph Glanvil (1636-1680) [Plymouth, Oxford, Bath]. Joseph Glanvil was rector of various churches, and became prebendary of Worcester Cathedral, and chaplain in ordinary to Charles II. He held that philosophy should limit itself to the elaboration of empirically given objects and follow a scientific Skepticism. In his *Vanity of Dogmatizing* (1661), he used philosophical Skepticism as a support for faith. Glanvil began with a Cartesian theory of causation but held that the attempt to grasp the whole system of things through reference to their causes is necessarily impossible. All facts are isolated without necessary connection with any others. He favored the Platonism of Cambridge over the Aristotelianism of Oxford and agreed with Henry More's theory of the pre-existence of the soul (*see* p. 137). He was impressed by superstitious stories, in spite of his philosophy, yet he defended the Royal Society in a work on the progress of knowledge since Aristotle. Glanvil also wrote in defense of Protestantism.

Antoine Arnauld (1612-1694) [Paris, Brussels]. Arnauld studied and taught theology with great success at the Sorbonne. He then became a follower of Jansenism and was embroiled in a controversy which led to disfavor and his expulsion from the Sorbonne. He was restored to favor under Louis XIV, but ten years later he fled to Brussels where he spent his last years in controversies with the Jesuits, Calvinists, and others. Arnauld was, with reservations, a follower of Descartes, but is noted chiefly for the formulation of *Port-Royal Logic* (1662), which has been the model for elementary logic textbooks since that time.

John Sergeant (1622-1707) [Barrow upon Humber, Cambridge, Lisbon, Rouen]. John Sergeant was converted to Catholicism, as a result of his studies in early Church history, and became an outstanding controversialist in defense of Catholic doctrine. During the "Glorious Revolution" in England he protected himself by using assumed names and passing himself off as a physician. His range of knowledge was said to be small and his ardent presumption great. A basic work was *Sure Footing in Christianity; or Rational Discourses on the Rule of Faith* (1665). The work was attacked by both Protestants and Catholics. Later, he also opposed Locke's theory of the subjective character of ideas and defended the immediate knowledge of things through pure understanding and reason.

Arnold Geulincx (1625-1669) [Antwerp, Lowen, Leiden]. Geulincx is noted for his theory of Occasionalism, which solved the problem of the relation between mind and body by declaring that there is no causal interaction. Each is set by Divine Power to run its own course without influencing the other. What happens in one is the "occasion" of what happens in the other, but without producing it. Finite bodies are modes of the Infinite Body, and finite spirits are modes of the Infinite Spirit. We must conduct ourselves with humility and learn to love God in pure unselfishness.

His most important work was *On Virtue* (1665), which he expanded later into the *Ethics*.

Henry More (1614-1687) [Grantham, Cambridge, Ragley]. The most mystical of the group of philosophers known as the Cambridge Platonists was Henry More. His parents were Calvinists, but Henry could not follow that austere doctrine, so he joined the Church of England. He became a fellow of Christ's College and received numerous offers of promotions, but refused all, preferring to live quietly at the college, which to him was paradise. He took orders, but did no preaching. He was much concerned over Quakerism (*see* p. 140), at first opposed to it, and later more sympathetic, with the thought that purity of heart was necessary for the grasp of true reason. More's *Divine Dialogues* (1668) was one of his most important works.

Richard Cumberland (1631-1718) [London, Cambridge, Peterborough]. When he was Bishop of Peterborough, Richard Cumberland published *A Philosophical Disquisition on the Laws of Nature* (1672), a Latin work highly commended by Pufendorf. It was written chiefly to oppose Hobbes's views. In this work Cumberland maintained that the laws of nature are unchanging propositions, which regulate the choice of good against evil and set standards of obligation which are independent of civil laws and decrees of government. All parties agree as to the nature of natural laws, whether they accept them as existing or not. He thinks that their existence is proved by reflection upon sensory experience. The basic principle of ethics is Universal Benevolence; no act which does not contribute to human happiness can be morally good. (This is opposed to the egoism of Hobbes.) Only benevolence is in accord with the plan of the universe. The foundation of rightness is the greatest good of the universe of rational beings. Individual good is absorbed into universal good. And happiness does not lie merely in sensory pleasures. Cumberland's thinking is reflected in the writings of a number of British moralists.

Samuel Pufendorf (1632-1694) [Chemnitz, Copenhagen, Heidelberg, Lund, Berlin]. Samuel Pufendorf traveled extensively. While a tutor at Copenhagen (in a family of a resident minister of Charles Gustavus, King of Sweden), he was imprisoned. During this time he meditated upon his recollection of the writings of Grotius and Hobbes and later published the results as *Elements of Universal Jurisprudence*. Heidelberg's first chair of the law of nature and nations was created for him. In *De Jure Naturae et Gentium (On the Law of Nature and of Nations,* 1672), he sought to complete the work of Grotius by analyzing Hobbes' thoughts and adding his own. All knowledge of law, Pufendorf held, flows from three sources—reason, civil statutes, and divine revelation—and produces three disciplines—natural law, civil law, and moral theology. Natural law is independent of revelation and takes men as they are. Religion is a means of realization of law and is originated by God. Natural law is limited to this life and is concerned with regulating external acts. He insisted, in opposition to Hobbes, that the state of nature is not one of war, but is one of precarious peace which has to be aided in order to preserve mankind. The State is a moral person, but its will is merely the sum of the individual wills of citizens. International law is not merely Christian but is rooted in all nations and is their common bond. He also delimited ecclesiastical and civil power, aided in the development of the theory of toleration, and influenced later German policy. Pufendorf's view was never acceptable to the Catholic Church. He was constantly opposed by Leibniz, and this opposition helped to obscure his real significance.

Nicolas de Malebranche (1638-1715) [Paris]. A follower of Descartes, Nicolas de Malebranche devoted his whole energy to the search for truth and wrote his views in a work entitled *Recherche de la Vérité (Search for Truth,* 1674). His conclusion was similar to Geulincx': it is God who gives us all our ideas about an external world corresponding to our experience. As Malebranche wrote, "We see all things in God."

Baruch Spinoza (1632-1677) [Amsterdam, The Hague]. Spinoza was also a devoted seeker of the truth. His own experience had led him to feel the pressure of social tradition in its effort to coerce human thought. He wrote treatises on the guidance of the intellect, on the State, and on the relation of political pressure to religious belief. In discussing theology, he, like Hobbes, raised questions about the internal evidence of the Bible as to its own authorship. These hold a place in the development of biblical criticism. On the question of the coercion of thought Spinoza's conclusion was that the State can by force determine overt action, but it cannot by the same means compel one to think certain thoughts; democracy is the form of government that is most true to humanity.

In his greatest work, published just after his death, he accepted the mathematical ideal that Plato and Descartes had upheld. For him it defined basic concepts and clearly stated all presuppositions as one does in a geometry text. Hence the work is entitled, *Ethics, Demonstrated in the Manner of Geometry* (1677).

To develop a basis for his ethical theory, Spinoza went back to the structure of the universe. In this he rejected Descartes' dualism and came to the same conclusion as Bruno that "substance," the ultimate subject of discourse, is infinite, and there cannot be more than one. This substance is God, or Nature, and has an infinite number of attributes; to us the most important of these are extension and thought. Each of these general attributes becomes expressed in particular modifications or modes—the particular objects we see in space, and the particular psychological experiences we have. The Ultimate Substance is neither matter nor mind. Seen as extended in space it is called matter, but seen under the form of thought it is called mind. The reconciliation of the differences between materialism and idealism is to be found in this distinction between the external and the internal views. Strictly speaking, Ultimate Reality is just "Substance."

Spinoza reasoned that man is so closely caught up in the structure of the universe that his only real freedom is intellectual, the freedom to contemplate and understand. Reason is the distinguishing mark of the human animal; the highest good of life, the goal of ethics, is to live according to reason and to perfect so far as possible the development of reason. Emotion is the disturbing factor in life, and what emotions need more than anything else is rational control. They lead men to live by the impulse of the moment instead of seeing things in the long range under the form of eternity, *sub specie aeternitatis*. Domination of man by the emotions alone is "human bondage"; rational ordering of the emotions is human freedom. To achieve this is difficult, but, as the closing sentence of the *Ethics* says, "But all things excellent are as difficult as they are rare."

The highest form of religion is the rational contemplation of God, or understanding of Nature; Spinoza expressed worship not by way of emotion but by way of intellect. For man as a rational creature the most appropriate love of God is intellectual—*amor dei intellectualis*. This kind of religion was of course unorthodox; hence Spinoza was formally placed under ban among the Jews and, not being a Christian, he was an outcast. However, he studied both the Old and the New Testaments. A century after his death his ideas began to wield great influence in philosophy.

Ralph Cudworth (1617-1688) [Aller, Cambridge]. One of the most noteworthy representatives of the Cambridge Platonists was Ralph Cudworth. His theory was set forth in *The True Intellectual System of the Universe* (1678). He maintained that there are eternal ideas of truth and goodness in the mind of God, which are the ultimate criteria for all judgments, and in which all knowledge and virtue participate. The impulse to seek these is innate in the human mind. Cudworth thought that nature is a system of harmonious workings of particular ends under Divine Providence. The soul is immortal, with a capacity to grasp absolute principles.

George Fox (1624-1691) [Drayton, Nottingham, Derby, London]. George Fox was the founder of the Society of Friends. During the period when he was apprenticed to a shoemaker, he felt an irresistible impulse to preach an inner appreciation of religion. Ultimate Truth he found not in books, not even in the Bible, but in one's experience of the presence of the Holy Spirit. Consequently, he rated low all institutionalism. Silent meditation, simplicity in living, and peaceful relations with one's fellow men were his fundamental principles. Fox's *Journal* was begun between 1678 and 1680.

Sir Isaac Newton (1642-1727) [Woolsthorpe, Cambridge, London]. At the same time that Leibniz contributed to it, Sir Isaac Newton aided in the growth of the theory which is now called the calculus. He also developed the theory of the spectrum and the structure of light, and invented the reflecting telescope. But his chief claim to fame rests upon the theory of universal gravitation and the laws of motion, an enormous synthesis or unification of previous scientific developments, and a scientific embodiment of the Cartesian faith in mechanical explanation. Newton's masterpiece is *Mathematical Principles of Natural Philosophy* (1687). He believed in absolute space, time, and motion as well as sensible space, time, and motion, in absolute and relative place. Space is the sensorium of God, the locus of God's knowledge. The existence of God is indicated by the order of the universe, as in the solar system and in the organs and behavior of animals.

John Locke (1632-1704) [Wrington, London, Oxford, Holland]. Born in the same year as Spinoza, John Locke's interest, like that of Bacon and Hobbes as well as Spinoza, was practical and social. His first important writings were his *Letter on Toleration* and his two *Treatises on Government.* Locke disagreed with Hobbes, insisting that since sovereignty is derived from a compact of the people it must always rest ultimately with them. But according to his own suggestion, he came to see that basic problems cannot be solved without an analysis of the structure of human experience. This he presented in his *Essay Concerning Human Understanding* (1690). The work began with a detailed consideration of whether men are born with innate ideas, as Descartes had suggested. Locke held that such ideas would be expected to appear very early in life and should be universally manifest in all men if they are truly innate. He was unable, however, to find any principles, either in theoretical understanding or in practical conduct, which fulfill these conditions; hence he concluded that there are no such ideas.

Then, Locke had to explain how ideas do come. And his answer was: through *sensation* and *reflection*. The former is the means of knowing the external world; the latter, which he sometimes called "internal sense," is the activity of the understanding itself. Beginning with simple ideas the mind builds up complexes, and holds them together through the ideas of substance, matter, spirit, and God. Qualities of bodies are primary or secondary, according to what they induce in our minds. The quantitative aspects of experience—such as size, shape, and motion—are primary; the qualitative aspects of experience—such as color, sound, taste, temperature, pleasure, and pain—are secondary. Substance, to which qualities "belong," is itself no quality and cannot be directly known. The mind also relates one thing to another, the two most important relations being identity and causality.

Men communicate their ideas by way of language, and Locke, therefore, devoted the third book of his *Essay* to the consideration of language. He found himself facing the problem of the relationship between *nominal* and *real* essences. General ideas, being abstractions framed by us, are nominal rather than real; thus he was inclined towards nominalism.

The fourth book of the *Essay* handled the crucial problem of the treatise: "How far does our attempt at knowledge succeed?" Locke's conclusion is that we have an intuitive knowledge of ourselves, a demonstrative knowledge of the existence of God, and a "sensitive" knowledge of the material world.

By arguing that experience begins as a kind of blank tablet, *tabula rasa,* and builds up a complex structure, Locke sought to discredit rationalistic claims that all knowledge can be deduced from "first principles."

Also, Locke justified the acceptance of the Christian religion on the ground of its fundamental reasonableness and value in practical living. Because of this view he is sometimes classed along with the deists although he did not formally ally himself with them.

Richard Burthogge (*c.* 1638-1694) [Plymouth, Oxford, Leyden, Bowden]. After being educated at Oxford, Richard Burthogge studied for and was awarded a medical degree at Leyden and, on his return to England, became a popular practitioner. He was a man of considerable learning, but also of pride and ambition. His writings championed tolerance in religion and the right of dissent. He gained reputation as a critic of Locke in his *Essay on Reason and the Nature of Spirits* (1694), explaining that all knowledge involves conformity with our power to know. Of the objects of the external world we know only phenomenal appearances, and our intellectual interpretations depend upon our modes of thought—in terms of substance, accidents, space, time, cause and effect. We must assume the existence of an external world in order to escape Skepticism. The nature of the world must be thought of as a spiritual principle which causes our experience.

John Toland (1670-1722) [Londonderry, Glasgow, Leyden, Oxford, London]. John Toland was an outstanding deist. He first became famous for his work *Christianity Not Mysterious* (1696), in which he maintained that there is nothing in the Gospels which transcends or conflicts with reason, but that priests and philosophers have transformed Christianity into a mystery. He was the first to be called a "free-thinker," and he coined the term "Pantheism."

Pierre Bayle (1647-1706) [Toulouse, Geneva, Sedan, Rotterdam]. Though he was the son of a Calvinist minister, Pierre Bayle was converted to Catholicism but, later on, reverted to Calvinism. He fled to Geneva, where he became acquainted with Cartesian philosophy. Bayle was appointed to the chair of philosophy at the Protestant University of Sedan, and when this university was suppressed he went to Rotterdam as professor of philosophy and history. The attempt to popularize literature was one of his activities; later, he gave his entire attention to the *Dictionnaire Historique et Critique,* which had great influence in France and especially upon Voltaire. Bayle's policy was to deal deferentially with "respectable prejudices," but to undermine them by presenting the opposite side in articles which were established by sound evidence. He was interested in doing justice to heretics, infidels, pagans, and atheists. He stated that theology and philosophy are unable to offer absolute certainty on any matter. He regarded reason and faith as mutually exclusive. He argued that freedom of thought is a natural right and that even an atheist can be a good citizen. Although he regarded the history of civilization as a record of man's effort to outgrow himself, he was not a revolutionary. Bayle objected to Spinoza's monism and favored Manichaeism.

9   The Enlightenment

The eighteenth century is often characterized as a period of enlightenment because of the vigorous intellectual activity in many areas. The problem of knowledge was discussed in detail; some thinkers emphasized the rational element in knowledge, while others accentuated the necessity for verification through sense data. In mathematics the theory of probability and the calculus were developed. The physical sciences saw renewed acknowledgment of the atomistic theory. The social sciences were studied and the following spheres were explored: the interpretation of history, human development, the ideal form of the state, international law, educational theory, and economics. The successful achievements of physics made it the model for a science of man. Religion was examined in many lights; for example, it was subjected to the criteria of reason. Comparative religion was studied, although there was continued interest in Mysticism. There were defenders and opponents of the idea of God; the essence of religion was debated, whether natural or supernatural, rational or revealed. More carefully than in any other period, the proponents of metaphysics analyzed the validity of the concept of matter and the nature of the objective world and attempted a re-interpretation in dynamic terms. New detailed analyses of man's being and place in nature were formulated, and, as a consequence, the science of psychology advanced. The status of the moral law was discussed intensively; on one hand its eternally objective character was maintained, and on the other its social, human origin was claimed.

John Norris (1657-1711) [Wiltshire, Oxford, Bemerton]. John Norris was a minister and a philosopher, and he was also one of the few English thinkers influenced by Malebranche. His position is seen in his *Essay Towards the Theory of an Ideal and Intelligible*

World (1701, 1704). Norris considered the intelligible world both in itself and in relation to human understanding. He opposed the theory maintained by Locke and the sensualists, though he agreed with Locke that there are no innate ideas. Also, he wrote in opposition to the Deism of Toland, holding that divine reason differs from human reason in degree though not in kind. In addition, Norris engaged in controversy with the Quakers over their interpretation of the "inner light." He was a student of Platonism and carried on correspondence with Henry More. In the spirit of Plato, he wrote the work entitled *Theory and Regulation of Love*. Norris believed that the contemplative love of God is the highest happiness.

Samuel Clarke (1675-1729) [Norwich, Cambridge, London]. The clergyman who became chaplain to Queen Anne and rector of St. James's, Westminster (London) was Samuel Clarke. He was a student of the theories of Newton and attempted to modify the theories of Descartes. Clarke was also somewhat of a classicist. He is best known for his Boyle Lectures of 1704-1705, published as *Discourse Concerning the Being and Attributes of God*. He regarded space and time as attributes of an infinite being. Clarke denied that the doctrine of the Trinity was held in the early Church and, thereby, started an active controversy with his contemporaries. He opposed deism, materialism, empiricism, and necessitarianism, and maintained the immortality of the soul. Clarke taught that the principles of morals are as certain as the truths of mathematics. They are based on reason, not on the consequences of acts, though goodness will be rewarded finally. These principles rest on the fundamental fitness of things. Applied to man, Clarke interpreted this to mean that men must treat one another as free agents.

Bernard Mandeville (1670-1733) [Dordrecht, Leyden, Hackney]. In his *Fable of the Bees* (1705) Bernard Mandeville pointed out the paradox in the relation of private conduct to public advantage. In private life desire for food, drink, and ambition, and envy of others are disapproved as selfish, yet they lead to civilization and social progress. According to Mandeville, it is difficult to have both material prosperity and moral uprightness.

George Berkeley (1685-1753) [Dysert, Dublin, London, Paris, Rhode Island, Cloyne, Oxford]. George Berkeley studied Descartes, Malebranche, and Locke and, from his early years, began to develop an idealistic interpretation of reality. In 1709 he published his *New Theory of Vision,* which was a purely psychological interpretation of three-dimensional space perception, through association of kinesthetic with visual sensations. In 1710 he published his *Principles of Human Knowledge,* and in 1715 his *Three Dialogues between Hylas and Philonous* appeared. In the latter he expounded his doctrine and met objections in the form of a conversation between two students, one of whom advocated his idealistic theory, which the other opposed.

Berkeley maintains that sensations are always in some knower's mind and that the contents of ideas are always sensations. Any object is thus only a package of sensations. The distinction Locke made between primary and secondary qualities—the former is supposedly independent of mind and the latter is supposedly dependent on it—vanishes upon careful analysis, all being equally functions of the knowing experience. The attempt to picture a material world beyond the sense realm duplicates the problem, giving a second realm with all the characteristics of the first. The concept of matter (material substance) is self-contradictory, being regarded sometimes as an active reality, sometimes as a purely passive, inert one. When men try to describe an object they are not seeing, they tacitly assume that some other observer is there seeing it.

Berkeley reasoned that knowledge is mental activity. Mind is the active principle of experience, and when we think of the universe as existing before there were any finite minds to experience it, we assume there is an Omnipresent Mind observing the universe through all time and eternity. Hence, Berkeley regards his interpretation of experience as a new proof of the existence of God. The individual realizes that at most moments in experience he does not originate his own ideas by means of deliberate efforts. This is an indication that something besides himself exists, but it must be understood as another spirit, not matter, because spirit is active and matter is not.

When objection is raised that we have no more idea of spirit than of matter, Berkeley concedes that knowledge of spirit is not attained by way of idea, but by way of a reflective process, which he designates by the term "notion" instead of "idea." Idea signifies the passive object of sense knowledge, whereas notion indicates the active side of the knowing process.

The result of Berkeley's thinking is the interpretation of the universe in dynamic, spiritual terms. He is not a solipsist or subjective idealist as he has often been called; he explicitly denies this in his *Third Dialogue.* In trying to clarify further the relation of finite to infinite mind, he moved in later years to an intellectual interpretation of the unity of finite with infinite mind, an appreciation of unity similar to that of the Mystic but attained by intellectual analysis, not by immediate intuition. In a sense we see God in all nature, as we see other persons through their bodily presence. But this is in both cases an interpretation through a mental process that is not merely sensory. Berkeley was really an objective idealist.

Anthony Ashley Cooper (1671-1713). The third Earl of Shaftesbury, later called Lord Ashley, was the author of *Characteristics of Men, Manners, Opinions, and Times* (1711), in which he based morality on an intuitive sentiment. As the organs of the body function together under the direction of the soul, so different individuals are united in higher unities—e.g., united in the species, and the species united finally in the life of God. Hence, the universe is a cosmos, a thing of beauty. Life is subject to a conflict of impulses, the selfish and the unselfish. Morality consists in a proper balance between these two. This harmony is felt by a moral sense analogous to the sense of beauty. Man is distinguished from the lower animals by rising to a reflective awareness of this moral sense. This condition of harmony, which is virtue, is also happiness. It is its own reward and needs no promise of a heaven hereafter, which indeed makes men mercenary in their motives. According to Lord Ashley, true religion is an aid to virtue, for it teaches the rule of the universe through a loving and protecting God who makes the universe a harmony.

Arthur Collier (1680-1732) [Wiltshire, Oxford, Langford Magna]. Arthur Collier was a student of the philosophy of Descartes and Malebranche. His chief work was *Clavis Universalis (Universal Key* or *A New Inquiry after Truth,* 1713), in which he attempted to prove the impossibility of an external world. Here, he rejects, with common sense, the theory of representative perception and holds that imagination and sense perception differ only in degree. The seeming externality of the visible world is erroneous, and a visible object is not really external. An external world would be both finite and infinite, movable and immovable. Furthermore, Aristotle's conception of matter as pure potentiality reduces it to nonexistence. The external cause of our experience is the operation of a divine power. Collier praised Norris' work. Although his own thinking is remarkably similar to that of Berkeley, it was quite independent. In theology, he was Anglican, and, in ritualistic practice, he favored the liturgy of the High Church, though he was not always strictly orthodox in his ideas. Collier had strong leanings toward Arianism.

Anthony Collins (1676-1729) [Heston, Cambridge, London]. The deistic train of thought was continued by Anthony Collins in his *Discourse on Freethinking* (1713), contending that the original meaning of Scripture had been perverted by priestly distortion. In other works, Collins defended *necessitarianism;*[1] he held that the soul might be material, but if it were immaterial it would not, therefore, necessarily be immortal.

G. W. Leibniz (1646-1716) [Leipzig, Mainz, Paris, Hanover]. In 1714, G. W. Leibniz published his *Monadology,* which is often taken as the summary of his doctrine of substance. In snatches of time from his duties as a man in public life, he managed a thorough study of mathematics and gave the calculus the notation which has

---

[1] The theory that every event in the universe is determined by causal necessity, excluding chance and freedom.

since been employed; he developed logic in new directions some of which supplied the roots for present-day symbolic logic; he constructed an idealistic metaphysics, approaching the subject from the side of Cartesian rationalism and balancing Berkeley's approach from the side of British empiricism; and he formulated a rebuttal (*New Essays on Human Understanding*) to Locke's *Essay,* which he did not publish because Locke died just as it was finished.

Leibniz' reply to Locke stated essentially that Locke had sought evidence of explicit innate ideas and had misconstrued Descartes' conception, which referred to latent tendencies to think in certain ways. Leibniz' position is expressed in the sentence: "There is nothing in intellect which was not first in sense, except intellect itself." It was from this standpoint that he had answered Locke's work, paragraph by paragraph. (Leibniz' *New Essays on Human Understanding* should be read along with Locke's *Essay* by all students of theory of knowledge.)

In his logical studies Leibniz recognized processes such as logical addition and multiplication which had not been given explicit formulation, along with those formulated by Aristotle and his followers. In this way he generalized logical science to cover more than the tradition, and made it applicable to mathematical modes of thought as well as to the qualitative modes of ordinary discourse.

In his metaphysical doctrine Leibniz analyzed all reality into units of force, replacing the inert atoms of materialism, and corresponding to the infinitesimal points which were the limiting constituent elements in differential and integral calculus. Each of these may be regarded as a perspective from which the universe can be viewed and is viewed with various degrees of clearness of consciousness. He called these units monads. There are body monads and soul monads, constituting the scale of reality from the lowest to the highest—God, the monad of monads. Each is unique and is not affected from without. Each lives out its own career, developing its own potentialities from within. In so far as their various careers interplay with each other, all are elements in a single system in which each is correlated with the others, just as mathematical variables are functions of each other. Thus, there is what Leibniz called a pre-established harmony among them, but it is logical rather than causal. Monads as active centers do not exist in space and in time; space and time are themselves the modes of expression of the consciousness the monad experiences.

Leibniz believed the universe is the expression of Perfect Reason. Therefore, it must be the best of all possible worlds. All apparent evil would be transformed by a larger view of the universe.

Christian Wolff (1679-1754) [Breslau, Leipzig, Halle]. Christian Wolff was a man with a wide range of interests. At the University of Halle he lectured on mathematics, physics, and all aspects of philosophy. He was an extreme rationalist, basing his teaching on the work of Leibniz and emphasizing the doctrine of pre-established harmony; but for the content of his rationalism, he appealed to experience. He divided the sciences into the theoretical and the practical. For many fields Wolff wrote textbooks, which were widely used in the universities. He helped to popularize interest in philosophy, but his lasting influence was on vocabulary rather than content. One of Wolff's chief works was *Rational Thoughts on God, the World and the Soul of Man, and also All Things in General* (1719).

William Wollaston (1660-1724) [Staffordshire, Cambridge, Birmingham]. William Wollaston was interested in philological and theological questions and wrote various treatises, most of which he burnt. His most important book was *Religion of Nature Delineated* (1722), a version of intellectualist theory of morals, like that of Samuel Clarke. According to Wollaston, every act involves a judgment as to its underlying relations; therefore, the decision as to whether an act is right or wrong depends upon the correctness of this judgment; and all virtue is an expression of the notion of truth. One should not treat a man like an inanimate thing because this is false. Wollaston's views led to some question of his orthodoxy; thus, he gave up his professional work as a clergyman.

Giovanni Battista Vico (1668-1744) [Naples]. Giovanni Battista Vico studied law, history, and philosophy, held the chair of rhetoric at the University of Naples, and was appointed historiographer to King Charles III of Naples. Though it was slow in gaining recognition, Vico's *Principles of a New Science Concerning the Common Nature of All Nations* (1725) was the basis of his fame and influence. In this treatise, Vico attempted to distinguish the essential from the accidental features of social phenomena and to discover the laws governing the formation, development, and decay of societies. These laws, he believed, exist eternally in the mind of God. He was especially influenced by reading Plato (who described the ideal man) and Tacitus (who described the actual man). Vico was also influenced by Francis Bacon and Grotius, who, respectively, stimulated him to investigate problems of history and to develop a philosophic jurisprudence. Vico became concerned with the latter subject when he tried to explain why varying codes exist even though the principle of justice is one and eternal. He found the answer in the changing history of humanity (which he approached through the study of Roman law), manifested in three stages, the divine, the heroic, and the human.

Matthew Tindal (*c.* 1656-1733) [Devonshire, Oxford]. Matthew Tindal was the son of a clergyman; he studied law and turned for a time to Catholicism. Later he became a Protestant freethinker whose writings attracted considerable attention in England and on the Continent, especially the celebrated *Christianity as Old as the Creation, or the Gospel a Republication of the Religion of Nature* (1730). This book attempted to remove the miraculous elements from religion and to show that its claim to reverence lies only in its morality. His treatise has been called the "bible" of deism. Tindal expounded the doctrine of "natural religion" (religion of reason), consisting of ideas based on rational knowledge without appeal to revelation and opposing subjective belief. He observed that natural religion is implicated in the constitution of the world and the natures of God and man; hence it is intrinsic and not dependent upon historical occurrences. Reason is a natural light by which God is necessarily known. Tindal believed this to be presupposed by revealed religion itself.

John Gay (1669-1745) [Cambridge, Bedfordshire]. The son of a country clergyman, John Gay was educated at Cambridge and elected a fellow there in 1723. He taught Hebrew, Greek, and ecclesiastical history. His only philosophical writing was an essay of sixteen pages called *Dissertation Concerning the Fundamental Principle of Virtue or Morality,* which appeared anonymously as a preface to a translation of *An Essay on the Origin of Evil* by Edmund Law (from the Latin by Archbishop King), published in 1731. It was based on associationism[2] in psychology, and utilitarianism[3] in ethics. Gay was influenced by Locke, and in turn had great influence on numerous writers—including David Hartley, and indirectly upon Bentham and James Mill—during the century which followed. He defined virtue as conformity to a rule of life, directing the actions of all rational creatures with respect to each other's happiness; to this all men are obligated, that is, are bound to as a condition for happiness. Gay wrote that the moral sense which men have is not innate, but is acquired from experience, their own or others'.

Joseph Butler (1692-1752) [Wantage, Oxford, Stanhope, London, Bath]. Joseph Butler wrote *Sermons on Human Nature* and *Analogy of Religion* (1733), in which he maintained that the basis of morality is conscience which speaks with a voice of authority and must be followed without regard to consequences. Its judgment is immediate, not a deduction from practical reason; nor is it a sense of harmony or utility. Conscience is not rooted in religion, although religion is its strong ally, especially in directing attention to the hereafter. According to Butler, the acceptableness of the idea of immortality rests on arguments from analogy with processes occurring in Nature.

David Hume (1711-1776) [Edinburgh, Paris]. David Hume, who worked as a secretary and librarian, is noted for the following

---

[2] The theory that all mental processes consist of the combination of simple sensory ideas originally distinct.

[3] The doctrine that the good is the useful, especially in producing the greatest amount of happiness in society.

153

works: *Treatise of Human Nature, Natural History of Religion, Dialogues concerning Natural Religion,* and *History of England.*

In the *Treatise of Human Nature* (1737) Hume attempted to carry forward, in his way, the analysis of human experience which Locke had undertaken in his *Essay.* Hume carried sense empiricism beyond Locke to the extreme, and, while agreeing with Berkeley that matter as something beyond sensation is an unverifiable inference, he drew the same conclusion about spirit. In this he ignored entirely Berkeley's recognition of the fundamental difference between knowledge of the mind itself and what is within the mind. He devoted attention wholly to the sensory contents of experience, refusing to make presuppositions on whose basis such contents are intelligible. He reduced all experience to "impressions" of sense and "ideas" which are the lingering images of them. Recognizing that "impressions" are irreducible to anything more ultimate, he classed them all as innate in this sense.

Hume believed that we do not perceive our own bodies, but of these, too, we have only sense impressions. There is no mind, only a succession of perceptions, a heap or collection of perceptions united by certain relations, and falsely supposed to be endowed with an underlying "personal identity."

One of the most important relations among phenomena is causation. But when Hume examined this he came again upon the difficulties that had been noted by Sextus Empiricus in the second century A.D. Sense empiricism can find no necessary connection between one phenomenon and another. All that is discoverable is uniform succession in certain cases. It is habit at work psychologically that produces the notion of cause and effect. The notion of power in a cause is a projection of our feeling of effort when we act.

The fundamental principle of explanation is association of ideas. In this connection, Hume revived the laws—suggested by Aristotle—of association by similarity and by contiguity.

His ethical theory centers action in that which proves agreeable or disagreeable and bases all consideration for others on a feeling of sympathy. He made an important attempt to explain the relations between moral feeling and rational moral analysis.

Hume realized that this theory had resulted in skepticism, and he was aware of the difference between the views he developed in his study and those he encountered in his practical contacts with his fellows. But he was unable to solve the problem and to reconcile the two. He presented the paradox of writing history when there is no substance which has a history. He was consistent, perhaps, in doing the one thing a phenomenalist can do, namely, record the succession of phenomena, though in his record he introduced much more than that. It is not surprising that when Hume wrote on religion in *Natural History of Religion,* he treated it merely from the psychological and historical standpoints. He based religion on fear, ignoring Cicero's suggestion that this develops superstition rather than religion. Hume's famous essays *Of the Immortality of the Soul* and *Of Miracles* state that belief in these must rest wholly on religious faith. Proof can never be adequate.

One of Hume's most significant contributions to philosophy was his classic questioning of many rationalistic assumptions. In his *Enquiry concerning the Principles of Morals,* he contended that the so-called dictate of natural law in morals is only the dictate of social utility. In his *Dialogues concerning Natural Religion,* he questioned the conclusiveness of the arguments and principles of natural religion. His skepticism about "necessary connection" in causal relation has remained a stimulus to one of the most active philosophic controversies.

Viscount Bolingbroke (1678-1751) [Battersea, London, Paris, Dawley]. One of the most brilliant of English statesmen and orators was Viscount Bolingbroke (Henry St. John), who was very active in British politics but whose life was marked by superficiality and selfish ambition. Politically, he was sometimes in favor, sometimes out of favor, and was called the Alcibiades of his time. He associated with Pope, Swift, and other men of letters, and was greatly admired by Voltaire for his brilliance and charm of manner. His literary style was imitated by Burke on occasion. In his *Letters on* *the Study and Use of History* (1735-1752) Bolingbroke wrote as a deist and violently attacked the doctrines of Christianity. In a period of political disfavor he participated in Alexander Pope's literary discussions and formulated the philosophy used by Pope in his *Essay on Man*. The impression of brilliance made by Bolingbroke on his contemporaries has not continued into later times.

Baron de La Brède et de Montesquieu (1689-1755) [La Brède, Bordeaux, Paris]. Montesquieu (Charles Louis de Secondat) spent much of his life in public affairs at Bordeaux. At the same time he engaged in study and presented papers on philosophy, politics, and natural science to the academy there. In early writings he satirized, anonymously, the social and literary conditions of his day. Then he traveled extensively through Europe, observing men and society. In 1748 he published his chief work, *Esprit des lois* (*Spirit of the Law*), the purpose of which was to show how the laws of a country are related to its social and geographical characteristics, such as the constitution of the government, customs, climate, religion, and commerce. It was a notable attempt to be empirical in the study of actual conditions. Its publication was opposed by Helvétius and others of his friends, and it was also put on the Index, but by other critics it has been called the most important book of the eighteenth century.

Julien Offray de La Mettrie (1709-1751) [St. Malo, Leyden, Paris]. In 1748 Julien Offray de La Mettrie published his *L'Homme Machine* (*Man a Machine*), a classic attempt at a materialistic interpretation of human life. During an illness, his observations of the effect of physical conditions upon psychological experience had led him to this theory. It met with so much opposition that he was forced to withdraw to Leyden. La Mettrie's ethical doctrines designated the aim of life as pleasures of the senses and self-love. His metaphysics was atheistic, and he denied the immortality of the soul.

David Hartley (1705-1757) [Illingworth, Bath]. From the empirical tendencies of British thought, David Hartley developed the system of associationist psychology which has influenced many thinkers. As a physician, he interpreted consciousness in terms of the action of brain substance, but did not adopt materialism. Hartley maintained that the soul receives sensations by means of vibrations. Simple ideas, by association, become united into complex ideas, which build up beliefs. Hartley's *Observations on Man, his Frame, his Duty, and his Expectation* was published in 1749.

Emmanuel Swedenborg (1688-1772) [Stockholm, London]. Emmanuel Swedenborg combined the interests of the biological and physical scientist and engineer with that of the mystic. His writings encompassed many fields. In astronomy, he proposed a cosmology similar to the nebular hypothesis. He conceived the universe as a harmonious organization of units of substance of various ranks. Swedenborg thought that the soul fashions its own body. It also has moments of direct experience of God, who reveals Himself in visions. God is the only true reality, whose essence is Divine Love, and whose body is Wisdom. Swedenborg's *Arcana Coelestia (Celestial Mysteries)* was published during the period 1749-1756.

Alexander G. Baumgarten (1714-1762) [Berlin, Halle, Frankfurt]. Alexander G. Baumgarten was a disciple of Wolff. He became famous for his study of aesthetics, making it a discipline on a par with other aspects of philosophy and giving it the name now used. Baumgarten's *Aesthetica* was published in 1750.

Henry Home (1696-1782) [Kames, Edinburgh]. Although he was a lawyer, Henry Home wrote on ethics and aesthetics. His *Essays on the Principles of Morality and Natural Religion* (1751) supported the theory of innate ideas and only apparent freedom for man. This statement aroused opposition on the part of the clergy. Home also wrote an influential work on aesthetics, maintaining that the sense of beauty lies in one's appreciation of the degree in which an object fulfills some end, whether or not that end is felt to be useful.

Jonathan Edwards (1703-1758) [East Windsor, Northampton, Princeton]. Jonathan Edwards preached a doctrine of divine sovereignty and the election of man. This was the central theme in his *Freedom of the Will* (1754). Here, he interprets freedom as a disposition of the heart, rather than as a self-determining power.

With the disposition of the heart, the foreknowledge possessed by God is compatible. He thought that the attitude of the heart makes one virtuous. For a time Edwards was a successful preacher, but the strictness of his doctrines led at length to estrangement of his congregation.

Denis Diderot (1713-1784) [Langres, Paris]. One of the leaders of the French enlightenment was Denis Diderot. At first, he advocated theism, but later he was an exponent of Pantheism. It was his view that philosophy must rest on experience. Diderot maintained that analysis leads to atoms, which even in inorganic things contain potential feeling. Out of these, organisms develop. Teleology must give way to description in science. The universe is an individual which maintains its balance through constant change of occurrences. Consciousness of self is due to the constancy and gradualness of psychic changes. Diderot's *Interpretation of Nature* was published in 1754.

Étienne Bonnot de Condillac (1715-1780) [Grenoble, Paris, Flux]. In his *Treatise on Sensation* (1754) Étienne Bonnot de Condillac described experience as being constituted by sensations, attention being accounted for by the intensity of sense experience and comparison as a kind of concomitance or association of one sensation with another. He regarded memory as a secondary effect. Nevertheless, he maintained Cartesian dualism of body and soul. Thus, Condillac reconciled his psychology with his Catholic theology.

Francis Hutcheson (1694-1747) [Drumling, Glasgow, Dublin]. Basing his views on those of Locke and Shaftesbury, Francis Hutcheson believed in a moral sense, which grasps right and wrong immediately. This process of moral judgment has been called "emotional intuitionism." General happiness is approved by all. He believed beauty is the unity of the many and is directly pleasing without reference to utility. Hutcheson was the first to use the phrase "the greatest good for the greatest number." His *System of Moral Philosophy* was published in 1755.

Edmund Burke (1729-1797) [Dublin, London]. Edmund Burke's early education was influenced by a member of the Society of

Friends, whose views were an important factor in his life. While at Trinity College (Dublin) Burke was interested in poetry, oratory —especially that of Cicero—history, and philosophy. He studied for the bar but found legal subjects distasteful. His early work *Vindication of Natural Society,* written in imitation and ridicule of Bolingbroke, was readily received by the public. Soon after appeared his *Philosophical Inquiry into the Sublime and the Beautiful* (1756), a work of no great significance but praised by numerous outstanding men, including Johnson and Lessing. Goldsmith and Hume became his friends. Burke studied carefully the conditions of the colonies and became private secretary to W. G. Hamilton, Secretary for Ireland. In the meantime, Burke became a prominent member of the literary club which met at the Turk's Head. In 1766 he entered Parliament and soon became known for his eloquence in spite of a manner of speaking not altogether pleasing. Thereafter he held various political offices. His work in Parliament was noted for its care, earnestness, brilliance, and high ethical tone, and when he retired, after thirty years of service, he received the thanks of the Commons and a liberal pension from the crown. Burke rendered distinguished service for the cause of humanity, working for the abolition of the slave trade, against the greed of stockholders in India, and for justice and conciliation with America. He wrote on many subjects connected with national affairs. His speeches impeaching Warren Hastings, Governor General of India, ruined the man politically even though he was acquitted. Burke's later years were marked by a strong opposition to the reforms of the French Revolution; this opposition was expressed in his writings, including *Reflections on the French Revolution.* Burke's first concern was for social stability. In general, objectivity made it impossible for him to cling closely to any political party, yet he strongly influenced the course of public affairs. Burke maintained that members of parliament are not instruments of their constituents, but men chosen by them to think independently for the good of the Commonwealth. Fairmindedness and impartiality are interesting qualities of Burke's thinking.

Joseph Boscovich (1711-1787) [Ragusa, Rome, Milan]. For many years Father Joseph Boscovich was professor of mathematics and philosophy at the Jesuit College in Rome. He is known for his proposal of a significant theory about the composition of matter, related to the metaphysics of Leibniz. Boscovich regarded matter as composed of indivisible points endowed with forces of attraction and repulsion, thus giving a dynamic interpretation. This theory was represented in his *Theoria Philosophiae Naturalis (Theory of Natural Philosophy)*, published in 1758.

Claude A. Helvétius (1715-1771) [Paris, Berlin]. Claude A. Helvétius was a literary man, holder of high public office, philanthropist, and philosopher. In his *De l'esprit (Of the Spirit,* 1758), he argued for the original equality of all men and attributed later differences to education and circumstances. Man's basic motive is self-interest. He believed that the interest of one and of all needs to become identified. Sensation is the basis of all human capacities. There is no absolute right or justice; these factors vary with the customs of individual cultures.

Jean Le Rond d'Alembert (1717-1783) [Paris]. Educated in law and medicine by the Jansenists, Jean Le Rond d'Alembert devoted himself finally to mathematics. In this field and also in mathematical physics his influence was of prime importance. D'Alembert wrote the preliminary discourse on the progress and relations of the sciences for Diderot's *Encyclopédie*. He also wrote on the theory of music. In religion d'Alembert was skeptical. His view of ethics was based on sympathy. *Elements of Philosophy* by d'Alembert was published in 1759.

Adam Smith (1723-1790) [Kirkcaldy, Edinburgh, Glasgow, London]. Adam Smith was primarily interested in the foundations of morals and in the methods of improving the condition of men. In his *Theory of the Moral Sentiments* (1759), he rests moral judgments on sympathy, the ability of a spectator to participate in the feelings of the actor and to accept the end of the action. Smith places its first manifestation in the tendency to imitate, and he claims that it results in the development of the attitude of an impartial spectator. Smith's popular fame rests with his economic treatise, *Wealth of Nations* (1776).

Voltaire (1694-1778) [Paris, London, Cirey]. An advocate of freedom of thought, and a literary, not a technical, philosopher, Voltaire (François Marie Arouet) represented natural religion, and was akin in spirit to the English deists, whose influence he helped to spread on the Continent. He opposed bigotry, intolerance, and social evils; he believed in a righteous God and in a universal morality, not confined to a particular code. In *Candide* (1759), he satirized Leibniz' optimism in believing that this is the best of possible worlds. *Le Philosophe Ignorant (The Ignorant Philosopher, 1766)* is one of the most direct expressions of Voltaire's position in philosophy.

Jean Jacques Rousseau (1712-1778) [Geneva, Paris, Montmorency, Bern, England, Ermenonville]. Jean Jacques Rousseau led an irregular life. He was of Huguenot ancestry, received his early education at the hands of relatives, and was later apprenticed to an engraver. He went to Paris, where he developed a new system of writing music and gained access to intellectual circles. He wrote for the stage and engaged in the discussion of the relative merits of French and Italian music. In 1754 Rousseau wrote a *Discourse on the Causes of Inequality among Men*. He also contributed articles on music and on political economy to Diderot's *Encyclopédie*. Then he presented *New Eloise* (1760), a plea for natural living with freedom of emotion; *The Social Contract,* on the ideal government, and *Emile,* a series of thoughts on naturalness in education, both appearing in 1762. Rousseau's religious thought, though vacillating, was essentially deistic. In his practical philosophy, he emphasized the priority of the "general will" over the will of the individual. He maintained that the state came into existence through an agreement among men upon conditions of living together. In the condition of nature all men are equal, but through the influences of society and civilization they become unequal. He advocated the revision of educational methods to make them in closer accord with "nature."

In spite of a favorable public response the authorities opposed him. He moved to England at Hume's invitation, and there he began his *Confessions;* after a time, he quarreled with Hume and returned to France, where he settled again in Paris. In his later years, he was subject to a delusion that plots were being made against him. Rousseau died at Ermenonville, near Paris.

J. H. Lambert (1728-1777) [Milhousen, Basel, Munich, Berlin]. Considered a noted mathematician, Lambert also studied logic and epistemology. His *Neues Organon (The New Organ,* 1764) attempted a study of a theory of knowledge that would be superior to Wolff's; this interested Kant, who corresponded with him. Lambert's work in astronomy is notable; he also undertook to develop a mathematical logic.

Thomas Reid (1710-1796) [Glasgow]. An appeal to common sense was the method which Thomas Reid believed would solve the problems of philosophy. He held that in perception we do not know a representative of an external thing but the thing itself, though he admitted that perception is unconsciously performed. All knowledge is built upon principles that are self-evident, and every man with common sense is aware of such principles. Reid recognized causality as one such principle and believed it should not be subjected to criticism. The trouble with the whole succession of skeptical philosophers from Zeno to Hume is that they neglect common sense, according to Reid. In 1764, he wrote *Inquiry into the Human Mind on the Principles of Common Sense.* Reid's influence was felt in the U. S., notably at Princeton.

Gotthold E. Lessing (1729-1781) [Kamenz, Leipzig, Berlin, Wolfenbüttel]. Gotthold E. Lessing made a name for himself as a poet (lyric and dramatic) and as a critic and philosopher of art. His *Laokoon* (1766), in which he discusses the limits of painting and poetry, has become a classic. For the most part, Lessing's later years were occupied with theological discussion, especially over the *Wolfenbütteler Fragmente,* defending the deistic point of view. He maintained in the play, *Nathan the Wise,* that noble character is independent of creed.

Moses Mendelssohn (1729-1786) [Dessau, Berlin]. A literary philosopher, Moses Mendelssohn was noted for the defense of immortality in his *Phädon* (*Phaedo,* 1767) and for his emphasis on belief in the existence of God. He was a pioneering advocate in Germany in behalf of the emancipation of the Jews, the separation of Church and State, and the freedom of conscience and belief.

Paul H. Dietrich d'Holbach (1723-1789) [Paris]. In his *Système de la Nature* (*System of Nature,* 1770), Baron d'Holbach argued in favor of materialism. Accordingly, he believed there is no mind independent of matter. He defined consciousness as agitation of the particles in the brain, a process similar to fermentation. Baron d'Holbach wrote that religion is conducive to superstition and that it leads to domination by priests, who fabricated the idea of God to keep the populace under their control.

James Beattie (1735-1803) [Lawrencekirk, Aberdeen, London]. At Aberdeen, where he was educated, James Beattie gained a reputation as a classical scholar. In 1760 he was appointed professor of moral philosophy at the university there. He attacked Hume's Skepticism in his *Essay on the Nature and Immutability of Truth* (1770), a volume which met with wide acceptance. Beattie's *Elements of Moral Science* was published during 1790-1793. Also, he wrote *The Evidences of the Christian Religion* and a series of essays on poetry and music. Beattie's style was graceful and clear, and he wrote with an appreciation of what is good and beautiful. He had many friends in literary circles in London; George III granted him a pension of £200 a year.

Leonhard Euler (1707-1783) [Basel, St. Petersburg, Berlin]. A Swiss mathematician, Leonhard Euler was interested in theology in addition to oriental languages and medicine. He was one of the founders of modern mathematics and introduced the abbreviations now used in trigonometry. He also wrote important treatises on the calculus and on astronomy. In his *Letters to a German Princess* (1772) he used the diagrams—which are now called Euler's diagrams, though not original with him—for indicating the relations of logical classes.

163

Joseph Priestley (1733-1804) [Yorkshire, Warrington, Birmingham, London, Pennsylvania]. Joseph Priestley was a nonconformist clergyman, a noted champion of Socinianism (*see* Sozzini, p. 120), and was also engaged in chemical experimentation. He mastered eight languages, was a capable mathematician, and studied logic and metaphysics. Erasmus Darwin, James Watt, and Benjamin Franklin were his friends. Priestley invented the pneumatic trough, for collecting gases in mercury. He wrote *History of Electric Science*. In 1774 he made a contribution of prime importance to chemistry when he discovered the element oxygen. Priestley was the author of papers opposing the British government's attitude toward the American colonies. His reply to Burke's *Reflections on the French Revolution* led not only to his being made a citizen of the French Republic, but also to the burning of his house and chapel by a mob. In addition, his books, manuscripts, and scientific instruments were destroyed. In 1794 he moved to America where he spent his remaining days. Priestley declined an offer of the Principalship of the University of Pennsylvania. He was a sincere seeker after truth, and his writings influenced Thomas Jefferson's thinking. In his philosophy he adhered to materialism, but maintained an electric theory of matter. According to Priestley, there is no difference between the body and the soul; they are of one homogeneous substance.

Lord Monboddo (1714-1799) [Monboddo, Aberdeen, Edinburgh, Gröningen]. John Burnett was a Scottish lawyer who was advanced to the bench by the title of Lord Monboddo. He made a collection of *Decisions of the Lords of Council and Session,* but is better known for his *Origin and Progress of Language* (6 vols., 1773-1792) and *Ancient Metaphysics* (6 vols., 1779-1791), a defense of Greek literature and philosophy. His works were erudite, his observations acute. Although scientifically ahead of his time, they were ridiculed by his contemporaries because of the paradoxes and eccentricities which marked them. According to Monboddo, man is of the same species as the orangutan, but man has gradually advanced from the animal condition, in which mind is immersed in matter, to a level on which mind acts independently of the body and to a social state determined by the needs of human life. In addition, Monboddo noted that language is a product of social living.

Richard Price (1723-1791) [Tynton, London]. As well as a metaphysician and moralist, Richard Price was a clergyman and a political philosopher. He wrote on the national debt of England and on the justice of the war with America. As a result of his friendship with Benjamin Franklin, his name became identified with the cause of the colonies. Price, with Priestley, was sympathetic toward the revolution in France; the two men remained friends despite differences of opinion on other doctrines. In *Letters on Materialism and Philosophical Necessity* (1778), Price maintained the freedom of man and the immateriality of the soul. His ethical doctrines were similar to those of Cudworth and in some aspects anticipated Kant.

Immanuel Kant (1724-1804) [Königsberg]. Immanuel Kant, who was of Scotch and German ancestry, was a teacher at the University of Königsberg from 1755 to 1797. The question of presuppositions on which "experience" rests, which Hume had failed to consider, became the central interest of the philosophy of Kant.

His early training was in the atmosphere of Leibniz' teachings. He read widely, remained a bachelor wholly devoted to study, and included astronomy in the scope of his interest. In the latter field he formulated a nebular hypothesis (perhaps on the basis of reading Swedenborg) to account for the evolution of the physical universe.

In time, he came upon the works of Hume which, he says, woke him from his dogmatic slumber. He came to the conclusion that the Leibnizian tradition placed too much confidence in human reason and led to dogmatism, whereas the Humean tradition represented too little confidence and led to Skepticism. Kant believed a careful study of the presuppositions, capacities, and limits of human reason was needed; this would be criticism.

This idea was first suggested at the time of his appointment as professor (1770) in a dissertation *On the Forms and Principles of the Sensible and Intelligible World,* and it was carried to completion in his *Critique of Pure Reason* (1781). Looking at experience from the standpoint of Leibniz, Kant saw that Hume had tried to reduce to phenomena (or sensory appearances), what can never be so reduced, namely the presuppositions or prior frameworks which determine for phenomena the form they have. There can be no specific items in space and time for one who has no capacity to perceive space and time. The assertion "this is an instance of spatiality" is impossible without the assumption of a logically prior general idea of spatiality. Kant says: no doubt, all knowledge begins *with* experience, but it does not follow that all comes *from* experience. The capacity for experience can not originate from experience. The case is similar with time. Space and time are *a priori* forms of experience, as Leibniz had suggested in a general way. Certainly our belief in the infinity of space and time is not a belief that has been empirically verified. The capacity to have experiences of a spatial and temporal character is an *a priori* possession of the knower. The particular occasions for exercising these capacities and the particular contents which result are *a posteriori* factors in experience. Knowledge is the result of the interplay of the two.

As, in the case of perception, the kind of experience one gets is determined primarily by the structure of perceiving, so in the intellectual processes the fundamental thing is the kind of structure knowledge-activity exhibits. To discover this Kant studied the forms which logic has presented and arrived at his list of categories, a revision of Aristotle's list of eight or ten. He found four groups coming under (1) quantity, (2) quality, (3) relation, and (4) modality, and giving respectively, (1) unity, plurality, totality; (2) reality, negation, limitation; (3) subsistence and inherence, causality and dependence, reciprocity; (4) possibility, existence, necessity. Kant believed these are the general forms under which we do all our thinking. If one asks by what right we bring all experience into conformity to our modes of thought Kant's answer is: that or nothing. Without this no thought about experience would be possible. These are the threads by which the self binds all experience together. But this process presupposes the unity of the self, the original, synthetic unity of apperception. Hume was on the wrong track when he tried to derive the unity of the self by association of ideas. He tacitly had to assume the unity of his own mind and apply its function in comparing and distinguishing separate ideas. The unity of the self is *a priori,* not *a posteriori.*

But since the forms of perception and thought are due to the structure of the knower, it follows that they can give no knowledge of *things-in-themselves* (noumena) beyond experience. Knowledge is of phenomena; noumena may in a sense be thought, but not known. We can not discuss the nature of the soul except in terms of its manifestations in empirical psychology. Nor can we talk about the material world in transcendent terms, terms referring beyond our possible experience. If we try to do so we get into antinomies, two incompatible points of view, each of which seems equally convincing. We think the world must have had a beginning, and also that it could not have had one; that matter must be infinitely divisible, but that it can not be; that there must be causality, but also that there must be freedom; that there must be a Necessary Being, but that we can never find one in experience.

Furthermore, Kant continued, when we try to prove the existence of God by the ontological argument (a necessary being), the cosmological (first cause), or the physico-theological (from universal order), we find there are unwarranted assumptions in each case. The soul, the universe, and God are regulative, not constitutive, ideas. They enable us to organize experience and give it unity; but we can not establish their validity beyond this. Theoretical (or scientific) reason is thus limited to "objects of possible experience."

The full discussion in the *Critique of Pure Reason* was not easy reading. Its intent was more briefly expressed by Kant in the *Prolegomena to Any Future Metaphysic,* stating the three fundamental questions of human interest—"What can I know? What ought I to do? What may I hope?"—and, developing the first question more technically, giving the answers to the further questions—"How is pure mathematics possible? How is pure physics possible? How far is metaphysics possible?" All of these are

167

phases of this central problem: "How are *a priori* synthetic judgments possible?" i.e., universal judgments which add to our knowledge and are necessary truths, but the validity of which can not be established by experience. The reply: such judgments do not anticipate the specific contents of experience, only its general forms.

The question "What ought I to do?" was more fully analyzed in Kant's *Foundations of the Metaphysic of Morals* (1785) and in his *Critique of Practical Reason* (1788). Morality is concerned with the conditions of the highest meaning of conduct, as science and philosophy are concerned with knowledge. In both cases, according to Kant, the final goal is to bring matters under the highest possible principles. Morality consists of actions in accordance with principles. An unprincipled man is an immoral man. And the principle here as in science is the principle of consistency, necessity, and universality. It is formulated in the statement, "So act that the maxim of thy deed may stand as universal law." That is, follow a rule that every other person may also follow, and ask no special privileges. A double standard, in any sense of the phrase, is wrong. Grant to others all the rights you claim for yourself. This is practical or moral reason, and since man is the rational animal the meaning may be stated in the form: Respect as ultimate the humanity of every man. Never regard humanity as a means to something else, but always as the final end. The particular rules of conduct, such as the commands of the decalogue, are specific modes of carrying out the general law.

As Kant developed the theory, morality is concerned with what ought to be, not with what is; it cannot be derived from a description of human behavior. It is prescriptive, not descriptive. It must therefore be *a priori,* not *a posteriori.* And the moral value of a life cannot be measured by its everyday success; it must be measured by its degree of embodiment of principle. A life lived according to principle is good regardless of material success or failure. Ultimately, the only good thing in the world is a good will. *Duty* is the key word, not *pleasure,* and the imperative call of duty is categorical, not conditional.

Morality presupposes certain postulates of practical reason. Above all, freedom is assumed (regardless of all the difficulties with the conception that arose in Kant's *Critique of Pure Reason*). Without it there would be no meaning to praise and blame, in fact no possibility of such a distinction. Secondly, immortality is presupposed because it is impossible completely to meet the demand "be ye perfect" in any finite life. If the moral law makes an impossible demand, then it is irrational and can not be moral. Thirdly, since this life shows much injustice to those who are most deserving, there must be belief in a God who will finally see that justice is done or there will be an eternal rift in the moral structure of the universe. Hence in moral practice these three fundamental features are presupposed in the universe though they could not be proved by the methods of theoretical knowledge.

Kant treated the third aspect of experience, that concerned with feeling and emotion, in his *Critique of Judgment* (1790). Of this there are two phases: one phase concerned with art, another concerned with the beauty of Nature. Art derives its beauty from the formal principles it expresses, and these are found chiefly in the factor of design. This is what gives objective meaning to the field, constitutes the basis of esthetic criticism, and makes esthetic appreciation disinterested. The unity of artistic design has features apparently purposive, but the purposiveness is within the object, not beyond it. Consequently, it is as if it were purposiveness without a purpose.

A sense of sublimity comes when greatness is added to beauty. Infinity is the greatest of all, an idea found in our minds. The sublime is that which awakens in us the idea of the infinite and arouses the feeling of awe.

In Nature, too, there is a unity, says Kant, which holds all things together and which is analogous to the unity of art. This gives Nature apparent design, lends it beauty, and suggests the teleological argument for the existence of God.

But our religious life remains subject to the limitations of our experience, according to Kant. Its emphasis must necessarily, then, be upon ethics rather than upon transcendent theology, as he explained in *Religion within the Limits of Mere Reason* (1794).

Note: The response to Kant's critical philosophy was varied. Traditionalists attacked it for being too negative in its results. It was approved by others for placing faith over knowledge. Many of the Romanticists believed it to be a support for their recognition of the individual's will and personal genius. Absolute idealists saw the structure of a new philosophy in its implications.

Ethan Allen (1738-1789) [Litchfield, Vermont]. In America, independent thought was exemplified by Ethan Allen. He was active in the political affairs of the region which became the state of Vermont, and he also advocated deistic doctrines in *Reason, the Only Oracle of Man* (1784). Allen believed in human responsibility and immortality, but rejected prophecy and revelation. He was strongly opposed to Jonathan Edwards.

Johann G. Herder (1744-1803) [Königsberg, Weimar]. A poet, critic, and preacher as well as a philosopher, Herder studied under Kant, and, at first, was a follower of his, but later he adopted divergent views. He emphasized the unity of reality and of personality. God and the world are one, and so are mind and nature, as Spinoza had suggested. The ages of man are greatest in which poetry, religion, and philosophy are inseparable. The individual and society likewise interpenetrate each other. The individual is a product of historical development, but also contributes to the outcome of history. Reason itself is a product of experience, which produces poetry and religion first. Herder's views are most significantly expressed in *Ideas on the Philosophy of Human History* (1784-1791).

Friedrich H. Jacobi (1743-1819) [Düsseldorf, Holstein, Munich]. Feeling was defended against the claims of reason by F. H. Jacobi. He believed that reason elaborates experience; feeling gives immediate awareness of spiritual things and God. Exact methods applied to spirit end in fatalism and atheism. Freedom can be felt only by intuition. Jacobi criticized Kant for inconsistency in first limiting causality to the categories within experience and then using it to describe the relation of the thing-in-itself to experience. In 1787 he wrote *David Hume, on Belief, or Idealism and Realism.*

Pierre Cabanis (1757-1808) [Cosnac, Warsaw, Paris]. Pierre Cabanis was a physician, statesman, and philosopher who upheld the people against the aristocracy in the French Revolution. He furnished speeches on public education to Mirabeau. He participated in the reorganization of French schools of medicine and taught in the medical school at Paris. He was also a member of the Council of 500 and, later, a member of the senate. Cabanis was a student of psychology, which he approached entirely from the physiological aspect. This led to the impression that he was a materialist and atheist, but he said he was not averse to belief in a spiritual and immortal soul and a personal God, though he did not attempt to relate these to his psychology. Cabanis' most important publication was *Relation of the Physical and the Moral in Man* (1788-99).

Jeremy Bentham (1748-1832) [London]. In his *Introduction to the Principles of Morals and Legislation* (1789), Jeremy Bentham attempted a reduction of human conduct to its ultimate motives. These are pleasure and pain. The fundamental pursuit is happiness, and the criterion of the value of deeds is their utility in leading to the greatest happiness of the greatest number. He regarded pleasure as the essence of happiness; in balancing one pleasure against another, consideration must be had for seven features: intensity, duration, certainty, nearness, productivity of further pleasures, purity, and extent (to the number of persons). Sum up the measures of each of these and the result is the value of the pleasure. The interests of the individual are inseparable from those of the community. The act, the circumstances, the intention, and the consciousness must be taken into account in estimating the moral value of an action. All virtue is based on prudence and benevolence.

His ethics is often contrasted with Kant's in that Bentham's was based upon regard for consequences, whereas Kant's was based upon principle.

Salomon Maimon (1754-1800) [Lithuania, Berlin, Nieder-Siegersdorf]. Salomon Maimon abandoned his orthodox Jewish training and followed the philosophy of Wolff and Mendelssohn. He studied Kant's philosophy and criticized it in his *Essay on the Transcendental Philosophy* (1790). Kant commended his criticisms but did not accept them wholly. Maimon criticized the "thing-in-itself" as without positive meaning, and he thought that Kant's discussion of causality did not completely answer Hume. The desire for completeness, according to Maimon, is the factor that impels us to attempt to transcend experience.

Dugald Stewart (1753-1828) [Edinburgh]. Substituting for his father, Dugald Stewart taught mathematics at the University of Edinburgh till, in 1785, he was appointed professor of moral philosophy. In 1792, his *Elements of the Philosophy of the Human Mind* appeared, and his *Outlines of Moral Philosophy* was published in 1793. His philosophy followed that of Reid and represented a reaction against that of Berkeley and Hume. He professed to follow the method of Francis Bacon but held that it was possible to establish fundamental laws of certainty and principles of knowledge. Stewart sought to explain habit as a result of association of ideas. The existence of the self is known through a suggestion of the mind which follows sensation but is not immediately joined to it. Certainty of the existence of objects outside us, he wrote, is derived from the repeated awareness of the same object and an unchanging order in nature. Moral laws were originally formed by reason and are not dependent upon either God or man. Stewart concluded that we are moral when we conduct ourselves in accordance with reason or conscience.

Johann Gottlieb Fichte (1762-1814) [Rammenau, Jena, Leipzig, Berlin]. The first great representative of the absolute idealistic school was Johann Gottlieb Fichte, who based his thought primarily on Kant's *Critique of Practical Reason*. The relatively negative result of Kant's *Critique of Pure Reason* indicated to Fichte that men walk by faith rather than by sight; they live by what they believe rather than by what they know. The moral interests of man must take precedence over his scientific interests.

The basic reality in man is his will; this is the true "thing-in-itself." And it is a microcosmic representation of the Whole Universe. Not only is man's chief concern the realization of his ethical obligations; the Whole Universe is a Moral Order working out its tasks on a grand scale. And, since Kant's philosophy had shown the impossibility of transcendent metaphysics and religion, God must be interpreted as the Absolute Spirit immanent in this Universe.

Fichte thought that the world of appearances in space and time is posited by the Absolute Spirit as the objectification of its will, as the raw material for duty. It is objective to man because he is finite; and the mistaken notion that what is outside of the human mind must be material has given rise to the customary forms of dualistic and even to materialistic philosophies. Actually, Fichte wrote, what is beyond us is Absolute Mind, as Berkeley had suggested. And as Spinoza had pointed out, Fichte continued, there is only one Substance in the universe, namely God, though Spinoza failed to see that even extension is a form of conscious experience. He insisted that Spinoza's "Substance" must be interpreted wholly in terms of spirit.

The opposition of subject and object is the real counterpart of the logical structure of thought. $A = A$, $A \neq$ non-A, can be given content by letting A be the Ego. Then Ego = Ego, and Ego $\neq$ non-Ego. Fichte wrote that this shows the ultimate identity of the Absolute Self, and the contrast between subject and object in experience, and also the contrast between one finite subject and another (cf. *Fundamental Principles of the Whole Science of Knowledge,* 1794). It was Fichte's idea that in society these various finite selves come into conflict with each other. Consequently, it is the function of morality and law to regulate these conflicts. In addition, he stated that it is the function of intelligence to educate citizens so that they see the necessity for the limitations that are placed upon them. Then, the intelligent citizen freely and willingly accepts the restraints of law and considers them as self-limitations, not external obstacles to action.

In the course of history the Absolute Spirit expresses itself most fully in the leading culture of each age. It was Fichte's conviction that the German people, then disunited and subject to the power of Napoleon, should unite and become the manifestation of the Absolute, which he considered Germany's proper place in history. His *Addresses to the German Nation,* delivered in 1808, had increasing influence in the course of the following century.

Friedrich W. J. Schelling (1775-1854) [Leonberg, Tübingen, Leipzig, Jena, Berlin]. The philosophy of nature was Friedrich W. J. Schelling's chief interest (cf. *Ideas on a Philosophy of Nature,* 1797). He wrote his views repeatedly; consequently his work has been divided into five periods. However, in the background of these varied expressions there is the basic influence of Kant's *Critique of Judgment.* Schelling, like Fichte, was an absolute idealist, but as he viewed the Universe the Absolute seemed analogous to a great artist expressing himself in the beauty and sublimity of nature. Schelling maintained that things contain a polarity, which causes them to swing from the unconscious pole to the conscious; this is the creative impulse working out its mastery of resistant material in all possible ways.

Friedrich Schleiermacher (1768-1834) [Breslau, Halle, Berlin]. The views of the Moravians, among whom he was educated, influenced Friedrich Schleiermacher's philosophy. He expounded the idea that the emotions are the fundamental seat of human nature. To this view he added a conviction regarding the limits of reason, though he valued the critical spirit. Thus, he combined Romanticism and criticism. Schleiermacher developed a representation theory of knowledge. The conceptions which criticism rejects are still valid as symbols of aspects of inner experience. Symbolizing activity is manifest in science, art, and religion. Schleiermacher spoke of dogmas as symbols, which when taken literally become myths. In ethics, according to Schleiermacher, reason and desire govern nature; will develops gradually through nature and becomes ethics in man. Each man expresses what is universal in an individual way. It was his conviction that religion centers in the feeling of dependence of the finite on the infinite, of man upon God.

Religious concepts are interpretations of immediate feelings. Schleiermacher's *Addresses on Religion* was published in 1799.

Friedrich Schlegel (1772-1829) [Hanover, Paris, Jena, Cologne, Vienna]. Friedrich Schlegel's earliest interest was in Greek and Roman literature, of which he wrote a history. He was an outstanding representative of the Romantic school in literature and philosophy, and he edited, with his brother, the *Athenaeum,* which was a publication consisting of their ideas. In 1799, Schlegel wrote a novel called *Lucinde,* in which he narrated his relations with the wife of a Berlin banker (later he married her in Paris) as an expression of the Romantic demand for freedom of self-expression and unlimited self-realization. He rooted this point of view in Fichte's doctrine of the self as the basic reality. Schlegel's lectures on philosophy at Jena were without success. After moving to Paris, he lectured on philosophy and studied languages, including Sanskrit, and published a volume on the language and wisdom of India. In addition, he published a collection of romantic poems from the Middle Ages. Among his later publications was a *History of Ancient and Modern Literature.* Schlegel and his wife, also a writer, joined the Catholic Church in Cologne.

The century opened on a group of thinkers who were unable to follow the doctrines of Kant. Hamann and Fries found it necessary to modify them, and later Trendelenburg criticized the major Kantian tradition.

This tradition took various turns and evolved into movements which were more than mere interpretations or criticisms. Whether in agreement or opposition, Herbart's realism, Hegel's absolute idealism, Schopenhauer's pessimism, and Comte's positivism were all developments based on Kantian thought. Coleridge introduced Kantian doctrine to England. Krause, Rosmini, Carlyle, Strauss, Emerson, and Feuerbach illustrate, in different ways, the influence of the German idealists, whose analytic emphasis caused reversion in some cases. Meanwhile the British tradition was carried on by the thinking of Paley, the Mills, and Hamilton.

Analysis of experience assumed a non-Kantian form in works of Maine de Biran, Beneke, Kierkegaard, and Stirner. Social problems were the chief interest of St. Simon and Engels. Independent theories appeared in the Deism of Jefferson and the syncretism of Cousin, while in the Church modernistic tendencies were seen in the thought of Lamennais and Gioberti. The interest in mathematical logic appeared in the thinking of Poisson, Cournot, and De Morgan and foreshadowed the increasing interest in this field, which has manifested itself in the past hundred years.

John G. Hamann (1730-1788) [Königsberg, Walbergen]. Although he disagreed with his philosophy, John G. Hamann was a personal friend of Kant. He considered life much more inclusive than knowledge, and hence gave analysis a low rating. According to him, thought is abstract. Religion is grounded in our whole being. He did not believe that Kant had refuted Hume. Hamann was convinced that life is a coincidence of opposites which do not destroy life though in thought they are incompatible. Reason can not live without tradition and faith. Matter and form, intuition and reflection, are only logically distinct, not really separate. Hamann's *Metacritique of the Purism of Pure Reason* was published twelve years after his death, in 1800.

Antoine Destutt de Tracy (1754-1836) [Bourbonnais, Strasbourg, Paris, Auteuil]. Antoine Destutt de Tracy was a colonel in the French army at the outbreak of the Revolution and was sent as a delegate to the States-General. At the time of Napoleon he became a senator and was later a peer under Louis XVIII. At Auteuil, with Cabanis and Condorcet, he engaged in scientific study. As a friend of Lafayette he accompanied him into exile, returned secretly, was caught and imprisoned. In prison he studied the philosophies of Locke and Condillac, upon whom he based his own sensualism, drawing a materialistic conclusion in metaphysics. De Tracy credited our knowledge of the external world to a basis of action and resistance. His principal work was *Elements of Ideology* (1801-15) which he based upon zoölogy; he also wrote *Treatise on the Will*.

William Paley (1743-1805) [Peterborough, Cambridge, London]. Combining hedonism and authoritarianism, William Paley reasoned that consideration of pleasure and pain motivates action, and what is harmful can not be an end for our sense of duty. What is useful on the whole is good and furnishes the content of the Divine Will for man. But it is this Divine Will which constitutes the ground of moral duty. In his *Natural Theology* (1802), Paley used the famous "watch argument"—if the intricacy of the structure of a watch indicates a designing intelligence, then all the more does the intricacy of the universe indicate the direction of a Divine Mind.

Jacob F. Fries (1773-1843) [Barby, Switzerland, Jena, Heidelberg.] In his *New Critique* (1807), Jacob F. Fries proposed to give Kantian criticism a new foundation in philosophical anthropology. He demanded that psychology discover the forms with which our knowledge operates spontaneously, then deduce the scientific concepts which express them. Fries accepted Kant's categories, but doubted Kant's justification of their use. Science can never go beyond the finite to the infinite. All reality has an inner spiritual side as well as an outer material side. Fries thought that faith presents this conclusion, though always by way of symbolic expressions.

Johann Friedrich Herbart (1776-1841) [Jena, Königsberg, Göttingen]. Johann Friedrich Herbart taught a philosophy which he called realism. He considered the Reals to be irreducible units of being, in terms of which philosophy elaborates the basic concepts of science (extension, action, inherence, causality, etc.). The universe is pluralistic, not monistic. Herbart named the soul as one of the Reals and credited it with expressing its own self-preservation through its ideas. Mental states are results of the conflict of opposing forces. Herbart tried to develop laws of psychology as definite as those of physics. He identified will with thought and interpreted freedom as the dominance of the strongest mass of ideas. Herbart's *Main Points in Metaphysics* was published in 1808.

Karl C. F. Krause (1781-1832) [Eisenberg, Jena, Dresden, Munich]. Karl C. F. Krause was the author of a system called *panentheism*—that God is in all things—which was to reconcile theism and Pantheism. He was influenced by the absolute idealists, but did not follow them directly. The self is something immediate and real, a union of body and spirit, the former belonging to Nature, the latter to the spiritual realm. Their interaction implies a higher being, God, who is Ultimate Reality, above the opposition of Nature and Spirit. Krause was convinced that nature is an organic whole, a total life. Humanity in the largest sense is the total realm of nature and spirit, of which the earthly is only a part. Man can realize his function only by perfecting society. Krause believed that ethics emphasizes the pure will to good. Law is recognition of the state under pure reason and permanent truth. Religion is the struggle of man for union with God. *Das Urbild der Menschheit (The Archetype of Man)* was published in 1811.

Maine de Biran (1766-1824) [Bergerac, Versailles]. Maine de Biran (F. P. Gonthier) emphasized the importance of self-consciousness as inner activity. Volitional activity is the origin of the categories and the source of morality. He was finally led to Mysticism by the belief that the life of the spirit is beyond the phenomenal realm. The mind experiences the resistance offered by the external world, and interprets the concept of substance and cause in terms of the activity of will. Maine de Biran was responsible for the increased reflection on French "spiritualism." Most of his works were published after his death; his *Essay on the Foundations of Psychology* (1812) is an important and typical treatise.

Count de St. Simon (1760-1825) [Paris]. Count de St. Simon (Claude Henri de Rouvroy) advocated a utopian socialism. Science should be applied to man and social relations for the purpose of improving them. St. Simon's conviction was that in the ideal society the learned and the industrialists should rule in the interest of the totality of the workers. He thought that the ideal state should be built on the principle that each worker is to be rewarded according to his capability and his work. Christianity is to be cleared of its transcendent and mystical core, and given only its social and ethical content. Count de St. Simon's doctrines are represented in his *Reorganization of European Society* (1814).

G. W. F. Hegel (1770-1831) [Stuttgart, Tübingen, Jena, Berlin]. Agreeing with Fichte as to the proper use of logical method, Hegel also agreed with Schelling in identifying logic with metaphysics. All three of these philosophers considered reality a living, evolving process. The Absolute is Universal Reason moving through eternity and embodying itself in the actual universe. Kant's *Critique of Pure Reason* was the root of Hegelian doctrine. Hegel maintained (as did Parmenides) that thought and being are one and elaborated his position in his *Logic* (1817). Here, he stated that the universe is rational, as indicated by the order seen in the heavens, in the laws of biology, in all things; and it is the function of philosophy to comprehend the reason in these things. This is what gives them meaning.

To Hegel, thinking was essentially an inductive process. He affirmed that new content is constantly appearing which has to be assimilated to the old, and the old has to be remade and brought up-to-date. Thinking follows the general dialectical formula of thesis, antithesis, synthesis (which has been noted in the thinking of philosophers before this time). Hegel reasoned that the all-inclusive ground of the universe differentiates itself into many different, even opposing, forms, creating a complex diversity in unity. In the course of evolution these opposites become reconciled and united in the whole. Later stages of development are the realization, the truth and purpose, of the earlier stages, in which the latter are taken up (*aufgehoben*). Thought then must take things not in isolation, but in connection with their origin and in relation to other things with which they are competing. Beginning with simple, abstract concepts it must move to more complex and concrete "notions." Knowledge is constituted by the entire system of concepts. The True is the whole, a totality which is never reached finally, but which keeps driving thought on in an endless process.

By the dialectical process, the categories of thought and reality can be traced, Hegel claimed, through the levels of Being, Essence, and Notion. Nature is the Absolute Idea externalized and particularized. Its unity has disappeared and it is struggling to regain unity and self-identity in the consciousness of man, who is the goal of nature. In this struggle there are three fundamental stages—mechanics, physics, and organic life. Spirit again appears in three stages—subjective, objective, and absolute. In the subjective, nature becomes conscious; in the objective, mind establishes law, morality, and the state—a society of free individuals each of whom willingly accepts the laws and customs of his people. Each citizen subjects his individual conscience to universal reason which is more fully expressed in the will of the group. Thus, Hegel speculated, the state is the larger and fuller expression of the individual. Progress is growth in the free acceptance of the law which makes social life possible.

The dialectic of history manifests the development of universal mind through the forms of particular states. Great personalities and great peoples are the means whereby the universal spirit, the

Absolute, realizes its ends. Hegel maintained that history is the expression of the movement of the Idea, developing assertion, opposition, and conflict, which results in an outcome in which neither side gains complete victory. The great sweep of history shows despotism in Oriental monarchies, unstable democracy in Greece, and constitutional government in Christianity. The last is the highest attainment of significant freedom.

Spirit reaches its absolute stage and its highest self-realization in art, religion, and philosophy. According to Hegel, art renders the infinite visible, religion symbolizes it as more than art, and philosophy brings it under the mastery of thought. Therefore, Hegel concluded, philosophy is the final goal of all development.

Samuel T. Coleridge (1772-1834) [Ottery St. Mary, London, Cambridge, Bristol]. As a liberal thinker, Samuel T. Coleridge lectured on literature, religion, and politics. He was interested in a plan to found a brotherly community on the Susquehanna River, but it did not develop. It is also interesting to note that Coleridge was a close friend of the Wordsworths. He was a careful student of German philosophy as well as of British, and he did a great deal to introduce a knowledge of Kant into England. His thought was marked by Pantheism and Mysticism, though in name he remained orthodox. His *Biographia Literaria* (1817) expresses many of his views.

Joseph de Maistre (1753-1821) [Chambery, Sardinia, St. Petersburg, Turin]. Joseph de Maistre was a French statesman and philosopher, a member of the senate of Savoy, and minister of the King of Savoy at St. Petersburg, where he did most of his literary work. He was a leader of the neo-Catholic movement, and he combatted the revolutionary doctrines in vogue at the time. De Maistre advocated an absolute monarchy. In *Du Pape* (*On the Pope,* 1819) he defended the temporal power of the pope and discussed the relations of the pope to the Church, to temporal sovereigns, to schismatics, and to civilization in general. De Maistre regarded the first essential in life to be order in society. Also, he wrote an examination of the philosophy of Bacon, attacked the thought of Locke, and strongly opposed Voltaire. He wrote a panegyric on the executioner as the foundation of social order. De Maistre considered the spiritual power of the pope superior to any temporal power and believed it should not be subjected to any restraint, whether by councils, by national churches, or by private judgment.

Arthur Schopenhauer (1788-1860) [Danzig, Göttingen, Berlin, Jena, Frankfort]. The contrast to the optimism of the absolute idealists is found in the pessimistic views of Arthur Schopenhauer. He got his start, as did Fichte, in the Kantian discussion of the role of will, and agreed that the will, in man and in the universe, is the thing-in-itself. His theory received its classic formulation in *The World as Will and Idea* in 1819. Here, Schopenhauer declared that the will has the capacity to objectify itself in phenomena and that, as a complex of presentations, the universe is idea. The World Will also differentiates itself into finite fragments, and these have their presentations; hence for me the World is my idea. But, Schopenhauer interpolated, will of itself is no more rational than irrational. An examination of the course of nature and of life does not present evidence of a rational process moving through all things. Rather it shows a blind purposeless impulse, a picture of more confusion than order. According to Schopenhauer, the absolute idealists, like Hegel, present not factual description, but wishful thinking. Schopenhauer read Buddhist works and related that they were truthful when they said that life is a process of desire and, in the nature of the case, could never be satisfied. Life in its essence is movement and restlessness. Therefore, a fair-minded man will necessarily be pessimistic because of the hopelessness of ever finding satisfaction in life.

There is no ultimate escape from pessimism, but there are three approximate means. The first is art, which expresses in concrete form the eternal ideas of Plato—ideas which are unaffected by the transitions of time and are universal in their significance. Music as a form of art is especially valuable, for it combines most completely the eternity of art and the restless movement of life. But the evil of life manifests itself in the fact that one cannot live at every moment on the high level of artistic appreciation.

Sympathy is a second means of partial escape from pessimism. It subordinates selfish individualism and minimizes the conflicts of living. It effects in some degree a unity among men and constitutes a basis for ethics.

Beyond both art and sympathy the third and deepest solution would be to renounce the very will to live. Schopenhauer believed the ascetics of Christianity and Buddhism had had the sense to see the real solution. Suicide will not do it, for this is based upon a dissatisfaction with present conditions. The proper attitude is *complete indifference* to living.

None of these solutions, however, are final. No one can live always in them. They are promises of salvation which are held before us only to be removed again. Schopenhauer considered this the final ground of pessimism.

Thomas Jefferson (1743-1826) [Shadwell, Philadelphia, Monticello]. Thomas Jefferson was educated in both classic and modern languages and in mathematics. He was an accomplished violinist, singer, and dancer, and an admirer of fine horses. He was a great liberal and advocate of democracy; he was trained as a lawyer, but cared less for practice at the bar than for politics and public service. Jefferson drafted the Declaration of Independence; and he prided himself upon being the author of the statute of Virginia for religious freedom, and father of the University of Virginia. In religion he was a deist, but he considered religious belief a purely individual matter. A compilation of the teachings of Jesus, which he made, is called "the Jefferson Bible." His *Autobiography* (1821) reveals his fundamental outlook on life.

F. Eduard Beneke (1798-1854) [Berlin, Göttingen]. After studying theology at Halle and Berlin, F. Eduard Beneke turned to philosophy. He believed that psychology is the basis of all knowledge, and that it should be placed on a strictly scientific basis. He sympathized more with the British thinkers than with the German and placed more value on the genetic method. Beneke opposed the conception of innate ideas, and that of mental faculties, though he did hold that the soul is endowed with a variety of powers which gradually acquire definiteness through responding to circumstances. An inner experience is our most direct knowledge of being, and from it we generalize in our metaphysics. In ethics, Beneke observed the way in which actions affect human welfare. His *Psychological Sketches* (1825-1827) was typical of his work.

Victor Cousin (1792-1867) [Paris, Berlin, Cannes]. Victor Cousin sought to unite Platonism, German philosophy, and Reid's common sense doctrine. Cousin thought that impersonal reason has a direct grasp of the Absolute. Included in his teachings is the idea that there are four basic types of philosophy—sensism, idealism, Skepticism, and Mysticism—each of which he believed to be partly true. The whole truth is to be found in a union of all their partial truths. The distinctive features of Cousin's thought are found in *Philosophic Fragments* (1826).

James Mill (1773-1836) [London]. *Analysis of the Phenomena of the Human Mind* was written in 1829 by James Mill. This philosopher was a follower of Hume and Hartley and explained all consciousness by way of association of ideas, even volition and emotion. Mill combined this idea with Bentham's utilitarianism in his evaluation of ethics. It was his conviction that there are three stages in the education of moral sentiments: the association of actions (1) with pleasure and pain, (2) with the pleasure or pain due to the praise or blame of others, and (3) with the expectation of future praise or blame.

Sir Willam Hamilton (1788-1856) [Glasgow, Oxford, Edinburgh]. Sir William Hamilton studied medicine and law and taught history and philosophy at Edinburgh. He regarded all sciences as branches of philosophy, and he defined the latter as the knowledge of effects through their causes. The primary task of philosophy is to examine the conditions of knowledge. Therefore, mind is philosophy's chief object, and metaphysics is its principal area of study. In other branches (sciences), mind is studied in special applications. Metaphysics is essentially philosophical psychology and is concerned with the phenomena of mind, its laws, and the results to be inferred from phenomena.

In logic, Hamilton undertook the quantification of the predicate, so as to make all judgments equations. This attempt was not successful, however. In psychology he classified phenomena into cognitions, feelings, and conations, each of which he considered in detail. Hamilton specified that to know is to condition; hence, the unconditioned is unknowable except through supernatural revelation. Furthermore, he insisted that although relativity applies to the self and the external world, our experience indicates that the self is unity and that the external world is permanent. Hamilton was of the opinion that causation results from the human mind's way of interpreting things in space and time. A few years after his death, Hamilton's *Metaphysics* and *Logic* were published.

Antonio Rosmini-Serbati (1797-1855) [Rovereto, Rome, Stresa]. In the early nineteenth century, philosophic thought was not inactive in Italy. Antonio Rosmini-Serbati was an Italian thinker who advocated idealism. He believed that thought consists of both matter (sensation) and form (intellect). He explained that the former gives multiplicity, the latter unity, which grasps Being in ideal form. Form is not a product of experience, but is innate, a divine endowment. According to Rosmini, the idea of Being is a principle of knowledge, not of existence; it is not identical with God. Yet, God is both real and ideal. Initial reality is purely indeterminate, distinguished only logically from the Word. He defined the soul, not as the substantial form of the body, but as sensibility in essence, united to the body by a fundamental bond of sensibility. It becomes intelligent through its intuition of Being. Some of Rosmini's opinions were condemned officially by the Church. One of his important works was *New Information on the Origin of Ideas* (1830).

James Mackintosh (1765-1832) [Aldourie, Edinburgh, London, Bombay]. James Mackintosh was awarded a degree in medicine from Edinburgh. Then he moved to London and became interested in politics. To Burke's *Reflections on the French Revolution* he wrote a reply, which won him many friends, including Burke. He was appointed secretary of the association of the Friends of the People. Afterwards, Mackintosh entered the legal profession and, at Lincoln's Inn, lectured very successfully on the law of nature and nations (1799). He was knighted in 1803 and appointed recorder at Bombay where he lived until 1812. Mackintosh then entered parliament as a Whig; he opposed the reactionary policies of the Tories, succeeded in reforming the criminal code, led the movement for Catholic emancipation, and supported the Reform Bill. Mackintosh's *Dissertation on the Progress of Ethical Philosophy during the Seventeenth and Eighteenth Centuries* (1831) met with strong opposition from the utilitarians.

Auguste Comte (1798-1857) [Montpellier, Paris]. Another philosophy, *Positivism,* which sprang from Kantian thought, was founded by Auguste Comte. Kant was right, Comte held, in limiting human knowledge to phenomena and in declaring the impossibility of transcendent metaphysics. One should renounce, therefore, all speculative philosophy, and limit oneself to the definite results of science (*Positivism*). Comte's *Course of Positive Philosophy* was published in the period 1831-1842. The evolution of mind is in three stages—the theological, the metaphysical, and the positive. The theological is the stage of primitive culture, in which all events are explained by reference to the wills of personal beings. In the metaphysical stage, explanations are in terms of impersonal forces and general concepts. But in full maturity the mind discards both of these and thinks in terms only of phenomena and their mathematical correlations (positive stage). Comte wrote that the sciences are capable of classification in a scale of increasing complexity and that they have, in history, become positive in a corresponding order. The sequence is mathematics, astronomy, physics, chemistry, biology including psychology and sociology (a term created by Comte).

He was especially interested in the field of sociology, which he developed under the headings of social statics and social dynamics. The former dealt with the conditions of social equilibrium, the latter with social progress. Comte stated the dependence of social statics upon the balance of the selfish and altruistic impulses of individuals. He was convinced that social dynamics indicates development from militarism through juridical society to industrial society.

In his later years, Comte attempted to construct a religion of humanity. He developed a Trinity consisting of humanity, world-space, and earth. Nature is alive throughout, and humanity is one family. It was Comte's view that individuals may select a particular hero as the object of special veneration.

Robert de Lamennais (1782-1854) [St. Malo]. After he became a Catholic cleric, Robert de Lamennais supported freedom on the part of the Church and advocated a democratic pope. This stand led to a break with the Church, following the publication of his *Words of a Believer* (1834). At this time, he turned to philosophic rationalism, advocating freedom and brotherliness. He wrote that universal human reason is the source of the truth the Church shows us. God is power, form, life, and love. Lamennais maintained that the finite comes from God and is sustained by Him.

Thomas Carlyle (1795-1881) [Ecclefechan, Edinburgh]. Thomas Carlyle was an essayist, historian, and lecturer who became a student of German philosophy. He found many suggestive ideas in this branch of thought and did much to call it to the attention of British minds. His *Sartor Resartus* (1834) was based upon the Kantian distinction between phenomena and noumena. Carlyle's *Heroes and Hero Worship* echoed Fichte's conception of the incarnation of the Absolute Spirit in great human personalities.

David F. Strauss (1808-1874) [Ludwigsburg, Tübingen, Darmstadt]. Associated with the followers of Hegel, David F. Strauss established his reputation by his *Life of Jesus* in 1835. His attitude was so radical that it aroused great opposition in orthodox circles. Strauss maintained that God and Man are united not merely in Jesus but in all mankind, an immanent rather than transcendent relation. He leaned toward Pantheism, yet with emphasis upon an inner religious experience.

Ralph Waldo Emerson (1803-1882) [Boston, Concord]. A poet and an essayist, Ralph Waldo Emerson was a leading representative of New England transcendentalism. For a short period he was minister of the Old North Church, but when he ceased to hold orthodox views of the sacraments he resigned and devoted his time to lecturing. *Nature* (1836), his first published book, expresses ideas typical of his philosophy. He maintained an idealistic view of life and the innate morality and friendliness of the universe. Also, he upheld the right of the individual to think freely in religion. He wrote that truth is too large to be compressed into a formula, and it tends always to become poetic. The sovereignty of ethics is the basic conviction of all Emerson's essays.

Siméon D. Poisson (1781-1840) [Pithiviers, Paris]. Medicine was Siméon D. Poisson's first study, but later he gave it up for mathematics. Lagrange, Laplace, and Legendre were impressed by him and recommended publication of one of his memoirs when he was only 18 years of age. Poisson wrote many papers, chiefly on mathematical physics; his *Researches on the Probability of Judgments* (1837) is of interest to logicians.

Bernard Bolzano (1781-1848) [Prague]. Bernard Bolzano became a Catholic priest and a professor of the philosophy of religion at the University of Prague. Due to disapproval of his theories and conduct, he was released from his appointment, though with a pension. His most important work was his *Wissenschaftslehre (Theory of Knowledge,* 1837). He opposed a subjectivist interpretation of truth and supported the conception of truth-in-itself, existing independently regardless of whether it is known or not. He believed that even the omniscient mind of God acknowledges this. According to Bolzano, there are elemental aspects of logic— percepts, propositions, and conclusions. Knowledge is gained under conditions which make it possible, and there are conditions necessary for its discovery. There is the true science of knowledge; in accordance with the principles of this science the whole field is divided into special areas and is expounded in appropriate treatises. Bolzano's metaphysics was based on a conception of monads, but, in contrast to the theory of Leibniz, he held that there is mutual influence among them. He undertook a philosophical representation of the dogmas of the Catholic church; also, he wrote a treatise on the bases for belief in immortality. In ethics he believed in an unconditioned obligating law. Bolzano's posthumously published *Paradoxes of the Infinite* (1851) proved important for the study of transfinite numbers.

William Whewell (1794-1866) [Lancaster, Cambridge]. Whewell was professor of mineralogy from 1828 to 1832, and professor of "moral philosophy and casuistical divinity" from 1838 to 1855. In 1841, he was made Master of Trinity College and, in 1855, became Vice Chancellor of the university. He was influential in reforming the method of teaching mathematics and in introducing moral and natural sciences into the curriculum. Later he became more conservative in his attitude toward university reforms. Whewell's reputation rests chiefly on his *History of the Inductive Sciences* (1837) and its sequel, his *Philosophy of the Inductive Sciences* (1840). He also wrote on ethics, metaphysics, Plato, Grotius, and the relation of physics to theology. Whewell was an intuitionist and an opponent of J. S. Mill.

Arnold Ruge (1802-1880) [Bergen, Kolberg, Halle, London]. As a student Arnold Ruge joined the national movement, for which he was imprisoned at Kolberg for five years. There he studied Plato and Greek poetry. After his release he taught at the University of Halle and edited the *Halle Annual for German Art and Science* (1837-1843), in which he defended Hegelian philosophy. As a result of official opposition to his political ideas he went to Switzerland, then to France and to England. Later, he supported Prussia against Austria, and Germany against France, and received a pension from the German government. His theology was pantheistic, and it represented God as the eternal and universal Substance, which comes to first consciousness in man. Ruge believed in the immortality of spirit in general, rather than that of the individual. According to his philosophy, dogmatic religion is surmounted by philosophical speculation.

Vincenzo Gioberti (1801-1852) [Turin, Paris, Brussels]. As a statesman and philosopher, Vincenzo Gioberti attempted a reconstruction of ontology, in which Being creates the Existent out of nothing. God is the only Being, the origin of human knowledge, and is apprehended by intuition. He identified civilization and religion, and he described the Church as the pivot of human life. Gioberti supported the acceptance of revelation and belief in immortality. Civilization tends to perfection, which finds its culmination in religion. The Pantheism of his writings led to their being placed on the Index. Gioberti's position is set forth in his *Introduction to the Study of Philosophy* (1839-1840).

Friedrich A. Trendelenburg (1802-1872) [Eutin, Berlin]. A thorough student of Plato and Aristotle, Friedrich A. Trendelenburg became involved in a controversy with Kuno Fischer over the latter's interpretation of Kant's doctrine of space. Trendelenburg's own thinking emphasized the presence of the ideal in the Real, the ethical end in the state and in history. The ideal and the ethical do not exist merely in abstract principles. Trendelenburg's *Logische Untersuchungen* (*Researches in Logic,* 1840), contains a thorough criticism of Hegel's views and a discussion of the problem of knowledge. His interpretation of mind in active dynamic terms considerably influenced American philosophy from 1875 to 1900.

Bruno Bauer (1809-1882) [Eisenberg, Bonn, Berlin]. A member of the Hegelian group of philosophers, Bruno Bauer was especially interested in the philosophy of religion. Christianity, he thought, was possessed of a historical core which had become overlaid with dogmatic interpretation. Bauer even maintained that the movement had been started by Seneca. In time, he doubted the inspiration of the Scriptures and was deprived of his lectureship because of his teaching. In his later years, he devoted his attention to historical and critical studies, but retained his opposition to traditional theology. Bauer's earliest typical work was his *Critique of the Evangelistic History of John* (1840).

Ludwig A. Feuerbach (1804-1872) [Landshut, Berlin, Erlangen]. Feuerbach's thought was influenced both by Hegel's philosophy and by the study of natural science. Early in his career, he expressed doubt about personal immortality, adopting a Spinozistic view and maintaining that Christianity had disappeared from human think-ing. In his *Essence of Christianity* (1841), Feuerbach translated theology into human terms. Religion, he wrote, is the consciousness of the infinity of man's own nature. "God" is this infinity, a name for the human self expressed in objective terms. The various aspects of the divine nature correspond to human needs. Feuerbach rejected revelation and sacraments.

Theodore Parker (1810-1860) [Lexington, West Roxbury, Boston]. Although he attended the full course at Harvard College and took all the examinations, Theodore Parker received no degree owing to non-payment of tuition fees. After he was graduated from the Harvard Divinity School, he became a Unitarian minister. Parker's rationalistic views set him apart from the conservatives, some of whom would not associate with him. His views first became noted as the result of a sermon on *The Transient and the Permanent in Christianity* (1841), which is regarded as one of the three great sermons of Unitarianism. He denied man's present need for the miraculous and supernatural aspects of Christianity. He became the minister of the Congregational Society in Boston and preached to thousands of hearers. Parker maintained that God, the moral law, and immortality are certainties of intuition. He regarded Jesus as a great humanitarian, and his critical attitude toward the Bible anticipated results of later scholarship. He was a strong abolitionist. Because he suffered from consumption, Parker traveled to England and to Italy; he died in Florence.

Antoine A. Cournot (1801-1877) [Lyons, Grenoble, Dijon]. Antoine A. Cournot was noted for his mathematical statement of economic problems and for his interest in the theory of probability. He disagreed with both the positivism and the rationalism of his day, and he recognized contingency and order as aspects of the Real. Man cannot reach certain truth, but he can approach it by increasing the probability of his statements. Cournot's *Exposition of the Theory of Chance and Probability* was published in 1843.

John Stuart Mill (1806-1873) [London, Avignon]. Among those who were sympathetic with the Positivism of Comte (*see* p. 186) was John Stuart Mill, who was given an intense private education by his father James Mill. J. S. Mill was, for thirty-five years, clerk and chief examiner of correspondence at the India House. His most important philosophical works were his *System of Logic* (1843), *Utilitarianism* (1863), and *Examination of Sir William Hamilton's Philosophy* (1865).

His primary interest was in social philosophy and his *Logic* was an attempt to formulate a thoroughgoing statement of how men actually make inferences from one set of particular facts to another. John Stuart Mill's central concept was "evidence." But an adequate discussion of evidence led him into the consideration of all the fundamental phases of knowledge. He regarded the first principles of mathematics as hypothetical rather than certain. The law of causation is, as Hume suggested, nothing but invariable sequence. Mill thought the syllogism of traditional logic a bit of circular reasoning because the major premise would have to be established by induction, which would include the conclusion in its summary.

The most noted part of Mill's *Logic* is the discussion of the canons of experimental inquiry, the methods whereby the invariable sequences called causal are established. These are the canons of agreement, difference, joint method, concomitant variations, and residues. What they amount to, in sum, is the rule: by changing the settings of phenomena, and varying them in different degrees, even to complete absence, it is possible to tell what phenomena vary together, though caution is still necessary in saying that one or the other event is cause; both may be effects of a common cause. And in complex situations, where causal connections are partially known, unexplained events must be traced to new causes. Mill thought that if, by some such methods, uniformities in human habits could be discovered, it would be possible to reduce social phenomena to a science analogous to the physical sciences.

Mill's effort to be purely empirical led him to reduce material bodies to "permanent possibilities of sensation," and mind to a succession of actual and possible states. However, he saw the weakness of such an account and was led to believe that there must be some other aspect to mind which serves to unite the separate states. Thus he moved away from the doctrines of Hume and toward those of Kant.

Also, Mill realized that for moral freedom it is necessary to limit the sway of causality; still, this was impossible in his interpretation of causal connection. He expected the ethical goal to be the greatest happiness for the greatest number. Here again, he recognized difficulties if happiness is merely pleasure and if the means of pleasure are ignored. Mill regarded only the pleasures chosen by enlightened minds as ultimately satisfying.

Sören A. Kierkegaard (1813-1855) [Copenhagen]. Sören A. Kierkegaard was a representative of extreme individualism. His fundamental position was that of religious atomism. He stated that the aim of all striving is to save one's own soul from the corrupt world. The entire wisdom of practical philosophy lies in the understanding of the unique value of the individual. Kierkegaard presented an aristocratic anarchy. Life as a member of a social circle corrupts and stupefies men. He believed philosophy is a matter of the inner life, which opposed the Hegelian view. The inner opposition of things is the deepest truth of existence: the world against God, the real against the ideal, the moment against the totality of life, time against eternity, faith against knowledge. Kierkegaard's *Either—Or* (1843) is typical of his writings.

Friedrich Engels (1820-1895) [Barmen, Manchester, Paris]. An active German socialist, Friedrich Engels collaborated with Karl Marx on the *Communist Manifesto* and also in a journalistic project in Paris. Engels and Marx worked together to form an international socialist movement. Engels participated in the German Revolution of 1848; he spent his remaining years in England. He wrote *The Condition of the Working Class in England* (1844), *The Origin of the Family,* and *Private Property and the State.* Engels engaged also in polemics against contemporary philosophers. He developed the Marxian conception of dialectical materialism and the Marxist theory of history. Engels regarded the State as an executive committee of the ruling class.

Max Stirner (1806-1856) [Bayreuth, Berlin]. Max Stirner (pseudonym of Kaspar Schmidt) taught for a while in Berlin and caused a sensation by his *The Ego and His Own* (1845). He thought previous liberals had not been radical enough. Stirner wrote that the individual is the true reality. Humanity and God are purely egoistic; each makes itself its own goal. The individual should do the same. Stirner was of the opinion that God, pope, emperor, and fatherland are all ghosts that must be demolished. He was convinced that all truth is discovered for one's own satisfaction; all effort is for one's own satisfaction. These are not for the Absolute Self, as Fichte said, but for the finite self. Stirner's theory is the acme of individualism and subjectivism.

Friedrich T. Vischer (1807-1887) [Ludwigsburg, Horrheim, Tübingen, Stuttgart]. After completing his education at Tübingen, Friedrich T. Vischer became vicar of a church at Horrheim. Then he spent two years studying aesthetics in the art centers of Germany and Austria. He joined the faculty of Tübingen and finally became professor of aesthetics. His independent thought led to his suspension from the university for two years, and, at Frankfort, he entered politics as a liberal. He was called to the polytechnic institute at Zurich, then to the institute at Stuttgart. As one of the most distinguished literary critics and a student of Hegelian aesthetics, Vischer wrote many significant articles and books. One of his most outstanding was *Aesthetics, or the Science of the Beautiful* (1847-1858).

Augustus De Morgan (1806-1871) [Madura, Cambridge, London]. As a mathematician and logician, Augustus De Morgan is noted for his contributions to the development of symbolic logic (*Formal Logic*, 1847) and to the philosophy of mathematics. His laws concerning negatives of complex terms, his treatment of relations, and his discussion of probability are outstanding results of his thinking.

The last half of the nineteenth century was marked by a more intensive development of the idealistic tradition; philosophers from Lotze to Creighton typified the maturing of this tradition as did others from France, Germany, Britain, and the United States. The mathematical formulation of logic and the philosophical study of the bases of mathematics received detailed treatment in England, Germany, and Italy. A strong influence was exerted on philosophy by the rapid advancement of natural science: the theory of evolution, instituted by Darwin and further expounded by Spencer and Haeckel; the study of the scientific method, interpreted with positivistic leanings by Ardigò and Avenarius; and the growth of experimental procedure in psychology, with contributions from Fechner, Wundt, and Lipps. An increase in the amount of attention given to the theories of history and society is evidenced in the doctrines of Gobineau, Lassalle, Marx, Simmel, Durkheim, and Plekhanov. Analysis of experience led Renouvier, Teichmueller, and Deustua to personalism. Investigation of the problem of meaning and truth impelled Peirce, James, and certain of the French philosophers to Pragmatism. Lachelier and Hermann Cohen founded Neo-Kantianism, and, through it, they reinterpreted critical idealism. New emphases in philosophy of religion were educed by Ritchl and the proponents of Neo-Scholasticism. Indeed, the intellectual activity of the time was so extensive that only small samples can be presented.

Jacob Moleschott (1822-1893) [Utrecht, Heidelberg, Zurich, Rome]. After studying at Heidelberg, Jacob Moleschott practiced medicine for two years at Utrecht. For the next seven years he lectured on physiology at Heidelberg, but was forced to resign because the authorities were alarmed at what appeared to be materialistic tendencies in his teaching. Moleschott's basic view was that physical conditions are the chief determinants in human life. Matter conditions life, life conditions thought, and thought conditions the will to improve. He went to Zurich, then to Rome as professor of physiology. His lectures were very popular, and his researches, especially on diet, were important. "No thought without phosphorus," said Moleschott. His *Kreislauf des Lebens (The Circuit of Life,* 1852) appeared in several successive editions.

Joseph Arthur de Gobineau (1816-1882) [Bordeaux, Paris]. A diplomat and orientalist, Joseph A. de Gobineau based his theory of history on the concept of race. In his view the advances and retreats of society are the effects of race mixture, which usually leads to degeneration; in this way, the strongest race assumes a position of predominance. In his *Essay on the Inequality of the Human Races* (1853-1855), Gobineau maintained the doctrine of "Nordic supremacy": originally, the white race had a monopoly on intelligence, strength, and beauty, but it lost these attributes through union with other races.

George Boole (1815-1864) [Lincoln, Doncaster, Cork]. George Boole provided symbolic logic with the basis which has led to its later development. He separated symbols of operation from the terms they connect and treated them as objects of calculation. Boole reduced logic to a kind of mathematics with two quantities, 1 and 0. 1 represents the universe of thinkable objects. Propositions were reduced to equations, and precise deductions were made in accordance with rule, in a system analogous to algebra. He dealt with propositions having any number of terms and developed an application to the theory of probability. Boole's chief work was *An Investigation of the Laws of Thought* (1854).

Henry David Thoreau (1817-1862) [Concord]. Henry David Thoreau was one of the New England transcendentalists. He was a lover of nature and made collections of plants for Agassiz, but he was not temperamentally suited for a serious scientific career. He built himself a cabin beside Walden Pond, where he lived in solitude for two years, and he devoted his time mainly to writing.

In 1854 Thoreau published *Walden, or Life in the Woods.* In it he extolled his individualism; he was indifferent to both money and fame.

Charles Bernard Renouvier (1815-1903) [Montpellier]. Charles B. Renouvier accepted Kant's phenomenalism, but rejected the concept of the thing-in-itself. Also he discarded the concept of substance—whether soul, absolute, or infinite spirit—and, likewise, the concept of matter or physical energy. According to Renouvier, only presentations exist, but these are neither subjective nor merely sensory. Personal experience is the ultimate fact. Freedom is man's basic characteristic. Renouvier believed in a finite God and in human immortality. His chief work was *Essais de Critique Générale* (*Essays in General Criticism,* 1854-1864).

Kuno Fischer (1824-1907) [Soudewalde, Heidelberg, Jena]. The views of Kant and Hegel strongly influenced Kuno Fischer's ideas. His fame rests upon his *History of Modern Philosophy* (1854-1877). Logic and metaphysics are identical for Fischer, and he regards Hegel's dialectical method as evolution. Fischer's writings were distinguished by a fine literary style.

Ludwig Büchner (1824-1899) [Darmstadt, Tübingen]. As a medical practitioner, Ludwig Büchner was appointed lecturer in medicine at Tübingen where he wrote his *Force and Matter,* which was published in 1855. The latter was a popular exposition of such frank materialism that it aroused strong opposition among authorities of the university and, as a result, Büchner was obliged to resign his position and return to the practice of medicine. Despite the protests, his work was widely read and was published in nineteen editions in German. He accepted the indestructibility of matter and force and supported the finality of physical force, identifying mind with the brain. To Büchner there seemed neither plan nor deity in the realm of nature. He also wrote other volumes expounding the various aspects of his position.

Alexander Bain (1818-1903) [Aberdeen, Glasgow, London]. One of the inner circle of friends and a close associate of J. S. Mill was Alexander Bain, who, for twenty years, was professor of logic at

Aberdeen and later was lord rector. As an influential teacher supporting empiricism, he established this doctrine as a rival of the common sense school and of idealism. Although active as a writer on psychology, ethics, logic, and other aspects of education, he was best known for his psychological works, *The Senses and the Intellect* (1855) and *The Emotions and the Will* (1859). Bain was influenced by the associationism of James Mill and rejected the speculative metaphysical discussion of the soul, making full use of the biological and physiological data available at the time. Yet he rejected materialism because he was not in favor of drawing metaphysical conclusions by a strict adherence to scientific method. Bain broke away from the passive mechanism of associationism and, in his exposition, discussed the spontaneity of emotions and volition. He regarded the soul not as a sum of atomistic elements but as a fluid continuum. He also used the genetic approach more than his British predecessors had done. Bain revived Hume's emphasis on belief and interpreted the feeling of opposition to one's will as the acceptance of the external world. He was instrumental in establishing the periodical *Mind*.

Rudolf H. Lotze (1817-1881) [Bautzen, Leipzig, Göttingen, Berlin]. A widely learned man, Rudolf H. Lotze's philosophy is drawn from the mechanistic interpretation of nature and also from idealism. He believed that ideals are worked out through mechanical means, but that the essence of reality is spiritual. Mechanism means simply the interplay of details. He was convinced that the idea of good is the end of all vital activity. What ought to be gives the explanation of what is. His writings included books on medical, psychological, and philosophical subjects. Lotze's *Microcosmos* (1856-1864) is one of his best-known and most pertinent works.

Albrecht Ritschl (1822-1889) [Berlin, Bonn, Göttingen]. Influenced by Hegel, Kant, and Lotze, Albrecht Ritschl criticized excessive use of Aristotelianism, which he believed to ignore the distinction between nature and spirit. He labeled Hegel's categories too confining and demanded more vital religious feeling. Faith is the heart of religious knowledge. Ritschl's *The Genesis of the Old Catholic Church* (1857) is an outstanding work.

Henry Thomas Buckle (1821-1862) [Lee in Kent, Damascus]. Before he was twenty years old H. T. Buckle was noted for his skill in chess and was regarded as one of the best players in the world. He traveled on the Continent; then he undertook the writing of a significant historical work, *History of Civilization in England*. In 1857, his first volume appeared and his reputation was established immediately; the second volume was published in 1861. Buckle's importance lies in his attempt to apply scientific method to historical problems. The work was an unfinished effort to show the laws operating in human progress. He was affected by the Positivism of Comte and John Stuart Mill and was convinced that spiritual life and cultural progress depend upon physical conditions of the environment such as climate, soil, and food supply. History, thus, is subject to the laws of nature. Buckle insisted that there is a necessary sequence in the course of things. Statistics are essential in the analysis of conditions. He regarded protective government and religion as retarding influences; progress must rest on the growth of scientific and philosophic knowledge. In this way, spirit will conquer nature. Buckle died at Damascus after traveling through Egypt and the Holy Land.

Henry Longueville Mansel (1820-1871) [Cosgrove, Oxford, London]. Ordained a priest, H. L. Mansel first became Waynflete Professor at Oxford, then was appointed dean of St. Paul's Cathedral, London. He edited the works of Sir William Hamilton, followed his line of thinking, and is credited with influencing Herbert Spencer's thought. Mansel opposed Hegelianism, which was becoming popular at Oxford, and he also opposed university reforms. In his *Limits of Religious Thought* (1858), he argued that the categories of substance or cause can not lead to an idea of the Absolute. Knowledge, according to his view, is limited to the finite and the conditioned; he insisted upon the psychological character of logical processes. He believed that because of these limitations all theoretical objections to the dogmas of religion are invalid. Reason can not interfere with holy things; these rest upon revelation. Mansel maintained that reason's only function is to decide whether or not the evidence supports the divine origin of dogma. Helpful indications are derived from our ethical standards.

Charles R. Darwin (1809-1882) [Shrewsbury, Edinburgh, Cambridge]. Charles R. Darwin studied medicine and theology, but was more interested in the study of nature. As a naturalist he embarked on a surveying expedition, which took nearly five years, and visited South America and islands in the Atlantic and Pacific oceans as far as Australia. On the basis of his observations and specimens, and his study of the breeding of animals and plants, he formulated his hypothesis of evolution to account for the facts disclosed in his *Origin of Species by Means of Natural Selection* (1859). He held that evolution occurred in nature as the result of competition in the struggle for existence. Minute chance variations proved to be advantageous in the struggle and were transmitted to descendants through inheritance. He applied his theory to human evolution in *The Descent of Man* and found sexual selection an important factor. Darwin also published many significant studies such as *The Expression of the Emotions in Man and Animals, Volcanic Islands* (geological formations), and *Formation of Vegetable Mould Through the Action of Earth Worms*. Darwin insisted that moral sentiment is based on sympathy and mutual help, factors favorable to survival, which offer a criterion for judgment of actions and, with language, take the form of praise and blame. More and more throughout his life he suspended his judgment in regard to questions of theology.

Gustav Theodor Fechner (1801-1887) [Grossärchen, Leipzig]. Combining a sense of fact and empirical procedure with high speculative impulse, Gustav T. Fechner founded psycho-physics as a systematic science. This resulted in a law correlating mathematically the intensities of stimulation and response (a geometrical increase of stimulus is necessary for an arithmetical increase in intensity of response). He interpreted atoms as centers of force. Reality is spiritual, but it has two manifestations—the psychic and the material. The interrelation of the psychological and the physical is not a causal interrelation but a type of correspondence. Fechner maintained that there are stages of consciousness in the universe, the higher including the lower; there is a planetary consciousness between the lowest individuals and the all-inclusive, God. There is plant soul as well as animal soul. The human soul is immortal, not in its substance but in its working. God is omniscient, the soul of the universe, which is his body. Fechner's ethics centered in eudaemonism. In addition, he developed experimental tests in aesthetics. *Elements of Psychophysics* (1860) by Fechner is a work which explains the core of his doctrine.

Herbert Spencer (1820-1903) [Derby, London, Brighton]. Herbert Spencer was an English philosopher who was sympathetic with the tendencies of Comte and John Stuart Mill. For a time he worked as a civil engineer and then as a journalist. He was not well-grounded in the history of philosophy, but his writings were widely read, and he did much to popularize the theory of evolution—which had been increasing in prominence for over a half-century. Spencer's *First Principles* (1860-62) presented his general view of the field of human knowledge and the course of evolution in the universe.

Beginning with a division of reality into the unknowable and the knowable, Spencer assigned the interest of religion to the first and the interest of science to the second. In the nature of the case, most of his work is concerned with the latter. There are three levels of knowledge: (1) common sense, which is unorganized; (2) the sciences, which are partially organized around special points of reference; and (3) philosophy, which is completely organized into one comprehensive system. The fundamental concepts of philosophy are: similarities and differences, self and not-self, and the physical realm which is analyzable into space, time, matter, motion, and force. The most important of these is force, from whose action result all phenomena in space and time and what is called matter in motion. The course of the universe is an evolution constituted by an integration of matter from a state of relatively indefinite, incoherent, "homogeneity" to a relatively definite, coherent, "heterogeneity"; motion undergoes a parallel transformation. After this has reached its maximum, a basic rhythm in the universe causes a reversal of the process and devolution occurs to its maximum. The pendulum swings back and forth throughout eternity.

Evolution is not only characteristic of the physical world, as shown in astronomy and geology, but also universal in the realms of biology, psychology, and sociology. In biology Spencer originated the phrase "survival of the fittest" in referring to the struggle for existence, a phrase adopted by Darwin in later editions of his *Origin of Species*. Mind is the substance which persists through all the flux of psychological states. It is not itself a phenomenon or a directly experienceable reality. Spencer attempted to reconcile the empiricists and *a priorists* by a theory of accumulation of experience by induction, *a posteriori,* in the race; this results in native endowments, which are *a priori* given to new individuals. Our knowing processes give us a *transfigured realism,* which mediates between idealism and realism. Society grows in a manner analogous to that of the organism, except that in society the whole serves the individual parts, whereas in the individual organism the parts serve the whole. Spencer was convinced that the moral sense is one of the results of evolution. It involves rational and utilitarian elements and is directed toward the production of ideal persons in an ideal society. Perfect life is marked by a maximum variety of interests and the longest possible duration.

Ferdinand Lassalle (1825-1864) [Breslau, Geneva]. Ferdinand Lassalle was interested in democracy and freedom and was once imprisoned for revolutionary activity. In 1861 he published *The System of Acquired Rights,* which is a treatise on property. Lassalle was the chief figure in the formation of the Universal German Workers' Union and formulated a theory of the historical development of the worker's condition, which included the feudal and the capitalistic eras and a coming trades association era.

Hermann Ludwig von Helmholtz (1821-1894) [Potsdam, Bonn, Heidelberg, Berlin]. Hermann von Helmholtz studied medicine at

Berlin and served as a surgeon in the army; he was a professor of physiology in several institutions and finally a professor of physics at Berlin. He was concerned with problems involving the inter-relations between physics and physiology, the fields of vision and hearing, and the relation of the conservation of energy to muscular action. Helmholtz' discussion of the conservation of force estab-lished his reputation at once. He also invented a very important instrument, the ophthalmoscope, for viewing the interior of the eye. In 1863 he published his famous monograph, *Sensations of Tone,* which is said to be the most important nineteenth-century work on acoustics. In *Physiological Optics* (1855-1866), Helmholtz for-mulated his theory of the perception of color, which states its dependence on three fundamental sensations—those of red, those of green, and those of blue. In addition, he contributed to the electromagnetic theory of light. In 1883, the German Emperor conferred the title of nobility upon Helmholtz.

Thomas Henry Huxley (1825-1895) [Ealing, Coventry, London, Eastbourne]. Thomas H. Huxley was without formal education, but mechanical engineering aroused his interest, and later he was concerned with biology and philosophy. As a surgeon in the British navy, he traveled to the Orient and studied forms of marine life, making significant discoveries in the field. He became a lecturer at the School of Mines and published an important study of the vertebrate skull. His view of evolution was presented in *Man's Place in Nature* (1863). Huxley served on numerous Royal Com-missions, including the London School Board, and had a strong influence on education. Owing to ill health, his later years were devoted to lecturing and writing. He was interested in theology and philosophy, but took a very critical position with respect to them and committed himself to neither materialism nor idealism. He accepted, with qualification, the Darwinian doctrine of gradual modification of species, but he held that transmutation might occur suddenly. Huxley believed that ethics cannot be accounted for by evolutionary naturalism. He introduced the terms "agnosticism" and "epiphenomenon" (applied to consciousness) to discussion.

Nineteenth Century: Second Half (1850-1899)

Friedrich Ueberweg (1826-1871) [Leichlingen, Bonn, Königsberg]. Friedrich Ueberweg is noted for the historical studies which he did for his *Logic* and especially for his *History of Philosophy,* which was begun in 1863 and continued by his disciples.

John Grote (1813-1866) [Cambridge]. John Grote, who maintained an idealistic position, was a professor of moral philosophy at Cambridge. He rejected the agnosticism of Kant and Hamilton and adhered to the idea that knowledge is the sympathy of human intelligence with an objective intelligence in the world. Knowledge attributes something that is within ourselves to that which is beyond ourselves; yet it is a discovery rather than a creation. The unity of a thing, for example, is a projection of the unity of the self. He believed Positivism to be incomplete and criticized it on that basis: it is useful but only preliminary to philosophic knowledge. The latter is concerned not with the object but with the process of knowledge. Ideals come not from positive history but from the demands of man's inner nature. Grote's only published work is the first volume of his *Exploratio Philosophica* (1865).

K. Eugen Dühring (1833-1921) [Berlin, Nowawes]. K. Eugen Dühring practiced law and then lectured on economics and philosophy, but blindness compelled him to give up academic work. For him reality is what appears in our experience. He opposed Kant's view that the forms of time and space have only subjective validity. The intellect constantly strives to form continuous and infinite series. But reality occurs only in finite units. Yet, Dühring continued, knowledge is due to the fact that human consciousness and nature follow the same laws. The forces of nature produce beings that exist, act, and enjoy their existence. He was certain that the cruel and painful are elements in the satisfactions of life. Moral progress produces both individualization and socialization. Contemplation of the order of the universe begets universal affection, which replaces traditional forms of religion. *Natural Dialectic* (1865) is an early expression of Dühring's views.

Friedrich Albert Lange (1828-1875) [Wald, Bonn, Zürich]. At the beginning of his career Friedrich A. Lange was concerned with problems of economics, in which he developed socialistic doctrines. However, his fame is the result of the acute criticisms of science, ethics, and economics contained in his *History of Materialism* (1866). He accepted materialism as a method, but did not identify the phenomena of consciousness as members of the material series. Lange labeled Spinoza's view correct. Religious ideas are valid as supplements to empirical reality. They should be evaluated on the basis of their utility for man. Lange made efforts to renew the Kantian theory of knowledge and, thus, fostered the Neo-Kantian movement.

Karl Marx (1818-1883) [Trèves, Paris, Brussels, London]. At first a student of Hegelian thought, Karl Marx was attracted later by that of Feuerbach. His primary concern was to present an interpretation of the historical trend in social structure. The social and economic situation contemporary with his early life was capitalism, which had been furthered by the Industrial Revolution. However, Marx believed capitalism to be only a temporary phase which would pass away into socialism, when the proletariat (workers) become intolerant of their exploitation by the heads of industry. He thought that the working classes around the world should become conscious of their common interests and develop an international solidarity that would oppose traditional idealism by substituting an ideology which centers in economic determinism and by recognizing the struggle between economic classes. This struggle is a concrete, practical dialectic and will go on until it develops a classless society—in which a man is no longer a commodity, in which the wholeness of each human life may be realized. Marx maintained that the new system would work for the welfare of all. As a journalist and by participating in revolutionary activity, Marx, chiefly in the company of Friedrich Engels, furthered the cause. His greatest work was *Das Kapital,* the first volume of which was published in 1867. The second and third volumes were published by Engels in 1885 and 1895, respectively.

Noah Porter (1811-1892) [Farmington, Berlin, New Haven]. After graduation from Yale College, Noah Porter became a Congregational minister. He studied Scottish philosophy and then spent two years in Berlin, where he was influenced by German idealism. Porter was elected professor of moral philosophy and metaphysics at Yale in 1846, and from 1871 to 1886 he was president of the college. His best-known writing is *The Human Intellect, with an Introduction upon Psychology and the Human Soul* (1868). He was an erudite man, and his writings were pre-eminent as textbooks for a generation. Porter used a wealth of historical orientation and clarification and aimed at scientific objectivity. In metaphysics he adhered to the idea that the universe is a thought as well as a thing and maintained that every one must assume the existence of God in order that thought and science may be possible. Porter thought little of the philosophy of Coleridge and his followers, but he used Kantian ethics to counteract evolutionism.

Felix L. Ravaisson-Mollien (1813-1900) [Namur, Rennes, Paris]. A pupil of Schelling, professor at Rennes, and later curator of antiquities at the Louvre, Felix Ravaisson-Mollien maintained that all philosophic systems tend toward "spiritualistic realism," though not with equal historical significance. Love, as desire and wish, is the presupposition of all effort. He was of the opinion that the inner free activity, which we sense intuitively, is the basis of causality and of all knowledge of the outer world. God is known directly through an immediate sense of the beauty and the harmony of the world. Ravaisson believed that God is personal and is reflected in our personality. Nature is a refraction of spirit. Art is a revelation higher than knowledge beauty is visible spirit. Above all stands heroic love which renou es itself and lives in another, as suggested by the suffering god in Greek myth and also enacted in Christianity. Ravaisson's views are expressed most fully in *Philosophy in France in the Nineteenth Century* (1868).

Eduard von Hartmann (1842-1906) [Berlin, Rostock]. Early in life Eduard von Hartmann was an officer in the army, but he resigned his commission because of injuries incurred in an accident. In his philosophy, he combined features of Hegel's rationalism with some of Schopenhauer's emphasis upon will, regarding the two as inseparable. It was his conviction that the mechanistic conception of nature is inadequate; atoms are minute wills with an unconscious idea of their destiny. The growth of an organism is guided by such an unconscious will. Also this is presupposed by instinct and the association of ideas. Individuals realize not only their own ends but also the ends of the universe, which is completely pervaded by this unconscious will. Consciousness is analytic, the unconscious is synthetic. There is more misery than happiness in the world, and hope for happiness here or hereafter is illusory. Hartmann, like Schopenhauer, came to the conclusion that the only solution is the renunciation of the will to live. Hartmann's best known work is *The Philosophy of the Unconscious* (1869).

John Henry Cardinal Newman (1801-1890) [London, Oxford, Littlemore, Birmingham]. John Henry Newman was impressive because of the strength of his personality, the perfection of his literary style, the power of his preaching, and the dramatic development of his religious thought and action. After preliminary years of study, tutoring, and preaching, he became identified with the Oxford movement for which he wrote many tracts urging the reaffirmation both of apostolic succession for the episcopate of the Anglican Church and of the sacraments as sources of divine grace. Newman sought an absolute authority to lean upon without reasoning the how or why of doctrine. He emphasized the difference between contemplation and assent and insisted on the priority of the latter for religious faith. He held that the two great items of faith are (1) the reality of God and (2) the sinfulness of man with consequent misery. Finally he left the Anglican Church and joined the Roman Catholic, in which he was later made a cardinal. In the course of his thinking, he realized the necessity of a growing revelation, although he did not accept the apparatus of scientific criticism. Newman's *Grammar of Assent* (1870) states the essence of his position.

Francesco De Sanctis (1817-1883) [Morra, Irpina, Zürich, Naples]. Combining philosophy and literary criticism, Francesco De Sanctis considered literature the expression of moral and social conditions and supported aesthetic criticism. Hegel's idealism was De Sanctis' background. His *History of Italian Literature* (1870) was a masterly work that helped to inspire the Italian philosophical revival in the nineteenth century. He linked poetry and civil history. De Sanctis' thinking carried considerable weight with Croce.

Hippolyte Adolphe Taine (1828-1893) [Vouzieres, Paris]. H. A. Taine is noted for his critical and historical essays. In 1854 he won the Academy prize for an essay on Livy, and in 1864 he was made professor of aesthetics and the history of art at the École des Beaux Arts in Paris. He was also a student of medicine and the sciences. Taine's philosophic stand coincided with naturalism, and he represented the scientific spirit in criticism. In France during the last half of the nineteenth century, this spirit was prevalent in many fields, including poetry, philology, fiction, drama, and art. Taine's attitude was unemotional, neither ironical nor enthusiastic. In a work on French philosophy he attacked the views of Cousin and his school. Taine wrote on the history of English literature, English philosophy, and English Positivism; on the philosophy of art; and the history of Italian art. In 1870 he wrote an important book *On intelligence (De l'intelligence)*. Taine also produced a work which made him famous, *Origins of Contemporary France (Origines de la France Contemporaire, 1871-1894)*. He has been called the high priest of the cult of misanthropy, and he expressed horror at the brutality of men and the folly of women. He was appalled by the *bête humaine;* he was terror-stricken at the possibilities of human folly. In 1878 Taine was elected to the French Academy.

Roberto Ardigò (1828-1920) [Padua, Casteldidone, Mantua]. As part of his education for the priesthood, Roberto Ardigò studied natural science and philosophy and, gradually, became a Positivist. After quitting the Church, he became professor of philosophy at the University of Padua. His conception of evolution was based upon inquiry into his own intellectual development. Ardigò applied his theory to the interpretation of the evolution of the solar system, in which smaller bodies develop within the larger; consequently, he concluded that an infinite continuum pervades all. He thought highly of Kant's theory of the synthetic unity of experience. Soul and body are not completely separate. Individuals are never independent of society. *Psychology of Positive Science* (1870) is typical of Ardigò's writing.

Jules Lachelier (1832-1918) [Fontainebleau, Paris]. Jules Lachelier was an educator and philosopher who followed the Neo-Kantian school and had strong idealistic leanings. Boutroux and Bergson were two of his students. One of his important works was *The Basis of Induction* (1871), in which he maintained there is no certainty unless the forms of thought constitute nature. Lachelier adhered to the primacy of thought over all other aspects of experience, including freedom.

Hermann Cohen (1842-1918) [Coswig, Marburg]. Hermann Cohen was one of the leaders of the Neo-Kantian movement and the founder of the Marburg school, which advocated Neo-Kantianism. He did away with the notion of the thing-in-itself and emphasized the connection between philosophy and the sciences. One of his outstanding works was *Kant's Theory of Experience* (1871) in which he stated that no reality is discoverable except what is posited by thought, and the laws of thought are supreme. Nothing is given; thought creates both object and subject. In ethics, Cohen continued, duty is the one goal of conduct and is expressed in respect for personality. It is found in the will of the community; the individual, as part of the community, should strive to realize its laws. Cohen also reinterpreted Plato in terms of modern idealism.

Julius Wilhelm Richard Dedekind (1831-1916) [Zürich, Brunswick]. J. W. Richard Dedekind made fundamental contributions to the foundations of arithmetic and analysis. These were important philosophically due to their bearing on modern logic. His outstanding book was *Continuity and Irrational Numbers* (1872), which deals with the theory of ideal numbers. Dedekind edited the collected mathematical works of Riemann, and some of the works of Dirichlet, and he also wrote on the vibrations of a liquid ellipsoid.

African Spir (1837-1890) [Elizabethgrad, Geneva]. While a Russian naval officer, African Spir became interested in writing and eventually turned to it. His thought was influenced chiefly by German philosophy. Primarily, Spir was concerned with the apparent incompatibility of the Law of Identity and the plurality and change of phenomena. The law comes *a priori,* not from experience. The concepts of substance and causality result from the combination of the data of experience and the Law of Identity. The Ultimate Substance of all things is God, who is not the cause but rather the ground of all. Identity with Him is the goal of all striving. In 1873, Spir published *Thought and Reality.*

Christoph von Sigwart (1830-1904) [Tübingen]. Theology and philosophy made up the greater part of Christoph von Sigwart's education, and he became professor at Tübingen. He wrote works on Zwingli, on Spinoza, and on ethics, but he is best known for his *Logic* (1873-1878). Sigwart brought logic into close relation with psychology, regarding the former as a technical normative discipline which serves to discover the criteria of correct thinking. He broadened logic to cover a general theory of method for scientific thought and, at the same time, brought its influence to bear upon positive science. He regarded all definitions as nominal, "real" definition being due to a confusion of logical and metaphysical questions. He influenced Bradley, Bosanquet, and Joseph, and he opposed the purely formal interpretation of logic, which dealt only in abstractions and ended in futilities. The difference between the psychic and the physical does not hinder their interaction. According to Sigwart, cause and purpose are not mutually exclusive. He thought ethics is eudaemonistic, social, and altruistic.

Paul Janet (1823-1899) [Paris, Bourges, Strasbourg]. Paul Janet was influenced by Cousin and was a representative of an eclectic doctrine, maintaining that each philosophical system presents a partial development of truth. Yet, he was biased in favor of idealism. Janet combatted materialism and biological mechanism, insisting that matter without force is an abstraction. Matter explains nothing until the properties of force and mind are attributed to it. He believed the proper standpoint in philosophy is a spiritualism that reckons with the facts of the natural sciences and, at the same time, recognizes the validity of final causes in life and mind. The soul is an immaterial force interacting with the body. Janet's *Final Causes* was published in 1874.

Gustav Teichmüller (1832-1888) [Braunschweig, Göttingen, Basel]. Influenced by Leibniz and Lotze, Gustav Teichmüller interpreted the self as the central fact of reality. He wrote that other types of philosophy deal primarily with phenomena. Substance and causality are derived from the experiences of the self. Teichmüller distinguished between consciousness and knowledge, and he recognized the importance of the unconscious. He was convinced that Christianity is the true religion because it emphasizes the importance of the individual. Teichmüller wrote *The Immortality of the Soul* (1874), which retains its importance even today.

William Stanley Jevons (1835-1882) [Liverpool, Sidney, Manchester, London]. W. S. Jevons was an economist and logician. After five years as assayer in the mint at Sidney, Australia, he was appointed professor of logic and mental and moral philosophy and lecturer in political economy at Manchester. In 1876 he accepted a teaching position at University College, London. Several of his works on logic were authoritative, but his most noted was *Principles of Science* (1874), which offers a mathematical foundation for logical procedures. His theory of the "substitution of similars"—i.e., "whatever is true of a thing is true of its like"—was the distinctive feature of his logic. Jevons built a "logical piano": when the keys of this machine were pressed to indicate premises, the conclusion was shown mechanically on the face of the machine. Although appreciating that portion of Boole's work which opposed Mill, Jevons revised some of Boole's symbols; he also contributed the view that algebra is subordinate to logic, not vice versa. In his writings on political economy, Jevons developed the theory of final utility (ascribed to a commodity): the minimum amount of demand, created by human want, for an economic commodity, which is necessary to induce continuance of production or use of the commodity.

Franz Brentano (1838-1917) [Marienburg, Wurzburg, Vienna, Florence]. Franz Brentano is noted for his *Psychology from the Empirical Standpoint* (1874), in which he defined psychical phenomena as those which "intentionally" contain an object in themselves. The act is mental, the content physical. In this way, he meant to overcome mentalism and maintain that the object is Real beyond consciousness. To Brentano the act of referring is immaterial and, as such, demonstrates the spiritual character of the soul. He maintained that further implications are indications of the wisdom and goodness of God. Brentano considered himself an Aristotelian. Actually, he began his career as a priest, but he eventually became an unorthodox Scholastic.

John Fiske (1842-1901) [Hartford, Cambridge]. Although trained for law, which he put to use only by trying and winning one case, John Fiske undertook a literary career. At Harvard, he lectured on the evolutionary aspect of philosophy and on history. As a public lecturer, he traveled both in America and abroad. In his *Outlines of Cosmic Philosophy* (1874), he applied the principles of evolution to philosophy. Fiske wrote extensively on American history as well as on the idea of God and the destiny of man.

Étienne Émile Marie Boutroux (1845-1921) [Paris]. Émile Boutroux was a student of Lachelier. In his *Contingency of the Laws of Nature* (1874), Boutroux propounded the significant thought that in the laws of nature there is a hierarchy, which renders accidental the application of any law in a given instance. One law supersedes another, and the operation of none is absolute. Thus, Boutroux reasoned, there can be freedom with respect to a specific law. Nature does not submit completely to the reign of law. Spirit is independent and free and is the basis of the explanation of the world. According to Boutroux, freedom is expressed in art, morality, and religion, all of which afford a higher than scientific knowledge.

George Henry Lewes (1817-1878) [London]. Known to the general public for his biography of Goethe (1855), George H. Lewes also participated in an unconventional union with the novelist George Eliot (Marian Evans). Early in life he was impressed with the Positivism of Comte. Lewes' *Biographical History of Philosophy,* one of the earliest comprehensive histories of thought in the English language, was widely read and reprinted repeatedly. The real purpose of the book was to expose the vanity of metaphysics. Later, he was influenced by Spencer's evolutionary point of view. Lewes was well read in biology and psychology as well as in philosophy, but he was unable to obtain a clear organization of his thoughts. He regarded the met-empirical as something whose existence may be granted but which remains unknowable. He was certain that whatever metaphysical problems are allowable must be treated in a strictly scientific manner. To philosophy Lewes assigned the task of seeking the widest possible generalizations and the most abstract ideas. He used the term "emergent" to refer to phenomena that are strictly new and not explicable because of the properties of their factors. The culmination of Lewes' thinking may be found in his *Problems of Life and Mind* (1874-1879).

F. Max Müller (1823-1900) [Dessau, London, Oxford]. While a student at Leipzig and Berlin Max Müller became deeply interested in Sanskrit, and later he published important translations of and treatises on Sanskrit literature. He was appointed to the chairs of modern languages and comparative philology at Oxford and became a well-known student of comparative religion, oriental studies, and linguistics. To the West he introduced oriental cultures and religions, especially those of India. Müller observed that in primitive culture language and religion go hand in hand and enlighten each other. To him, religion is the awareness of the infinite, and it passes through three fundamental stages—the physical, the anthropological, and the psychological—and culminates in Christianity. His reputation spread to the Orient and he received many honors. As editor of *The Sacred Books of the East* (1875-1900) Müller made the sources of oriental religions accessible to western readers. Furthermore, he made a noteworthy translation of Kant's *Critique of Pure Reason.*

Henry Sidgwick (1838-1900) [Skipton, Cambridge]. An advocate of higher education for women, Henry Sidgwick assisted in the founding of Newnham College at Cambridge. In his *Methods of Ethics* (1875) he criticized most of the standard formulations of intuitionism and introduced a rational basis for utilitarianism. Sidgwick rejected egoistic hedonism and adhered to a social utilitarianism based on universal moral principles. Furthermore, he was a member of the Society for Psychical Research, and he was co-editor of *Mind*.

Sir Leslie Stephen (1832-1904) [London, Cambridge]. Leslie Stephen was editor of the *Cornhill Magazine* and of the *Dictionary of National Biography,* for which he wrote four hundred of the biographies. But his chief claim to fame rests with his *History of English Thought in the Eighteenth Century* (1876), which mingled Buckle's ideas with the doctrine of evolution. Stephen's philosophy was agnostic and utilitarian, and he wrote about the English utilitarians, the science of ethics, and social rights and duties. He felt that theologians sidestepped the claims of intellectual honesty and covered up difficulties with loose thinking and evasions. Stephen insisted that choice is determined not by judgment of what is pleasantest but by the judgment that is pleasantest to make. Hence, one does not always choose what one knows is for his ultimate good. He called individuals the tissue of society and stated that they are only relatively independent of the social body. Morality is distorted by social pressure and does not consider, first of all, the interests of the individual. Stephen claimed that pleasure must be accounted for by the conditions which make acts pleasant in specific cases. Survival in the evolutionary process, Stephen wrote, is more ultimate than pleasure, though men do not consciously realize this fact.

Karl Ludwig Michelet (1801-1893) [Berlin]. Karl L. Michelet assisted in the publication of Hegel's works and was one of his most loyal followers. He wrote on ethics, the history of philosophy, the history of human progress, and Hegel's dialectical methods. Michelet's *History of Philosophy as Exact Science* (1876-1881) is one of his important contributions to the field.

Pope Leo XIII (1810-1903) [Capineto, Brussels, Rome]. In the encyclical letter, *Inscrutabili Dei Consilio* (1878), Pope Leo XIII, as in later documents, gave a new impetus to the study of Scholasticism. He insisted that Thomas' wisdom should be gleaned from the sources; over-subtle and unprofitable problems should be abandoned; the doctrines of the Scholastics, which were not in line with doctrines accepted in later times, should not be proposed for reception; and the Scholastic system should be enlarged and perfected with new developments. Thus, he directed that the significance of the past be newly appreciated and the original documents be studied afresh. Out of the effort to realize these goals the Neo-Scholastic movement developed.

Chauncey Wright (1830-1875) [Northampton, Cambridge]. In addition to physics and mathematics, Chauncey Wright was interested especially in astronomy. He taught mathematical physics at Harvard, where he also lectured on psychology. During this time, he was a member of the "Metaphysical Club" to which James and Peirce also belonged. Wright wrote articles on the theories of J. S. Mill, Spencer, and Bain, and he defended Darwin's theory of natural selection. Wright maintained that the only justification of abstract principles in science is their utility in enlarging our concrete knowledge of nature. It must be possible to make sensuous verification of the results of their use. The consequences of metaphysical and theological speculation are practical and moral. Wright doubted that there is a universal pattern in history; he supported utilitarian morals. He was of the opinion that the process of the universe is cyclic, not endlessly evolutionary. The distinction between subject and object is not intuitive but is the result of analysis for purposes of social communication. Scientific ethics should be free from fears and aspirations and, at the same time, be purely objective. Wright insisted that the evolution of self-consciousness was accomplished by putting old capacities to new uses. Philosophical speculations should be valued for their motives rather than their results. His principal work was *Philosophical Discussions,* published in 1877.

Nineteenth Century: Second Half (1850-1899)

Charles S. Peirce (1839-1914) [Cambridge, Baltimore, Milford]. For short periods of time, Charles S. Peirce lectured at Harvard and Johns Hopkins universities, but most of his life was spent in the service of the U. S. Geodetic Survey. He engaged in experimental work on the density of the earth and on the wave lengths of light. In an article, in the *Popular Science Monthly,* called *How to Make Ideas Clear* (1878), Peirce introduced the method of consideration of empirical consequences as the test of the meaning of an idea. He coined the term "Pragmatism" and founded the pragmatic movement in philosophy. Peirce was influenced by Kant and, indirectly, by Darwin. He interpreted logic as the general theory of signs, and hence he considered it as the heart of philosophy. Peirce was one of the very early contributors to the development of mathematical logic. His view of ethics was that the finitude of things compels the identification of interests with those of an unlimited community. The desire of beings to come together makes love an evolutionary force.

William K. Clifford (1845-1879) [Exeter, London, Cambridge, Madeira]. First of all, William K. Clifford was a mathematician and had won honors in that subject at Cambridge. In 1871 he became professor of mathematics and mechanics at University College, London. He wrote many papers on mathematics for the London Mathematical Society and also gave popular lectures on *Ether, Atoms,* and the *Sun.* In addition, he was interested in the theory of knowledge and in ethics. Beginning with a view similar to that held by Berkeley and Hume, Clifford maintained that the immediate facts of experience are sense impressions. *Objects,* therefore, are data appearing to us. Other selves are *ejects,* which are projected by inference from one's own consciousness. The proof of the reality of the external world is a social process. Clifford called the substance of which the world is made "mind stuff." This is raw material that constitutes sensations and things, which are the same stuff from two different points of view. The methodology of science he regarded as pragmatic. Clifford's ethics centered in belief in a Tribal Self to which the individual must be subject. His religion was worship of the universe, "cosmic emotion," which differed from organized Christianity (which he regarded as an enemy of humanity). *Lectures and Essays* and *Commonsense of the Exact Sciences,* both by Clifford, were published in 1879 and 1885, respectively.

Arthur J. Balfour (1848-1930) [Whittinghame, Cambridge, London]. Arthur J. Balfour was a Conservative member of Parliament and, in numerous ways, proved himself a leader in politics. Yet, in the midst of his active political career, he found time to engage in philosophic reflection, publishing in 1879 his *Defense of Philosophic Doubt.* This was followed by *The Foundations of Belief, Being Notes Introductory to the Study of Theology* (1895). Balfour's philosophy was basically theistic, was grounded in religious faith, and was directed against naturalism. For him, doubt was a preliminary stage which preceded rational certitude which is, in turn, attained in religion. Furthermore, he was interested in science, literature, music, and the fine arts. Balfour maintained that science rests on postulates accepted on faith, as does religion. Both are based on "inevitable beliefs." Science like religion postulates a rational Ultimate Cause of the World. In 1915 he published *Theism and Humanism.* Balfour was elected chancellor of the University of Cambridge in 1919. He was also a member of the Society for Psychical Research.

Gottlob Frege (1848-1925) [Jena]. Gottlob Frege is generally regarded as one of the greatest mathematical logicians of his time. His *Begriffschrift* (*Treatise on Concepts,* 1879) effected a transition from Boole's algebra to a more generalized logistic system. (This was so technical that it was "largely unknown to or misunderstood by his contemporaries.") Propositional functions and calculus, quantifiers, and the notion of hereditary property appear; he also included a logical analysis of mathematical induction. This work was the basis of important developments in Frege's later writings.

Wilhelm Wundt (1832-1920) [Neckarau, Heidelberg, Leipzig]. Distinguished in physiology, psychology, and philosophy, Wilhelm Wundt founded the first psychological laboratory and also made extensive studies in folk-psychology. According to Wundt, consciousness is the basis of all knowledge. All our experience is mental, though there are external causes of it. The categories of experience would not arise and endure if the external world did not agree with them. Whether one emerges a materialist or idealist depends upon whether one begins with external or internal experiences. It was also Wundt's belief that the cosmic mechanism conceals a spiritual reality, resembling ourselves. Theory of knowledge gives the psychic element priority in reality, and psychology shows that life is primarily will. He maintained that soul is not a substance but a pure activity. To ethics Wundt attributed the unification of individual wills in a universal will, which is absolute. Reality is a totality of striving beings, manifested in phenomenal forms. In his *Logic* (1880-1883), Wundt discussed, in detail, the laws of thought which affect knowledge of the truth.

John Venn (1834-1923) [Hull, Cambridge]. John Venn was originally a lecturer in moral science and in 1903 became president of Gonville and Caius College, Cambridge, of which he wrote a biographical history. He is noted for his work in logic, the most important phase of which is typified by *Symbolic Logic* (1881). Venn's aim was to improve upon the systems of Boole and Jevons and to make symbolic logic more useful. He refused to merge logic with mathematics because he believed the methods of calculation in the two fields to be distinct, though both are branches of a single symbolic language. Traditional logic had not been superseded; it still had a proper place in the field of thought and value. The later development of logic is the result of further generalization. Venn originated a set of diagrams to represent the interrelations of logical classes for up to five classes. He credited logic with explaining and systemizing the facts of the world throughout their entire extent. Remaining close to concrete experience, Venn also wrote *Logic of Chance* and *Empirical Logic*.

Friedrich Jodl (1849-1914) [Munich, Prague, Vienna]. Ethics and its history were the special interests of Friedrich Jodl. His works show the effects of Positivism and, consequently, he insisted that knowledge does not transcend experience. Our forms of perception and thought are determined by the relations of things. To ethics he assigned concern with practical ideals; ethics is independent of religion, metaphysics, and politics. The concept of humanity which calls for an enlargement of the interests of the Self makes it unnecessary to appeal to a transcendent reality. Morality is dependent upon an over-individual will.[1] In ontology, Jodl maintained an identity theory, with resultant parallelism of the physical and psychical where neurological conditions have occasioned consciousness. The soul is the unity of psychic experience. Jodl's *History of Ethics in Modern Philosophy* (1882) is a typical work.

Wilhelm Dilthey (1833-1911) [Biebrich, Berlin]. Basing philosophy on inner experience, Wilhelm Dilthey represented a positivistic idealism. The function of philosophy is to raise the inner motives of a culture to consciousness of themselves and a realization of their goals. Not merely thought, but the entire psychic life belongs to knowledge. Dilthey distinguished between the sciences of the spirit and natural sciences; the sciences of the spirit have to do with immediate reality, values, and norms. They deal with reality, as it appears in history and society, and with culture systems and their objectifications. The external world which appears in phenomena is a correlate and an opposite of our self. Dilthey's *Introduction to the Sciences of the Spirit* was published in 1883.

Thomas Hill Green (1836-1882) [Birkin, Oxford]. In his *Prolegomena to Ethics* (1883) Thomas Hill Green presented the first distinguished formulation of English absolute idealism. To him, a metaphysical background is necessary in order to give ethics any significance. The central questions concern the facts of consciousness, and the simplest explanation that is necessary to account for them. It was Green's opinion that what is required to explain experience must necessarily be true. Despite the truth there is in biological evolution, it does not give an adequate account of human consciousness. The ultimate whole is not matter, but spirit, a

---

[1] Cf. Emerson's over-soul, page 188.

realm of thought relations, involving the self, the cosmos, and God. Self is first in the order of knowledge, but God is first in the order of being. He decided that the mind as the unifying factor is implied in the unification of the plurality in the world. This indicates a process of self-realization of the world in our mind. Mind within can be known only by reflection upon self; thus the meaning of action can be discovered. Green believed it important that man look forward primarily to a moral ideal to be attained, rather than back to a biological past. This centers in an ideal of personal character, rather than in the well-being of the race.

George Sylvester Morris (1840-1889) [Norwich, Vt.; Hanover, N. H.; Ann Arbor, Mich.; Baltimore, Md.]. George S. Morris served in the Civil War, studied philosophy and theology in Germany for several years, and was appointed professor of modern languages and literature at the University of Michigan. Later he was professor of philosophy (1881-1889) at that university, and he also lectured at Johns Hopkins University. His thinking was influenced both by Kant and by Aristotle. Morris supported the idea that acts of thought are motions and can be assimilated to other types of motion and to the laws of natural energy. Thought is less a logical sequence than a series of living activities. It was from this standpoint that he criticized Spinoza, Leibniz, and Hegel. To Morris philosophy is the science of the life of the body in action. He tried to place philosophy on a scientific basis, without subordinating it to other sciences, expressing it in a dynamic idealism, which was larger and freer in its method than any special science, but not less scientific. Morris' *Philosophy and Christianity* was published in 1883.

Carl Stumpf (1848-1936) [Wiesentheid, Prague, Berlin]. Facets of Brentano's philosophy carried weight with Carl Stumpf, whose claim to fame rests primarily on his studies in the psychology of music, though he also wrote on metaphysics and theory of knowledge. The psychical is a kind of energy which has a physical equivalent. Stumpf wrote that the world as a whole is a causal system in which each phase plays a part. Plurality rests on a transcendental unity, which works through evolution in accordance with a plan. He considered phenomena of sense as neither physical nor psychical, but consisting of the material out of which these are built. Phenomenology analyzes sense phenomena down to their simplest elements. Spirit is prior to Nature in that the former is immediately given, the latter inferred from it. Stumpf's *Psychology of Tone*, out of which his thinking developed, was published in the period from 1883 to 1890.

James Martineau (1805-1900) [Norwich, Derby, Liverpool, Manchester, London]. Early in his youth James Martineau was apprenticed to an engineer at Derby, but later his attention turned to the ministry and he entered Manchester College (Unitarian). He worked as a preacher at Liverpool for a quarter of a century. In 1840 he was appointed professor of mental and moral philosophy and political economy at Manchester. In 1857 he moved to London where the college had been since 1853, and in 1869 he became principal. Martineau avoided extreme positions on the relation between Church and State, but felt he could trust statesmen more than ecclesiastics. He propounded a scheme for state co-ordination of religious sects without affecting their doctrine, polity, or discipline, but recognizing their historic achievement, character, and capacity. The proposal was an unpopular one.

Martineau's *Types of Ethical Theory* (1885) was an outstanding work. Although in the beginning his great interest was empiricism, his reflections upon the problems of the inner life, of responsibility, and of duty led him to abandon naturalism for idealism. He studied the latter in Germany, mainly through Trendelenburg's lectures on the history of philosophy. His dominant interest was moral and religious philosophy. It was Martineau's view that causality is not merely phenomenal; it is grounded in a non-phenomenal world. Freedom of the will and the authority of God are the supporting pillars of his thought. Concisely, his central idea is the self and its moral consciousness, which finds its completion in religion.

Francis Ellingwood Abbot (1836-1903) [Boston]. Francis E. Abbot was graduated from Harvard and from Meadville Theological

School. After five years as a Unitarian minister, he resigned because of his convictions. He became a journalist and edited *The Index,* a weekly journal of religious topics. Abbot's *Scientific Theism* (1885) is an expanded version of a lecture on the idea of God, an answer to the question: "Is Pantheism the legitimate outcome of modern science?" He tried to secure academic recognition among philosophers but was unsuccessful. He was one of the founders of the *Free Religion Association* which was devoted: (1) to the study of rational religion without a priesthood, (2) to a moral code independent of theology, (3) to a God without a dogmatic system, and (4) to a religion of action. Abbot criticized Kant's distinction between phenomena and noumena, and he developed an objective relativism. His realism was based on an analysis of the objectivity of relations, which he believed is exhibited by scientific experiment and observation. Knowledge is the result of dynamic correlation of the cosmos and the mind. Abbot maintained an organic, biological psychology and an organismic cosmology.

Ernst Mach (1838-1916) [Turas, Vienna, Graz]. Positivistic interpretation of science is seen in Ernst Mach's work, a typical sample of which is his *Analysis of Sensation* (1886). Taking the consequences of Berkeley, Hume, Kant, and Comte into consideration, Mach regarded what is called matter as merely a complex of sensations, as is also the self. He rejected *a priori* principles. Science should follow Ockham's razor and, governing itself by the principle of economy of thought, make its theories as simple as possible. To science Mach delegated the function of describing the irreducible contents of consciousness and discovering their connections, in the same instance avoiding metaphysical interpretations. Hypotheses are temporary expedients, which must be replaced by direct observations. He believed concepts to be shorthand symbols for groups of sensations. Knowledge is an instrument for action; the will is prior in life. Mach thought that a world view serves to bring us into relation with our environment.

Friedrich Wilhelm Nietzsche (1844-1900) [Röcken, Leipzig, Basel, Weimar]. Friedrich W. Nietzsche interpreted life in terms of evolution, centering in the biological urge toward survival and taking the form of a "will to power." This is the essence of life and the criterion of value. Life is a constant effort to give form to the unformed inner impulse. He studied classical philology, in which he held a professorship at Basel until ill health forced him to resign his position; but he continued strenuous literary activity.

He was absorbed in the contrast of the "Dionysian" (frenzied, spontaneous) with the "Apollonian" (measured, orderly) view of life, and he insisted that the former is superior to the latter. This led him to glorify Schopenhauer and Wagner for a time, though he rejected their pessimism. Nietzsche's work was marked by an expansive optimism, scorning past and present in the hope of a more glorious future. Moral standards need to be transformed to bring them to honest admission of the true urge of life and to free them from the leveling tendencies of tradition—the Christian standards have favored the weakling, so they have failed to contribute to the progress of the race. Traditional standards have favored *Sklaven-moral* (*slave-morality*) not *Herren-moral* (*master-morality*). The function of knowledge is to contribute to power. Nietzsche wrote that the heroic type of person, not the average man, should set the values of life. The mass of mankind is an instrument for the service of the great. Thus, he speculated, evolution should move on to the superman. Power constitutes nobility, and the aim of life is to produce supermen; strife and severity weed out the weak, hence they are good from the standpoint of the well-being of the race. Nietzsche's view was that only those should survive who can prove themselves masters of their environment. Our knowledge is not a means of attaining to the ultimate nature of reality. To Nietzsche it is an instrument of survival. The process of evolution repeats itself in endless recurrent cycles. A characteristic statement of his thought is found in *Beyond Good and Evil* (1886). Nietzsche was a poetic rather than a technical philosopher. His insights are flashes of intuition rather than carefully analyzed inferences.

Johannes Volkelt (1848-1930) [Lipnik, Basel, Leipzig]. Johannes Volkelt made a careful study of Kant's views and gave special attention to the theory of knowledge. He recognized two kinds of certainty: one of immediate consciousness and one of necessity of thought. Volkelt maintained that immediate experience is not enough; there is an unavoidable reference beyond experience. This idea leads to metaphysics; in addition to this there is "philosophy of life" which is more than the hypothetical results of science. He defined religion as a demand for union with the basis of all being. Volkelt was also interested in aesthetics, which he considered relative to religion. His *Experience and Thought* was published in 1886.

Ferdinand Tönnies (1855-1936) [Oldenswort, Kiel]. Ferdinand Tönnies' thought was induced to some extent by Schopenhauer's metaphysical voluntarism and was also related to Positivism. He attended mainly to social philosophy and included sociological, as well as philosophical, thought in his analyses. His chief publication was *Gemeinschaft und Gesellschaft* (*Community and Society,* 1887), in which he wrote that community living is group life, in which individuals are organically bound to each other. Social life, on the contrary, is more individualistic and more mechanistic than organic. One of Tönnies' observations was that an irresistible tendency toward the mechanization of life increasingly dissolves community existence. According to his theory, modern socialism will not restore communal living, but will produce more individuals with equal rights. Tönnies stated that the original community life was rooted in a generic will; the mechanical society is a product of free activity carried on by the intellect.

Bernard Bosanquet (1848-1923) [Rock Hall, Oxford, St. Andrews, London]. Following the same line of thought as Hegel, Bernard Bosanquet, in his *Logic or the Morphology of Thought* (1888), emphasized the wholeness of the Real. The universe is a system of members, each of which is unique and, as such, makes its special contribution to the nature of the whole. Bosanquet was convinced that all knowing strives toward this sort of inclusive totality. He applied his theory to ethics, individual and social; individual actions are moral in so far as they accord with the total will. The same

224

limitation has bearing on policies of state, as well as on individual action.

Richard Avenarius (1843-1896) [Paris, Zürich]. Richard Avenarius is noted for his theory of experience, which he expounded in *Critique of Pure Experience* (1888-1890). He claimed that the fundamental necessity of human thought is biological economy. He valued Spinoza because of his reduction of all ideas to a single one. Avenarius was aware that problems arise in experience when there is a state of tension between individual and environment, calling for a greater or lesser expenditure of energy than the individual is ready to give. When stimulus and energy on hand are equivalent the individual feels at home. This philosopher also stated that the enlargement of experience produces new problems. Each problem disappears when adjustment has been achieved. Adjustment may be purely individual, but it must be free from subjectivity to be a real solution. The point of view of pure experience is reached in quantitative description. Avenarius was anxious to formulate a symbolic language for philosophy like that of mathematics.

Edward Caird (1835-1908) [Greenock, Oxford, Glasgow]. As a pillar of the neo-Hegelian movement in Britain, Edward Caird contributed to the establishment of the vocabulary of Kantian and Hegelian doctrine. He succeeded in presenting the spirit of Hegel without the form which was forbidding to many and held that Hegel represented a great idealistic tradition, in both philosophy and literature, originating with the Greeks. For Caird, Kant was the key to Hegel, and Hegel the fulfillment of Kant. The essence of reality is identity in difference. The Absolute is not rigid, complete, and closed; it is a living, developing process, unfolding itself dialectically. He described the principle of unity in all things as God. This idea is at work in all rational consciousness, progressively manifesting itself in the evolution of religion and culminating in Christianity. Caird had sympathy with Spencer's evolutionary philosophy, but, to make it acceptable, he Hegelianized it. He had complete confidence in the ability of reason to illuminate the Ultimate Real. Caird's *Critical Philosophy of Kant* (1889) has been called the most thorough, comprehensive, and weighty exposition ever written in English.

Alejandro Deustua (1849-1940?) [Huancayo, Lima]. The special interest of Alejandro Deustua was the concept of freedom. He recognized two kinds—static and dynamic. The former accounted for the order in the universe, and the latter for the novelty. He wrote that the world, as we experience it, is the result of a synthesis of the two; this synthesis is more dynamic than static. A conception of values results from it. Deustua's *The Ideas of Order and Liberty in the History of Human Thought* (1889) is an important work.

William T. Harris (1835-1909) [Killingly, New Haven, St. Louis]. William T. Harris was Superintendent of Schools in St. Louis from 1867 to 1888 and United States Commissioner of Education from 1889 to 1906. In 1867 he established the *Journal of Speculative Philosophy,* the first periodical of its kind in English. Also he founded the St. Louis Philosophical Society, the predecessor of the American Philosophical Association. Harris was a member of the Concord school. Furthermore, he was an enthusiastic follower of Hegel and published, in 1890, *A Critical Exposition of Hegel's Logic.*

Alfred Fouillée (1838-1912) [La Pouëze, Donai, Bordeaux, Paris]. On the basis that the mechanistic interpretation of nature is compatible with human freedom, Alfred Fouillée undertook to mediate the tenets of idealism and science. His primary suggestion was that of "idée-force," as in his *L'Évolutionnisme des idées-forces* (1890). An idea does not merely represent an external fact; it is a force which tends to work itself out. This applies to the idea of freedom as well as to other ideas; the idea of freedom precedes the fact. Fouillée added that the universe is inseparably linked to our ideas. There results a monism in which matter and mind are different aspects of one reality. However, the mental aspect is the one immediately known to us; hence we must interpret everything in terms of mind.

William James (1842-1910) [Cambridge]. William James is well-known for his *Principles of Psychology,* which he wrote in

1890. This work is a philosophy of human experience, rather than a textbook in psychology, and is marked by a vivid, concrete, pragmatic presentation which characterized all James's work. His psychological theory was dynamic, and his interpretation of religion was centered in faith, "the will to believe." The essential thing is to see that reality is not finished; it is always in the making. This is the fundamental meaning of evolution. James followed Fichte in believing that the kind of philosophy one adheres to depends upon the kind of man one is. There is pluralism in this respect in experience as well as in the structure of the universe. The Absolute, implying a "block universe," tied things too closely together for James.

In a sense, he renewed Kant's distinction between empiricism and rationalism; but James's Pragmatism offers a *via media,* a corridor theory which allows a man to choose and live by the philosophy that fits him best and works most satisfactorily for him. Life is practical and oriented toward the attainment of the greatest satisfaction. The utilitarianism of John Stuart Mill appealed to James. Truth and goodness he defined in terms of long run, over-all expediency in ways of belief and behavior. Absolute truth is a distant vanishing point toward which our temporary truths may converge. James's corridor theory provided access to "radical empiricism" or "neutral monism." Thus he became the inspiration for much of Neo-Realism.

Ernst Schroeder (1841-1902) [Karlsruhe]. Ernst Schroeder was a professor of mathematics for twenty-six years. In his *Lectures on the Algebra of Logic* (1890-1895) he presented a detailed consideration of the logical foundations of mathematics; he also developed Boole's system with improved symbolism, giving a well-rounded summary of the work which had been done in the field up to his time. Schroeder's original contributions emphasized propositional functions and theory of relations.

Georg Simmel (1858-1918) [Berlin, Strasbourg]. The strength of Kant's views weighed heavily on Georg Simmel, and from them he developed a pragmatic interpretation of knowledge before this movement had reached its height in America. An individual perspective determines for each person what Nature and what history mean to him. He was of the opinion that there is a relativism in all knowledge; no one gains a strictly objective view; there are no laws in history. Simmel divided ethics into the descriptive and the normative; the former is concerned with actual practices, the latter with ideals. He recognized a realm of ideal demands in addition to the realms of physical, psychical, and natural law. According to his theory, the deepest demands of morality are concerned not with particular acts but with the character of life itself. Duty is the same whether fulfilled or not. Simmel sympathized with the Mystic, and he thought that the soul might have a kind of existence different from "substantial" survival. He was also deeply interested in social psychology and sociology, whose function he believed to be the determining of the forms of mutual association, rather than concern with its content. Simmel's *Introduction to Moral Science* (1892) was an early expression of his views.

Francis H. Bradley (1846-1924) [Glasbury, Oxford]. This philosopher's name is most often associated with *Appearance and Reality* (1893). Francis H. Bradley has been called the "Zeno of modern philosophy" because of the dialectical argument he used to support his theory. Careful examination seemed to him to show that all finite experiences are full of contradictions and, therefore, unreal. Only the Absolute Whole is strictly real. Bradley argued the inadequacy of the hedonistic tradition in ethics; he maintained the necessity for reference to the total system of thought in logic. The mind desires to comprehend the universe, not merely piecemeal, but as a whole. He credited appearances with a degree of reality, but not with the Ultimate Reality that is sought. The Ultimate Real is a harmony of many in one. It is not only formal thought but also immediate feeling. Its nature is suggested to us, but not exhausted in finite experience. Bradley stated that neither discursive thought nor immediate feeling alone is adequate for knowledge; the two must be combined. Error, ugliness, and evil are resolved but not obliterated in the Absolute. Nature as quantitative construction is a scientific fiction; to this must be added our experience of joy, sorrow, beauty, and emotion. According to his view, even soul and body are abstractions and, therefore, fictions. Bradley believed we escape solipsism[2] because the Whole is in every experience. The Absolute is super-personal, containing all history and progress, though not subject to these.

Émile Durkheim (1858-1917) [Les Vosges, Paris]. Émile Durkheim maintained a theory of a collective consciousness, distinguishable from the individual and having characteristics of its own, in general more coercive than those of the individual and within which the individual develops. The group, a unity within which division of labor occurs increasingly, maintains itself through customs, duties, and accepted conventions. Herein lie social values and moral ideas. Durkheim noted that community minds differ from one another; hence there are different moral standards. In time, these change. He explained that conceptions of truth are also primarily determined by the community, as are goodness and beauty. There are no absolute metaphysical or theological presuppositions. In 1893, Durkheim wrote a treatise *On the Division of Social Work*.

Maurice Blondel (1861-1939) [Dijon, Aix]. A French representative of pragmatic philosophy, Maurice Blondel modified his Pragmatism by means of an idealistic tendency. He was influenced by Maine de Biran and Boutroux. One of his important works was *Action* (1893). Later Blondel showed a strong theological interest. According to him, activity of the spirit is the basis of all knowledge and living. He stated that human will can overcome the world, but it must believe in God in Whom all activity finally comes to rest.

Wilhelm Windelband (1848-1915) [Potsdam, Leipzig, Zürich, Heidelberg]. Wilhelm Windelband is noted as a historian of philosophy, but he also developed a philosophy which was centered in the theory of value. In general, his position was idealistic, but independent. He insisted that science is concerned with facts, philosophy with values. The distinctive disciplines of philosophy—

---

[2] The theory that oneself alone exists.

logic, ethics, aesthetics—are normative, not merely descriptive. In the conception of what "ought" to be there are an *a priori* and a theological element not present in description. Furthermore, Windelband emphasized the difference between natural science and history; the former is concerned with generalizations, the latter with individuals (especially with important individuals) and with events as unique occurrences. Windelband's *History and Natural Science* was published in 1894.

Giuseppe Peano (1858-1932) [Turin]. A logician, mathematician, and student of language, Giuseppe Peano introduced a new symbolism into mathematical logic, which has proved more acceptable than previous systems. He recognized the uniqueness of the concept of membership in a class and distinguished it from inclusion of one class in another; inclusion of classes was also distinguished from implication among propositions. Peano's *Formulaire de Mathématiques* (*Formulary of Mathematics*) was developed during the years 1894-1908. He made positive contributions to mathematics and was also interested in Latin without inflections as an international language.

Wilhelm Ostwald (1853-1932) [Riga, Leipzig]. Wilhelm Ostwald was a noted chemist and winner of the Nobel Prize in 1909. He regarded energy as the Ultimate Reality, rejecting materialism and mechanism as ultimate concepts. The properties of matter are special manifestations of energy (chemical, electric, etc.). He described consciousness as another manifestation. Interaction between the physical and mental is possible as transition from one form of energy to another. An expression of Ostwald's view is found in *The Overcoming of Scientific Materialism* (1895).

George Trumbull Ladd (1842-1921) [Painesville, Bowdoin, New Haven]. George T. Ladd is noted for his writings on psychology, philosophy, and education. After being graduated from Western Reserve University and Andover Theological Seminary, he held pastorates for ten years, taught at Bowdoin, and then was appointed professor of philosophy at Yale where he taught for twenty-four years. He lectured in Japan, India, Honolulu, and Korea as well as in many places in the United States, and received many honors at home and abroad. He was one of the pioneers of experimental psychology in America. The psychological laboratory at Yale was founded by him. Ladd's philosophy was theistic and placed personality in a central position. In many respects his ideas were similar to Lotze's thought, and he wrote important documents on German idealism. His *Philosophy of Mind, an Essay in the Metaphysics of Psychology* (1895) is typical of his point of view, which worked from psychology into the problems of knowledge, metaphysics, ethics, and religion.

Georg Cantor (1845-1918) [St. Petersburg, Halle]. Georg Cantor was an outstanding mathematician, who is noted for his contributions to the foundations of analysis, and for his theory of transfinite numbers. Between 1895 and 1897 he published his *Foundations of the Theory of Transfinite Groups.*

George V. Plekhanov (1856-1918) [Tambov, St. Petersburg, Geneva]. The founder of Russian philosophic Marxism, George V. Plekhanov joined the populist revolutionary movement. However, he rejected terrorist methods. For forty years he lived in Geneva and became the intellectual leader of the Social-Democratic party, having a great deal of influence upon Lenin. For a time they were joint editors of *The Spark*. Plekhanov supported World War I, but was unsympathetic toward the Revolution of 1917. In spite of his independent ideas, he is regarded by Soviet thinkers as an important interpreter of Marx. Plekhanov's *Essays on the History of Materialism* (1896) expresses his position.

George Frederick Stout (1860-1944) [Cambridge, Aberdeen, Oxford, St. Andrews]. Three primary interests pervade the thinking of Stout: (1) an interest in the exact description of psychological process, (2) an accurate consideration of the problem of knowledge, and (3) the analysis of self-consciousness. He interpreted psychology in a broad sense. It is concerned not merely with empirical details, nor with physiological processes, nor with special problems of experimental techniques. He believed it finds its real meaning in the highest and most complex activities of experience. Error is to be interpreted as confusion of imaginative appearance with objective reality. Stout declined to separate the psychical from the physical as sharply as did the Cartesian tradition. He insisted that the world is fundamentally one. Self-consciousness is the point of central interest because it presents the knowledge of the empirical self both from within and from without. Finally, reality is to be interpreted spiritually; it includes Nature but it is not exhausted by it. Stout's *Analytic Psychology* (1896) was an outstanding work.

Heinrich Rickert (1863-1936) [Danzig, Freiburg, Heidelberg]. Windelband and Heinrich Rickert represented the same type of philosophy—an idealistic system based on Fichte's views and emphasizing norms of value as the core of philosophy. Value is dependent upon the assent of consciousness, which is more than individual, and is guided by obligation. History, science, and philosophy have their distinctive interests in the individual, the universal, and the axiological. Rickert's view is represented by *The Limits of Natural Scientific Conceptions* (1896).

Leonard Trelawney Hobhouse (1864-1929) [Oxford, London]. Noted for his versatility, Leonard T. Hobhouse's wide range of interests covered not only philosophy but also journalism, politics, and sociology. His *Theory of Knowledge* (1896) sounded the keynote of all his writing. Philosophy, according to him, must keep in close touch with the facts discovered by empirical science, but must also effect a synthesis of being in all its orders and gradations, never closing itself to the recognition of new discoveries. Hobhouse was open-minded toward the contributions of all schools of philosophy and was stimulated by Spencer's evolutionism, which he restated and applied in *Mind in Evolution, Morals in Evolution,* and *Development and Purpose.* Furthermore, he made important investigations in animal psychology. Cognition begins with presentation and returns to it in the end. He stated that apprehension covers the entire content of consciousness and constitutes the criterion of truth. The only *a priori* factor that exists is the mind's ability to handle sense content. One judgment must be supported by confirmation by other judgments. To him, mind is an essential constituent in the universe but a mechanical principle must also be recognized. "Organism," however, is the most important of all aspects of reality. The function of ethics is to show the operation of reason in practice. Hobhouse described the highest type of society as one which is based on co-operation not on competition.

John M. E. McTaggart (1866-1925) [Cambridge]. J. M. E. Mc-Taggart was one of the most thoroughgoing English idealists. His thought grew out of an intensive study of Hegel, though it went beyond this philosopher. McTaggart departed from the prevailing theistic interpretation and developed an atheistic one, tending toward pluralism. He devoted three books to the study of Hegel. In the first one, *Studies in the Hegelian Dialectic* (1896), he defended Hegel against the charge of abstract formalism which ignores concrete experience. The final synthesis in the Absolute Idea is the approach to the concrete whole. The dialectical movement is itself subject to development. Negation is less important as thought develops, making explicit what was implicit before and growing as a plant out of a seed. McTaggart's later treatise, *The Nature of Existence* (1921) was a study based on *a priori* principles of the concepts of substances, qualities, and relations. As a result of this study he came to the conclusion that the universe is finally one interrelated structure and is, in essence, spiritual. The Absolute is a system of immortal selves, among whom the most important bond is love. In addition, McTaggart developed a detailed theory of time.

Theodor Lipps (1851-1914) [Walhalben, Munich]. Theodor Lipps studied mathematics, theology, philosophy, and natural science and was influenced especially by Husserl and the Neo-Kantians. According to his theory, philosophy is the science of inner experience and, therefore, the basis of psychology, logic, ethics, esthetics, and metaphysics. Lipps was certain that psychology is especially close to philosophy, but he believed that there are psychological processes which are deeper than those reported by empirical psychology. The normative disciplines are pervaded by psychology.

Lipps made a special study of optical illusions which led to his theory of "empathy." Through empathy, every object is involuntarily regarded as living and as something into which the observer projects his own feelings. Empathy combines intuition and inference, providing knowledge of the inner experience of other sensitive beings. Lipps's doctrine was developed in *Space-perception and Geometrical Optical Illusions* (1897).

Christian von Ehrenfels (1859-1932) [Rodaun, Prague]. Although he was influenced more by Meinong, Christian von Ehrenfels is regarded as one of the leaders of the Brentano school. His conception of "Gestaltqualität," the feeling produced by a complex as a totality, met with great sympathetic response. Ehrenfels named "desire" as the basic root of life and of consciousness. Whether it is the production or modification of an object or a process, it is an act directed to some end. Desire is not a specific element of consciousness, but a general attitude toward things and activities. There are, according to Ehrenfels, struggles of motives, the winner being the one which promises the most for happiness. He stated that the "value" of a thing is its desirability. There are intrinsic values and instrumental values. He defined the highest moral value as effort toward the greatest possible well-being of the Whole. Ehrenfels' *Systematic Theory of Value* was published in 1897. In addition, he wrote several dramas.

Shadworth Holloway Hodgson (1832-1912) [Boston, Oxford, London]. Shadworth H. Hodgson did not hold an academic position, but instead he devoted his life to the study of philosophy. He was one of the founders of the Aristotelian Society and was its president for several years. Hodgson attempted to combine psychology and logic in an analysis of experience which is without presuppositions. This gave him consciousness and object, two aspects of the same reality from which all other propositions must be derived by reflection. In his theory he derived the conception of existence from memory lasting through duration; the item of experience remembered is first of all a quality and secondly a thing. This is the simplest case of perception of existence. Hodgson stated that consciousness can not be explained by the causality of matter, for matter itself is a concept derived from consciousness. The search

234

for a condition upon which consciousness depends points to an unseen realm behind the visible one. According to his view, its direct features are unknown to our type of consciousness, but our practical interests lead us to clothe it in the only imagery we have. Thus we must think of it as conscious and personal, with knowledge that goes beyond ours to a grasp of the Real and the ideal. He believed this gives religion a basis. Hodgson's *Metaphysic of Experience* (1898) is the maturest presentation of his position.

James E. Creighton (1861-1924) [Ithaca]. James E. Creighton is known chiefly for his *Introductory Logic* (1898), which was written from the standpoint of the Aristotelian tradition combined with the idealism of Bosanquet and Bradley. Creighton was also attracted by Kant's views although he thought Kant's doctrine was too self-centered. He believed in the continuity and unity of experience through time and in society; he maintained that every student of philosophy must be well-grounded in the history of thought, and accepted thought as a social and co-operative process. To philosophy he ascribed humanistic, spiritual, and poetic qualities, rather than natural-scientific. Creighton was not a prolific writer; for the most part he expressed his views in critical articles. He was one of the founders of the Eastern Division of The American Philosophical Association and served as its president. For many years, he edited *The Philosophical Review* and was active in connection with *Kantsudien (Kant Studies)* a famous periodical.

Alfred H. Lloyd (1864-1927) [Montclair, New Jersey; Andover, Massachusetts; Ann Arbor, Michigan]. Alfred H. Lloyd spent thirty-six years (1891-1927) as teacher of philosophy and dean of the graduate school at the University of Michigan. His *Dynamic Idealism, an Elementary Course in the Metaphysics of Psychology* (1898) presented a monistic view of the world with emphasis upon objectivity and the importance of the actuality of thinking. He stated that the universe lives and thinks. To live critically is the essence of mental activity, according to Lloyd. He answered James's *The Will to Believe* with a volume called *The Will to Doubt*. Life is a dialectical process, a struggle of opposites. He was more concerned with the application of his philosophy than with expounding it. His style was subtle and ironical. In another of his writings Lloyd discussed the psychology of post-war politics. He thought the study of history uncovers the progressive increase in the degree of individual freedom accorded to the members of society.

Ernst Haeckel (1834-1919) [Potsdam, Jena]. Ernst Haeckel, a noted zoölogist, developed an evolutionary hylozoistic metaphysics which was similar to that of the early Greeks. For the traditional interests in God, freedom, and immortality, he substituted a naturalistic monism emphasizing the true, the good, and the beautiful. Haeckel's most popular work was *The Riddle of the Universe* (1899).

James Ward (1843-1925) [Hull, Cambridge, Leipzig]. James Ward broke away from his early training as a Congregational minister and entered upon an academic career. He became professor of mental philosophy at Cambridge and was twice Gifford lecturer, at Aberdeen and at St. Andrews. He gained a reputation, at first, as a writer on psychology and was influenced by Lotze, Wundt, and other German thinkers. Through his voluntarism and humanism in psychological theory, Ward did a great deal to counteract the influence of associationism. In *Naturalism and Agnosticism* (1899) he attacked the methods of natural science for being inadequate (because of abstractness) to give a complete account of the structure of reality. On the basis of the continuity of nature, the immediacy of the knowledge of the self, and the difficulties of dualistic interaction theory, Ward adhered to panpsychism in metaphysics. In his later writings he developed a theism offering a world-ground to whose activity finite monads owe their freedom as creative agents. Ward viewed objectivity as a reference not to an independent being but to a intersubjective discourse.

David Hilbert (1862-1943) [Göttingen]. David Hilbert was a mathematician whose contributions to different branches of mathematics and its foundations in logic place him among the highest in the field. His discussion of the bases of Euclidian geometry was published in *Foundations of Geometry* (1899). Hilbert is noted as the leader of the formalist school of mathematics. This school maintains that mathematics is a process of manipulation of symbols, without content, in accordance with certain rules. Simply, it is a kind of game played with marks on paper. In addition to this, Hilbert stated that there is a "meta-mathematics" consisting of real assertions *about* mathematics.

The dominant type of philosophy in the first half of this century has been idealism, which is represented by many prominent thinkers, among them Eucken, Royce, Taylor, Calkins, Muensterberg, Hocking, Unamuno, Gentile, and Temple; without explicitly using the designation, Bergson and Whitehead occupy similar positions. The personalist tendency is typified by Howison and Bowne in the United States and by Romero in South America.

In the meantime, two forms of realism—the active rivals, New Realism and Critical Realism—were being developed. A few of the supporters of New Realism are Moore, Meinong, Perry, and Alexander; Critical Realism is favored by such thinkers as Santayana and Lovejoy.

The studies of the foundations of mathematics and the mathematical formulation of logic have been carried on vigorously after Hilbert by Russell, Zermelo, Brouwer, Wittgenstein, Ramsay, Gödel, Carnap, Tarski, and Quine; later Feigl, Sellars, and Black.

The field of ethics has not been subordinated. Interest in it has developed among men of many continents—Foerster and Ross in Europe, Tufts in North America, and Korn, Nuñez, and Xirau in South America. As a result of the thinking of Lenin, Huizinga, and Morris R. Cohen, social philosophy has become of increasing concern and has been linked with aspects of psychology by such men as McDougall, Weber, and Lévy-Bruhl. Psychology has been restated into behaviorism by Watson, into individual psychology by Stern, and into Gestalt psychology by Wertheimer and his co-workers. In another area of psychology, psychoanalysis has been developed by Freud, Adler, Jung, and Jaspers.

Instrumentalism, with emphasis on scientific method and social appeal, is represented by Poincaré, Schiller, Dewey, Lewis, Mead and their followers, Murphy, Lepley, and White. Phenomenology has developed under Husserl, Scheler, Nicolai Hartmann, and Heidegger. The religious aspect of experience has received special attention in the work of Höffding, Berdyaev, and Barth; Grahmann, Geyser, and Maritain have been concerned with Scholasticism. Neo-Kantian doctrine has continued in the thought of Cassirer, Natorp, and Ortega y Gasset; scientific method has had great influence on Driesch, Turro y Darder, and Schlick. The philosophy of physical science has been the special interest of Planck and Frank. Aesthetics has also had its devotees, outstanding among whom are Croce, Kuelpe, and Kallen.

George H. Howison (1834-1916) [Maryland, Harvard, California]. The movement called "personal idealism" was brought to a focus in the thinking of George H. Howison. He argued that absolutism was incompatible with human freedom and responsibility. The primary fact of all experience is the existence of minds. It was Howison's conviction that nature consists of the interrelated system of experiences of minds and is thus an ideal world, recognized by the society of minds. In this society God stands as the leading mind, the uniting bond between minds, and the perfect type of all. He is not to be interpreted as creator and ruler, but rather as end and ideal.

Howison opposed what he considered the pantheistic and solipsistic tendencies of absolute idealism and interpreted the *a priori* as human, not absolute in status. He did not write a great deal, but *The Limits of Evolution* (1901) is an important expression of his views.

Harald Höffding (1843-1931) [Copenhagen]. Harald Höffding, a Danish thinker, wrote on psychology, the history of philosophy, and the philosophy of religion. He called attention to the significance of Kierkegaard as a philosopher. He named his own philosophy *critical monism,* a type of idealism which insists that though ultimate reality is strictly unknowable the only approach to an interpretation of it is by way of conscious experience and its unity. Höffding's *Philosophy of Religion* (1901) is a well-known work; an important point is his definition of religion as the conservation of value.

Rudolph Eucken (1846-1926) [Aurich, Jena]. Winner of the Nobel Prize for Literature in 1908, Rudolph Eucken presented an idealism which is more activistic than intellectualistic. The ground of all being is a universal life which is the basis of nature, of humanity, and of history. He insisted that evolution moves from inorganic nature to organism, mind, spiritual independence, and self-consciousness. Individuality develops within the universal life. Naturalism presupposes the mental world, and intellectualism has to embody logic in experience. Mind yearns for the infinite; we experience free, self-active spirit in ourselves. He thought that the sense of contrast between man's actual situation and his spiritual possibilities produces the conviction that a higher power is working within. Life is a struggle between alternatives. Eucken taught the need for a cultural renewal and influenced such men as Spranger and Scheler. *Der Wahrheitsgehalt der Religion* (*The Truth of Religion*), which was published in 1901, is typical of Eucken's work.

Max Planck (1858-1947) [Kiel, Berlin]. As a physicist Max Planck introduced to science the concept of "quantum"—the unit in which energy travels—which is comparable to an atom of matter. He formulated the following: the magnitude of the quantum of radiant energy of a given frequency is equal to the product of the frequency multiplied by his constant h. Planck's theory has had important consequences in the interpretation of the structure of the physical world. His doctrine is to be found in a paper *On the Elementary Quanta of Matter and Electricity,* in *Annalen der Physik IV* (1901).

Edmund Husserl (1859-1938) [Prossnitz, Göttingen]. In his *Logische Untersuchungen* (*Logical Investigations,* 1901), Edmund Husserl undertook to detach logic from psychology. He originated a new point of view which he called "phenomenology." This is a kind of realism which holds that the objects of thought have a being independent of the processes by which they are apprehended. It avoids the usual concern with matter and mind, as something outside the pure phenomena of experience. It is concerned only with the analysis of immediate data, after these are phenomeno-logically "reduced" or detached, in consciousness, from all preconceptions and all natural facts. To Husserl, analysis of consciousness reveals that it involves an act of being conscious, an object of consciousness, and a datum by which the object is known. The object is given, not constructed by consciousness, and is not the "appearance" of any "reality." It is the content of "pure" experience. Husserl regarded his system as neither idealism nor materialism. Nor is it any form of metaphysics. This discrimination of states of consciousness from their actuality or possibility in a world he called "epoché" or "bracketing."

Josiah Royce (1855-1916) [California, Baltimore, Cambridge]. Although agreeing with the absolute idealistic position, Royce thought it needed restatement such as he made in *The World and the Individual* (1901, 1904). Bradley had spoken of the function of thought as dealing with relations, and he concluded that it succeeded only in cutting things apart. To Royce, this meant the relations did not relate. Rather, he employed a synthesizing process and called his own position *synthetic idealism*. In line with the general trend of idealism he insisted that the primary problem of philosophy is the problem of knowledge. Knowledge is more than perception and conception; it is interpretation. The path of knowledge is the path the mind must inevitably follow in reaching reality. With Parmenides, he believed that thought and being are one. In fact, the movement from the general and incomplete "internal meaning" of an idea to the concrete and perfected "external meaning" is the attainment of the Real, which is the goal of the idea. This Royce named as the aim of every philosophic system, although different temperaments follow different paths in order to reach it. Fundamentally, these temperaments are four: the realistic, the mystical, the critical rationalistic, and the synthetic idealistic. Each one is impressed with a certain phase of reality and emphasizes it over other phases. According to his view, every system has some degree of truth in it. Men could not live by what is entirely false; it would fail them absolutely.

These are the phases of reality with which, Royce believes, the four temperaments are impressed. The realist professes the objectivity of the Real in contrast with the subjectivity of the finite ideas that are seeking it. The Mystic emphasizes the immediacy and final satisfactoriness of reality when it is attained. The critical rationalist observes the analytic structure of reality. The synthetic idealist grasps the fact that the true is the Whole.

Every finite aspect of the Universe, Royce maintains, must be interpreted as a unique expression of the Absolute. Nature, animals, and man all get meaning in their settings and relations as well as in internal structure. World movements and religious systems, like Christianity, are also to be interpreted in this manner. It is through this method that man gains a sense of his moral value and of the significance of living.

Glimpses of the Absolute Principles, which tie all details together, are obtained by use of the "reflexive" method, which reveals truths presupposed even in the attempt to deny them. Consequently, Royce declared that so-called relativism must come to see that when it denies that there is any absolute truth it asserts thereby what it accepts as an Absolute Truth. The formulation of final principles is the goal of metaphysical logic. Royce considered that the construction of a principle of loyalty, which will allow and encourage loyalty to all subordinate loyalties, is the final goal of ethics and the solution of the problem of living together nationally and internationally.

Jules Henri Poincaré (1854-1912) [Nancy, Caen, Paris]. A French representative of the most recent type of Positivism (that which includes pragmatic tendencies), J. Henri Poincaré stated his position in such works as *Science and Hypothesis* (1902). Here his concern is with the philosophy of science, and his approach is that of the mathematician. He asserted that the postulates of science are conventions determined by fitness with experience and by the demand for consistency. *A priori* truth is akin to mathematical induction. In the latter, if the truth of a formula in a given case implies its truth for an immediately succeeding case, then an infinite series of instances follow. Poincaré noted that this is an algebraic process and does not apply in the same way to geometry. In this case the simplest explanation is the best and will be superseded when a simpler and more convenient one is discovered. In physical science experiment is the only acceptable test of truth, and it alone can give new truth. According to Poincaré's theory, the truth of theories consists in their ability to co-ordinate the facts which are presented by sense.

Note: Italian thought of the early twentieth century was marked by a revival of idealism. Its aim was to defend the place of spirit in the universe; it regarded mind as self-creating, and as the Ultimate Reality.

Benedetto Croce (1866-1952) [Percasseroli, Naples]. In a series of volumes beginning with *Aesthetic as Science of Experience and Universal Linguistic* (1902), Benedetto Croce, Italian Senator and Minister of Education, advocated the revived doctrine of idealism. Experience is the one thing of which we are certain, and it does not have a transcendent reference. Croce stated that the distinction between subject and object is itself a distinction within experience, and the object known is a mental construct. Reality is universal, self-constructing mind or spirit. It contains much diversity according to the various modes of conscious life. The latter, Croce asserted, has two fundamental modes—the theoretical and the practical.

The theoretical is either intuitive or intellectual; the intuitive gives the content of knowledge, the intellectual gives the arrangement. Intuition is a general process creating the content of imagination and feeling as well as the data of knowledge; it is immediate expression and is the preeminent faculty of the artist and poet. According to this philosopher, their intuitions are more vivid, and they have more skill than average persons in expressing them. Concepts generalize the content of intuitions. Real concepts, like quantity, existence, beauty, are present in all experience. He considered that mathematics and the sciences develop pseudo-concepts, mental fictions, which are not valid in reference to reality as a whole, but only in the special areas for which they are generated.

Croce insisted that practical consciousness has to do with action. It is dependent upon the theoretical; we must know in order to act. Practical consciousness takes two essential forms—economics and ethics. The former centers in individual advantage; the latter in social ends. The latter depends upon the former, and there can be no moral activity without economic action, though the reverse may be true; thus they are closely related to each other.

Croce repeated Hegel's phrase, "Philosophy is history," but re-interpreted it to give more emphasis to change and to progress than he thought Hegel had. But in studying reality, mind is studying, interpreting, and creating itself; this activity, Croce concludes, is the core of history.

Ferdinand C. S. Schiller (1864-1937) [Oxford, Los Angeles]. In his *Humanism* (1903) F. C. S. Schiller formulated a relativistic view of knowledge. Later, he expressed a deliberate preference for the philosophy of Protagoras over that of Plato. The presuppositions of human knowledge he regarded as practical postulates, rather than absolute axioms. Schiller acknowledged that man is a doer rather than a knower: his practical interests come first. Moral and religious concerns play a fundamental part in what man believes is true, as knowledge. All that man ever succeeds in reaching is opinion; nothing is ever final. In addition, Schiller declared formal logic to be a social problem rather than a guide to life.

Alfred E. Taylor (1869-1945) [Oxford, St. Andrews, Edinburgh]. An absolute idealist, with strong Neo-Scholastic sympathies, A. E. Taylor was an Anglo-Catholic in conviction. For a while he emphasized ethics, but eventually he shifted his attention to theology, basing his beliefs on cosmology and conscience as well as on religious experience. His *Elements of Metaphysics* (1903) is a statement of the essence of his position. The task of metaphysics is to bring the results of the natural sciences, morality, and religion into mutual harmony. Taylor was convinced that there is no evolution of Ultimate Reality; evolution is a relative conception.

Bertrand A. W. Russell (1872-   ) [Trelleck, Cambridge]. Through his *Principles of Mathematics* (1903) Bertrand Russell gained a position of prime importance in logical theory, one that he has kept ever since. He further developed his theory with A. N. Whitehead in *Principia Mathematica* (1910-1913). Russell has moved toward Positivism in his interpretation of matter and mind, though in the statement of the nature of knowledge, in his later works, he has employed a representational theory. During one period of his thinking, he interpreted reality as a system of perspectives. These are not to be understood as dependent in any way upon a knowing mind. Objects are particular sets of closely related perspectives. On the basis of a physicalistic interpretation of reality, Russell, in his well-known essay *A Free Man's Worship* (1918), expressed a pessimistic outcome for life so far as the human being is concerned. On occasions his interpretation of the Real has been in terms of a neutral stuff, like that of Neo-Realism. The process which occurs in knowing is inseparably connected with a brain. The clarity of Russell's writing won him the Nobel Prize in literature for 1950.

George E. Moore (1873-1958) [Cambridge]. An outstanding representative of realism in England, G. E. Moore regarded the function of philosophy as the analysis of common sense, not its destruction. This analysis should apply to the knowledge of things and of other persons. Moore contends that nature is non-mental and is directly known in perception. The knowledge process does not effect any change in the object. In refuting idealism he noted a distinction between the act of sensing an object and the object itself. According to his theory, the awareness of whiteness is not itself white. The whiteness is objective, the awareness subjective. Mental activity is diaphanous, referring to the objective which is presented through sensation. Relations are external not internal, as idealism has held. Moore's *Principia Ethica* was published in 1903; in his ethical theory he regarded the good as "indefinable" and something immediate, to be grasped by a direct intuition, not by analysis.

Friedrich W. Foerster (1869-   ) [Berlin, Vienna, Munich, Paris, Zürich]. Friedrich W. Foerster is noted for his discussions of education and ethics. which were at first independent of religion since his own youthful training was without religion (later he adopted Catholicism). He criticized frankly the moral tenets of Hitler's National Socialism. His *Jugendlehre* (*Doctrine of Youth*) was published in 1904.

Ernst Zermelo (1871-   ) [Zürich, Freiberg]. Ernst Zermelo was a professor of mathematics and, understandably, his most important contributions were to mathematical theory. His contributions were outstanding, especially in regard to functions of a real variable and particularly to his "axiom of choice," which he later showed to be identical with Russell's multiplicative axiom.[1] Zermelo's purpose was to show that every class can be well-ordered. His proof avoids the assumption of the *theory of types*.[2] His position is controversial and has been criticized on the ground that his conception of "existence" is merely equivalent to "freedom from contradiction." Zermelo's theory is set forth in his *Proof that Every Class can be Well-ordered* (*Mathematische Annalen,* 59, 1904).

George Santayana (1863-1952) [Madrid, Harvard, Rome]. A poet and essayist as well as a philosopher, George Santayana is an outstanding representative of Critical Realism, a form of naturalism. The objects of knowledge occupy either of two statuses; they may be existing substances or subsisting essences, though it is impossible to prove the independent existence of either type of object. Santayana stated that we believe in the objectivity of substance on the basis of animal faith. The ultimate substance of the real world is matter in motion. He also asserted that the operation of the universe is mechanical and is unaffected by mind, the function of which is purely contemplative. The fundamental character of the universe is neither moral nor rational. Santayana continued that mind itself

---

[1] According to Russell: "Given any class of mutually exclusive classes, of which none is null, there is at least one class which has exactly one term in common with each of the given classes."

[2] The *theory of types* distinguishes formulas regarding *individuals* from formulas regarding *classes* of individuals.

is a product of matter in motion; under certain conditions it becomes conscious of itself. It develops likes and dislikes, which are the root of values—goodness, beauty, imagination. But values belong in in the realm of essence, not of existence. Santayana was convinced that a fundamental error of philosophies and religions lies in their confusing ideals with existences. Truth, goodness, and beauty are the real divinities, independent of each other, and often hostile, though the function of reason is to effect as great a harmony as possible. Santayana's *Life of Reason* (1905-1906) was the earliest expression of his doctrine.

Ernst Cassirer (1874-1945) [Breslau, Marburg, Berlin]. Ernst Cassirer, a representative of the Neo-Kantian school, was interested in its relation to science. The history of modern philosophy seemed to him to support his position, which he elaborated in his interpretation of mathematics, chemistry, and the theory of relativity. His *Problem of Knowledge* (1906) is an outstanding work. Later, Cassirer's position was expressed in the study of symbolic forms in general. The categories employed for organizing experience and knowledge at any period are expressions of the needs of that age.

Alexius Meinong (1853-1920) [Lemberg, Graz]. Originally a disciple of Brentano, Alexius Meinong developed his own doctrine, a *theory of objects*. An object is anything "intended" by thought and may be either a physical existent or a subsistent such as a mathematical entity; it may be actual, possible, or impossible, for actuality is a matter of indifference. Objects are determined either by self-evidence or by assumption. His theory applies to emotions as well as to cognitions, imaginary emotions being possible, as in the case of a spectator of a drama. Meinong's *On the Status of the Theory of Objects in the System of the Sciences* was published in 1907.

Hastings Rashdall (1858-1924) [London, Oxford, Carlisle]. Hastings Rashdall's early reputation was won by his three volumes on *The Universities of Europe in the Middle Ages* (1895). His *Theory of Good and Evil* (1907) embodied the substance of his lectures at Oxford University. His theory was a form of "ideal utilitarianism," combining the thought that ethics must be teleological with the rejection of the assumption that pleasure is the end. It was his conviction that good actions must tend to produce for all mankind an ideal good which includes pleasure and something more than pleasure. Rashdall emphasized also the necessity for applying ethical theory to practical life. He participated in the development of the philosophy of personal idealism. In addition, he published a volume of university sermons and wrote in defense of Anglican clergymen who did not assent to literal interpretation of every article in the creed. His *Idea of Atonement in Christian Theology* (Bampton Lectures, 1919) gave him a place in theology as well as in history and philosophy. The justification of man Rashdall interpreted as the enkindling in him of the love of God, which expresses itself in regeneration of life.

Henri Bergson (1859-1941) [Paris]. Henri Bergson's *Creative Evolution* was published in 1907. This is the work by which he is most generally known. In his early years he had given close attention to mathematics; later, he made an intensive study of biology. To him, as to many others, the evolutionary process is the basic fact of the universe. But, Bergson stated, evolution does not explain anything; it is primarily the record of the path which the world-movement takes. He asked, as Aristotle had, "But why was there any evolution at all?" This question is a fundamental one. And, like Aristotle, Bergson thought evolution needed some cause; otherwise the universe might have lain asleep through eternity. In Bergson's judgment the movement is due to a vital impulse (*élan vital*) which carries things forward. This impulse is creative and fresh at every moment. The universe is not merely unrolling a scroll on which all things are written from the first. That would be radical mechanism. Nor is it working to a goal set from the beginning. That would be radical finalism. In either case we should have to say that from first to last *all is given,* (*tout est donné*). However, Bergson chooses a third alternative, one in which there is no fixed beginning and no fixed ending: the vital impulse creates its path as it goes. When we look back over the past we gain the illusion that all was predetermined, because the past is inexorable.

Even worse we then project the illusion into the future and believe that the future is fatally fixed. If the future were thus fixed we could predict it as definitely as we can trace the past. But the future is the realm of alternatives. Therefore, Bergson reasoned, the present is the point of selection and determination of what becomes the inexorable past. The creative impulse shoots forward like a rocket from which the dying embers fall back dead. This creative impulse is life; the dead past is matter against the inertia of which life is always struggling. But, according to Bergson, we falsify time when we represent it as a line in space every point of which we can view equally at once. This spatializes time; and time is not spatial. He named life as the ultimate concept. All the universe is alive; if we use theological terms this creative power is God. We gain the feeling of the movement of life by immediate consciousness, the sort of thing by which insects, through instinct, solve the problems of survival without intellectual analysis. Bergson maintained that intellect develops mathematics and is most successful in dealing with matter, with the static. Finally, evolution brings these two capacities together in intuition—a discipline of immediate knowledge that has the power of instinct and intelligence united.

Mary W. Calkins (1863-1930) [Wellesley]. Mary W. Calkins was a staunch defender of objective idealism and a trenchant critic of various forms of realism. She was very sympathetic with Royce and combined absolutism with personalism. Her study of Gestalt theory suggested psychological support for her doctrine. Miss Calkins wrote on psychology, ethics, and metaphysics. *The Persistent Problems of Philosophy* (1907) is a notable example of her thinking.

Alfred Adler (1870-1937) [Vienna]. Alfred Adler began his work with Freud, but later he withdrew and established his own school supporting individual psychology. He emphasized the *ego* in place of *libido* (desire, or striving), minimizing the importance of sex in psychic causation, and giving special attention to feelings of inferiority and attempts at compensation. Inferiority complexes, Adler found, rest on either physical or psychic deficiencies and lead to exaggerated efforts at correction. He regarded these efforts as expressions of the will to power. Attempts at compensation lead to frustration and to construction of excuses based on "difficulties." The basic areas of frustration are community life, vocation, and love. The solution he offered was that through self-knowledge one is led to redirect one's activities into more wholesome channels. Adler's views are set forth in his *Study of Organic Inferiority and Its Psychical Compensations* (1907).

Borden P. Bowne (1847-1910) [Boston]. Borden P. Bowne was a professor at Boston University, who taught a theistic idealism, to which he gave the name *personalism*. His followers have formed a school with this designation. Bowne's volume entitled *Personalism* was published in 1908. Essentially, his view is that all knowledge must be interpreted from the standpoint of human personality, the term representing a point in a scale from which one must read up or down.

James H. Tufts (1862-1942) [Ann Arbor, Chicago]. James H. Tufts was a noted teacher of ethics whose work was done mostly at the University of Chicago. He was influenced by Kant and Green and was especially interested in the social aspect of ethics. In 1908 Tufts's collaboration with Dewey produced the widely used *Ethics*.

Hans Driesch (1867-1941) [Kreuznach, Naples, Heidelberg, Berlin]. Originally a biologist and a follower of Haeckel, Hans Driesch later became a philosophical interpreter of this science. To him life is autonomous, not a mechanical result. Driesch revived the concept of entelechy to account for the direction of growth of an organism, a feature not explained by physics and chemistry. The entelechy is not a form of energy; it inhibits the expenditure of energy, working to certain ends. It interplays with the body, being affected as well as affecting. Each organism is an individual, and each biography is unique. Driesch supported his view by the experimental study of embryology. He believed in a phylogenetic as well as an individual entelechy. He was also interested in the problem of the mind-body relation. Nature as a whole is partly spatial, partly not. God is the entelechy of the world-structure. One of Driesch's outstanding works is *Science and Philosophy of the Organism* (1908).

Luitzen Egbertus Jan Brouwer (1882-   ) [Amsterdam]. L. E. J. Brouwer is known for his work in mathematics, especially in topology,[3] and for establishing the school of intuitionism. He considers mathematics prior to logic and philosophy. His view calls for the abandonment of certain parts of classical mathematics and the reconstruction of other parts. Of particular interest in respect to logic is Brouwer's rejection of the application of the Law of the Excluded Middle to propositions requiring a quantifier with a variable having infinite range. In 1908 he wrote the *Unreliability of the Principles of Logic.*

Hugo Muensterberg (1863-1916) [Danzig, Freiburg, Harvard]. As a psychologist and philosopher, Hugo Muensterberg was interested in the social applications of psychology and in the problem of value. His position was akin to the idealism of Fichte, and he considered that there are *a priori* principles of reason which give results transcending the results of psychology. *The Eternal Values,* published in 1909, was one of Muensterberg's outstanding works.

Leon Brunschvicg (1869-1944) [Paris]. As a representative of an idealistic philosophy, which was influenced by Spinoza, Kant, and Schelling, Leon Brunschvicg emphasized the creativity of thought in science and culture. To philosophy he attributed the function of reflecting upon knowledge, not of increasing it. In its historical development science produces content, which transforms common sense. Reality is the plastic product of spirit. Brunschvicg's position was expressed in *Contemporary Idealism* (1909).

Vladimir I. Lenin (1870-1924) [Simbirsk, Leningrad]. The chief exponent of dialectical materialism (begun by Marx and Engels) was Vladimir Lenin. He adapted it for use as a party tool, then as a political doctrine, choosing it as the practical means for serving his interests. He regarded idealism as the last stronghold of vested interests, which were supported also by religion; he believed that

---

[3] The doctrine of those properties of figures which are unaffected by change of form not due to joining or tearing, e.g., twisting or turning.

both of these must be eliminated. Lenin's first training was for the law. For many years he was a political refugee from Russia in various countries, devoting his attention to social science and philosophy, and writing notebooks containing critical comments on works of philosophers, especially Hegel. In his *Materialism and Empirio-Criticism* (1909) he opposed what he regarded as misinterpretations of Marx, especially the positivistic approach. He gave special attention to capitalistic imperialism and to the doctrine of the State. Lenin contributed to the concept of the dictatorship of the proletariat, the distinction between communism and socialism, and the idea of the necessity for world revolution.

Paul Natorp (1854-1924) [Düsseldorf, Marburg]. As a Neo-Kantian of the Marburg school Paul Natorp applied his point of view to the interpretation of Plato and to scientific method. In 1910, he wrote *The Logical Basis of the Exact Sciences*. Here, he considered logic and epistemology to be independent of psychology. The Laws of Thought are neither Natural Laws nor teleological ones. They are criteria of truth. Natorp thought that Kant's thing-in-itself is really a limit-concept, an ideal never reached. He spoke of objects as the constants of knowledge. His ethics is Kantian (formal) and Platonic and with social emphasis. Natorp asserted that ethics, pedagogy, and social philosophy are phases of "social pedagogy," or theory of the "formation" of the will. Religion rests on objectless feeling, the undefined character of which is transformed into the feeling of infinity. To Natorp, the core of religion was the idea of humanity, based on a common moral consciousness.

John Dewey (1859-1952) [Burlington, Ann Arbor, Chicago, New York]. John Dewey was a representative of the same tendency as Pragmatism, but he called his philosophy instrumentalism, partly to indicate that thinking is only one of the functions of life, and, like other functions, is an instrument for living, not an end in itself. So, he conceived logic, not as a formal process expressed most typically in mathematical deductive processes, but rather as a methodology, the aim of which is the discovery of new truth. Thinking is solving problems. When there are no problems life settles down to automatic processes or aesthetic contemplation. Dewey agreed that life is movement, as the evolutionists have insisted. It does not continue long in any state. It is a process of continual reconstruction in thoughts and in practical habits. The central problems of one age are not those of another age. Issues come and go; we solve most of our problems by outgrowing them. At a given time, when we face a problem, we undertake to clarify the issue, canvass alternative solutions, deduce anticipated consequences, and check by immediate experience the hypothesis that is most completely verified by life. In his early years, Dewey was subject to the influence of Hegelianism, and certain features of it linger through his thought though he did not class himself as an idealist. He defined "experience" as the general field within which life goes on. The dichotomy into mind and matter is unwarranted. The quest for certainty is an endless quest; because of its endlessness, it is a futile one. The solution of the most pressing human problem, the problem of living together, is a perpetual process. Dewey recognized that adjustment to the environment is constantly attempted, but the adjustment, itself, partly remakes the environment, whose conditions are ever changing. So, the real situation is a fluid one, in which external and internal changes are temporarily being balanced. An early expression of Dewey's view is found in *The Influence of Darwin on Philosophy* (1910), and his views are developed further in *Experience and Nature* (1925) and *The Quest for Certainty* (1929). In the history of thought, Dewey is essentially a humanist, placing metaphysical interpretation in the background. Religion, in Dewey's *A Common Faith,* is interpreted in naturalistic and humanistic terms.

Paul Haeberlin (1878-   ) [Bern, Basel]. Paul Haeberlin wrote on the psychology of philosophizing, defining philosophy as a world-view that will overcome the contradictions in a given culture. Philosophy assumes that there is an absolute truth and engages in the quest for the universal plan for conduct. Norms are not individual; they are objective and constitute the will of God. Piety is devotion to them. He wrote that all truth is psychic in character,

253

and matter is phenomenon. All interaction is psychic; the uncomprehended level is called physiological. Pedagogy is the application of philosophy to growing mankind. Its aim is the fulfillment of one's calling. Haeberlin's *Science and Philosophy* was published during 1910-1912.

William McDougall (1871-1938) [Oxford, Harvard, Duke]. William McDougall made significant contributions to physiological and experimental psychology, and then he became interested in social psychology. He was impressed with the importance of considering the basic motives in social living, which he called instincts. He listed fourteen important ones, from the tendency to escape from danger, through sex interest, to amusement. These are the bases of purposive activity, which pervades life. He stated that the impulses may be classified under two great headings, the self-regarding and the self-denying sentiments. The raw material of instinct can be modified by learning. McDougall defended a dualistic interaction theory of human personality in his *Body and Mind* (1911).

John E. Boodin (1869-1950) [Sweden, Carleton, Los Angeles]. An advocate of a form of idealism, John E. Boodin was sympathetic toward Pragmatism too. He explained knowledge through "functional realism" in which perceptions are functions of nature and of the organism in perspective relation to each other. The cosmos consists of a hierarchy of levels of reality. Finite entities are configurations in a system of mutual relations. Boodin evaluated science as inadequate to state all that occurs; there is a teleology in nature. The whole undergoes a cosmic evolution which expresses a cosmic idealism. God is the totality of all fields. In addition, Boodin developed a theory of non-serial time. His *Truth and Reality* (1911) is a typical work.

Hans Vaihinger (1852-1933) [Nehren, Halle]. Hans Vaihinger is noted as a student and interpreter of Kant's philosophy. He called his own position idealistic positivism, and was of the opinion that we find it necessary in theory and practice to formulate certain fictions as indispensable bases of science, art, and morality. Practical interests dominate, and our basic concern is to control situations. In order to accomplish this, he reasoned, we reconstruct the raw data of successive and coexistent phenomena by means of our categories, but in so doing we distort the Real. Vaihinger labeled the True as that representation which enables us to act successfully. We attain no absolute truth. Things, forces, causes, the self, are useful fictions. Legitimate misrepresentations are allowable practically. A concept does not have to be true in order to work as if it were true. Vaihinger's *The Philosophy of the 'As If'* was published in 1911.

W. Ernest Hocking (1873-1966) [Cleveland, Berkeley, Yale, Harvard]. W. Ernest Hocking maintained an absolute idealism of a very concrete and pragmatic type. *The Meaning of God in Human Experience* (1912), his first outstanding work, is sometimes valued beside the work of William James in the philosophy of religion. Hocking also wrote on comparative religion. Furthermore, he was deeply concerned with the philosophy of the State, and he advocated a combination of the best elements in laissez faire and collectivism, a synthesis recognizing the value of the individual.

Martin Grabmann (1875-1948) [Wintershofen, Vienna, Munich]. An outstanding student of medieval thought, Martin Grabmann was also an adherent of medieval studies and gave special attention to Thomas and to questions regarding the authenticity and chronology of works ascribed to him. In 1912, Grabmann published *Thomas Aquinas, an Introduction to His Personality and Thoughtworld.*

Ralph B. Perry (1876-1957) [Harvard]. One of the collaborators in the neo-realistic movement is Ralph B. Perry, who is, in addition, an ardent disciple of William James. His *Present Philosophical Tendencies* (1912) was a typical expression of his position. In this work he referred to the realistic tendency in opposition to the idealistic metaphysics represented by Royce. Perry claimed that neo-realism placed metaphysics before epistemology, reversing the order of idealism. Knowing was interpreted as a specific type of relation and one of the functions of the organism, as were nutrition and reproduction, specifically the reaction of a nervous system and brain. Perry made a careful analysis of the concept of "independence," the relation used by Royce as crucial in the distinction between idealism and realism. He rejected Berkeley's claim that sense qualities are the contents of Mind and accepted James's suggestion that qualities are mental or physical according to their connections. Perry concluded that relations are external and knowledge is a relation; knowing an object brings it to light but does not construct or reconstruct it.

Max Wertheimer (1880-1943) [Frankfort, Berlin, New York]. Since he was one of the founders of Gestalt psychology, Max Wertheimer rejected the concept of distinct psychic units as suggested by associationism and analytic psychology. Rather, Gestalt psychology insists upon the importance of configuration on all levels of experience. Parts receive their character from the whole in which they stand. Wertheimer's study of apparent movement led him to this view. His *Experimental Studies in Visual Perception of Movements* appeared in *Zeitschrift für Psychologie,* in 1912.

Oswald Külpe (1862-1915) [Candau, Würzburg, Bonn]. Oswald Külpe was a psychologist and philosopher and made recognized contributions to experimental aesthetics. His psychology was dualistic; he believed that the transformation of psychical to physical energy is possible. The soul he believed to be a unitary subject of experience. According to his view, philosophy is concerned with constructing a world-view, studying the presuppositions of science, and developing new special fields. In logic Külpe opposed psychologism. He supported moderate rationalism and the possibility of critical metaphysics. He attributed a genetic and an *a priori* aspect to ethics; the general will is a real moral factor. Külpe's *Die Realizierung* (*Realization*) was published between 1912 and 1922.

Miguel de Unamuno y Jugo (1864-1936) [Bilbao, Salamanca, Paris]. Miguel de Unamuno y Jugo was a linguist and educational administrator. His personality was essentially mystical, as it was expressed in his poetry, essays, and novels. His writing denotes passionate meditation. He emphasized the importance and immortality of the individual and placed faith above reason. Unamuno opposed corruption in government and, as a result, was exiled from Spain. Although he was granted amnesty, he chose to live in France until political changes in Spain favored his return in 1930. His greatest work was *The Tragic Sense of Life* (1913).

John B. Watson (1878-1958) [Chicago, Baltimore, New York]. The founder of Amerian "behaviorism" was John B. Watson. This field began with the study of animal psychology and was extended to include the study of man. The difficulty of establishing, with scientific objectivity and precision, the inner experiences of subjects observed led to the abandonment of the attempt to do so and to the exclusion of reference to these experiences. He believed that those aspects of life which cannot be directly observed should be interpreted as implicit motor behavior. Watson's *Behavior* was published in 1914.

Edward Spranger (1882-   ) [Leipzig, Berlin]. Edward Spranger's emphasis upon descriptive as opposed to explanatory psychology reflects influences of Dilthey and of Neo-Kantianism. Spranger is interested in the philosophic basis of the social sciences and in the understanding of history. Society is constituted by objective spirit. All particular values are relative, but hovering over life are norms which culminate in the demand that each man live up to the highest that is possible for him. He classified men into six general types. Spranger was interested also in the application of his psychology and philosophy to education. His *Lebensformen* (*Forms of Life*) was published in 1914.

Douglas Clyde Macintosh (1877-1948) [Breadalbane, Toronto, New Haven]. Calling his own philosophy *critical epistemological monism,* Douglas C. Macintosh aimed at a position somewhere between absolute dualism and absolute idealism; in his judgment, the former is committed to agnosticism. He believed that extreme monism is unable to allow the occurrence of error. The object of knowledge and the real object are numerically one, though not necessarily identical in all their qualities—some qualities are due to the activity of consciousness. Primary qualities are revealed; secondary qualities are created in conscious experience. His *Problem of Knowledge* was published in 1915. In the philosophy of religion Macintosh sought to find in experience those aspects of life which constitute the roots of religious beliefs.

Sigmund Freud (1856-1939) [Vienna, Paris, London]. When a young student of medicine in Vienna, Sigmund Freud became interested in neuroses and their treatment. Later he studied at Paris and Nancy and developed his own method, which in its early stages, made use of hypnotism for recalling repressed ideas from the unconscious level. In later stages, he used free association of ideas and interpretation of dreams. The most fundamental conceptions in Freud's doctrine of human behavior and personality are: the unconscious, conflict and repression, the influence of the infantile period, and the importance of sex. Freud's *Introductory Lectures on Psycho-analysis* (1916) summarizes his theory.

Max Scheler (1874-1928) [Munich, Jena, Cologne]. At first a follower of Kant and Eucken, Max Scheler eventually became a member of Husserl's school of phenomenologists. His primary interest was in ethics and religion. Scheler believed in the objective existence of values and a hierarchy reaching from the pleasant, through the noble, the true, beautiful and good, to the holy. In philosophy of religion he maintained theism and the necessary connection of ethics and religion. He defined the psychic as anything appearing in immediate relation to a self; the physical is what is expressed in space and time. He was also interested in Catholicism, sociology, and humanism. Scheler's *Formalism in Ethics and the Material Ethics of Value* (1916) is an outstanding example of his writing.

Giovanni Gentile (1875-1944) [Castelvetrano, Palermo, Pisa, Rome]. As Senator and Minister of Public Education during the period 1922-1924, Giovanni Gentile reformed the public school system of Italy. A follower of Hegelian philosophy as interpreted in his *Theory of Mind as Pure Act* (1916), Gentile emphasized the creativity of mind and viewed the Real as cosmic mind. Experience, especially self-consciousness, is a plurality in unity, both knower and known. This is the key to the interpretation of reality. Mind begets its own objects. From the subjective point of view it is fundamentally artistic creativity. In objective expression it becomes religious. Gentile's philosophy has been called *actualism*. He formulated a philosophy (theoretical justification) for fascism and the conception of the ethical state to which the individual is entirely subordinate.

Carl Gustav Jung (1875-1961) [Zürich]. C. G. Jung is a pioneer in the field of psycho-analysis. Originally associated with Freud, he drew away from him and founded the analytic school. He regards neuroses as resting on an immediate, exciting cause as much as upon a situation in the past. Jung has generalized the conception of libido, after the analogy of the term energy, regarding it as assuming various expressions and thus capable of sublimation. He has interpreted dreams on a basis of present conflict, not necessarily sexual, and he has classified persons as introverts, extroverts, or ambiverts. Jung believes that the unconscious level of life is very important and is both individual and racial, the latter being prominent in inherited characteristics. In 1916, Jung wrote *The Psychology of the Unconscious*.

A. Seth Pringle-Pattison (1865-1931) [Edinburgh, Cardiff, St. Andrews]. Although, influenced by Hegelianism, A. Seth Pringle-Pattison criticized it because it seemed too formal in structure to do justice to concrete personality. Each self is unique, relatively independent of every other person and even of God. Later, he expressed closer agreement with the idea of the Absolute, though still maintaining the uniqueness of each individual self. From this comes moral responsibility for actions. In his *Idea of God in the Light of Recent Philosophy* (1917), Gifford Lectures at Edinburgh, Pringle-Pattison's thought developed to a systematic and rounded form. Here, he stated that man and Nature are organic to each other, but it is in man that Nature comes to consciousness of her self and to enjoyment of her being. This unity makes knowledge possible. God also is organic to man and Nature and immanent in them. But, according to Pringle-Pattison, the development of the individual is a contribution to the enrichment of the Whole.

Rudolph Otto (1869-1937) [Peine, Göttingen, Marburg]. Rudolph Otto was a professor of the history and philosophy of religion. He traveled widely in Russia, India, and Africa. He made a special study of Indian Mysticism and translated some of its texts into German. Otto's best-known book is *The Idea of the Holy* (published in German in 1917), which was recognized around the world; it was translated into many languages and reprinted in numerous editions. He maintained religious experience to be of a unique kind, distinct from all other experience. Otto was influenced by Schleiermacher's theory of the feeling of dependence as the core of religious feeling. He asserted that religion has roots in feeling and reason and has its own *a priori* categories. The basic category is the "holy," constituted by various elements—moral, rational and non-rational. He identified this non-rational element as the root of both the moral and the rational, which have dominated discussion of religion. Furthermore, Otto wrote works on Luther, on the life of Jesus, and on Mysticism. He participated in politics between 1913 and 1921 as a member of the National Liberal Party in Prussia.

Joseph Geyser (1869-1948) [Erkelenz, Minster, Freiburg]. Joseph Geyser is an outstanding representative of Neo-Thomism. He has been especially interested in epistemology and psychology and has opposed Kantian doctrine in favor of Aristotelianism. Also he has agreed with Husserl's anti-psychologism.[4] He has been an energetic critic of materialism in psychology. In 1917 Geyser wrote a work entitled *Aristotle's Theory of Knowledge.*

William Stern (1871-1938) [Berlin, Breslau]. William Stern was a student of individual psychology, the psychology of childhood and youth, and applied psychology—especially in relation to testimony. He introduced the conception of the *intelligence quotient* as the ratio of mental age to chronological age. He based his personalistic philosophy on the concept of individual differences. He regarded

---

[4] Opposition to approaching problems of logic and epistemology by way of psychology.

each individual as a psychophysical, teleological unit, displaying unity in variety, and combining existence and value. Stern's *Psychology and Personalism* was published in 1917.

Moritz Schlick (1882-1936) [Rostock, Vienna, Berkeley]. Founder of the Vienna Circle (a school of philosophers supporting Logical Positivism) of Scientific Empiricism, Moritz Schlick was influenced by Wittgenstein and Carnap. Schlick regarded the logical clarification of meanings as the first task of philosophy and as necessary to end the conflict of systems. He applied his view to logic, methodology, and ethics. Schlick revised the statement of the meaning of truth, distinguished immediate experience from relational knowledge, and disclosed the definitions implicit in postulate systems. He rejected Kantian *a priorism,* and he interpreted the mind-body problem in terms of a double-language theory. Schlick's *General Theory of Knowledge* appeared in 1918.

Ramon Turro y Darder (1854-1926) [Malgrat, Madrid, Barcelona]. In addition to having military experience, Ramon Turro y Darder was a biologist and a philosopher. He attained distinction in veterinary science, biology, physiology, and psychology. He made a careful study of the circulation of the blood, modifying the mechanistic interpretation of the process. He was in the enviable position of being respected even by those who did not accept his views. He stimulated numerous followers to become active scientists by encouraging them in scientific projects; he also collaborated with the publishers of foreign scientific journals. He studied endocrinology and bacteriological immunity. In philosophy he was a Positivist, but sympathetic with Aristotle's realism; he opposed subjectivistic and metaphysical psychology, and he limited scientific method to determining antecedents of phenomena, not ultimate essences. Turro y Darder's views on these topics marked him as an agnostic. He supported the idea that physiological sequences and psychic sequences are conjoined but not connected. His biology was anti-vitalistic. In his *Filosophia Critica* (*Critical Philosophy,* 1919), he contrasted subjective with objective conceptions of the universe and favored the objective. Science rests on philosophical

261

presuppositions, but philosophy is chaotic in its inner contradictions and countless systems. To philosophy he assigned the task of developing unity on the basis of the primordial concepts of philosophical inquiry. Turro y Darder was primarily interested in methodology, but he also considered the relation of art to science.

Karl Jaspers (1883-   ) [Oldenburg, Heidelberg]. Psychopathology is Karl Jaspers' method of approach to the problems of philosophy. He has classified mental cases into two groups: the first has relations that are understood, and the second has relations that are not yet understood. In a manner similar to Dilthey's, Jaspers has attempted to construct a psychological system of worldviews. He believes that three methods of philosophizing have occurred in the history of thought: (1) world orientation, showing the limitations of science; (2) elucidation of existence, based on penetration into the deepest experiences of man; and (3) metaphysics, seeking for the one ultimate being basic to all the plurality of systems. He advocates giving psychology and history important places in philosophy. Jaspers' *Psychology of World-views* was published in 1919.

Samuel Alexander (1859-1938) [Sydney, Oxford, Manchester]. In his *Space, Time, and Deity* (1920), Samuel Alexander stated the philosophy of evolution: space and time are inseparable. This is the basic presupposition of all reality, the matrix within which evolution occurs. But, he wrote that Aristotle and Bergson were right in insisting that there is another presupposition necessary to explain the movement of evolution. This he called a *nisus,* an urge to move to a more complex form of reality. This new form is superior to the previous one and in comparison with the former is more divine.

These three fundamental concepts—space, time, nisus—give the basis for the course of the universe throughout all eternity. Time and the nisus are so closely related that often Alexander writes of time itself as creative. The new qualities that emerge at every decisive forward step are unpredictable on the basis of the past. Reality is creative and its new forms unique. Only empirical observation of them can tell what they are. He maintained that each has to be "enjoyed" directly in order to be known. Thus the process is called *emergent evolution*. He described the steps, so far, as matter, life, and mind, and placed deity always ahead. The nature of deity is always at least what all preceding things have been, but ever moving on to something which the other forms could not grasp. Alexander believed that it will always be so. God is forever in the making and will always be more than is describable or comprehensible.

The basic values of life—truth, goodness, and beauty—are likewise always in the making. Alexander considered that up to this point Pragmatism has been right, but he called his doctrine realism, to put emphasis upon the objective side of knowledge.

Furthermore, he wrote that finite beings are elements in the process and gain their eternal significance through the role they play (the place they occupy) in the history of the universe.

Max Weber (1864-1921) [Berlin, Heidelberg, Munich]. Max Weber was a jurist, became a student of economics, and attempted to make his economic views socially effective. He undertook extremely critical estimates of current economic theories and tried to reveal the religious roots of the rationale of modern culture—in particular, the influence of Protestant ethical teaching on the "capitalistic spirit." He founded the *Archiv für Sozialwissenschaft* (*Journal of Social Science*) and undertook a study of economics and society. It was an investigation of the behavior of a man in relation to his fellow men. A theory of "chance" played a large part in Weber's thinking, i.e., the chance of realizing expectations. To this theory he added the concept of "ideal type," by which he judged individual complexes. He considered that empirical science is not concerned with how men ought to act, but with how they can and will. A participant in practical affairs, he was concerned with the Treaty of Versailles and the German Republic and its constitution. Weber published *Collected Essays on the Sociology of Religion* in 1920.

C. Lloyd Morgan (1852-1936) [London, South Africa, Bristol]. Although his earliest studies emphasized mining and works-management, C. Lloyd Morgan's later studies included biology under Huxley. After lecturing five years in South Africa, he became professor of zoölogy and geology at Bristol, and later Vice-Chancellor of the University. A man widely read in literature and history as well as in natural science, Morgan emphasized psychology before concentrating upon purely philosophical interpretation. He had a strong influence upon behavioristic psychology. His scientific knowledge made him restrained in his generalizations. Only in 1922-1923 did he formulate a comprehensive synthesis of his ideas in *Emergent Evolution.* His theory of knowledge stemmed from Berkeley and Hume, but Morgan regarded mind as more than a mere observer of facts; it is a co-operator in the shaping of the objective world. The non-psychic thing is a skeleton, unknowable yet believed to exist, which cognition clothes with flesh and blood. He supported his theory by continuous appeal to empirical facts. Emergent evolution, the title of Morgan's treatise, refers to crucial points in evolution at which new, unpredictable qualities and connections arise, caused by a power operating in the universe.

Lucien Lévy-Bruhl (1857-1939) [Paris]. Lucien Lévy-Bruhl approached morality and religion by way of sociology and comparative anthropology. He had previously made a notable contribution to the study of primitive religion, emphasizing the pre-logical, mythical character of primitive thought. He subscribed to the idea that positivistic study shows morality to be the condition of social solidarity. Lévy-Bruhl rejected *a priori* norms and followed a historical method of investigation. Also, he performed significant work on the history of French philosophy. *Primitive Mentality* by Lévy-Bruhl was published in 1922.

Joseph A. Leighton (1870–1954) [Orangeville, Ont.; Geneva, N. Y.; Columbus, O.]. Philosophy of personality is Joseph A. Leighton's main interest. Personality is for him the highest expression of reality and the criterion of value. This special interest has led him into the study of ethics, social philosophy—including the philosophy of history—education, metaphysics, and religion. Although not formally allied with it, Leighton has been sympathetic with the personalist school. At times he has called his philosophy "critical realism," but not in the same sense in which Santayana and his associates used the term. Leighton's early training was under the absolute idealists, and his position is as much objective idealism as it is realism. His most important work is *Man and the Cosmos,* which was published in 1922.

Alejandro Korn (1860-1936) [San Vicente, La Plata, Buenos Aires]. Anatomist, psychiatrist, philosopher, and editor of *Valoraciones (Evaluations),* Alejandro Korn was Argentina's outstanding philosopher. Influenced by Nietzsche and Bergson, he was an opponent of dogmatic Positivism, believing that mechanistic science is hostile to ethics, which is based on freedom. Korn was concerned primarily with freedom and worked for the union of economic and ethical liberty. According to his view, the free soul operates on the basis of intuition, the ground of all knowledge. The experience of freedom leads to the act of evaluation, which comes from the struggle for liberty. He believed personal faith to be the ground of both knowledge and action. Korn's position, which is essentially personalistic and leans toward voluntaristic absolutism, is expressed in the essay *Creative Liberty* (1922).

Ludwig Wittgenstein (1889-1951) [Cambridge]. Ludwig Wittgenstein is noted as the author of *Tractatus Logico-philosophicus* (1922). In this work, he sets forth the conditions which symbolism must satisfy. The essential feature of symbolism is sameness of structure in a statement and in the state of affairs it represents. The sameness is not itself asserted by a statement; it is directly shown. A considerable portion of philosophy represents an attempt to state what can only be shown, and, therefore, it results in meaningless efforts to say the "unsayable." Wittgenstein insists upon the tautological character of logical and mathematical truths, i.e., they are functions whose "truth-value" is always "truth." He has rejected "metaphysics," as he called what lies beyond experience and observation. His thinking carries a great deal of weight with Logical Positivists, though he later modified his own views. Wittgenstein was also interested in the theory of an ideal language, which would be complete, formal, and allow for the resolution of all philosophical problems.

Nicholai Berdyaev (1874-1948) [Kiev, Moscow, Berlin, Paris]. A noted philosophical theologian, Nicholai Berdyaev was exiled and threatened with expulsion from the Greek Orthodox church. Expelled from the Soviet Union by the Communists, he went to Berlin and then to Paris where he established the Academy of the Philosophy of Religion. He was influenced by the ideas of German Mysticism and idealism, and he criticized both Scholasticism and communism. As a Christian personalist, Berdyaev adhered to the finiteness of God. In addition, he considered the philosophy of history worthy of attention. Berdyaev's *The Meaning of History* (1923) is a typical work.

José Ortega y Gasset (1883-1955) [Madrid, Marburg, Buenos Aires]. José Ortega y Gasset is a refined humanist, trained in the Neo-Kantian school. His thought is less mystical than Unamuno's; his work is psychological and critical. But Ortega y Gasset insists that life is prior to thought, and he is not a strict rationalist. A man is constituted both by his inner self and his circumstances. Life and reason are the two poles of a problematic situation; they have to be made to function together. Life is always in the making, a realization of purposes and values. The future is the core in the correlation of all time. This process exists on a large scale in history, from which Ortega y Gasset draws philosophic implications; he also extracts inferences from politics, and in addition from recent scientific developments, e.g., relativity. His *The Theme of Our Time* was published in 1923.

Paul Elmer More (1864-1937) [St. Louis, New York, Princeton]. A teacher, editor, literary critic, lecturer, and essayist, Paul Elmer More's thinking consisted of both Platonic philosophy and Christian doctrine and emphasized the dualism of bodily and spiritual interests. More's final position was a "humanistic" ethical theism, based upon man's sense of goodness and purpose and formulated in Anglo-Catholicism. His interests ranged over the Orient and Occident, through ancient and modern thought, and included a special concern with Sanskrit. More set forth and explained his philosophy in a series of volumes, *The Greek Tradition,* begun in 1923 and finished in 1931.

William Pepperell Montague (1873-1953) [Chelsea, Berkeley, Columbia]. One of the founders of New Realism is William P. Montague. He has also called his theory animistic materialism. He maintains that consciousness is a form of energy and that knowledge is the self-transcending implication of brain states. Consciousness is a relation between entities which exist independent of knowledge. Montague described sensation as a state of potential energy. Secondary qualities, as well as primary qualities, are objective. He developed a monism, but regarded it as realistic, not idealistic, and he acknowledged the difficulty of explaining error. He believed that heredity and consciousness could be explained mechanistically. Faith he interpreted in terms of probability. Montague's *Ways of Knowing* was published in 1925.

Manuel Nuñez Regüeiro (1880-   ) [Montevideo, Santa Fé]. A man with a wide range of activities, including those of a diplomat, journalist, novelist, poet, essayist, and biographer, Manuel Nuñez Regüeiro is interested in Kant's questions concerning knowledge, moral obligation, and final hope. Science does not answer these questions; it lacks the conception of purpose. He believes that at the bottom of everything is the problem of value, which raises man above matter and gives meaning to life. The possibility of realizing the ideal life comes only through Christian truth. *The Fundamentals of Philosophy* by Regüeiro was published in 1925.

Charlie Dunbar Broad (1887-   ) [London, Cambridge]. Charlie Dunbar Broad is a realist, who bases his notion of method, fundamental concepts, and propositions on the sciences; he has sought a justification of physical science from the realist's point of view. In order to gain a total view of experience, he has added aesthetics, religion, ethics, and politics to science. He has worked out a way of applying Whitehead's method of extensive abstraction to physics; also, he has studied the relation of measurement to relativity. Broad is an emergent materialist, deriving everything from matter or energy alone. Primary and secondary qualities, classes, and laws are emergents. He describes the *psyche* or soul element as a material product which survives after death for a time, with the possibility of combining with a new material body. To him *sensa* are temporary existents, neither physical nor mental. Broad's *Mind and its Place in Nature* was published in 1925.

Kurt Koffka (1886-1941) [Frankfort, Northampton]. Along with Köhler and Wertheimer, Kurt Koffka was a founder of Gestalt psychology. He emphasized the factor of insight as important in learning and labeled the trial and error theory of Thorndike as too mechanical. Learning always involves an element of novelty. He did important work on imagery and thought. In 1925 Koffka's *Growth of Mind* was published.

Frederick James Eugene Woodbridge (1867-1940) [Windsor, New York]. F. J. E. Woodbridge was one of the founders of the *Journal of Philosophy* and was also a member of the realist school. He asserted the concept of structure over that of substance and regarded consciousness not as an end-term in a relation but as a special relation of meaning among objects. Woodbridge was strongly opposed to subjective idealism. Knowledge of a thing does not transform it. Mind is not external to reality in knowing it, but is a result of the expanding process of the real. By being in consciousness, real things represent each other. Woodbridge expounded his doctrine in *The Realm of Mind,* which was published in 1926.

Nicolai Hartmann (1882-1950) [Riga, Marburg, Berlin]. Nicolai Hartmann began his philosophic career as a member of the Marburg School, but he gradually moved toward a realistic position which opposed Neo-Kantianism. To the end he regarded a theory of knowledge as impossible without assuming a metaphysic. Hartmann accepted the thing-in-itself concept and held, too, that there is an irrational content underlying logic. However, he was sympathetic with phenomenology and sought a presuppositionless description of phenomena. He stressed humanism over supernaturalism. Hartmann's *Ethics,* written in 1926, is an important work.

Martin Heidegger (1889-   ) [Masskirch, Freiburg, Marburg]. Trained under Husserl, Martin Heidegger has carried his teacher's phenomenology still further. Although influenced by eclectic Neo-Scholasticism, Heidegger undertook an approach to philosophy which differed from that of the Greek tradition. He felt it necessary to destroy existing philosophies. He has interpreted anew the *a priori*, has sought independence from the special sciences, and has tried to analyze the conceptual meanings of individual phenomena without reference to the problems of knowledge and reality. The result, which he embraces, is an idealistic philosophy of man as a creative workman. Heidegger was influenced by Kierkegaard's views and came to think of the heart of consciousness as "concern," the core of "dread," the basic attitude toward the world. He considered that this ultimate fact is concealed by the routine of daily life. To philosophy he has delegated the task of calling attention to it. It was his idea that the final meaning of Being and Time involves a sense of the significance of choice, conscience, and death. Heidegger's *Being and Time* (*Sein und Zeit,* 1927), an explicit expression of his view, has attained considerable prestige in Germany.

Joaquin Xirau (1895-   ) [Figueras, Barcelona, Mexico]. Joaquin Xirau has been a student of law, literature, and philosophy and has lectured at many universities, including Paris, Cambridge, and Oxford. He has also studied under Ortega y Gasset and has been influenced by the views of Husserl and Heidegger. But Xirau thinks of philosophy in terms of ethics and the perfection of human personality, rather than in terms of the analysis of abstract concepts. In 1927 he wrote *The Sense of Truth.*

Alfred North Whitehead (1861-1947) [Cambridge, London, Harvard]. An evolutionist of a unique type, Alfred North Whitehead asserted, "the safest general characterization of the European philosophical tradition is that it consists of a series of footnotes to Plato." Beginning as a mathematician, Whitehead achieved outstanding reputation for his generalization of algebra, for his logic of mathematics, and for his work with Bertrand Russell in *Principia*

Mathematica. After studies in *The Principles of Natural Knowledge, The Concept of Nature,* and *The Principles of Relativity,* he went on to cosmology and, in *Process and Reality* (1929), developed a doctrine which has been classed as Aristotelian, as panpsychist, and as a form of idealism. He recast the vocabulary of philosophy in order to escape many of the associated connotations of the past, and often he used terms in their more literal sense. In his theory of knowledge, he was able to use rationalistic analysis in the greatest detail, yet he emphasized the concept of feeling as a term characterizing in a very general way the sensitivity that all factors of the universe have for each other. Reality is not to be interpreted in atomistic terms. It consists of *events,* which have their spatial and temporal aspects and, in addition, are the expressions of the "ingression" of eternal objects (universals) into individual instances, as illustrated by every assertion of identification in the form: "this is a tree." God is the system of eternal objects thus expressing itself in the actual universe, a process, not static in entity. Whitehead considered the units of description, such as surfaces, lines, and points, as limiting goals of a process of "extensive abstraction."[5] To reason he ascribed the function of helping men to live, to live well, to live better. In the course of time men undertake many adventures of ideas, adhering to those that bring most meaning to life.

Clarence Irving Lewis (1883-1964) [Stoneham, Berkeley, Cambridge]. Clarence I. Lewis was noted for his work in logic, epistemology, and axiology. In logic he originated the theory of strict implication, recognizing that *Principia Mathematica,* by Whitehead and Russell, was based on material implication. Also, he argued for the enlargement of logic into new forms. In epistemology he entertained a conceptualistic Pragmatism, maintaining that there is a choice of conceptual systems for application to the explanation of particular experiences. Lewis favored naturalism in ontology,

---

[5] A method of approximation from common experiences to ever more exact definitions.

rather than Logical Positivism. He regarded idealism and realism as equally unprovable. In his theory of value he adhered to a realistic allocation beyond the apprehending mind. Lewis' *Mind and the World-Order* (1929) is an exposition of his theory of knowledge.

Wolfgang Köhler (1887-   ) [Reval, Frankfort, Teneriffe, Berlin, Swarthmore]. Formerly a pupil of Stumpf, Wolfgang Köhler was one of the founders of Gestalt psychology. He is especially noted for his study of the mentality of apes. Köhler expounded his views in *Gestalt Psychology,* which was published in 1929.

Johan Huizinga (1872-1945) [Leyden]. Professor of general history and political geography, and a member of the Committee on Intellectual Co-operation of the League of Nations, Johan Huizinga was noted for his philosophy of culture. He described this as a situation in which there is a harmonious balance of material and immaterial interests, together with an ideal which unifies the efforts of the members of society. Huizinga's *Ways of Culture* was published in 1930.

Arthur O. Lovejoy (1873-1962) [Berlin, Baltimore]. Arthur O. Lovejoy is a member of the Critical Realist group and is a sharp critic of New Realism, especially in so far as the impossibility of error and illusion in that theory is concerned. Lovejoy has defended dualism and has insisted upon the necessary distinction between appearance and reality. He has written on Pragmatism, against behaviorism, on primitivism, and on Romanticism, and he has uncovered the doctrines of the Cambridge Platonists which anticipated those of Kant. He was the first editor of the *Journal of the History of Ideas.* Lovejoy's *Revolt Against Dualism* (1930) is an outstanding work.

Edgar S. Brightman (1884-1953) [Middletown, Boston]. A leader of the personalist movement, Edgar S. Brightman was well-known especially for his writings on the philosophy of religion. The evidence for the existence of God lies in the rationality of the universe, the occurrence of novelty, the existence of personality and values, and the character of religious experience. The most distinc-

271

tive feature of Brightman's view is the theory of the limitation of the activity of God by a factor called The Given. This factor is not a product of divine creativity, but is one which God finds present in his own reality and which He constantly struggles against. The existence of The Given accounts for the problem of evil and reveals the meaning of the Christian conception of a suffering God. Although Brightman's interpretation of the nature of God is unorthodox, it seemed to him to be required by the facts of evolution, of consciousness, of the dialectic of reality, and of religious experience. A clear presentation of Brightman's position is found in his *The Problem of God* (1930).

John Henry Muirhead (1855-1940) [Glasgow, Oxford, Birmingham]. John Henry Muirhead's education was in the Hegelian tradition since he studied under E. Caird and Green, but Muirhead modified Hegelianism to suit the changing times. He was concerned with the application of idealism to the problems of ordinary life. Morality and social and political life were, therefore, of prime interest to him. His ethical doctrine was one of eudaemonism (theory of well-being), which, with its strong emphasis on duty, restrained excessive hedonism and rationalism. Duty must not be regarded as abstract, but as connected with human interests. Morality is free obedience to law imposed by man on the animal impulses of his nature. Furthermore, Muirhead incorporated what seemed to him valid evolutionary doctrines. In spite of change there is a universal norm, a single evaluating principle from which moral judgments derive their normative intention. He wrote that moral progress is evaluated in the light of this criterion. *Platonic Tradition in Anglo-Saxon Philosophy* (1931) represents the culmination of Muirhead's thinking.

Morris R. Cohen (1880-1947) [Minsk, New York]. Morris R. Cohen was a student of social, political, and legal philosophy. He advocated a concrete use of reason in thinking, and he used the principle of polarity in his interpretations. Cohen criticized the neo-realistic view of independence and favored a naturalistic ontology. *Reason and Nature* (1931) is one of his best-known works.

Frank P. Ramsey (1903-1930) [Cambridge]. Working with Wittgenstein's views as a basis, Frank P. Ramsey made important modifications in the doctrine of *Principia Mathematica*. He simplified the theory of types, improved the definition of identity, and omitted the axiom of reducibility.[6] He presented pertinent discussions of universals and particulars, probability, induction, and causation. Ramsey's *Foundations of Mathematics* (1931) is a collection of his philosophical essays.

Kurt Gödel (1906-   ) [Austria, Princeton]. Mathematician and logician, Kurt Gödel is best known for his Incompleteness Theorem—in certain complex logical systems there are undecidable propositions such that neither they nor their negations are provable, though one or the other proposition in the contradictory pair must, according to the principle of excluded middle, be true. That is to say, applying a method which arithmetizes syntax and using a line of reasoning similar to the Epimenides paradox, Gödel proved that there can be no logical system which is adequate to develop all truths—even all those of elementary mathematics. Gödel's *On Formally Undecidable Propositions* (1931) is a typical statement.

Walter T. Stace (1886-   ) [London, Ceylon, Princeton]. A doctrine of phenomenalism, akin to the philosophies of Poincaré and Vaihinger, is upheld by Walter T. Stace. He maintains that all beliefs are built up out of one's own immediate experience or one's inferences from such experience. Sense data are private, but not, therefore, mental. Physical objects, indeed all the external world, are mental constructions, which can not be finally proved or disproved. The concept of "thing" is useful for its predicative value and helps us in regulating action. Stace's *Theory of Knowledge and Existence* was published in 1932. In addition to this, he has written on the history of philosophy, aesthetics, and ethics.

Alfred Tarski (1901-   ) [Poland, Harvard, Berkeley]. Alfred

---

[6] The assumption that there is a type of function which can take a given object as argument, which is formally equivalent to a function of a type in question.

Tarski has been concerned chiefly with the logic of mathematics, dealing especially with such fundamental concepts as "truth," "truth-functions," "meta-mathematics," and "meta-language." He contributed to the founding of formal semantics and conceived truth as a syntactical property. Tarski's *Wahrheitsbegriff in den formalisierten Sprachen* (*The Truth-concept in Formalized Languages*) appeared in 1933.

Rudolf Carnap (1891-   ) [Vienna, Prague, Chicago]. One of the leaders of the Vienna Circle, Rudolf Carnap also has developed Logical Positivism (Scientific Empiricism), which rejects all metaphysics. In addition, he has advanced the unity of science by his efforts in favor of a common language for all sciences. In this connection, he has contributed to semantics, to logical syntax, and to the application of formal logic to mathematics. Following Tarski, Carnap has pointed out the necessity for a hierarchy of languages. He has also supported physicalism, a revised form of behaviorism, although he insists that objects of experience are only quasi-objects. *The Logical Syntax of Language* (1934) is typical of Carnap's work. In his theory of knowledge he does not assume atomic facts. To Carnap, the test of meaninglessness is the impossibility of theoretical, as well as practical, verification.

George H. Mead (1863-1931) [Chicago]. As a kind of Pragmatist and one who has been called a "social behaviorist," George H. Mead's basic view was contained in the *Philosophy of the Act* (at first, a theory and, in 1938, the title of a work). In this work he states that all reality is an active process. The past is constantly growing, and the present existence is always precarious. He insisted that action transcends statements even when these are objective. Mead followed Wundt in his theory of the social character of thought, and he conceived mind in terms of social acts. The self develops by way of social language. Hence symbolic processes are very important. He regarded Royce's philosophy as an escape from, rather than interpretation of, life. Mead's *Mind, Self, and Society* was published in 1934.

Willard Van Arman Quine (1908-   ) [Akron, Oberlin, Harvard]. At the present time, Willard V. Quine is one of the leading workers in the field of symbolic logic and has contributed numerous articles to philosophical journals, besides writing books on logic on both the elementary and advanced levels. *A System of Logistic* (1934) expresses his approach to the subject. In his articles, Quine has discussed the positions of contemporary logicians; he has developed methods of generating a part of arithmetic without the use of intuitive logic and of dealing with classes without presupposing a theory of types. Moreover, Quine has reinterpreted fundamental concepts (such as truth and negative degree) and processes (such as substitution and derivability).

William Temple (1881-1944) [Manchester, York]. As an archbishop, William Temple defended an idealistic theism. He regarded teleology as the basic principle of reality. To theism he attributed the belief that the ground of the universe is a good will. Will and act are directed to the future; time is real. Temple supported a theory of levels in reality, leading to Value as supreme and to God as the union of Value and reality. He asserted that life reveals what matter really is, soul reveals life, and spirit reveals soul. Everything exists to express creative will. Temple drew ideas from the doctrines of Bosanquet, Platonism, and Scholasticism, and from the aims of Marxism. His *Nature, Man and God* was published in 1935.

Hans Reichenbach (1891-1953) [Hamburg, Berlin, Stamboul, Los Angeles]. Hans Reichenbach was a leader of the Logical Positivists at Berlin. He gave special attention to the philosophy of science; he dealt, in detail, with space, time, induction, and probability and developed a statistical definition of the latter. He also related probability to a theory of truth. Reichenbach explored the nature of geometry and the nature of relativity, reconciling Kant's views and relativity through a reinterpretation of the *a priori,* the principles which constitute an object. To him, these are not apodictic, but subject to reconstruction as a result of experience. He rejects the aprioristic theory of time and space. Reichenbach's *Theory of Probability* (1935) is a pertinent expression of his point of view.

Twentieth Century: First Half (1900-1949)

Alfred J. Ayer (1910-   ) [Cambridge]. One of the chief popularizers of Logical Positivism (Scientific Empiricism) is Alfred J. Ayer. His basic work is *Language, Truth, and Logic* (1936). In this, he makes a fundamental distinction between factual and value judgments, or description of fact and emotional expression, holding the former to be open to public verification and the latter to be private and unverifiable. Ayer represents the British expression of the Positivist movement, especially strong in Cambridge.

Note: The Positivists agree with Hume on causality and induction, interpret philosophy as logical analysis and clarification of everyday language, insist that mathematical and logical truths are tautological, and reject the traditional type of metaphysics.

Étienne Gilson (1884-   ) [Paris]. Étienne Gilson represents a reconciliation of Thomism and Existentialism. Influenced by Bergson and Lévy-Bruhl, he engaged at first in historical research on the scholastic doctrines which were sources of Descartes' thinking. Then he studied other outstanding figures of the Middle Ages, such as Augustine and Bonaventure; later he stated his own interpretation of philosophy, in general, and of the theory of knowledge, in particular. Gilson has emphasized the importance of revelation in addition to reason. God is Being itself, as the act of existing, the First Cause, giving to creatures the ability to be efficacious causes in turn. Furthermore, Gilson has displayed an interest in social philosophy and human culture. His *Spirit of Mediaeval Philosophy* was written in 1936.

José Vasconcelos Calderon (1882-1959) [Mexico]. José Vasconcelos Calderon has been a leader in the educational, political, and philosophical life of Mexico. His philosophical writings deal with the history of thought—especially in Mexico—esthetics, metaphysics, ethics, and the history of culture in Latin America. Vasconcelos has stressed the views of Bergson and Nietzsche and has emphasized feeling and will over reason in life. On the other hand, he is less sympathetic toward Platonic and mathematical formalism. Art stands high, in his estimation, because of the way in which it unifies varied elements into organic creativity. He stresses the importance of revelation in religion. Vasconcelos' *Estetica* was published in 1936.

James B. Pratt (1875-1944) [Elmira, Williamstown]. James B. Pratt was especially interested in the philosophy and history of religion and in problems which stemmed from this interest. His writings deal with the psychology of religious belief, the religious consciousness, the relation of the material to the spiritual realm, and the place of personality in the natural world. Pratt made an extensive, first-hand study of the religions of India; besides this, he studied Buddhism in the various countries where it predominates. He co-operated in a volume on Critical Realism, criticizing sharply the neo-realistic theory of perception and illusion. Pratt also disagreed with the neo-realistic theory of value on the ground that it made insufficient allowance for subjectivity. Perception is always mediate, involving a reference of a quality to something beyond, though it may be difficult to determine the truth or falsity of this reference. He considered that the self is a substance, whose tool is the body with which it interacts. The continuity of thought is the evidence of the independent existence of the self. In personality he recognized clues to the nature of the universe. The latter is organic rather than mechanical, and, in the sphere of human development, it is something essentially purposive and creative of values. Pratt's *Personal Realism* appeared in 1937.

Jacques Maritain (1882-   ) [Paris, Toronto, New York]. A student of Bergson, Jacques Maritain was later converted to Catholicism. He also studied with Driesch. He opposed Descartes' formula "I think, therefore I am" with the assertion "I know that something exists." Maritain also distinguishes philosophy of nature from natural science and maintains a science of phenomena independent of idealism. Although more a philosopher than a theologian, he is sympathetic toward Mysticism and insists that all particular interests look finally toward the Beatific Vision. Maritain has applied a personalistic view to Thomistic social theories and ethics, favoring democratic reform rather than the organic theory of the State. He believes true humanism is theocentric and supports the spiritualization of the means of temporal action. Problems of practical concern, such as anti-Semitism, have received his active attention. Maritain's discussions of esthetic experience have been penetrating. A typical work is *Degrees of Knowledge* (1937).

Francisco Romero (1891-   ) [La Plata, Buenos Aires]. After receiving a military education, Francisco Romero served in the Argentine army for twenty-one years. At present, he is a professor at the University of Buenos Aires and Director of the Philosophical Library of the Losada Publishing House, and he participates in the publication of several magazines. He is the author of numerous articles and books presenting the problems of knowledge, discussing structuralism in world views—especially in contemporary philosophy—and interpreting the study of personality in values and in history. Romero's *The Philosophy of Personality* was published in 1938.

Karl Barth (1886-   ) [Basel, Safenwil, Bonn]. Karl Barth is a prominent figure in Existentialism, Neo-orthodoxy, and Crisis Theology. According to him, crisis lies in the triumph of faith over reason. Philosophy is opposed to faith. He defines contrition as the surrender of reason. Dialectical theology maintains that God is revealed as transcendent, to the extent that man can not know the divine mind. Moreover, Barth states that man can only trust Him for salvation and for the truth of the Christian revelation. The chaotic state of human affairs shows how helpless man is in dealing with life. Barth's views are summed up in *The Knowledge of God and the Service of God* (1938).

William David Ross (1877-1940) [Urso, Oxford]. Known chiefly as the editor and translator of the works of Aristotle and Theophrastus, W. David Ross has also written articles and books on ethics. In this field, he delivered the Gifford Lectures, at the University of Aberdeen, which were published as *Foundations of Ethics* in 1939.

Brand Blanshard (1892-   ) [Michigan, Swarthmore, Yale]. *The Nature of Thought* (1940) by Brand Blanshard is a detailed analysis of idealism, and it insists that, even on the level of perception, what is given as sensuous is pervaded with elementary thought and judgment. He restates the idealistic position in the light of the realistic criticism in recent theory of knowledge, and he takes account of the contributions made by Pragmatism and behaviorism. But Blanshard acknowledges that his position proves to be in a direct line with that of Royce.

Philip Frank (1884-   ) [Vienna; Prague; Cambridge, Massachusetts]. As a member of the Vienna Circle, Philip Frank's thinking was influenced by Mach. Frank is concerned with the unity of science, especially the concepts useful in both physics and philosophy (causality, mechanism, etc.). Frank's *Between Physics and Philosophy* was published in 1941.

Jean-Paul Sartre (1905-   ) [Paris]. Heidegger's atheistic existentialism has been extended and popularized by Jean-Paul Sartre. He sees man without God as a forlorn creature, without standards of truth or value beyond his own subjectivity. Since there is no ontological pattern for human nature, man is "condemned to be free"; he must develop himself and deliberately commit himself to values freely chosen but not regarded as absolute.

According to Sartre, man cannot escape from his own isolation. The existence of another is revealed, as he says, by the "awareness of someone staring at me." Although man can co-operate with others, there is no communication with any other person's subjectivity. We are all objects to one another, but we need others in order to understand what we ourselves are.

Politically, Sartre is close to Marx, though he rejects materialistic determinism. Society should constantly transcend itself in the direction of greater freedom.

He has made phenomenological investigations into the psychology of the emotions and of the imagination. Emotion, Sartre has stated, is an unreflective type of consciousness. It is a method by which consciousness directs the body in order to change its relation with the world and, in this way, to transform the world. In a sense it is a degradation of consciousness inasmuch as, objectively speaking, the transformation is non-effective. Imagination, like emotion, is a distinct existential level, a total synthetic organization of consciousness.

Sartre's novels, plays, and literary criticism show the application of existentialist principles; *L'Être et le Neant* (*Being and Nothing,* 1943) contains these philosophical formulations.

Horace M. Kallen (1882–   ) [Silesia, Harvard, Wisconsin, N.Y.C.] H. M. Kallen has been a progressive thinker throughout his career. He has been interested strongly in aesthetics, but his attention has ranged widely over the entire human situation. He has been concerned with the social and political realms, even with international relations and the prospect for world peace. Modern educational theory and the critical evaluation of moral practices and of religion and its problems have received his attention. In recent decades the hope of freedom for oppressed people has been of great interest to him. He has followed the current trend and has been concerned with the future trend of thought in American philosophy.

He has found in art the impulse to express the freedom of the human spirit. In *Art and Freedom* (1943), he followed this expression through the course of Western thought; he traced in biography and history, the interrelations of the ideas of beauty, use, and freedom from Plato to modern times through Romanticism and the recent industrial age.

Arthur E. Murphy (1901–1962) [Chicago, Providence, U. Illinois, Cornell, U. Washington, Texas]. A. E. Murphy is an instrumentalist in his basic ideas; he emphasized the point of view of Dewey in his early writings and also the work of Mead, whose Carus lectures he edited. He has also given attention to the philosophy of Whitehead and Moore.

Murphy disagreed with Lovejoy's defense of dualism, holding that there are various kinds of dualism, and that fundamentally the position makes too great a concession to common sense.

In *The Uses of Reason* (1943), he examined the function of reason and of evaluation. He defended the adequacy and efficacy of reason for the process of living, in the determination of truth, moral values, and social behavior. He defended it against those who advocate other means of determining truth, or who disparage its employment; cynics, behaviorists, ultra-conservatives are among those he attacks. Appeal to higher intuition, to infallibility based on claims of superrationality, is to be feared as well as subrational emotionalism. The one corrective for errors in reason is better use of it. It must be used with wide outlook, not subject to arbitrary presuppositions, in the search for truth and security. Thus, it becomes the means of sanity and of the organization of life.

Moral judgments must rest on appeal to facts, and reason must guide this appeal. Social action, also, must rest upon reason, employing as its criteria appeal to facts and their relevance to practical aims, co-operative social spirit, and a liberal attitude, though liberality must take cognizance of tradition and the existing spirit of the people.

Murphy joined with others in opposition to authoritarian attempts to interfere with the sense of equality, the intrinsic value of each individual, and concern for free association and interest in others. The scientific spirit is essentially democratic and calls for freedom from restriction in education, communication, political action, and so on.

Philosophic ideas are of serious character, not mere toys or instruments, and must be applied in significant fashion to the problems of society, in the direction and improvement of daily life.

Ray Lepley (1903–) [Ohio, Peoria (Ill.)] Ray Lepley's first significant contribution was made in *Verifiability of Value* (1944), in which he followed the method of Dewey's Instrumentalism—a method analogous to that in which facts are critically determined—as a means of criticising values. Later he edited a group of essays (*Value,* 1949) in which various writers had considered the nature of Value. This was a significant, though indirect, tribute to Dewey in his ninetieth year and sought to give concrete expression to questions raised by Dewey some years before and the suggestions he had made. *The Language of Value* (1957)—an attempt to clarify the linguistic problems which have a bearing on the theory of value and its practical application—which Lepley edited is held by some to be a model of co-operative activity in philosophy.

Filmer S. C. Northrop (1893–) [U. Wisconsin, Yale]. Filmer S. C. Northrop has given much attention to various aspects of the philosophy of science, including the theory of relativity, probability and causality in physics, and the relation of physical theory to the theory of living organisms. He has followed the development of first principles through the course of history of science and philosophy.

In recent years Northrop has been deeply concerned with the world situation and the entire field of human thought and has attempted to bring together the major philosophic movements of East and West, South and North, Communism and Democracy. This effort is seen especially in *The Meeting of East and West* (1946) and in *Ideological Differences and World Order* (1949). The latter volume of essays by a score of writers (including Northrop) from the fields of jurisprudence, art, politics, anthropology, etc., edited by Northrop. In 1947 he was made Professor in the Yale Law School.

Lewis Mumford (1895–) [Palo Alto, Dartmouth, U. Pennsylvania, N.Y.C.]. L. Mumford is a public-spirited, socially-active writer on the fringe of technical philosophy, with numerous books on the historical development and present status of mankind, and with anxious fears for the future of democratic civilization.

Mumford aired these fears in *Values for Survival* (1946). His basic question was: What shall the modern man do to be saved? He regarded the tendency toward Fascism and its grasp of political power as the chief threat to democracy. So-called "liberalism" of mind had weakened the foundations of democracy. It had falsified true liberalism which was worldwide and humanistic in its outlook and had come to suffer from emotional anesthesia. The future of man is at stake and must be assured by a militant democracy which resumes its responsibility for the sacredness of human life.

This constitutes the challenge to Education, a call for the development of new devotion to the whole of human society. It faces the issue which Plato confronted in his day, but advises that we must face it more successfully than he. The spirit of the humanities must be revived, and even the leaders of the nations defeated in war (as Germany) must see the importance of this new ideal.

Mumford's *Conduct of Life* (1951) is a further challenge to a renewal of proper orientation to life that will transform men by carrying them beyond their ambiguous moral conceptions to a higher fulfillment of the meaning of life, giving it significance in the light of its place in the total cosmos.

Joseph L. Blau (1909–   ) [Columbia]. Joseph Blau has been concerned with Jewish life and thought, including the Christian interpretation of the Cabala in the Renaissance. He has written on the social theories of Jacksonian democracy and on the roots of religious freedom, advocating separation of church and state.

In 1946 he published *American Philosophical Addresses, 1700–1900*, a book declared indispensable for the understanding of American philosophy. It is a record of the cultural development of America and deals with the country's intellectual and social problems. He presents the biographical stories of influential persons living in particular periods, shows the ways in which their thinking grew from and developed within contemporary conditions, and indicates the contributions made by the writers to each period. It covers American democracy, education and social problems, philosophy of science, and religion, and includes some figures commonly neglected.

John D. Wild (1902–   ) [Chicago, Harvard]. John Wild has written on Berkeley and Existentialism, but has been especially interested in Platonic philosophy. In *Plato's Theory of Man* (1948) he presented a "Realistic Philosophy of Culture," calling attention to the historic setting in which Plato lived, a post-war era of disillusionment similar to the present. Plato diagnosed the cultural diseases of his time and attempted to formulate a natural order to guide men in their strife for a healthy state. From a study of Plato's

283

work modern man may derive benefit in understanding human nature and human culture. Such study will clarify the relation of Aristotle to Plato and their fundamental harmony. This will also throw light on the classical and medieval tradition.

Plato was not a supernaturalist. He tried to present a naturalistic interpretation of civilization, and show the way in which the true order of life had become inverted. This is shown in the *Republic, Parmenides, Theatetus,* and *Sophist.*

In *Plato's Modern Enemies and the Theory of Natural Law* (1953) Wild corrects misinterpretations of Plato as an enemy of freedom (a dogmatist, militaristic totalitarian, and reactionary racialist). Misunderstanding of Plato's moral philosophy led to the view that he was opposed to democracy.

His influence was the root of the theory of natural law, according to Wild. He based ethics on the natural tendencies of the human person regarded as a dynamic, developing organism.

Gilbert Ryle (1900–   ) [Oxford]. From his earliest years Gilbert Ryle was interested in philosophical arguments and dilemmas. He advocates analytic method expressed in ordinary language, a position for which he is criticized by Russell.

In 1949 Ryle presented his view—which in the opinion of many is an important one—in *The Concept of Mind.* He offered his theory as a means of escape from assumptions of which he himself had been the victim. His book begins with a statement of the dualism of Descartes, which he regards as erroneous, the error lying in a mistaken subsumption of mind and matter under a single category of existence. He starts off his own theory with acceptance of a "public world" in which are to be found the entities of the realm of common sense and ordinary life. In this world no ghostly apparitions to be called "minds" are discoverable, not even by inference from sense experience. Mind is a set of abilities, liabilities, inclinations to do or undergo certain processes in the ordinary world of every day. We "know" how to do certain acts, and we know that certain facts are true, but we never know minds as substances. He also rejects the theory that there are 'sense data.'

All aspects of experience are matters of behavior, though Ryle does not explicitly ally himself with the behaviorist. From this point of view he interprets volition, emotion, sensation and observation, imagination, and intellect.

Herbert Feigl (1902–   ) [Austria, Vienna, Iowa State, U. Minnesota]. Feigl joined with Sellars in editing *Readings in Philosophical Analysis* (1949). Analysis, in their view, grows out of influences from the Cambridge school, the logical positivists of the Vienna Circle, and the scientific empiricists of Berlin. The points of view of Realism and Pragmatism are most prominently represented. Two-thirds of the readings are taken from American publications; the rest, from English, German, and Austrian.

The content of the work covers the nature of logic and mathematics, language, meaning, and truth. In epistemology the problems of *a priori* knowledge, induction, and probability are treated. Description and explanation in empirical science are interpreted. Metaphysics is touched relatively lightly as to data, reality, and the mind-body problem. In ethics disagreement in judgments and the question of freewill are considered.

The last topics connect with a more recent co-operative work on *Concepts, Theories, and the Mind-Body Problem* (1958), suggesting the connection of philosophical analysis with psychology—an interest which Feigl has also carried into other works.

Max Black (1909–   ) [Baku, U. Illinois, Ithaca]. Black has been a student of mathematics, logic and scientific method throughout his life and has written extensively on these subjects, giving attention as well to logical positivism and language.

In *Language and Philosophy* (1949) he considered the use of language in throwing light upon philosophical problems. He maintained that some widely-held doctrines about language need to be revised. In the course of his discussion he argued that solipsism is meaningless because it is self-contradictory; vagueness is a deviation from precision, as a mathematical variable approaches a limit; and the justification for induction in spite of theoretical difficulties is that it is empirically trustworthy.

Black also discussed the views of Tarski, Russell, Wittgenstein, and others, in addition to theories of emotive meaning. A further expression of his views is to be found in *Problems of Analysis* (1954).

Morton White (1917–   ) [Columbia, Philadelphia, Harvard]. Morton White has been strongly influenced by the philosophy of Dewey. His conception of history is that it is not mere chronology, but that it includes generalized interpretation. In 1949 he wrote *American Social Thought, the Revolt Against Formalism,* in which he discussed the positions of five liberal leaders in social philosophy in the twentieth century. They were concerned with methodology, ethics, and political philosophy. Knowledge and action are guided by reasonable results, not by formal principles in moral and social situations. Because life is a shifting process, traditional ethics and law do not fit it closely. One must recognize the concrete facts of life as well as high ideals. This calls for creative intelligence which should be encouraged by education, and which will of necessity undo some of the past.

In *Toward Reunion in Philosophy* (1956) he discusses the inter-mingling of types of philosophy: the analytic, the positivistic, and the pragmatic have in common their opposition to Absolute Idealism. The central problems are those of existence, the *a priori,* and values. These White presents as: What is (entities and postulates), What must be (*a priori*), and What should be (ethics), and their synthesis.

Twentieth Century: Second Half

All the major aspects of philosophy have been of interest in the latest decade. Problems of knowledge have concerned Goodman, Flew, and Pap. Instrumentalism has been emphasized by Hook and problems of science, by Einstein, Bridgman, von Mises, Toulmin, Nagel, Wiener, and Woodger. Metaphysics has concerned Weiss, Sheldon, and Robinson. Discussions of religion have come from Lamprecht, Ducasse, Tillich, Marcel, Niebuhr, Morris, and Kaufmann. Ethics has been of special interest to Baumgardt, Schneider, and Adler; aesthetics, to Boas and Pepper. A number of significant historical studies have been made by Miller, Mayer, Balz, McKeon, Moore, Radhakrishnan, Toynbee, Wolfson, Luce, Schilpp, and Randall.

Albert Einstein (1879–1955) [Ulm, Berne, Berlin, Princeton]. Although he is commonly known as a Nobel Prize winning scientist, Albert Einstein was also a philosopher. His work involved a view of the physical universe and led to reflections on the final meaning of experience. He was interested in the realm of human relations and indicated his position by advocating complete disarmament, a socialist society, social justice, and limited world government. He supported the Zionist plan for a homeland for Jews.

In 1950 Einstein published a *Generalization of the Gravitational Theory,* which he hoped would bring all physical phenomena under a single concept or law. His position was controversial; it was a basis of much discussion and gave rise to many further problems.

Percy W. Bridgman (1882–1961) [Cambridge (Mass.), Harvard]. Percy Bridgman is a Nobel Prize winner in physics—for research dealing particularly with phenomena under high pressure —and an outstanding philosopher of science.

He has been concerned not only with the empirical results of physics, but with the interpretation of the methods used in research, the nature of physical theory—especially thermodynamics—and basic physical concepts. He formulated the conception of operational definition.

P. W. Bridgman is interested also in the social obligations of science and its relation to intelligent citizenship. Freedom, time, and cosmic concern have a part in the *Reflections of a Physicist,* which were formulated in 1950. In all his thinking he is concerned with *The Way Things Are* (1959).

Sterling P. Lamprecht (1890–   ) [Cleveland, U. Illinois, Amherst]. British philosophy, especially the thought of Locke, has interested Sterling P. Lamprecht. He has also favored the thinking of Dewey and Santayana.

In *Our Religious Traditions* (1950) he reviewed the past from a standpoint influenced by the thought of Woodbridge. He dealt with the "Heritage of Judaism," the "Genius of Catholicism," and the "Adventure of Protestantism," considering their great contributions, respectively, as the idea of the covenant, catholicity, and the right to be different. His aim was to promote mutual understanding, not unity of organization. All must be appraised, he said, in the light of the Greek mind with its emphasis upon moral unity.

In Lamprecht's philosophy of religion, God as a person is a possible concept though, he believes, the arguments offered as proofs of existence have never met the demands of empirical science. Men are too concerned about their religious beliefs and go too far in committing themselves on emotional bases to fixed doctrines. Religion is significant, but should be taken with a light touch and a sense of humor. It should enrich life, not bring it stagnation. His own religion is naturalistic.

George Boas (1891–   ) [Providence, U. California, Johns Hopkins]. George Boas has written extensively on the history of philosophy, with much emphasis on French thought. He has made a detailed study of primitivism in antiquity and has considered too the aesthetic aspect of philosophy.

In *Wingless Pegasus, a Handbook for Critics* (1950) he considered, as he says, the problems the critics would face if serious. His approach, influenced by Perry, was naturalistic, straightforward, and literal, without "purple passages" and "fine writing." He assessed the situation from the standpoint of facts, not feelings. In the light of actuality he was forced to be pluralistic and relativistic, his views being determined by history, not by metaphysics. He was greatly influenced by study of psychology and anthropology.

Boas has considered alleged rules, and values, the significance of form, the difference and interrelations of liking and approbation, the question of a hierarchy of values, and ultimate standards. Finally he has admitted that there is an aspect of art which is not analyzable, a kind of ineffable factor.

Paul Weiss (1901–   ) [N.Y.C., Bryn Mawr, Yale]. Since he has had an interest in metaphysical problems from the first, Paul Weiss has considered their place in contemporary American philosophy and their implications for moral issues, individual and general.

He holds a naturalistic view of reality, in which order and variety, continuity and discontinuity, necessity and freedom, are fundamental characteristics. In *Man's Freedom* (1950) he applies this background to human life, holding that it is through freedom that man realizes his own nature. Through freedom he becomes unpredictable in behavior, creative in action, a socialized being. His moral significance depends on this: his aim at some common good, however it be conceived, should be an ideal good which unifies varied efforts. Working toward it requires the learning of techniques. All men are bound by the requirements to love and to create.

In *Modes of Being* (1958) Weiss sets forth the structure of reality under the four types: actuality, ideality, existence, and God. Actualities are beings in space and time, each one unified, but none perfect. Idealities are possibilities, realities with the attributes of the good, a future status and perfection. Existence is being engaged in a passage from one position to another. God is the explanatory concept for teleology, cosmological relations, and ontological status.

Each mode may be approached negatively by considering what would be the consequence if it were not true. Being, the Cosmos, is constituted by the synthesis of all the modes.

Sidney Hook (1902–   ) [N.Y.C.]. Sidney Hook, an outstanding progressive in thought, upholds the pragmatic philosophy of Dewey and concerns himself especially with trends in contemporary thinking. He has given special attention to the development of nineteenth-century philosophy from Hegel to Marx and Engels. He has supported movements in defense of freedom and equality of individuals and has considered the problem of values, their determination and testing. His philosophy is naturalistic and opposed to the tendencies which place primary emphasis upon the classics of the past. In 1950 he edited a collection of papers by various writers the purpose of which was to pay tribute to Dewey on the occasion of his ninetieth birthday; this collection was published, in the same year, as *John Dewey, Philosopher of Science and Freedom* and dealt with the leader of Instrumentalism's influence on conceptions of art, social inquiry, legal reasoning, education, and other basic topics.

In 1958 Hook edited a symposium on *Determinism and Freedom in the Age of Modern Science,* which manifested intense interest in the problem of social freedom.

Perry Miller (1905-1963) [Chicago, Harvard]. The thought of New England—including the orthodoxy of Massachusetts, the Puritan mind, and especially the thought of Jonathan Edwards—has been an area of deep interest to Perry Miller.

In 1950 he assembled a rich mine of sources in *The Transcendentalists,* beginning with forerunners of the movement, continuing through its period of emergence, into full flower, and showing its literary and critical, political and social, as well as its philosophical and religious phases. The collection consists of one hundred and seven papers including sixteen by Orestes Brownson, thirteen by George Ripley, six each from James F. Clarke, Theodore

Parker, and Margaret Fuller; then on down to fewer for the other transcendentalists.

Frederick Mayer (1921–   ) [Redlands]. The problems of philosophy that effect education have been the concern of Frederick Mayer. He has stressed the essentials of high level living and has handled the troubles of youth, education against delinquency, and education for maturity and the good life. He has made suggestions for new directions in university education and discussed patterns in philosophy, emphasizing a skeptical approach and a naturalism of the type of Santayana. In 1950 he completed the second volume of his *History of Philosophy,* covering a succession of thinkers from Machiavelli to Spengler.

C. J. Ducasse (1881–   ) [Angouleme, Brown U.]. With a comprehensive outlook in the field of philosophy, Ducasse has written on many aspects of it—logic and philosophy of science, art and aesthetics, education and religion.

In *Nature, Mind and Death* (1951) he centers on the mind-body problem. First of all the conceptions of the "mental" and the "material" need to be rendered less vague than they usually are; this vagueness haunts questions about sensations or sensa. He disagrees with Moore's refutation of idealism; sensations are mental. The mental is noetic, or conational, or affective. Belief in the physical world is due to the conviction that pressure intuitions are caused by events that are not mental intuitions. Such physicopsychical experiences are the source of knowledge of the physical realm, the world being the basis of continuities in experience. He avoids the difficult problem of perceptual illusion.

Mind is a substance, when the term "substance" is rightly understood. Interaction of mind and body occurs causally. Survival of mind after death is possible, though the alternative forms conceivable are not empirically verified.

A Philosophical Scrutiny of Religion (1935) is a precise, nonpartisan, non-dogmatic treatment of the nature and function of religion. Ducasse is unsympathetic toward arguments for a transcendent God, though opposed to a mere naturalistic humanism. He favors a type of dualism over behavioristic naturalism and is open-minded about phenomena classed as paranormal. He admits that religion has had its perversions and misuses, leading to Satanism and witchcraft, yet on the whole he believes the balance is in its favor as a useful social factor, supporting altruism and courage. Evil is to be accepted simply as a natural aspect of the physical world. What religion needs most is direction toward ethical goals.

Richard von Mises (1883–1953) [Lemberg, Strassburg, Istamboul, Harvard]. Von Mises was a specialist in applied mathematics, dealing with various problems in physics and with the theory of probability and statistics. He defended the frequency theory in probability, admitting that this involved a certain degree of skepticism, and he relied upon pragmatic convention and an anthropological warrant.

His *Positivism, a Study in Human Understanding* (1951) was based upon a work first written in German some years before. As a positivist von Mises was opposed to traditional metaphysics of transcendent reality. He traced his views from Comte through Mach and Poincaré to Carnap, Frank, and Schlick. He disapproved of vagueness and generalities beyond experience. He covered the whole range of interest, from language as the instrument used in all discussion, through the process of analysis, the nature of exact theories, causality, and probability, including a proper attitude toward alleged miracles. He discussed the application of scientific method to history and the biological and social fields, to the problems of the *a priori* and totality, to poetry and art. Finally he reckoned with human behavior and the relations that lead to ideas of "ought," "will" and "must," the essence of law, ethics, and the overall orientation which is the essence of religion.

Each section and chapter and finally the whole book is summarized with a brief statement of his meaning—making his work one extremely easy to understand, a model of exposition.

Paul Tillich (1886-1965) [Prussia, Berlin, Dresden, Frankfurt, N.Y.C., Harvard]. Paul Tillich has been rated as the most important influence in the resurgence of religious thought in these times. His position was that of Neo-orthodoxy, a defense of supernaturalism, greatly influenced by Kierkegaard.

In *Systematic Theology* (1951, 1957) he treated the question of reason and revelation, interpreting the latter in a broad sense as concerned not merely with what is beyond reason, but as any process of making Truth evident. The Being of God becomes the identity of "Being" and "God." God is personal, and as every person is self-transcendent, is not beyond the universe, nor merely within it, but within it yet infinitely transcending it.

The revelation of God is centered in Christ, who symbolizes the estrangement of man from God and the reconciliation with him. Man's significance is not found in the search for the historical Jesus; this has not been successful. It is found in the new Being that one gains in the life of the Church. This is the power of salvation which has universal significance beyond the literal expression of dogma.

Love, Power, and Justice (1954) presents a synthesis of various interpretations. Their unity, Tillich believed, absorbs their separateness and tensions. They are rooted in being, intelligible only as such, and are cosmic powers, not merely human reactions. The three interpenetrate. The Power of Being is God. The will to power is the striving for the divine likeness and is supported by love and justice. Evil is due to estrangement from our real nature.

Biblical Religion and the Search for Ultimate Reality (1955) sees in the Bible story a set of symbols pointing beyond to a search for Ultimate Reality, centering in the problem of the Divine-human relationship and the divine manifestation in history. There are implied all the questions of ontology—regarding the nature of the Real, and man's place in relation to it—with which philosophy has occasion to deal.

Gabriel Marcel (1889–   ) [Paris, Sens]. The careers of philosopher, dramatist and critic, and musical composer have been combined by Gabriel Marcel. He wrote on the relation of the philosophy of Coleridge to that of Schelling, and became a Catholic Christian existentialist in touch with Teutonic existentialism as well as that of Sartre. He has reflected deeply on the existence of God and the meaning of "existence" as applied to God.

From the first he has been impressed with the mystery of existence and has been interested in the relation of faith to reality. He read the philosophy of Royce and regarded it as a transition from Absolute Idealism to Existentialism. The essential point to remember about man is that he is a traveler, living in a time of crisis. But he is more than a finite self; he is a partner in a vast enterprise. Through communion and transcendence he engages in hope, bowing before God. Life is a captivity, in which there is a contrast of despair and hope. Final hope for escape must come through response to the Infinite Being to whom one owes everything unconditionally.

In *Faith and Reality* (1951) G. Marcel continues an analysis begun earlier. Ontology is concerned not merely with *my* being but with the essence of existence. It is to be understood only by way of the conception of intersubjectivity, the basic fact that "we are," with others; and oneself is understood only through communication and life shared with others.

The unity underlying all is realized through love, which says of another "thou shalt not die." True existence can not cease; it transcends things and locations. Man regarded as a mechanism is deprived of substance. Faith is belief in some one, a pledge, attended by humility and prayer, recognizing dependence upon God. By grace one is free to radiate one's influence into an infinite world. Charity is intersubjectivity.

H. Nelson Goodman (1906–   ) [Boston, Philadelphia]. Goodman has made a special study of logical theory and the theory of knowledge and has written various articles on topics in this field. In 1951 he wrote *The Structure of Appearance,* an exceptionally strong attempt to apply the methods of symbolic logic to the realm of phenomena, in accordance with his conviction that the problems of philosophy should be so treated. He does not commit himself explicitly to phenomenalism or nominalism, though his position is akin to these. It is a detailed attempt to eliminate confusion, an attempt so exact that it perplexes any but a careful reader.

In three Parts, H. G. Goodman deals first with the nature and methods of logical philosophy, second with the requirements of accurate logical construction, and third with the choice of extralogical vocabulary. He then goes on to types of systems and the relation of qualities to particulars. Finally he considers the ordering of qualities and a calculus of shape and measure, coming at length to the temporal realm and the physical world.

A. G. N. Flew (1923–   ) [Oxford, Aberdeen, Keele]. Flew has gained recognition as a result of his interest in the field of logic, theoretical and applied. In editing *Logic and Language* (1951, 1954), two volumes of essays, he dealt with basic questions concerning linguistics, problems of time and of induction, sense data, verifiability, etc., even to questions of social, political, and religious concepts. This he did without the use of formal symbolisms such as those in common use in the works of others.

The categories, the meaning of "existence," causal connections, and knowledge of other minds, were also considered.

Flew's *Essays in Conceptual Analysis* (1956) continued the line of thought into discussion of theories of meaning, explanation, validity, etc., the relation of metaphysics to logic, and the meaning of four-dimensional space.

Albert G. A. Balz (1887–1957) [Charlottesville]. Although his interest ranged over the entire history of philosophy from the Greeks down, A. G. A. Balz studied in detail the philosophy of Hobbes and Spinoza, with emphasis upon political philosophy. He also gave attention to French thinkers. His leadership in philosophy, psychology and the humanities was acknowledged especially in the South.

His masterwork was *Descartes and the Modern Mind* (1952) and was awarded the Nicholas M. Butler Medal by Columbia University. It was the fruit of his lifetime study. In Descartes he found the mind which determined our modern intellectual tradition and gave impulse to the attitude which has generated science and technology, remolding a tendency coming from at least as far back as Aquinas. The basic motive is inquiry, the essence of thought (*cogito*), working out its implications down to the present. Thus Descartes attempted to build a philosophical superstructure on science.

Epistemology is the heart of philosophy, according to Balz. "Wisdom" has to make adjustments between "claims" regarding Nature and "doctrines" about ends to be served.

David Baumgardt (1890–   ) [Erfurt, Berlin, N.Y.C.]. Baumgardt has given attention to the fields of ethics, Jewish philosophy, and Romanticism.

In *Bentham and the Ethics of Today* (1952) he holds that a revaluation of Bentham's method offers a way to a sounder basis for ethics in spite of the revision and supplementation which his moral philosophy needs. Both positivism and metaphysics should be taken seriously and not opposed to each other. Bentham is consistent in his hedonist positivism, but has been much misjudged. This book presents the genetic development of Bentham's thought regarding motives, fictions, and criticism of bills of rights. It traces the connections with pre-Benthamist thought and comments on the importance of his thought for contemporary ethical systems.

The author proceeds from Bentham's earliest anonymous writings, *Fragment on Government* and *Comment on the Commentaries,* through the *Introduction to the Principles of Morals and Legislation* and the works edited by Louis Dumont de Genève to his later *Table of the Springs of Action,* and juristic, economic, and religious writings. There follows an essay on whether Benthamism is "bankrupt." The six short Appendixes contain hitherto unpublished statements by Bentham.

Richard P. McKeon (1900–   ) [N.J., Paris, N.Y.C., Chicago]. Richard McKeon was educated in the United States and in Paris and became an eminent classicist, philosopher, and administrator. He has held high place in international organizations and has had important influence in the teaching of philosophy, in the rapprochement of nations, and international movements toward peace. His studies have ranged from Aristotle through the Middle Ages to modern times; he has shown an especial interest in Asoka

(India) and also has been interested in the thought of Spinoza.

In *Freedom and History, the Semantics of Philosophic Controversies* (1952) McKeon treated fashions in philosophy against their historical backgrounds and their theoretical assumptions. Historical semantics and philosophical semantics represent the chief emphases of the man of action and the man of reflection. Analysis he classified under three types, dialectical (treating freedom and history as expressions of the nature of man), logistic (dealing with general law), and problematic (enquiry concerning the assembling of data). Oppositions among conceptions are developed in the oppositions of philosophic doctrine and political action.

In *Thought, Action and Passion* (1954) he assembled from various occasions essays presenting history as an endless dialogue recurring repeatedly to certain fundamental themes: love, truth, freedom and imitation, expressed in science, morals, art, and rhetoric.

Charles A. Moore (1901–   ) [Chicago, Yale, Hawaii]. C. A. Moore has been active in developing contacts between philosophy in the West and the Orient. This is evident in *Essays in East-West Philosophy,* which was edited in 1952 and is a report of the second East-West Philosophers' Conference at the University of Hawaii in 1949. It dealt with the methodologies employed in Japanese Buddhism in Chinese epistemology, and in Indian and Western philosophy. Metaphysics was represented by Chinese, Buddhist, and Western thought. A third section contained essays from China, India, and the West on social, ethical and spiritual issues, including legal ideas, and theory of value.

Wilfrid S. Sellars (1912–   ) [U. Michigan, Iowa State, Minneapolis, Yale]. Sellars joined Feigl in editing a volume of papers from various sources on *Philosophical Analysis* (1949). He and Feigl also founded a new periodical, *Philosophical Studies.*

He joined another colleague in editing *Readings in Ethical Theory* (1952) which is composed of papers and chapters, from mainly British and a few American writers, representing ethical discussions resulting from statements of G. E. Moore in 1903. The materials included represent the points of view of naturalism, intuitionism, and emotive theory, and some papers treat the psychology of conduct and sense of obligation. Freedom, guilt and responsibility, and the process of justification were also discussed.

Sarvepalli Radhakrishnan (1888–   ) [South India, Benares, Calcutta, Delhi]. Radhakrishnan is one of India's most distinguished scholars and statesmen. He has done much to interpret the mind of India to the English-speaking world. He has presented the religious spirit of India and its idealistic philosophy and has compared it with the thought of the West; he has translated and edited the philosophical classics of India and, with C. A. Moore, has made the outstanding sources (among them some not generally known) available in English. As Vice President of the Indian Union, his interest in the history of civilization has been both theoretical and practical.

Radhakrishnan edited with colleagues the *History of Philosophy, Eastern and Western* (1953) and in doing so helped to break down the line of division between the two philosophic traditions. By bringing both East and West into a single scope the work represents a landmark in the history of philosophy, even though it still separates the two into distinct volumes.

The volume on Eastern thought runs from pre-Vedic influences to contemporary thought in India, China, and Japan and is presented by outstanding scholars of the countries discussed. It covers the traditional sources, the schools (orthodox and heterodox), and later developments, with some reference also to mathematics and scientific knowledge, and aesthetics.

Included in the treatment of Western thought is brief consideration of Persian and Islamic thought along with the usual line of Presocratics through the Medieval to contemporary British, Italian and American Idealism, and also Logical Positivism and Existentialism.

Ronald B. Levinson (1896–   ) [Harvard, U. Maine]. Ronald B. Levinson justifies his treatise *In Defense of Plato* (1953) on the ground that Plato's thought is still very much alive and is being held responsible for certain present-day corruptions of which he is not the ancestral advocate. The critics have emphasized faults more than they have recognized merits. The result has been a distorted view of Plato as a man and a thinker. He is treated as being in the setting of our culture rather than in his own—and even that is seriously misrepresented. The accusations are much more easily made than refuted; hence the treatment had to be rather lengthy.

Among the questions touched upon are Platonic love, the status of the slave, whether he was a totalitarian, freedom of inquiry, and the philosopher king. On all these points Plato is not as vile as he has been painted, though Levinson sympathizes with those who fear the danger of regulative proposals for ordering the ideal state.

Stephen E. Toulmin (1922–   ) [Leeds, Oxford, Cambridge]. S. E. Toulmin studied the place of reason in ethics and came to the conclusion that its function is to effect a harmonizing of activities, both in individual and in social relations.

In *The Philosophy of Science* (1953) he sought to show the logic of the physical sciences and their program by looking at the field from the position of the scientist himself. It is necessary to see what the scientist does rather than to listen to what he says. His chief work is to construct a model that will show concretely what happens in the physical world. He proceeds by analogies and examples. This is more significant than attempting to find universal laws and first principles. To this end he tries experiments, working not at random but with a particular problem in view. He is always ready to change his course and try new techniques. He knows that induction is not a simple accumulation of experiments and is aware of the uncertainty in all results. Uniformity is always subject to degrees of precision.

Toulmin has written on the uses of argument, also; he believes that it does not hold closely to the rules of traditional logic.

Wilmon H. Sheldon (1875–   ) [Massachusetts, Princeton, Dartmouth, Yale]. The conception of polarity has been the center of Wilmon H. Sheldon's thinking.

In *America's Progressive Philosophy* (1942) he found at the heart of things process—a process which is productive of novelty. Out of it come various points of view and various philosophies; but these do not merely rival each other. They are supplemental, rooted in contrasts—idealism and naturalism, monism and pluralism, rationalism and irrationalism—but they finally lead to what may be called a scholastic synthesis.

The criterion of reality is presentedness, force, coherence, action. Out of these come ever new realizations of possibilities, which are compatible with each other. This is the career of Nature.

In *God and Polarity, a Synthesis of Philosophers* (1954) he carries out these ideas on a larger scale. Systems exist together and give a solid precipitate of truth. They are aspects of an inclusive system which is headed by a single First Cause, called God. The fundamental aspect of Reality is process, leading to progress. The final nature of Reality is more than intellect; it is also conation and affection, and in these respects is "irrational." The strife of philosophers would come to a close through what the Christian has called a "charitable" attitude.

Arnold Toynbee (1889–   ) [London, Oxford]. A philosophical historian, noted for his activities and studies in international relations and the history of civilization, including religion, Toynbee joined the contributors to the volume *Man's Right to Know* (1954) published in connection with the 200th anniversary of the founding of Columbia University.

His *Study of History,* begun in 1934, reached its tenth volume in 1954 and dominates the field of the philosophical study of history. Its influence is widespread among academic persons, theologians, and others. This great work is a massive documentation of fears and hopes, appealing to popular sentiments. It was well received especially by those who look to religion for rescue from their fears of cultural disaster.

Reinhold Niebuhr (1892–   ) [Missouri, Detroit, Union Seminary]. R. Niebuhr has applied himself with exceptional keenness to the study of human nature in its religious and social aspects, with resulting new interpretations of sin, salvation, transcendent goals, and final judgment. He has followed the course of faith through the path of history and is deeply sensitive to man's needs and to the desperate condition into which man has brought himself.

In *Christian Realism and Political Problems* (1954) Niebuhr has analyzed current issues and criticized the optimism of liberals who fail to assess rightly the evil in human behavior. In his view there are two domains in which man lives: that of Nature, and that of History. Science deals with the realm of Nature, in a manner disinterested of outcomes; but History is concerned with man's participation in outcomes and so is never disinterested. Throughout the course of time, evil is always flourishing; hence repentence is always in order. Repentance must be not merely in general terms, but in terms of specific sins. The new life in the Gospel, however, does not promise historical success. Man is responsible for relative victories, in communities, nations, and cultures. But the final victory is God's. Man must stand humbly before facts, grateful for a measure of truth and justice, recognizing the finitude of everything human. There is a degree of irrationality in all the given. The notion of the perfectibility of man, endless progress, and world government are erroneous. Meliorism is all that man can hope for.

Ernest Nagel (1901–   ) [Czechoslavakia, N.Y.C.] Ernest Nagel is noted for his studies of logic and the philosophy of science with emphasis on theory of probability. His rationalistic bent is evident in *Sovereign Reason, and Other Studies in the Philosophy of Science* (1954). This is a collection of essays written from a naturalistic point of view and holding that there is no total context of experience; science and art are in the empirical flux. Criticising the views of others he finally accepts Dewey's philosophy, which excludes pontifical dogmatism, oracular wisdom, or condescending absolutism.

He has maintained the possibility of forming a scientific theory in the social sciences of the same sort as that employed in the physical sciences.

Nagel's papers, written during the preceding twenty-five years, are gathered together in *Logic Without Metaphysics* (1957). Here he interprets "logic" as connoting structure, articulation, assumptions and methods and covers various topics from symbolism, truth and verification, to a naturalistic conception of logic, and an alternative to Marxism.

Philip P. Wiener (1905–   ) [N.Y.C., So. California, C.C.N.Y.]. Philip Wiener had an early interest in the foundations of geometry and in the thought of Leibniz. He also has been interested in the philosophy of science. He studied the origins of Pragmatism and the philosophy of Peirce in detail. He edited a volume of *Readings in the Philosophy of Science* (1953) and, in 1954, translated for the first time into English Duhem's *Aim and Structure of Physical Science,* which is a clear and sustained interpretation of the logic of physics (written in 1906) explaining it as construction of models for intelligibility rather than universal laws. He acknowledged the influence of historical settings and regarded the unity of science as organic in structure. (In religious belief Duhem was a Catholic.)

Daniel S. Robinson (1888–   ) [U. Wisconsin, Miami U. (O.), Butler U., U.C.L.A.]. Robinson has written texts in philosophy, including logic, ethics, and philosophy of religion. He has also edited anthologies of modern philosophy, assembled logical writings of Royce, and the less known writings of Gomperz. In 1955 he presented *Crucial Issues in Philosophy;* here he interpreted current problems and leading personalities from the standpoint of idealism.

Harry A. Wolfson (1887–   ) [Wilno, Harvard]. H. A. Wolfson has concentrated on Jewish thought, its relation to classical, especially Aristotelian, tradition, and its influence upon Christian ideas. In *The Philosophy of the Church Fathers, Vol. I* (dealing with *Faith, the Trinity and the Incarnation,* 1956), he traces from his earlier study of Philo the relation of faith and reason and the use of allegorical method. He follows the course of the issue through such Church Fathers as Tertullian, Origen, and Augustine. He presents the development of the conception of the Trinity, the use of the idea of the Logos, and the influence of Platonic ideas in such a way as to lead to the central three Mysteries: Generation, the Trinity, and Incarnation. He contrasts with these the Gnostics and heretical sects.

Herbert W. Schneider (1892–   ) [Ohio, Columbia]. Among many dimensions of interest Herbert W. Schneider has included special emphasis upon political philosophy and its relations to recent movements. He has made careful study of Fascism, its roots and expression in European governments. He has also been interested in American thought—from Franklin, Samuel Johnson, and the Puritans, to the present. He attended to the forms of religion, too.

In *Three Dimensions of Public Morality* (1956) in the presence of the World's disintegration he followed the interconnections of the ideas of liberty, equality, and fraternity. Questions of human rights, public needs and security, and fundamental civic virtues concern all peoples, and cannot be separated from each other.

J. H. Woodger (1894–   ) [Great Yarmouth, U. London]. J. H. Woodger has been interested in scientific method, especially as it applies to biology. He has written on the construction of technical theories, on the theory of development, and on the structure of language as used in biological science. In 1956 he edited the volume, *Essays, by Tarski, on Logic, Semantics and Metamathematics* which included the noted one on *Der Wahrheitsbegriff in den Formalisierten Sprachen* (*The Truth-concept in Formalized Languages*) (see page 274).

Charles W. Morris (1901–   ) [Denver, Houston, Chicago, Gainesville]. Charles W. Morris has been interested in the entire field of philosophy, but in his early years he emphasized theories of mind, the nature of the self, and the structure of society. At the same time he was very sympathetic with the pragmatic philosophy of G. H. Mead. Later he placed emphasis upon scientific empiricism in its various aspects and in the movement of the Unity of Science. He held that scientific method unites aspects of meaning emphasized separately by pragmatism, empiricism, and formalistic doctrines.

In 1956 C. W. Morris re-issued *Paths of Life, a Preface to a World Religion,* in which after examining four types of life he used the Buddhist figure of Maitreya as a goal beyond present ideals for men. In the same year he published *Varieties of Human Value;* this was an attempt at a scientific examination of thirteen different beliefs, described by students from various nations, about the good life. Five different dimensions (1. social restraint, 2. enjoyment, 3. withdrawal, 4. receptivity, 5. self-indulgence) and their determining factors were discovered, three of them (1, 2, and 4) common to the United States, India, and China.

Arthur A. Luce (1882–   ) [Dublin]. A. A. Luce, student of the history of philosophy, has been especially concerned with the work of George Berkeley. In 1948 he published a biography of Berkeley (in connection with a definitive edition of his works), an account of his personal life without reference to his thinking.

He presented a vigorous defense of what he termed Berkeley's empirical realism at the two hundredth anniversary of Berkeley's death (1953).

In 1957, with T. E. Jessop, he published the ninth volume of their new edition of the *Works of Berkeley,* covering everything from the Philosophical Commentaries (or Commonplace Book) through the *Principles of Human Knowledge, Three Dialogues between Hylas and Philonous,* and correspondence with Johnson, down to his sermons and letters, and notes on the letters.

Stephen C. Pepper (1891–   ) [N.J., U. California]. Throughout his career Stephen Pepper has looked at philosophy from the standpoint of aesthetics. He has written on aesthetic qualities, on the basis of criticism in art, and on principles of art appreciation.

Recently he has applied the general problem of aesthetics to the field of value as a whole. In *The Sources of Value* (1958) he included such topics as ethics, theory of knowledge, economics and anthropology as areas in which conceptions of "good" and "bad" are employed. He notes the various methods by which standards of goodness have been gained and chooses "desire as purposive" as the basic feature. These rest upon instinctive appetites and aversions, referring to goals, often potential, and a state of quiescence.

Evaluations are judgments, first descriptive, then quantitative. Out of these come a sense of obligation and applications to personality integration and social and cultural patterns. They contribute to survival value, and to legislation.

Paul A. Schilpp (1897–   ) [Hesse-Nassau, C. Pacific, North-western U.]. P. A. Schilpp has been a progressive and vigorous defender of freedom of thought and has been concerned with ethics, philosophy of religion, and the future prospects of higher education. But his reputation the past twenty years rests chiefly on his editing of a series of volumes, each of which treats the philosophy of a noted contemporary personality: beginning with Dewey, and Santayana, continuing through Russell, G. E. Moore, Cassirer, Einstein, and Radhakrishnan, to Karl Jaspers. Each volume has an autobiographical or biographical section and a series of descriptive or critical essays on the man's philosophy, followed when possible by a response from the philosopher himself. A bibliography of the person's writings concludes the volume.

J. H. Randall, Jr. (1899–   ) [Grand Rapids, Columbia]. J. H. Randall has been strongly historical-minded, concerned with group responsibility, and with the formation of modern mentality. He has considered the part that religion in general has played in modern culture and has studied the place of knowledge in Christianity.

He has studied American philosophy, giving special attention to certain outstanding personalities who have had part in it.

In *Nature and Historical Experience* (1958) Randall presents a theory of history and a naturalistic metaphysics. The temporal dimension of reality he regards as fundamental; hence history is essential, and ideas play a causal part in reality. Problems are temporary, but despite this are not to be lightly regarded. They grow out of the past, which limits the present by way of the materials it hands over to it. With time, the understanding of the past itself changes; and the future is an open realm. The result is histories rather than "history." There is no perennial philosophy.

Mortimer J. Adler (1902–   ) [N.Y.C., Columbia, Chicago]. M. J. Adler has been an active advocate of thought, general culture, and education. He has written on art and music appreciation, effective reading, and on moral issues, especially in their social and legal aspects. In the history of thought he has been especially occupied with the philosophy of Thomas Aquinas. His educational

305

theory has disagreed with that of Dewey. He holds that the core of education is acquaintance with the great thoughts of the past as formulated in the great books. His *The Idea of Freedom* (1958) is the result of several years' investigation of the basic agreements on the concept of freedom, in spite of variations in a dozen modes of expression, in the history of Western thought through 2500 years.

Walter A. Kaufmann (1921–   ) [Princeton]. W. A. Kaufmann has been a critical writer in the field of philosophy of religion, including the development of Existentialism and Nietzsche. In 1958 his *Critique of Religion and Philosophy* was an examination of Existentialism, Positivism, and contemporary religious systems—Christianity, Judaism and Zen Buddhism, along with various recent thinkers in religion. The work voiced the objections of numerous American philosophers to current orthodoxies. He stood for the pursuit of particular truths rather than Truth and the various arts, without authoritarian standards. "God" is the expression, he says, of man's ontological interest and the objectification of the urge to higher existence.

Arthur Pap (1921–1959) [Zurich, C.C.N.Y., U. Oregon, Yale]. An advocate of analytic philosophy, Arthur Pap has in *Semantics and Necessary Truth* (1958) undertaken an inquiry into the foundations of this type of philosophy. He has traced the history of the conception through earlier thinkers—Leibniz, Kant, Locke and Hume—and then has presented its structure in contemporary thought. The *a priori* and the necessary he regards as identical; the empirical is contingent. The aim of his discussion is to clarify the relation of the *a priori* to linguistic conventions and to analytic and synthetic judgments. He also comments upon implicit and ostensive definition, logical truth, and logical necessity .

His definite conclusions are few; the problems remaining are numerous.

Appendix

Appendix

Schools of Philosophy and Their Adherents

The following bold face terms identify the chief schools of, or emphases in, philosophy. Below each definition are names of representatives* of the particular philosophical group. The lists of adherents presented are typical, rather than exhaustive. The overlapping of terms makes it difficult to label the different aspects of an individual's beliefs and, in many cases, makes it impossible to classify him under a single school of thought.

The tenets of the various groups are fully discussed in the works listed under Reference Books, pages 319–323.

Absolutism—In epistemology, metaphysics, or ethics, the theory claiming that there is a final and always relevant standard of belief, reality, and action.

Plato	Fichte	Bosanquet
Augustine	Schelling	Caird
Mohammed	Hegel	Bradley
Thomas Aquinas	Cousin	McTaggart
Spinoza	Newman	Royce
Cudworth	Green	Hocking
Leibniz		Barth

Agnosticism—The theory that the final answer to basic questions is always "I do not know."

Protagoras	Nicholas of Cusa	Spencer
Gorgias	Montaigne	Huxley
Pyrrho	Kant	Lewes
Carneades	Cournot	Stephen
Sextus Empiricus	Mansel	Barth

---

* Read down each column for chronological sequence.

Altruism—The ethical doctrine that one must emphasize the good of another over one's own good.

Jesus	Butler	Sidgwick
Seneca	Comte	Höffding
Cumberland	J. S. Mill	Royce

Animism—The theory that objects ordinarily considered inanimate have something within them analogous to a human soul.

| Thales | Zeno (Stoic) | Schelling |
| Xenocrates | Leibniz | Fechner |

Asceticism—The religious and ethical doctrine that one's highest merit is attained by withdrawing from the ordinary world and concentrating upon an inner spiritual realm, with severe self-discipline.

| Antisthenes | Richard of St. Victor | Olivi |
| Diogenes of Sinope | Bonaventure | Thomas à Kempis |

Atheism—The belief that the idea of God is not tenable in any connection.

| Leucippus | Protagoras | Diderot |
| Democritus | La Mettrie | McTaggart |

Atomism—The theory that the ultimate structure of reality is constituted by separate indivisible units (usually matter).

Leucippus	Epicurus	Gassendi
Democritus	Lucretius	Boyle
	William of Conches	

Communism—A social philosophy which advocates the allowance of private rights and possessions only by the consent of the whole society.

| Engels | Plekhanov |
| Marx | Lenin |

Conceptualism—A theory of the status of universal concepts which says that they are neither wholly independent of absolute mind nor the creations of finite minds. They are subjective to God, but objective to man.

| Remi of Auxerre | Abelard | Thomas Aquinas |
| Avicenna | | Duns Scotus |

Critical Idealism—The theory that all known facts are within the realm of experience; whether or not there is anything beyond experience is indeterminable (*see also Agnosticism*).

Kant	H. Cohen	Natorp
Maimon		Cassirer

Critical Realism—The theory that there is in the structure of reality a third realm of "essences" in addition to the mental and the physical realms.

Santayana	Lovejoy	Pratt

Criticism—The theory that knowledge is reached neither by Dogmatism nor by Skepticism, but by an intermediate method which avoids both.

Kant	Beneke	Husserl
Fichte	Lange	Cassirer
Fries	H. Cohen	Natorp
Schopenhauer		Vaihinger

Determinism—The view that the course of the universe is definitely fixed and allows no meaning to the term "freedom" (*see also Mechanism*).

Democritus	Gottschalk	Siger
Mohammed		Bruno

Dialectical Materialism—The view (supported chiefly by Russian communism) that ultimate reality is material; its mode of operation is through a constant struggle of opposites, allowing only temporary synthesis and peace.

Engels	Plekhanov
Marx	Lenin

Dogmatism—Excessive definiteness of belief, especially without adequate supporting reasons. This is usually made in the form of an accusation against a theory with which one disagrees (e.g., Kant against Wolff).

Dualism—The theory that reality is composed of only two irreducible substances, e.g., matter and spirit.

Zoroaster	Lactantius	Arnauld	Ducasse
Pythagoras	Boehme	Locke	
Mani	Descartes	Bayle	

Egoism—The ethical doctrine that the object of prime importance is oneself, the serving of whose interests is the highest end.

Protagoras	Schopenhauer	Stirner
Hobbes		Nietzsche

Empiricism—Literally, this is an appeal to experience, but usually it emphasizes the importance of sense experience over thought in the process of verification.

Epicurus	Hobbes	Hutcheson	Mach
R. Bacon	Locke	de Tracy	Poincaré
Telesio	Hume	J. S. Mill	Northrup
F. Bacon	Montesquieu	Bain	Lee
Gassendi	Condillac	Clifford	

Evolutionism—The theory that the basic process of the universe is one in which later things develop from earlier; in conduct the highest good is to realize this process to the greatest possible degree.

Epicurus	Ardigò	Harris
Zeno (Stoic)	Fiske	Hobhouse
Monboddo	Lewes	McTaggart
Schelling	Stephen	Croce
Hegel	Wright	Bergson
Comte	Nietzsche	Alexander
Spencer	Caird	Morgan
Huxley		

Existentialism—Recently, this theory has emphasized the self as the Ultimate Real and its inner struggles as basic fact of existence.

Kierkegaard	Heidegger	Marcel
Jaspers	Barth	Sartre

Hedonism—The ethical doctrine supporting pleasure as the highest good and the goal of living and that man's obligation is to seek pleasure.

Democritus	Condillac	Bentham
Aristippus	Helvétius	J. S. Mill
Epicurus		Sidgwick

Humanism—The doctrine that emphasizes the prime importance of the human factor in the universe.

Protagoras	Zwingli	Feuerbach
Erasmus	Comte	Schiller

Hylozoism—The theory that regards matter (hylē) and life (zōē) as inseparable in the real world.

Thales	Archelaus	Cardano
Anaximenes		Haeckel

Idealism—In epistemology, the theory that ideas are the essential factors in knowledge; in metaphysics, the view that all reality is of the essence of spirit; in ethics, the doctrine that ideals are the objects to be pursued in action.

Plato	Hegel	Green	Hocking
Plotinus	Emerson	Caird	Unamuno
Berkeley	Renouvier	Fouillée	Robinson
Leibniz	Lotze	Bradley	
Fichte	Boutroux	Royce	
Schelling	Wundt	Croce	

Instrumentalism—The term, as applied by Dewey and his followers, concerns the function of ideas as instruments of living, not as goals of living (*see also Pragmatism*).

Epicurus	Avenarius	Lepley	Hook
Wright	Dewey	White	Morris
Nietzsche	Murphy	Bridgman	

Intuitionism—The view that Ultimate Truth is reached not by analysis but by an immediate grasp of its contents.

Nicholas of Cusa	Whewell	Croce
Rosmini	Parker	Bergson
Gioberti		N. Hartmann

Logical Empiricism—See *Scientific Empiricism.*

Logical Positivism—An early name for *Scientific Empiricism.*

Materialism—In metaphysics, the theory that ultimate reality is constituted by a substance called "matter," which is possessed primarily of physical properties. In ethics, it is the pursuit of physical well-being over all other things.

Strato	La Mettrie	de Tracy
Lucretius	Holbach	Moleschott
Hobbes		Büchner

Mechanism—The consideration that reality is ultimately a machine, not a living organism (*see also Determinism*).

Democritus	La Mettrie	Digby

Meliorism—The theory that the world is neither the best possible nor the worst possible, but lies between and is capable of improvement.

Emerson	James

Monism—The theory that there is only one Ultimate Reality, whether spirit, matter, or neutral substance.

Thales	Spinoza	Fouillée
Anaximenes	La Mettrie	Bradley
Parmenides	Feuerbach	Royce
Speusippus	Dilthey	Bergson
Plotinus	Bosanquet	Perry
Proclus	Avenarius	Gentile
Bruno		Montague

Mysticism—The belief that Ultimate Truth is to be attained by a great intuition, not by analysis, and that contact with the Ultimate Real is by an immediate merging with it.

Ammonius Saccas	Damascius	Tauler
Plotinus	Richard of St. Victor	J. Gerson
Hermes Trismegistus	Hugh of St. Victor	Weigel
Jamblichus	Joachim	Boehme
Proclus	Bonaventure	H. More
Dionysius the Areopagite	Eckhart	Coleridge

Naturalism—The theory that the Ultimate Real is most adequately designated "nature" rather than "spirit" or a dualistic pair of realities.

Prodicus	Strato	Cardano	Weiss
Democritus	Duns Scotus	Bruno	

Galileo	Hobbes	Morris
Herbert	Voltaire	Haeckel
Grotius	Taine	M. Cohen

Neo-Realism—A form of neutral monism in which reality is regarded as constituted by abstract qualities, not being mental contents except in certain contexts and being physical in others.

| Perry | Montague |

Neutral Monism—The theory that reality is neither physical nor spiritual, but is of a third type which expresses itself sometimes as spirit, sometimes as matter.

| Spinoza | Perry |
| James | Montague |

Nominalism—The theory that universal concepts are merely names, or impulses of the voice.

| Eric of Auxerre | William of Ockham | Buridan |
| Roscelin | | Pierre d'Ailly |

Occasionalism—The theory that matter and spirit do not interact causally; what happens in one is the occasion for something to happen in the other, both of which are brought about by a higher being (*see also Parallelism*).

| Geulincx | Malebranche |

Optimism—The view that this is the best of all possible universes or that occurrences will work out to the best possible results in the long run.

Zoroaster	Paul	Thomas Aquinas
Plato	Augustine	Leibniz
Jesus		Royce

Panpsychism—The view that all the universe is pervaded by life and soul.

| Thales | Telesio | Clifford |
| Anaxagoras | Fechner | Ward |

Pantheism—The belief that the universe taken as a whole is God.

| Zeno (Stoic) | Marcus Aurelius | Theodoric |
| Epictetus | Duns Scotus | William of Conches |

Joachim	Spinoza	Rosmini
Amalric	Toland	Lamennais
David of Dinant	Coleridge	Feuerbach
S. Franck	Schopenhauer	Ruge
Bruno		Spir

Parallelism—Similar to occasionalism, this school of philosophy emphasizes the thought that mental and physical phenomena run parallel to each other.

Spinoza	Fouillée
Lange	Jodl

Personalism—The theory that the ultimate constituents of reality are persons. All facts are contained in some person's experience.

Howison	Calkins	Vaihinger
Rashdall	Bowne	Brightman

Pessimism—In opposition to optimism, Pessimism holds that this is the worst of all possible worlds; or all things work ultimately to evil.

Ecclesiastes	von Hartmann
Schopenhauer	Taine

Phenomenalism—The theory that the world is made up of mere appearances with nothing substantial beneath them.

Comte	Renouvier	Mach

Physicalism—This school lays less stress upon matter than upon energy in reference to the ultimate reality. This is a more recent term than *Materialism*.

Priestley	Ostwald

Pluralism—The view that there are numerous (more than two) kinds of irreducible reality.

Empedocles	Leibniz	Howison
Anaxagoras	Herbart	Bowne
Leucippus	James	Pringle-Pattison
Democritus		

Positivism—A view which emphasizes positive assertions rather than negative ones and finds positive content in sense data.

Comte	Jodl	Durkheim	von Mises
Buckle	Mach	Poincaré	
Ardigò	Tönnies	Dewey	

Pragmatism—The theory that the test of the truth of a belief is in the way in which it works, the latter being left to the judgment of the believer in the idea, as well as the choice of what idea is tested (*see also Instrumentalism*).

Peirce	Tufts
James	Boodin

Rationalism—The doctrine that thought is the clew to the nature of reality and of ethical good.

Heraclitus	Zeno (Stoic)	Wolff
Parmenides	Duns Scotus	Wollaston
Zeno (Eleatic)	Averroes	Tindal
Plato	Descartes	Herbart
Aristotle	Spinoza	Hegel
Clement of	Toland	Caird
Alexandria	Leibniz	Bradley

Realism—The theory that reality is ultimately independent of any knowledge of its existence.

Anselm	William of	Herbart	Moore
Odo	Conches	Hamilton	Meinong
William of	Amalric	Spencer	Boodin
Champeaux	Alexander of	Brentano	S. Alexander
Bernard	Hales	Husserl	Broad
Gilbert	Machiavelli	Russell	Wild

Relativism—This theory of knowledge, reality, and conduct opposes any conception of absoluteness.

Prodicus	Comte	Renouvier
Bayle	Mansel	Dewey
Mandeville	Abbot	

Scientific Empiricism—This theory of knowledge emphasizes scientific method and appeals to sense evidence.

Schlick	Ayer	Goodman	Nagel
Wittgenstein	Ryle	Flew	Wiener
Carnap	Feigl	Sellars	Woodger
Reichenbach	Black	Toulmin	Pap

Skepticism—The belief that human efforts to know are futile.

Cratylus	Timon	Aenesidemus
Pyrrho	Carneades	Sextus Empiricus

Nicholas of	Montaigne	Glanvil
Autrecourt		Hume

Solipsism—The view that one's own experience is the only fact reliably verifiable.

> An accusation made against Berkeley, but not admitted by him; it was admitted at times by Hume.

Subjective Idealism—See *Solipsism*.

Theism—The belief that the conception of God can be defined and used in an acceptable fashion.

Ikhnaton	Abelard	Newton
Amos	Bernard	Berkeley
Xenophanes	Descartes	Leibniz
Aristotle	Hobbes	Newman
Augustine	Pascal	Balfour
Mohammed	Cudworth	Martineau
Anselm		James

Transcendental Idealism—See *Critical Idealism*.

Transcendentalism—The belief that there is an ultimate reality that transcends human experience.

Aristobulus	Hugh of St. Victor
Philo	Emerson

Utilitarianism—The ethical doctrine that the good of any action is tested by its contribution to results, especially to human happiness.

Gay	J. S. Mill	Wright
Bentham	Sidgwick	Stephen
James Mill		Rashdall

Voluntarism—The theory that reality is of the nature of will rather than knowledge, feeling, or inert matter.

D. Scotus	Schopenhauer	Tönnies
Kant	Renouvier	Rickert
Fichte	Bain	Ward
Herbart	von Hartmann	Royce
Maine de Biran		

Reference Books

Encyclopedias

D. Runes, *Dictionary of Philosophy*
Encyclopaedia Britannica
Encyclopedia Americana
International Encyclopedia
Catholic Encyclopedia
Jewish Encyclopedia
Encyclopedia of Islam

General Histories of Philosophy

Boas, G., *The Major Traditions of European Philosophy*, Harper, 1929.
Brinton, C., *Ideas and Men*, Prentice-Hall, 1950.
Fuller, B. A. G., and McMurrin, S. M., *History of Philosophy*, Holt, 3rd ed., 1955.
Jones, W. T., *History of Western Philosophy*, Harcourt, 1952.
Lamprecht, S., *Our Philosophical Traditions*, Appleton, 1955.
Mayer, F., *History of Philosophy*, American Book, 1951.
Radhakrishnan, S., *et al.*, *History of Philosophy, Eastern and Western*, Macmillan, 1953.
Randall, J. H., and Buchler, J., *Philosophy: An Introduction*, Barnes & Noble, 1942.
Sahakian, W. and S., *Ideas of The Great Philosophers*, Barnes & Noble, 1966.
Thilly, F., and Wood, L., *History of Philosophy*, Holt, 3rd ed., 1957.
Turner, W., *History of Philosophy*, Ginn, 1929.
Ueberweg-Heinze, *et al.*, *Geschichte der Philosophie*, Mittler, 1916.

Special Periods

Benrubi, I., *Contemporary Thought in France*, Williams and Norgate, 1926.

Reference Books

Boas, G., *Dominant Themes of Modern Philosophy*, Ronald, 1957.

Burnett, J., *Greek Philosophy, Thales to Plato*, Macmillan, 1914.

Gilson, E., *The Spirit of Medieval Philosophy*, Scribners, 1936.

Goodenough, E. R., *An Introduction to Philo*, Yale Univ., 1940.

Hamison, L. H., *Russian Marxists and the Origins of Bolshevism,* Harvard, 1955.

Havens, G., *The Age of Ideas* [French], Holt, 1955.

Hawkins, D. J. B., *Crucial Problems of Modern Philosophy*, Sheed, 1958.

Hicks, R. D., *Stoic and Epicurean*, Scribner, 1910.

Hudson, W. H., *The Story of the Renaissance*, Cassell, 1912.

Inge, W. R., *The Philosophy of Plotinus*, Longmans, 1948.

Jones, W. T., *Contemporary Thought in Germany*, New York, 1931.

Latourette, K., *A History of the Expansion of Christianity: The First Five Centuries*, Harper, 1937.

Leff, G., *Mediaeval Thought from Augustine to Ockham*, Penguin, 1958.

Lévy-Bruhl, L., *History of Modern Philosophy in France*, Open Court, 1899.

Mace, C. A., *British Philosophy in Mid-Century*, Macmillan, 1957.

Mason, C., *Socrates, the Man Who Dared to Ask*, Beacon, 1953.

Metz, R., *A Hundred Years of British Philosophy*, Macmillan.

Oates, W. J., *The Stoic and Epicurean Philosophers*, Random House, 1940.

Patrick, M. M., *The Greek Skeptics*, Columbia Univ., 1940.

Perry, R. B., *Present Philosophical Tendencies*, Longmans, 1912.

Rogers, A. K., *English and American Philosophy Since 1800*, Macmillan, 1922.

Ross, W. D., *Aristotle*, Barnes & Noble, 1955.

Roth, Leon, *Spinoza*, Barnes & Noble, 1929.

Royce, J., *The Spirit of Modern Philosophy*, Houghton Mifflin, 1892.

Runes, D., *Twentieth Century Philosophy*, Philosophical Library, 1943.

Schneider, H. W., *A History of American Philosophy*, Columbia Univ., 1946.

Simmons, J. S., *Continuity and Change in Russian Soviet Thought*, Harvard, 1955.

Stern, A., *Sartre, His Philosophy and Psychoanalysis*, Liberal Arts, 1953.

Warnock, G. J., *English Philosophy since 1900*, Oxford, 1958.

Zeller, E., *Plato and the Older Academy*, Longmans, 1888.

Sources in English

Adler, M. J., *The Idea of Freedom,* Doubleday, 1958.

Avey, A. E., *Readings in Philosophy,* Appleton, 1924.

Bailey, C., *Epicurus, the Extant Remains,* Oxford, 1926.

Bakewell, C. M., *Source Book in Ancient Philosophy,* Scribner, 1939.

Barton, G. A., *Archaeology and the Bible,* American Sunday School Union, 1937.

Budge, E. A. Wallis, *The Book of the Dead: Introduction and Chapters I-XV,* Barnes & Noble, 1951.

Burnett, Whit, ed., *This is My Philosophy* [of twenty living philosophers], Harper, 1957.

Burtt, E. A., *The English Philosophers from Bacon to Mill,* Random House, 1939.

Bury, J. B., *Sextus Empiricus,* Loeb Classical Library, 1933-36.

Cassirer, E., *et al., The Renaissance Philosophy of Man,* Univ. of Chicago, 1948.

Clark, G. H., *Selections from Hellenistic Philosophy,* Crofts, 1940.

Demos, R., *The Dialogues of Plato Translated into English,* Random House, 1937, Introduction by Demos; trans. by Jowett.

Freeman, K., *Ancilla to the Early Greek Philosophers,* Harvard Univ., 1948.

Great Ages of Philosophy, Mentor, 1956.

Hartshorne, C. L., and Reese, W. L., *Philosophers Speak of God,* Chicago, 1953.

Lewy, H., *Philo, Selections,* Oxford, 1946.

Martin, Gottfried, *Kant's Metaphysics and Theory of Science,* Barnes & Noble, 1955.

Martin, H., *The Inquiring Mind: Introductory Philosophic Studies,* Barnes & Noble, 1947.

McKeon, R., ed., *The Basic Works of Aristotle,* Random House, 1941.

Nahm, M., *Selections from Early Greek Philosophy,* Crofts, 1947.

Oates, W. J., *Basic Works of St. Augustine,* Random House, 1948.

Paton, H. J., *The Moral Law or Kant's Groundwork of the Metaphysic of Morals,* Barnes & Noble, 1950.

Pegis, A. C., *The Basic Writings of St. Thomas,* Random House, 1945.

Rackham, H., *Aristotle's Ethics for English Readers,* Barnes & Noble, 1943.

——, *Cicero, De Natura Deorum and Academica,* Loeb Classical Library, 1933.

Rand, B., *The Classical Moralists,* Houghton Mifflin, 1950.

——, *Modern Classical Philosophers,* Houghton Mifflin, 1936.

Randall, J. H., *et al., Readings in Philosophy,* Barnes & Noble, 1950.

Robinson, D. S., *Anthology of Modern Philosophers,* Crowell, 1938.

Russell, Bertrand, *Mysticism and Logic,* Barnes & Noble, 1954.

Ryle, G., *Concept of Mind,* Barnes & Noble, 1949.

Schopenhauer, Arthur, *The Essential Schopenhauer,* Barnes & Noble, 1962.

Smith, T. V., *Philosophers Speak for Themselves,* Univ. of Chicago, 1934.

Vaihinger, H., *The Philosophy of "As If,"* Barnes & Noble, 1935.

The following selections from the Modern Student's Library, published by Scribner

Aristotle	Hobbes	Medieval Philosophy
Bacon	Hume	Plato
Berkeley	Kant	Schopenhauer
Descartes	Locke	Spinoza
Hegel		

The following titles from the Modern Library, published by Random House:

Dante, *Divine Comedy*

Dewey, *Human Nature and Conduct*

Edman, *The Philosophy of Santayana*

Emerson, *Essays*

Machiavelli, *The Prince*

Marx, *Capital*

Nietzsche, *Thus Spake Zarathustra*

Pascal, *Thoughts*

Philosophy of William James

Russell, *Selected Papers*

Voltaire, *Candide*

The following works from Everyman's Library, published by E. P. Dutton:

Bede, *Ecclesiastical History*

Boehme, *The Signature of All Things*

Boyle, *The Sceptical Chymist*
Burke, *Reflections on the French Revolution*
Butler, *Analogy of Religion*
Carlyle, *Sartor Resartus*
Darwin, *The Origin of Species*
Epictetus, *Moral Discourses*
à Kempis, *Imitation of Christ*
The Koran
Leibniz, *Philosophical Writings*
Lessing, *Laocoön*
Lucretius, *On the Nature of Things*
Marcus Aurelius, *Meditations*
Thomas More, *Utopia*
Newman, *Apologia pro Vita Sua*
Plutarch of Chaeronea, *Moralia*
Rousseau, *The Social Contract and Discourses*
Smith, *Wealth of Nations*
Swedenborg, *The True Christian Religion*
Thoreau, *Walden*
Xenophon, *Cyropaedia*

Index

Abarbanel, Isaac ben Jehudah, 114
Abbot, Francis E., 221f.
Abelard, Peter, 86, 87, 90
Abraham, 93
Abraham ben David, 90
Abraham ben Ezra, 89
Absolute, 69, 130, 140, 141, 160, 173,
    174, 179-181, 184, 187, 199, 207, 218,
    219, 225, 227-229, 233, 239, 242, 244,
    249, 253, 255, 259, 265
Abstraction, extensive, 267, 270
Academics, The (Cicero), 46
Academy, 20, 23, 29, 30, 43, 67, 72,
    113
Action (Blondel), 229
Address to the Greeks (Tatian), 56
Addresses on Religion, 175
Addresses to the German Nation, 174
Adelard, 78
Adelard of Bath, 86
Adler, Alfred, 238, 249f.
Adler, Mortimer J., 305-306
Aenesidemus, 46
*Aesthetic as Science of Experience and
    Universal Linguistic*, 243
Aesthetica (Baumgarten), 157
Aesthetics, 36, 157, 162, 169
*Aesthetics, or the Science of the Beauti-
    ful* (Vischer), 194
Against Celsus (Origen), 60
Against Heresies (Irenaeus), 57
Against the Academics, 68
Against the Christians (Julian), 66
Against the Ethicists, 58
Against the Logicians, 58
Against the Nations (Arnobius), 63
Against Wolfhelm (Manegold), 85
Agassiz, L., 196
Agnosticism, 203, 214, 261
Aim and Structure of Physical Science,
    302

Alan, 92
Albert the Great, 76, 88, 94-98, 101
Albo, Joseph, 112
Alcibiades, 155
Alcuin, 78
Aldhelm, 77
Alexander, S., 262f.
Alexander V, Pope, 111
Alexander of Aphrodisias, 59
Alexander of Hales, 76, 94f., 97
Alexander the Great, 30, 31, 48
Alhazen, 90
Allegorical Interpretation of Genesis
    (Philo Judaeus), 49
Allegory, 49, 64
Allen, Ethan, 170
Almaric of Bena, 93
Ambrose, 66, 67, 68, 78
Amelius Gentilianus, 62
Amenemope, 6
*American Philosophical Addresses,
    1700-1900*, 283
*American Social Thought, The Revolt
    Against Formalism*, 286
America's Progressive Philosophy, 299
Americus Vespucius, 111
Ammonius Saccas, 59, 61
Amos, 8
Analogy, 153
Analysis of Sensation (Mach), 222
*Analysis of the Phenomena of the
    Human Mind* (James Mill), 184
Analytic Psychology (Stout), 232
Anaxagoras, 15
Anaximander, 11, 12
Anaximenes, 11, 12
Ancient Metaphysics, 164
Andronicus, 45
Anselm, 84, 86, 91, 95, 106
Anti-Claudian (Alan), 92
Antinomy, 167

Antiquities (Josephus), 73
Antisthenes, 23
Antitheses (Nicomachus), 54
Aphraates, 65
Apocrypha, 67
Apollinaris, 65
Apollonius, 74
Apologia (Pico), 115
Apology (Justin), 55
Apology (Plato), 23
Apology (Xenophon), 29
A posteriori, 166, 168
Apostolic succession, 53, 57
Appearance and Reality, 228
A priori, 166, 168, 202, 210, 222, 230,
    239, 242, 251, 256, 269, 275
Aquasparta, Matthew of, 103
Arcana Coelestia (Swedenborg), 157
Archelaus, 16
Archimedes, 46
Archiv für Sozialwissenschaft, 263
Ardigò, Roberto, 208
Arianism, 66
Aristippus, 23
Aristobulus, 44
Aristocles, 23
Ariston, 23
Aristophanes, 22
Aristotelianism, 83, 121, 132, 198, 212,
    260, 270
Aristotelicae   Animadversationes, 119
Aristotle, 20, 30ff., 36, 38, 45, 46, 52, 54,
    56, 59, 63, 65, 67, 73, 74, 76, 78, 80,
    81, 82, 86, 88, 90, 91-101, 104, 106,
    108, 109, 111, 113, 115, 116, 126, 136,
    149, 154, 166, 190, 220, 248, 261, 262,
    278
Aristotle's Theory of Knowledge, 260
Arithmetic (Diophantus), 71
Arius, 65
Arkesilaus, 43
Arnauld, 136
Arnobius, 63
Ars Magna (Lully), 102
Art, 182, 206, 212, 243, 259, 276

Art and Freedom, 280
Artaxerxes II, 28
Asceticism, 62, 66, 86, 134, 183
Association, 154, 156, 172, 184, 198, 207,
    236, 256, 258
Assyrian Law Codes, 7
Assyrian Tablets, 8
Astronomy, 12, 16, 18, 29, 71, 72, 97,
    110, 112, 114, 115, 121, 128, 157, 165
Astronomy, Handbook on, 104
Athanasius, 65
Atheism, 156, 233
Athenaeum (Schlegel), 175
Athens, 17
Atom, 17, 22, 40, 45, 89, 108, 133, 158,
    200, 207, 270
Augustine, 48, 66, 67, 68f., 78, 79, 82,
    84, 94-96, 104, 106, 117, 129, 276
Augustinus (Jansen), 129
Aurora (Boehme), 125
Autobiography (Jefferson), 183
Avenarius, Richard, 195, 225
Averroes, 91, 109, 221
Averroism, 101, 102, 109, 115
Avicebron (ibn-Gabirol), 83, 89, 95
Avicenna, 81, 118
Ayer, Alfred J., 276

Baba, 6
Babylonian Tablets, 5
Bacon, Francis, 124, 126, 133, 135, 141,
    152, 172, 181
Bacon, Roger, 96
Bahya, 82
Bain, Alexander, 197f., 215
Balfour, A. J., 217
Balz, Albert G. A., 295-296
Barnabas, 51
Barth, K., 239, 278
Bartholomew the Englishman, 94
Basis of Induction, The, 209
Bauer, Bruno, 190
Baumgardt, David, 296
Baumgarten, A. G., 157
Bayle, Pierre, 143

Index

Bazaar of Heraclides, The, 71

Beattie, James, 163

Beauty, 26, 27, 61, 158, 163, 169, 174, 206, 229

Becket, Thomas à, 90

Bede the Venerable, 77

Behavior (Watson), 257

Behaviorism, 257, 264

Being and Nothing (Sartre), 280

Being and Time (Heidegger), 269

Beneke, F. E., 176, 183

Bentham and the Ethics of Today, 296

Bentham, J., 153, 171

Berdyaev, N., 239, 266

Berenger, 82

Bergson, H., 209, 238, 248f., 262, 265, 276, 277

Berkeley, George, 147f., 150, 154, 172, 173, 216, 222, 256, 264

Bernard of Chartres, 87-89, 93

Between Physics and Philosophy (Frank), 279

Beyond Good and Evil, 223

Biblical criticism, 133, 139

Biblical Religion and the Search for Ultimate Reality, 293

Biel, G., 113, 117

Biographia Literaria, 181

Biographical History of Philosophy (Lewes), 213

Black, Max, 285-286

Blanshard, Brand, 278f.

Blau, Joseph, 283

Blondel, M., 229

Boas, George, 288-289

Body and Blood of the Lord, On (Lanfranc), 83

Body and Blood of the Lord, The (Paschasius Radbertus), 78

Body and Mind (McDougall), 254

Boehme, J., 125

Boethius, 72f., 80, 89, 92, 99

Boethius, On, 89

Bolingbroke, Viscount, 155, 159

Bonaventure, 95, 97, 103, 276

Boodin, J., 254

Book of Beliefs and Convictions, 81

Book of the Dead, 4

Book of Deuteronomy, 9

Book of Gomorrha, 82

Book of The Kazars, The, 89

Booklet on the Rational Use of Reason (Gerbert), 81

Boole, George, 196, 211, 217, 218, 227

Bosanquet, Bernard, 210, 224, 235, 275

Boscovich, Joseph, 160

Boutroux, Emile, 209, 212, 229

Bowne, B. P., 238, 250

Boyle, Robert, 135, 146

Bradley, Francis H., 210, 228, 235, 241

Brentano, Franz, 212, 234, 247

Brevity of Life (Seneca), 51

Bridgman, Percy, 287-288

Brightman, Edgar S., 271

Brittany, Roscelin of, 86

Broad, C. D., 267

Brouwer, L. E. J., 238, 251

Bruno, Giordano, 121, 139

Brunschvicg, Leon, 251

Buckle, H. T., 199, 214

Buechner, L., 197

Buridan, John, 109

Burke, Edmund, 155, 158f., 164

Burthogge, Richard, 142f.

Butler, Joseph, 153

Cabanis, 171

Caird, Edward, 225, 272

Caligula (Emperor), 51

Calkins, Mary W., 238, 249

Calvin, John, 119

Campanella, 126f., 129

Candide (Voltaire), 161

Cantor, Georg, 231

Capella, Martianus, 71

Cardano, Girolamo, 119

Carlyle, Thomas, 176, 187

Carnap, Rudolf, 238, 261, 274

Carneades, 43, 44, 45, 46

Cassiodorus, 73

Cassirer, Ernst, 239, 247, 305

Categories (Aristotle), 31
Category, 31, 166
Catholic Faith (Isidore), 74
Causality, 42, 46, 126, 135, 154, 162, 167, 170, 172, 185, 192, 206, 211, 221
Cause, 32, 57, 61, 69, 100, 101, 108, 114, 122, 129, 133, 210, 220, 276
Celestial and Ecclesiastical Hierarchy (Pseudo-Dionysius), 72
Celestial Mysteries (Swedenborg), 157
Chalcidius, 64
Chance, 32, 191
Change, 13-16, 23, 32, 33, 44
Characteristics of Men, Manners, Opinions and Times, 148
Charlemagne, 78
Charles I (England), 134
Charles II (England), 134, 135
Charles III (Naples), 152
Charles Gustavus, 138
Charmides (Plato), 24
Charron, Pierre, 124
Chosroes, King of Persia, 73
Christ, 65, 75, 93, 110, 120
Christianity, 54, 58, 115, 127, 142, 179, 190, 191, 213, 217, 223, 225, 267, 272, 278
Christianity as Old as the Creation, (Tindal), 152
Christian Faith, On the, 66
Christian Realism and Political Problems, 301
Christianity not Mysterious, 143
Chronicle (Eusebius), 64
Chronology, 64, 72, 77, 78
Chrysippus, 43
Chrysostom, 78
Church, 53, 54, 57, 58, 60, 61, 64, 68, 73, 89, 107, 113, 116, 117, 163, 187, 189, 190
Church, On the (Huss), 111
Cicero, 45, 68, 73, 155, 159
City of God (Augustine), 70, 116
City of the Sun, 126f., 129
Clarke, Samuel, 146, 151

Classification, 27, 31, 63
Clavis Universalis (Collier), 149
Cleanthes, 43
Clement of Alexandria, 58, 59, 63
Clement of Rome, 52
Clifford, W. K., 216
Clitomachus, 44
Cohen, Hermann, 195, 209
Cohen, Morris, 238, 272
Coins, Treatise on (Nicholas), 110
Coleridge, S. T., 76, 176, 181, 206
Collier, Arthur, 149
Collins, Anthony, 149
Columbus, Christopher, 111
Commedia (Siger of Brabant), 101
Comment on the Commentaries, 296
Commentaries on Aristotle, 110
Commentaries on Aristotle's Ethics, and Physics (Buridan), 109
Commentary on Aristotle, 90
Commentary on the Apocalypse, 92
Commentary on the Book of Sentences (William of Ockham), 109
Commentary on the Dream of Scipio (Macrobius), 67, 85
Commentary on Matthew, 78
Commentary on Paul's Epistles, 71
Commentary on the Pentateuch, 109
Commentary on Plato's Timaeus (Chalcidius), 64
Commentary on the True and False Religion (Zwingli), 117
Common Faith, A (Dewey), 253
Common sense, 162, 184
Common Sense of the Exact Sciences, (Clifford), 217
Communist Manifesto, 193
Community and Society, 224
Compendium of Logic, 109
Comte, A., 186, 191, 199, 201, 213, 222
Concept of Mind, The, 284
Concept of Nature, The, 270
Concepts, Theories, and the Mind-body Problem, 285
Conceptualism, 87

Concerning the Cause, The Principle and the One (Bruno), 121

Concerning the Lives and Opinions of Eminent Philosophers, 59

Conciliator of the Differences of Philosophy (Peter of Abano), 104

Condillac, 158, 177

Condition of the Working Class in England (Engels), 193

Conduct, 5-9, 17, 30, 42, 44f., 47, 49f., 52f., 62, 77, 115, 171, 253

Conduct of Life, 283

Confession of Augsburg, 118

Confessions (Augustine), 69

Confessions (Rousseau), 162

Conflict, 62, 259

Congruism, 123

Conics, 71

Conscience, 110, 153, 172

Consciousness, 34, 43, 110, 205, 218, 230, 241, 267, 268

Consolations of Philosophy, 73

Constance, Council of, 111

Constantine (Emperor), 63

Constantine the African, 83

Contemplation, 35, 60

Contemporary Idealism, 251

Contingency of the Laws of Nature (Boutroux), 212

Continuity, 32, 33

Continuity and Irrational Numbers (Dedekind), 209

Corpore et Sanguine Domini, De, 83

Corpus Hermeticum, 63

Cosmic Philosophy, Outlines of, 212

Cosimo de Medici, 113

Cournot, A. A., 176, 191

Course of Positive Philosophy, 186

Cousin, A., 176, 184, 208, 210

Cratylus (Plato), 23

Creation, 7, 8, 69, 81, 87, 96, 100, 109, 125, 133, 190

Creation of the World, On the, 49

Creative Evolution (Bergson), 248

Creative Liberty (Korn), 265

Creativity, 249, 251, 258-262, 269

Creighton, J. E., 195, 235

Crescas, H., 111, 112, 114

Critical Philosophy, 261

Critical Philosophy of Kant, 225

Critique of the Evangelistic History of John (Bauer), 190

Critique of Judgment, 169, 174

Critique of Practical Reason (Kant), 168, 177

Critique of Pure Experience, 225

Critique of Pure Reason (Kant), 166, 167, 169, 172, 179

Critique of Religion and Philosophy, 306

Crito (Plato), 24

Croce, B., 239, 243f.

Cromwell, O., 132, 134

Crucial Issues in Philosophy, 302

Cudworth, R., 140, 165

Culture, 263, 271, 276

Cumberland, R., 137

Cynics, 22, 23, 29

Cyprian, 60

Cyrenaics, 22, 23, 40

Cyrus, the Younger, 28

d'Ailly, Pierre, 111

d'Alembert, J. L., 160

Damascius, 72, 73, 74

Dante, 36, 91, 93, 101, 103

Darwin, C., 195, 200, 202, 215, 216

Darwin, E., 164

David Hume on Belief, or Idealism and Realism (Jacobi), 171

David of Dinant, 95

Decisions of the Lords of Council and Session (Monboddo), 164

Dedekind, Richard, 209

Defender of Peace, 107, 109

Defense of Philosophic Doubt, 217

Definition, 21, 27, 31, 84, 261

Degrees of Knowledge, 278

Deism, 127, 142, 143, 146, 149, 152, 156, 161, 162, 170

de Maistre, Joseph, 181
Democritus, 22
Demonstratio Evangelica, 64
De Morgan, Augustus, 194
Deposition (Arius), 65
Derby, 221
De Sanctis, 207
Descartes, 124, 129, 136, 138, 139, 141, 146, 147, 149, 276, 277
Descartes and the Modern Mind, 295
Descent of Man (Darwin), 200
Design, 16, 177
Desire, 234
Destruction of Destruction, 91
Destruction of the Philosophers, 86
Determinism, 17, 102, 149
Determinism and Freedom in the Age of Modern Science, 290
de Tracy, D., 177
Deustua, A., 226
Development and Purpose, 232
Dewey, John, 229, 250, 252, 305
Dialectic, 87, 180, 193, 205, 228, 233
Dialogue on Christianity, 122
Dialogue on the Two Greatest Systems of the Universe, 128
Dialogues (Plato), 113
Dialogues Concerning Natural Religion (Hume), 154, 155
Diatessaron (Tatian), 15, 56, 65
Dictionary of National Biography (Stephen), 214
Dictionnaire Historique et Critique (Bayle), 143
Diderot, D., 158, 160, 161
Dietrich of Freiburg, 104
Differences Among the Various Academics (Numenius), 55
Difficulties and Solutions of First Principles (Damascius), 73
Digby, K., 182
Dignity of Man, Oration on, 115
Dilthey, W., 219, 257, 262
Diogenes of Sinope, 29
Diogenes Laërtius, 59

Dionysius Exiguus, 72
Diophantus, 71
Dioptrics (Descartes), 132
Dirichlet, P. G. L., 209
Discourse on the Causes of Inequality among Men (Rousseau), 161
Discourse Concerning the Being and Attributes of God (Clarke), 146
Discourse on Free Thinking, 149
Discourse on Method, 130
Discourses on Livy, The, 116
Disputationes Metaphysicae, 123
Dissertation Concerning the Fundamental Principles of Virtue or Morality (Gay), 153
Dissertation on the Progress of Ethical Philosophy (Mackintosh), 186
Divination, On (Cicero), 46
Divine Dialogues (More, H.), 137
Divine Institutions (Arnobius), 64
Divine Names, Concerning, 72
Division of Nature, On the, 79
Division of Social Work, On the (Durkheim), 229
Docta Ignorantia, De, 113
Doctrine of Youth (Foerster), 246
Donation of Constantine, 113
Donatus, 67
Doubt, 130, 133, 217
Dream (Lucian), 55
Driesch, H., 239, 250, 277
Dualism, 8, 12, 131, 158, 173, 254, 256, 266, 271
Ducasse, C. J., 291-292
Dühring, E., 204
Duns Scotus, 106, 111
Durkheim, E., 195, 229
Duties, On (Cicero), 46
Duties of the Heart (Bahya), 82
Duty, 168, 177, 209, 228, 272
Dynamic Idealism (Lloyd), 235

Ecclesiastical History (Evagrius), 74
Ecclesiastical History of the English Nation (Bede), 77

Ecclesiastes, 44

Eckhart, Johannes, 104

Eclogues (Stobaeus), 72

Education, 23, 36, 100, 103, 117, 161, 173, 254

Education of Cyrus (Xenophon), 29

Edwards, Jonathan, 157, 170

Ego and His Own, The (Stirner), 194

Ehrenfels, Christian von, 234

Einstein, Albert, 287, 305

Either-Or (Kierkegaard), 193

El Amarna, 7

Eleatic, 16, 23

Election, 117, 157

Elementary Quanta of Matter and Electricity, On the (Planck), 240

Elements (Euclid), 86

Elements of Ideology, 177

Elements of Metaphysics, 244

Elements of Moral Science (Beattie), 163

Elements of Philosophy, 160

Elements of the Philosophy of the Human Mind (Stewart), 172

Elements of Psycho-physics, 201

Elements of Universal Jurisprudence (Pufendorf), 138

Elihu, 39

Eliot, George, 213

Eloise, 87

Eloquent Peasant, 6

Emanation, 69, 104, 121

Emergence, 216, 263, 264, 268

Emergent, 213

Emergent Evolution (Morgan), 264

Emerson, R. W., 176, 187

Emile (Rousseau), 161

Emotions and the Will, The, 198

Empathy, 223, 224

Empedocles, 15, 16

Empiricism, 40, 86, 120, 154, 198, 215, 216, 227

Enchiridion Harmonikes, 54

Encyclopédie (Diderot), 160, 161

Ends, On (Cicero), 46

Encomium Moriae (Erasmus), 115

Energy, 220, 230, 250, 267

Engels, F., 176, 193, 205, 251

Enneads (Plotinus), 62

Enquiry Concerning the Principles of Morals (Hume), 155

Eodem et Diverso, De (Adelard), 87

Ephesus, 71

Epictetus, 53

Epicurus, 40, 41, 45

Epimenides, 273

Epiphenomenon, 203

Epistle of Barnabas, 51

Epistle of the Hebrews, 51

Epitome and Collection from Ockham (Biel), 113

Erasmus, D., 115, 117

Eric of Auxerre, 80

Erigena, 79, 80, 93, 95

Error, 40, 130, 231, 257, 267, 271

Essais De Critique Générale, 197

Esprit, De l' (Helvétius), 160

Esprit des Lois (Montesquieu), 156

Essay on the Human Understanding (Locke), 141, 142, 150

Essay on Man (Pope), 156

Essays (Montaigne), 120

Essays, by Tarski, on Logic, Semantics, and Metamathematics, 303

Essays in Conceptual Analysis, 295

Essays in East-West Philosophy, 297

Esse et Essentia, De, 104

Essence, 246

Essence of Christianity, 191

Essence and Substance of God, On the (William of Champaux), 86

Essence of the Soul (Alcuin), 78

Essentia et Substantia Dei, De, 86

Estetica (Vasconcelos), 277

Eternal Values, The, 251

Ether, Atoms and the Sun, 216

Ethics, 5, 6, 7, 8, 14, 16, 19, 21, 22, 23, 29, 30, 34, 38, 41, 46, 51, 107, 110, 127, 137, 139, 154, 156, 170, 174, 178, 183, 184, 188, 189, 190, 193, 201, 203,

206, 209, 210, 215, 216, 218, 219, 224, 228, 233, 244, 248, 252, 265, 272
Ethics (Aristotle), 34
Ethics (Dewey and Tufts), 250
Ethics (Geulincx), 137
Ethics (Hartmann, N.), 268
Ethics Demonstrated in the Manner of Geometry (Spinoza), 139, 140
Être et le Néant, l' (Sartre), 280
Eucharist, 74, 117
Eucken, Rudolf, 24, 238, 258
Euclid, 22, 86, 90
Eudoxus, 29
Euhemerus, 42
Euler, Leonhard, 163
Eusebius, 64
Euthydemus, 25
Euthyphro (Plato), 34
Evagrius, 74
Evans, Marian, 213
Evidences of the Christian Religion (Beattie), 163
Evil, 69, 125, 151, 183, 272
Evolution, 13, 15, 16, 40, 42, 119, 131, 133, 165, 179, 180, 186, 197, 200, 201, 203, 208, 212, 213, 214, 215, 219, 221, 223, 225, 227, 232, 236, 240, 244, 248, 253, 254, 262, 263, 264, 269, 272
Évolutionnisme des Idées-forces, l' (Fouillée), 226
Exalted Faith, 90
Examination of Sir William Hamilton's Philosophy (J. S. Mill), 192
Excellence of Scripture, The, 103
Excluded Middle, 14, 251
Exigit Ordo Executionis, 108
Existence of Evil (Proclus), 72
Existentialism, 276, 278, 279
Experience, 225, 234, 253
Experience and Nature (Dewey), 253
Experience and Thought, 224
Experiment, 97, 104, 114, 126, 164, 192, 243, 250
Experimental Studies in Visual Perception of Movements, 256

Evaluations (Korn), 265
Exploratio Philosophica, 204
Exposition of Porphyry, On the, 88
Exposition of the Theory of Chance and Probability (Cournot), 191
Expression of Emotion in Man and Animals, The (Darwin), 200

Fable of the Bees (Mandeville), 146
Faith, 50, 57, 58, 84, 87, 91, 99, 107-108, 111, 116, 117, 118, 121, 135, 144, 155, 170, 177, 178, 198, 207, 217, 227, 246, 257, 265, 267, 278
Faith and Reality, 294
Faith, Hope and Charity, 78
Faith, the Trinity and the Incarnation, 302
Farabi, al-, 80, 90
Fate (Proclus), 72
Fate, On, 59
Fate, On (Cicero), 46
Fechner, G. T., 195, 200
Feeling, 170, 270, 276
Feigl, Herbert, 285
Feuerbach, L., 176, 190, 205
Fichte, J. G., 172, 175, 179, 182, 187, 194, 227, 251
Ficino, M., 113
Fiction, 255
Fidanza, John, 97
Filosofia Critica, 261
Final Causes (Janet), 211
First Principles (Spencer), 201
Fischer, K., 190, 197
Fiske, J., 212
Flesh of Christ, On the, 58
Flew, A. G. N., 295
Flood, 6, 7, 8
Florence, 103, 113, 128, 191
Florilegium (Stobaeus), 72
Foerster, F. W., 238, 245
Force, 41, 160, 186, 200, 201, 203
Force and Matter (Buechner), 197
Formalism in Ethics and the Material Ethics in Value (Scheler), 258

Index

Formal Logic (De Morgan), 194
Formally Undecidable Propositions (Gödel), 273
Formation of Vegetable Mould, 200
Forms and Principles of the Sensible and Intelligible World (Kant), 165
Forms of Life (Spranger), 257
Formulary of Mathematics, 230
Fouillée, A., 226
Foundations of Belief (Balfour), 217
Foundations of Ethics (Ross), 278
Foundations of Geometry, 236
Foundations of Mathematics, 273
Foundations of the Metaphysics of Morals (Kant), 168
Foundations of Psychology, Essay on (Maine de Biran), 179
Foundations of the Theory of Transfinite Groups (Cantor), 231
Fountain of Knowledge, 77
Fountain of Life, The (Gabirol), 83
Four Books of Sentences, The, 90
Fox, George, 140
Fragment on Government, 296
Franck, S., 118
Frank, P., 239, 279
Freedom, 22, 23, 24, 35, 42, 46, 69, 70, 71, 79, 84, 87, 102, 109, 114, 118, 119, 125, 129, 133, 157, 165, 167, 169, 170, 175, 178, 180, 181, 187, 193, 197, 202, 206, 212, 221, 224, 226, 236, 239, 240, 265, 271
Freedom and History, the Semantics of Philosophic Controversies, 297
Freedom of Thought, 116, 119, 139, 144, 161, 163, 183, 188
Freedom of the Will (Edwards), 157
Free Man's Worship, A, 245
Free Religion Association, 222
Free Will, On the (Pelagius), 71
Frege, Gottlob, 217
Freud, S., 258
Friendship, S., 258
Friendship, On (Cicero), 46
Fries, J. F., 176, 177

Fundamental Doctrines (Origen), 60
Fundamental Principles of the Whole Science of Knowledge (Fichte), 173
Fundamentals of Philosophy, 267

Gabirol, ibn-, 83
Galen, 56, 90, 118
Galileo, 33, 128, 135
Gassendi, 133
Gaunilon, 84
Gay, John, 153
Gemeinschaft und Gesellschaft, 224
General Theory of Knowledge, 261
Generalization of the Gravitational Theory, 287
Genesis of the Old Catholic Church, The (Ritschl), 199
Genetic Method, 183, 271
Gentile, Giovanni, 238, 258
George III, 163
Gerard of Cremona, 90
Gerbert, 81
Gerson, John, 111
Gerson, Levi ben, 109
Gestalt, 256, 268, 271
Gestalt Psychology (Köhler), 271
Geyser, Joseph, 239, 260
Ghazali, al-, 86, 91
Gilbert de la Porrée, 88
Gilgamesh Epic, 6
Gilson, Étienne, 276
Gioberti, Vincenzo, 176, 189
Glanvil, Joseph, 135
Gnosticism, 56, 57, 60, 63
Gobineau, 195, 196
God, 6, 7, 8, 13, 16, 26, 27, 34, 42, 44, 49, 53-57, 59, 60, 61, 63, 69, 70, 72, 76, 80, 82, 84, 87, 89, 90, 92, 93, 95, 96, 98, 100, 101, 105, 107-114, 117, 119, 121, 125, 127, 130, 139-141, 148, 150, 157, 158, 161, 163, 167, 169, 170, 173, 178, 185, 187, 189-191, 193, 194, 197, 201, 206, 210, 212, 220, 221, 225, 229, 239, 249, 250, 253, 254, 259, 263, 266, 270-272, 275, 276, 278

God and Polarity, a Synthesis of Philosophers, 300
God in the Light of Recent Philosophy (Pringle-Pattison), 259
Gods, 17, 19, 22, 40, 42, 45f., 63f.
Gödel, Kurt, 196, 238, 273
Goethe, J. W. von, 212
Goldsmith, O., 159
Good, 22-24, 26, 27, 29, 40, 41, 43, 57, 100, 113, 120, 137, 139, 163, 177, 198, 227, 228, 245, 248
Goodman, Nelson H., 294-295
Gorgias, 17, 18
Gorgias (Plato), 25
Gonthier, F. P., 179
Gospel (Barnabas), 51
Gospels, 52, 54
Gottschalk, 79
Grabmann, Martin, 255
Grace, 69, 71, 117, 118, 119, 129
Grammar of Assent (Newman), 207
Great Art (Lully), 102
Greek Tradition, The, 267
Gregory of Antioch, 74
Gregory of Tours, 74
Gregory the Great, 74
Gregory VII, 74, 85
Gregory X, 101
Grosseteste, 96
Grotius, H., 123, 127, 138, 152
Growth of Mind (Koffka), 268
Guide for the Perplexed, 92

Habakkuk, 9
Haeberlin, Paul, 253
Haeckel, E., 195, 236, 250
Halle Annual for German Art and Science (Ruge), 189
Hamann, J. G., 176
Hamilton, Sir William, 176, 184, 199
Hamilton, W. G., 159
Happiness, 22, 23, 30, 35, 39, 41, 100, 133, 137, 146, 153, 158, 178, 193
Happy Life, On the (Augustine), 68
Happy Life, The (Seneca), 51

Harmony, 16
Harmony, pre-established, 151
Harrington, James, 134
Harris, W. T., 226
Hartmann, Nicolai, 268
Hartmann, Eduard von, 206
Hastings, Warren, 159
Healing (Avicenna), 82
Hebrew, 4, 7, 8
Hebrew Patriarchal Stories, 7
Hedonism, 23, 40, 177, 214
Hegel, G. W. F., 176, 179, 182, 197, 198, 206, 208, 214, 220, 224, 225, 226, 233, 244
Heidegger, Martin, 239, 269, 279
Heidelberg, 112, 138, 195
Helmholtz, H. L. von, 202
Helvétius, 157, 160
Henry IV (Germany), 82, 85
Henry V, 85
Henry VIII (England), 117
Heracliteans, 23
Heraclitus, 13
Herbart, J. F., 178
Herbert, Lord Edward, 127
Herder, J. G., 170
Hermes Trismegistus, 63
Heroes and Hero Worship, 187
Hesoid, 13
Hexapla, 60
Hilbert, David, 236, 238
Hildebrand, 82
Hippias, 17, 18
Hippocrates, 90
History, 8, 12, 50, 77, 92, 122, 144, 152, 155, 170, 181, 190, 199, 205, 208, 215, 230, 236, 244, 266
History and Natural Science, 230
History of Ancient and Modern Literature (Schlegel), 175
History of Calamities (Abelard), 87
History of the Christian Church (Eusebius), 64
History of Civilization in England (Buckle), 199

History of Electric Science, 164
History of England (Hume), 154
History of English Thought in the Eighteenth Century (Stephen), 214
History of Ethics in Modern Philosophy (Jodl), 219
History of the Franks, 74
History of the Goths, 73
History of Ideas, Journal of the, 271
History of Materialism (Lange), 205
History of Materialism, Essays on the (Plekhanov), 231
History of Italian Literature, 208
History of Modern Philosophy, 197
History of Philosophy, 204, 291
History of Philosophy as Exact Science (Michelet), 214
History of Philosophy, Eastern and Western, 298
History of the Inductive Sciences (Whewell), 189
Hitler, 246
Hittite Code, 7
Hobbes, Thomas, 133
Hobhouse, L. T., 232
Hocking, W. E., 255
Hodgson, S. H., 234
Höffding, Harald, 239
Holbach, P. H. D. d', 163
Holy, idea of, 260
Holy Spirit, On the (Ambrose), 66
Home, Henry, 157
Homer, 13, 18, 65
Homilies (Aphraates), 65
Homme Machine, L', 156
Honolulu, 320
Honorius, Emperor, 67
Hook, Sidney, 290
Horrheim, 194
Hosea, 8
Howison, G. H., 238, 239
How to Make Ideas Clear, 216
Hugh of St. Victor, 89, 91
Huizinga, Johan, 238, 271

Humanism, 113-117, 236, 252, 253, 266, 268, 277
Humanism (Schiller), 244
Human Intellect, The (Porter), 206
Human Knowledge, On, 103
Hume, David, 153, 159, 162, 163, 165, 166, 172, 177, 192, 198, 216, 222, 264, 276
Huss, John, 111
Husserl, Edmund, 233, 239, 240, 258, 260, 269
Hutchison, Francis, 158
Huxley, T. H., 203, 264
Hylozoism, 11, 119, 236
Hymn to the Most High, 43
Hypatia, 71

Idea, 24f., 27f., 30, 80, 94, 98, 130, 140, 142, 147, 154, 180, 182, 226
Idea of Freedom, The, 306
Ideal, 204, 222, 228
Idealism, 14, 122, 132, 139, 147, 150, 170, 174, 185, 188, 198, 204, 206, 208, 210, 218-221, 225, 226, 229, 232, 233, 235, 239-245, 248-251, 254f., 266, 270, 272, 275, 278f.
Idea of Atonement in Christian Theology (Rashdall), 248
Idea of the Holy (Otto), 260
Ideas of Order and Liberty in the History of Human Thought, 226
Ideas on a Philosophy of Nature (Schelling), 174
Ideas on the Philosophy of Human History (Herder), 170
Identity, 14, 15
Ideological Differences and World Order, 282
Ignatius, 53
Ikhnaton, 7, 8
Imitation of Christ (à Kempis), 112
Immortality, 5, 25, 26, 30, 40, 42, 45, 46, 52, 55, 59, 68, 90, 91, 92, 99, 102, 107, 109, 115, 116, 120, 140, 146, 149,

153, 163, 169, 170, 171, 189, 190, 197, 201, 233, 257
Immortality of the Soul, 116
Immortality of the Soul, Of the, 155
Immortality of the Soul, On the, 94
Immortality of the Soul, The, 211
Incarnation, 45, 52, 84
Incarnation of the Word of God, 65
In Defense of Plato, 298
Index, The (Abbot, ed.), 222
Individual, 211, 250, 257, 259-261
Individualism, 193-195
Individuality, 25, 98, 107, 240
Induction, 31, 68, 99, 126, 179
Indulgences, 111, 117
Inequality of the Human Races, Essay on (Gobineau), 196
Infinite, 15, 121, 139, 146, 169
Influence of Darwin on Philosophy, The (Dewey), 253
Innate, 46, 130, 140, 141, 146, 150, 153, 154, 157, 184, 188
Inner Light, 122
Inquiry into the Human Mind On the Principles of Common Sense, 162
Inscrutabili Dei Consilio, 215
Institutes of the Christian Religion (Calvin), 119
Instrumentalism, 252
Intellect and Demons, On the, 115
Intellective Soul, On the, 101-102
Intelligence, On (Taine), 208
Intelligence Quotient, 260
Interaction, 131, 136, 210, 254
On Interpretation (Aristotle), 31
Interpretation of Nature, 158
Introduction to Arithmetic, 54
Introduction to the Categories, 63
Introduction to the Principles of Morals and Legislation, 296
Introduction to the Sciences of the Spirit (Dilthey), 219
Introductory Lectures on Psychoanalysis (Freud), 258
Introductory Logic (Creighton), 235

Introduction to Moral Science, 228
Introduction to the Principles of Morals and Legislation, 171
Introduction to the Study of Philosophy (Gioberti), 190
Intuition, 27, 31, 189, 191, 243, 245, 249
Investigation of the Laws of Thought (Boole), 196
Ion (Plato), 24
Ipuwer, 6
Irenaeus, 56
Isaiah I, 8
Isaiah II, 12
Isidore, 74
Isocrates, 29
Itinerarium Mentis in Deum, 97

Jacobi, F. H., 170
Jamblichus, 64
James, William, 3, 195, 215, 226, 235, 255, 266
Janet, Paul, 210
Jansen, Cornelius, 129
Jaspers, Karl, 238, 262, 305
Jefferson, Thomas, 164, 176, 183
Jeremiah, 9
Jerome, 66
Jesus, 48, 49, 53, 54, 55, 60, 62, 64, 67, 71, 85, 104, 260
Jesus Christ the Saviour, Concerning (Sozzini), 120
Jevons, W. S., 211, 218
Joachim of Floris, 92
Job, Book of, 39
Jodl, Friedrich, 218f.
John, Gospel of, 52, 57
John, Bishop of Jerusalem, 70f.
John of Damascus, 77
John Dewey, Philosopher of Science and Freedom, 290
John of Jandun, 107, 109
John of Salisbury, 90
John XXI, Pope, 101
John XXII, Pope, 107, 108, 109
Johnson, Samuel, 159

Index

Joseph, H. W. B., 210
Joseph, Saadia ben, 81
Josephus, 73
Journal (Fox), 141
Journal of Social Science, 263
Journal of Speculative Philosophy, 226
Journey of the Mind to God, 97
Jovinian, 67
Judaism, 9, 89
Jugendlehre (Foerster), 246
Julian (Emperor), 65, 66
Jung, C. G., 238, 259
Jure Naturae et Gentium, De, 138
Justice, 6, 8, 159
Justin, 54
Justinian (Emperor), 73, 74

Kallen, Horace M., 280
Kant, Immanuel, 84, 124, 162, 165ff.,
    171, 172, 173, 176-179, 181, 182,
    186, 190, 193, 197, 198, 204, 209,
    213, 216, 220, 222, 223, 225, 227,
    235, 250, 251, 252, 258, 267, 271
Kant Studies, 235
Kant's Theory of Experience (H.
    Cohen), 209
Kapital, Das (Marx), 205
Kappel, 117
Kaufmann, Walter A., 306
Kempis, Thomas à, 122
Kierkegaard, Soren, 193
Kindi al-, 78, 80, 90
King, Archbishop, 153
Knowledge, 24, 26, 29, 40, 41, 45, 58,
    68, 69, 83, 84, 95, 98, 99, 104, 108,
    112, 122, 127, 129, 130, 132, 133,
    136, 138, 140, 142, 143, 147, 162,
    166, 167, 172, 174, 177, 178, 180,
    183, 185, 188, 201, 204, 218, 219, 222,
    223, 227, 228, 232, 241, 245, 250, 254,
    255, 257, 264, 265, 267, 268, 274, 278
*Knowledge of God and the Service of
    God, The* (Barth), 278
Koffka, Kurt, 268
Köhler, Wolfgang, 268, 271

Korn, Alejandro, 265
Krause, K. C. F., 176, 178
Kreislauf des Lebens, 196
Kuelpe, Oswald, 239, 256

Laches (Plato), 24
Lachelier, Jules, 209
Lactantius, 63
Ladd, G. T., 230
Lafayette, Marquis de, 177
La Grange, J. L., 188
Lambert, J. H., 162
Lamennais, Robert de, 176, 187
Laments of Nature (Alan), 92
La Mettrie, Julien Offray de, 156
Lamprecht, Stephen P., 288
Lanfranc, 82
Lange, F. A., 204
Language, 21, 25, 36, 142, 165, 175,
    230, 265, 274
Language and Philosophy, 285
Language of Value, The, 281
Language, Truth and Knowledge
    (Ayer), 276
Laokoon (Lessing), 162
La Place, P. S., 188
Lassalle, Ferdinand, 202
Law, 7, 14, 19, 28, 36, 41, 42, 51, 60,
    72, 83, 100, 107, 120, 123, 128, 138,
    152, 156, 173, 180
Law, Edmund, 153
Law of Nature and of Nations, On the
    (Pufendorf), 138
Law of War and Peace, On the, 128
Laws (Plato), 28, 46
Learned Ignorance, On, 113
Lebensformen (Spranger), 257
Lectures and Essays (Clifford), 217
Lectures on the Algebra of Logic
    (Schroeder), 227
Legendre, A. M., 188
Leibniz, G. W., 138, 141, 144, 149,
    151, 160, 161, 165, 166, 188, 211, 220
Leighton, J. A., 264
Lenin, Vladimir I., 231, 238, 251

Lepley, Ray, 281-282
Leo XIII, Pope, 215
Lesser Socratic Schools, 23
Lessing, G. E., 159, 162
Letter on Toleration (Locke), 141
Letters on Materialism and Philosophical Necessity (Price), 165
Letters on the Study and Use of History (Bolingbroke), 155, 156
Letters to a German Princess, 163
Leucippus, 17
Leviathan (Hobbes), 133
Levinson, Ronald B., 298-299
Levi, Judah ha-, 89
Lévy-Bruhl, Lucien, 238, 264, 276
Lewes, 102
Lewes, G. H., 212
Lewis, C. I., 239, 270
Lexicon (Suidas), 81
Liber Gomorrhiana, 82
Liber Pantegni (Constantine), 83
Libido, 259
Life, 33, 182, 222, 227, 235, 240, 249, 252, 253, 259, 266, 275
Life of Jesus (Strauss), 187
Life of Reason (Santayana), 247
Life of St. Anthony of Padua, 103
Light of the Lord (Crescas), 111
Limits of Evolution, The, 239
Limits of Natural Scientific Conceptions, The (Rickert), 232
Limits of Religious Thought, 199
Lipps, Theodore, 195, 233
Livy, 208
Lloyd, A. H., 235
Locke, John, 136, 141, 146, 147, 150, 153, 154, 158, 177
Logic, 31, 34, 41, 56, 57, 73, 78, 85, 101, 102, 119, 122, 126, 136, 150, 162, 173, 179, 185, 188, 192, 194, 195, 199, 202, 210, 211, 216, 217, 218, 227f., 230, 235f., 240, 244f., 251f., 261, 265, 269f., 273-276
Logic (Aristotle), 63, 73, 91
Logic (Hamilton), 185

Logic (Hegel), 179
Logic (Sigwart), 210
Logic (Ueberweg), 204
Logic (Wundt), 218
Logic and Language, 295
Logical Basis of the Exact Sciences (Natorp), 252
Logical Syntax of Language, 274
Logic of Chance (Venn), 218
Logic, Empirical (Venn), 218
Logic, or the Morphology of Thought (Bosanquet), 224
Logic Without Metaphysics, 301
Logische Untersuchungen, 190
Logos, 14, 41, 49, 52, 54, 56, 57, 58, 60, 65
Lombard, Peter, 90, 92, 109
Lotze, R. H., 195, 198, 211, 231, 236
Louis XVIII, 177
Louis of Bavaria, 107
Love, 8, 9, 15, 49, 53, 55, 58, 100, 122, 136, 146, 157, 187, 202, 216, 233, 248
Lovejoy, A. O., 238, 271
Love, Power, and Justice, 293
Luce, Arthur A., 304
Lucian, 55
Lucinda (Schlegel), 175
Lucretius, 45
Luke, 52
Lully, Raymond, 102
Luther, Martin, 106, 116, 117, 260
Lyceum, 20, 31, 36, 42, 45, 59, 86
Lyons, General Chapter of, 103
Lysis (Plato), 24

Mach, Ernst, 222, 279
Machiavelli, Niccolo, 106, 116
Macintosh, D. C., 257
Mackintosh, James, 185
Macrobius, 67f., 85
Maimon, Solomon, 171f.
Maimonides, Moses, 92, 114
Maine de Biran, 176, 178f., 229
Main Points of Metaphysics, 178

Index

Malebranche, Nicholas de, 138, 145, 147, 149

Man, 21, 34, 41, 49, 56, 90, 91, 93, 99, 102, 120, 125, 127, 134, 148, 164, 178, 180, 187, 189, 191, 194, 223, 259, 267, 269, 279

Man Measure, 17

Man and the Cosmos, 265

Mandeville, Bernard, 146

Manegold of Lautenbach, 85

Mani, 62

Manichaeism, 62, 64, 66, 68, 94

Mansel, H. L., 199

Man's Freedom, 289

Man's Place in Nature (Huxley), 203

Man's Right to Know, 300

Marburg school, 209

Marcel, Gabriel, 293-294

Marcion, 54

Marcus Aurelius, 55

Maritain, Jacques, 239, 277

Mark, 51, 52

Marsh, Adam, 95

Marsilius of Inghen, 112

Marsilius of Padua, 107, 109

Martineau, James, 221

Marx, Karl, 193, 195, 205, 231, 251, 252, 279

Mary, 51, 67, 71

Materialism, 40, 45, 133, 139, 156, 163, 164, 173, 177, 193, 195, 205, 218, 251, 260, 267

Materialism and Empirio-Criticism (Lenin), 252

Mathematics, 13, 15, 18, 26, 29, 54, 71, 72, 92, 97, 110, 114, 120, 128, 129, 134, 139, 141, 149, 163, 167, 186, 189, 192, 194, 209, 211, 218, 231, 236, 237, 242, 243, 246, 249, 251, 269, 275

Mathematical Principles of Natural Philosophy (Newton), 141

Matter, 32, 41, 61, 81, 120, 121, 123, 125, 131, 135, 147, 149, 154, 160, 192, 197, 210, 222, 234, 249, 254

Matthew, 52, 54

Matthew of Aquasparta, 93, 103

Maurus, Rhabanus, 78-80

Maximus Confessor, 74

Mayer, Frederick, 291

McDougall, William, 238, 254

McKeon, Richard P., 296 297

McTaggart, J. M. E., 233

Mead, G. H., 239, 274

Meaning of God in Human Experience, The (Hocking), 255

Meaning of History (Berdyaev), 266

Mecca, 76, 77

Mechanism, 22, 114, 132, 135, 141, 198, 207, 224, 246, 250, 261, 267

Medicine, 6, 16, 56, 118

Medina, 76

Meditations (Marcus Aurelius), 55

Meditations (Descartes), 130

Mediterranean, 48

Meeting of East and West, The, 282

Megarics, 22

Meinong, Alexius, 234, 238, 247

Melissus, 16

Memorabilia of Socrates, 28

Mendelssohn, 163, 172

Meno (Plato), 24

Mercy, 51

Metacritique of the Purism of Pure Reason (Hamann), 177

Metaphysical Disputations, 123

Metalogicus (John of Salisbury), 90

Metaphysics, 34, 59, 110, 185

Metaphysic of Experience, 235

Method, 21, 22, 262

Methods of Ethics, The, 214

Micah, 8

Michelet, K. L., 184, 214

Microcosm, 173

Microcosmos (Lotze), 198

Miller, Perry, 290-291

Mill, James, 176, 184, 192, 198

Mill, J. S., 153, 176, 189, 191f., 197, 199, 201, 211, 215, 227

Mind, 16, 17, 61, 68, 133, 154, 173, 184, 185, 186, 190, 192, 197, 198, 202, 211,

212, 214, 216, 218, 220, 229, 239, 240, 244, 258, 259, 264, 268, 273, 274
Mind and the World Order, 271
Mind in Evolution (Hobhouse), 232
Mind and its Place in Nature, 268
Mind, Self and Society (Mead), 274
Mirabeau, Count de, 171
Miracle, 127, 152, 191
Miracles, Of (Hume), 155
Miracles, On (Gregory of Tours), 74
Miscellanies (Clement), 58
Mises, Richard von, 292
Mnemon (Artaxerxes II), 28
Modalists, 60
Modes of Being, 289
Moderation, 35, 36, 41, 44
Moleschott, Jacob, 195f.
Monad, 121, 150, 188, 236
Monadology (Leibniz), 149
Monasticism, 67, 73, 78, 79, 85, 92, 112
Monboddo, Lord, 164
Monica, 66, 68
Monism, 11, 170, 226, 227, 232, 235, 236, 239, 257, 267
Monothelitism, 75
Montague, W. P., 267
Montaigne, Michel, 120
Montanism, 57, 58
Montesquieu, 156
Moore, Charles A., 297
Moore, G. E., 238, 245
Moralia (Gregory the Great), 74
Morality, 87, 116, 120, 129, 146, 148, 151, 153, 155, 158, 161, 168, 172, 173, 177, 179, 200, 202, 204, 212, 223, 234, 244, 259, 264
Moral Order, 173
Moral Philosophy, System of, 158
Moral Philosophy, Outlines of, 172
Morals in Evolution, 232
More, Henry, 135, 137, 146
More, P. E., 266
More, Sir Thomas, 115, 116
Morris, Charles W., 303-304
Morgan, C. L., 263f.

Morris, G. S., 220
Moses, 58, 88
Motion, 15, 33
Mohammed, 76
Muirhead, J. H., 272
Mueller, F. M., 213
Mumford, Lewis, 282-283
Münsterberg, H., 238, 251
Murphy, Arthur E., 280-281
Music, 12, 16, 18, 54, 74, 119, 182
Myriobiblion (Photius), 80
Mystery, 70, 107
Mystical Theology, Concerning, 72
Mysticism, 59, 62-64, 85, 89, 91, 92, 97, 104, 110, 118, 125, 137, 148, 157, 179, 181, 242, 256, 266, 277

Nagel, Ernest, 301-302
Naples, 98, 114, 120, 152
Napoleon, 177
Nathan The Wise (Lessing), 162
Natorp, Paul, 239, 252
Natural History (Pliny the Elder), 52
Natural History of Religion, 154-155
Naturalism, 119, 121, 134, 208, 217, 246, 270, 272
Naturalism and Agnosticism, 236
Natural Theology, 112, 177
Nature, 42, 79, 81, 98, 121, 126, 133, 137, 139, 169, 170, 172, 174, 178, 180, 182, 187, 188, 206, 209, 212, 221, 228, 239, 242, 254, 259
Nature According to Its Own Principles, On (Telesio), 120
Nature and Historical Experience, 305
Nature, Man and God (Temple), 275
Nature, Mind, and Death, 291
Nature of Bodies, On the, 132
Nature of Existence, 233
Nature of the Gods, On (Cicero), 46
Nature and Immutability of Truth, Essay on the (Beattie), 163
Nature of the Soul, On the, 132
Nature of Thought, The, 278
Neo-Kantianism, 205, 209, 247, 252, 266

Index

Neo-Platonism, 67, 68, 72, 73, 78-81, 83, 89, 93, 97, 101, 118, 122
Nestorius, 71
Neues Organon (Lambert), 162
New Critique (Fries), 177
New Eloise (Rousseau), 161
New Essays on the Human Understanding (Leibniz), 150
New Information on the Origin of Ideas (Rosmini), 185
Newman, Cardinal, 195, 207
New Testament in Greek, 115
New Theory of Vision, A, 147
Newton, Sir Isaac, 141, 146
Nicaea, Council of, 64, 65
Nicholas of Autrecourt, 108
Nicholas of Cusa, 112, 121
Nicholas of Oresme, 110
Nicomachus, 54
Niebuhr, Reinhold, 300-301
Nietzsche, F. W., 222f., 265, 276
Nifo, Agostino, 115
Nippur Tablets, 6
Nisus, 262
Nominalism, 80, 86, 108, 109, 111, 112, 133, 142
Norris, John, 145, 149
Northrop, Filmer S. C., 282
Novum Organum, 126, 135
Number, 12, 16, 29, 30, 42, 64, 81
Number of Syllogisms, On the, 56
Numenius, 55, 62
Numerals, 77
Nuñez Regüeiro, Manuel, 238, 267

Object, 247
Observations on Aristotle, 119
Observations on Man (Hartley), 157
Occasionalism, 136
Odo of Tournai, 85
Old Age, On (Cicero), 46
Olivi, P. J., 103
Ontological argument, 84, 95, 100, 167
Opposition, 125, 177, 178, 180, 181
Optimism, 151, 161, 223

Opus Maius (Roger Bacon), 97
Opus Oxoniense (Scotus), 107
Opus Tripartitum (Eckhart), 104
Order of Execution Demands, 108
Order, On (Augustine), 68
Organicism, 207, 222, 233, 250, 277
Organic Inferiority and Its Physical Compensations (Adler), 250
Organon (Aristotle), 31
Origen, 52, 59
Origin, 5, 6, 7
Original Sin, On (Ode of Tournai), 85
Origin and Progress of Language (Monboddo), 164
Origin of Evil, On (Law), 153
Origin of Species (Darwin), 200, 208
Origin of the Family (Engels), 198
Origins of Contemporary France, 208
Ortega y Gasset, José, 239, 266, 269
Ostwald, Wilhelm, 230
Otto, Rudolph, 260
Our Religious Traditions, 288
Overcoming of Scientific Materialism (Ostwald), 230
Oxford, 93, 96, 102, 110, 116, 135, 142, 199, 213, 247, 269

Paley, William, 176, 177
Panaetius, 44, 45
Panentheism, 178
Panpsychism, 16, 120, 236, 270
Pantheism, 42, 52, 88, 89, 92, 93, 95, 118, 121, 143, 158, 181, 187, 189
Pap, Arthur, 306
Pape, Du (De Maistre), 181
Papacy, 70, 74, 93, 109, 110, 111, 127, 181, 182, 187
Papias, 53f.
Paracelsus, 118
Paradox, 219
Paradoxes (Franck), 118
Paradoxes of the Infinite, 189
Parallelism, 219
Parallel Lives (Plutarch), 85

Parker, Theodore, 191
Parmenides, 13, 14, 16, 17, 179, 241
Parmenides (Plato), 27, 284
Pascal, Blaise, 134
Paths of Life, a Preface to a World Religion, 303
Patricius, 68
Patrizzi, Francisco, 122
Paul, 43, 50-52, 54, 72, 73, 79, 117
Paulus Diaconus, 78
Peace of mind, 39, 55
Peano, Giuseppe, 230
Peccato, Originali, De (Odo), 85
Peckham, John, 102
Peirce, C. S., 195, 215, 216
Pelagius, 70
Pepper, Stephen C., 304
Perry, R. B., 238, 255f.
Persistent Problems of Philosophy (Calkins), 249
Personalism, 249, 250, 265, 266, 271
Personalism (Bowne), 250
Personality, 118, 187, 258, 264, 269, 277, 278
Personal Realism (Pratt), 277
Perspectives (Witelo), 100
Pessimism, 182, 183, 207, 208, 245
Peter, 50, 51, 52, 107
Peter of Abano, 104
Peter of Spain, 102
Phaedo (Plato), 25
Phädon (Mendelssohn), 163
Phaedrus (Plato), 26, 106
Phenomena, 166, 182, 186, 231, 277
Phenomenalism, 155, 197, 273
Phenomenology, 240, 258, 268, 279
Philebus (Plato), 27
Philip V of Macedonia, 30
Philo Judaeus, 48, 52, 58
Philolaus, 16
Philosophe Ignorant, Le, 161
Philosophical Analysis, 297
Philosophical Discussions, 215
Philosophical Disquisition on the Laws of Nature (Cumberland), 137

Philosophical Inquiry into the Sublime and the Beautiful, 159
Philosophical Scrutiny of Religion, A, 291
Philosophical Review (Creighton, ed.), 235
Philosophical Studies, 297
Philosophic Fragments (Cousin), 184
Philosophy, On (William), 89
Philosophy and Christianity, 220
Philosophy in France in the 19th Century (Ravaisson), 206
Philosophy of Epicurus, The, 133
Philosophy of the Act (Mead), 274
Philosophy of the "As If," 255
Philosophy of the Church Fathers, The, 302
Philosophy of the Inductive Sciences (Whewell), 189
Philosophy of Mind (Ladd), 231
Philosophy of Personality, The, 278
Philosophy of Religion, 239
Philosophy of Science, The, 299
Photius, 80
Physicalism, 245, 274
Physics (Aristotle), 101
Physiological Optics (Helmholtz), 203
Pico, John, 114
Pindar, 65
Planisphere (Ptolemy), 89
Planck, Max, 239, 240
Plato, 20, 23, 29, 30, 31, 43, 45, 46, 48, 49, 54, 56, 58, 59, 62, 64, 65, 67, 72, 85, 89, 90, 97, 102, 106, 113, 122, 139, 146, 152, 182, 189, 190, 209, 244, 252, 276
Plato's Modern Enemies and the Theory of Natural Law, 284
Plato's Theory of Man, 283
Platonic Tradition in Anglo-Saxon Philosophy (Muirhead), 272
Platonism, 55, 61, 66, 74, 87, 88, 94, 96, 113, 115, 129, 133, 135, 137, 184, 266, 271

Pleasure, 23, 30, 35, 40, 41, 168, 171, 177, 184, 214

Plekhanov, G. V., 195, 231

Pliny the Elder, 51f.

Plotinus, 61, 69, 91, 113

Pluralism, 15, 17, 22, 178, 227

Plutarch of Athens, 67

Plutarch of Chaeronea, 52

Poetics (Aristotle), 36

Poincaré, J. H., 242, 273

Poisson, 176, 188

Polarity, 174, 272

Polemo, 30

Policraticus (John), 90

Politics (Aristotle), 35, 97

Polycarp, 53, 56

Polytheism, 64

Pomponazzi, Pietro, 115, 116

Pope, Alexander, 155, 156

Porphyry, 62, 63, 64, 73, 80, 113

Port Royal Logic (Arnauld), 136

Porter, Noah, 205f.

Posidonius, 45, 65

Positivism, 186, 199, 208, 213, 218, 219, 222, 224, 242, 245, 254, 261, 265, 274, 275

Positivism, a Study in Human Understanding, 292

Postulate, 169, 244

Potentiality and actuality, 32, 34f.

Power and Use of Money, On the (Biel), 113

Praeparatio Evangelica, 64

Pragmatism, 216, 227, 229, 254, 263, 270, 274

Pragmatism (James), 227

Praise of Virginity, In (Aldhelm), 77

Pratt, J. B., 277

Predestination, 69, 79, 107

Present Philosophical Tendencies (Perry), 255

Price, Richard, 165

Priest of Seneferu, 5

Priestley, Joseph, 164, 165

Primitive Mentality, 264

Prince, The (Machiavelli), 116

Principles (Albo), 112

Principia Ethica (Moore), 245

Principia Mathematica (Whitehead and Russell), 245, 269, 270, 273

Principles of Human Knowledge (Berkeley), 147, 304

Principles of Mathematics, 244

Principles of Natural Knowledge (Whitehead), 270

Principles of Morality and Natural Religion, Essays on (Home), 157

Principles of a New Science Concerning the Common Nature of All Nations (Vico), 152

Principles of Philosophy, 130

Principles of Psychology, 226

Principles of Science (Jevons), 211

Pringle-Pattison, A. Seth, 259

Prior Analytics (Aristotle), 31

Private Property and the State, 193

Probability, 43, 46, 68, 191, 194, 195, 267, 275

Problem of God, The, 272

Problem of Knowledge, The, 247

Problem of Knowledge, The (Macintosh), 258

Problems (Aristotle), 104

Problems of Analysis, 286

Problems of Life and Mind, 213

Process and Reality (Whitehead), 270

Procession of the Holy Spirit, 103

Proclus, 72, 97, 104, 113

Prodicus, 17, 19

Prolegomena to Any Future Metaphysic (Kant), 167

Prolegomena to Ethics (Green), 219

Proof that Every Class Can Be Well-ordered (Zermelo), 246

Properties of Things, On the, 94

Proslogium (Anselm), 84

Protagoras, 17, 21, 24, 244

Protagoras (Plato), 24

Protagoras (Cicero), 46

Providence, 42, 55, 118

Providence, On (Proclus), 72
Provincial Letters (Pascal), 134
Psalms, Interpretation of, 80
Psalms, Paraphrase of, 65
Pseudo-Dionysius the Areopagite, 72, 79, 91, 96, 105, 113, 122
Psychological Sketches (Beneke), 184
Psychology (Aristotle), 34, 91
Psychology from the Empirical Standpoint (Brentano), 212
Psychology and Personality, 261
Psychology of Positive Science, 209
Psychology of Tone (Stumpf), 221
Psychology of the Unconscious, 259
Psychology of World Views, 262
Psychoanalysis, 258
Psychopathology, 262
Psychophysics, 200
Ptahhotep, 5
Ptolemy, 89, 90, 97
Pufendorf, Samuel, 137
Purgation, 36
Pyrrho, 38, 43
Pyrrhonism, Outline of, 57
Pythagoras, 12, 16, 55, 64
Pythagorean Numbers, 30
Pythagorean Way of Life, On, 64

Quadrivium, 7
Quaestiones (Olivi), 103
Quaestiones Disputatae, 103
Quakers, 137, 140, 146, 149
Qualities, 142, 147, 258, 267, 268
Quantum, 240
Questions Concerning Four Books of Sentences (Marsilius), 112
Quest for Certainty, The, 253
Quierzy, 79
Quine, W. V., 238, 274f.

Radbertus, Paschasius, 78
Radhakrishnan, Sarvepalli, 298, 305
Ramsey, F. P., 238, 273
Ramus, Petrus, 119
Randall, J. H., Jr., 305

Rashdall, Hastings, 247f.
Rationalism, 27, 150, 151, 187, 191, 206, 214, 242, 256
Rational Thoughts on God, the World and the Soul of Man, and also All Things in General, 151
Ravaisson-Mollien, F. L., 206
Raymond, Bishop of Toledo, 90
Raymond of Sabunde, 112
Readings in Ethical Theory, 297
Readings in Philosophical Analysis, 285
Readings in the Philosophy of Science, 302
Realism, 84-89, 178, 202, 206, 222, 227, 240, 242, 245, 246, 255, 263, 267, 268, 271, 277
Reality, 10-15, 17, 22, 27-30, 34, 41, 61, 69, 81, 88, 95, 99, 101, 104, 107, 114, 122, 133, 150, 157, 170, 178, 179, 185, 190, 198, 200, 204, 209, 212, 216, 218, 219, 224, 225, 227, 228, 230, 232, 234, 235, 239, 241, 243-245, 251, 254, 255, 258, 259, 262, 264, 269, 270, 274, 275
Realization (Külpe), 256
Realm of Mind, The, 268
Reason and Nature (M. Cohen), 272
Reason, 14, 34, 35, 41, 42, 56, 58, 84, 87, 91, 110, 114, 120, 127, 128, 132, 139, 142, 143, 146, 151-153, 168-170, 172, 177, 179, 180, 225, 247, 270
Reason and the Nature of Spirits (Burthogge), 143
Reason the Only Oracle of Man, 170
Rebus Naturalibus, De, 122
Reductione Artium ad Theologiam, De (Bonaventure), 97
Reflections of a Physicist, 288
Reflections on the French Revolution (Burke), 159, 164
Reformation, 108, 119
Refutation of the Cardinal Principles of Christians (Crescas), 111
Reichenbach, Hans, 275
Reid, Thomas, 162, 172, 184
Reims, 79, 84, 86, 88

Index

Relation of the Physical and the Moral in Man (Cabanis), 171

Relativism, 16, 17, 19, 20, 44, 222, 228, 242, 244

Relativity, 14, 15, 267, 275

Religion, 8, 12, 42, 50, 56, 68, 79, 91, 126, 127, 132, 134, 138, 140, 148, 152, 153, 155, 163, 170, 174, 175, 176, 178, 187, 188, 189, 190, 191, 193, 199, 201, 204, 205, 207, 211, 212, 213, 216, 217, 221, 222, 224, 225, 227, 235, 240, 242, 244, 252, 253, 258-260, 263f., 266, 277

Religion Within the Limits of Mere Reason (Kant), 170

Remi of Auxerre, 80

Renouvier, C. B., 195, 197

Reorganization of European Society (St. Simon), 179

Repentance, On (Ambrose), 66

Reply to Burke's Reflections on the French Revolution, 185

Republic (Plato), 26, 27, 29, 62, 90, 284

Republic (Cicero), 46, 68

Researches in Logic, 190

Researches on the Probability of Judgments (Poisson), 188

Responsibility, 9, 35

Resurrection, 104, 114

Revelation, 84, 85, 89, 93, 107, 112, 118, 123, 126, 127, 152, 170, 185, 190, 191, 200, 207, 276

Revolt Against Dualism, 271

Rhetoric (Aristotle), 36

Richard of St. Victor, 90f.

Rickert, Heinrich, 232

Riddle of the Universe, The, 236

Riemann, G. F. B., 209

Rigorism, 103, 129

Rising Dawn (Boehme), 125

Ritschl, Albrecht, 195, 198

Robert of Lincoln, 93

Robinson, Daniel S., 302

Romanticism, 170, 174, 175

Romero, Francisco, 238, 278

Roscelin, 86, 87

Rosmini-Serbati, Antonio, 176, 185

Ross, W. D., 238, 278

Rousseau, J. J., 161

Rouvroy, C. H., 179

Royce, Josiah, 238, 241f., 249, 255, 256, 274, 279

Ruge, Arnold, 189

Ryle, Gilbert, 284-285, 305

Russell, B., 238, 244, 246, 269f., 305

Sabellius, 60

Sacrament, 67, 117, 118, 191, 207

Sacraments, On the (Hugh), 90

Sacred Books of the East, 213

Sagesse, De la (Charron), 125

St. Germain of Auxerre, 80

St. John, Henry, 155

St. Simon, Count de, 176, 179

Salvation, 50, 61, 62, 117, 118, 119, 122, 129, 183, 193, 278

Same and the Different, On the, 87

Santayana, George, 238, 246f., 305

Sartor Resartus (Carlyle), 187

Sartre, J. P., 279

Satires (Timon), 43

Satirical Dialogues (Lucian), 55

Saturnalia (Macrobius), 67, 68

Satyricon (Capella), 71

Savonarola, 114

Scheler, Max, 239, 240, 258

Schelling, F. W. J., 174, 206, 251

Schiller, F. C. S., 239, 244

Schlegel, Friedrich, 175

Schleiermacher, Friedrich, 174, 260

Schlick, Moritz, 239, 261

Schilpp, Paul A., 304-305

Schmidt, Kaspar, 194

Schneider, Herbert W., 303

Schopenhauer, A., 176, 182f., 206, 233

Schroeder, Ernst, 227

Science and Hypothesis, 242

Science and Philosophy, 254

Science and Philosophy of the Organism (Driesch), 251

Scientific Theism (Abbot), 222

Sebokht, Severus, 77
Secondat, C. L. de, 156
Sein und Zeit (Heidegger), 269
Sellars, Wilfrid S., 297-298
Self, 111f., 127, 129f., 158, 166f., 172, 175, 178f., 185, 194, 204, 211, 216, 220-222, 258f., 274, 277
Self-consciousness, 215, 231, 232, 259
Semantics and Necessary Truth, 306
Seneca, 47, 51, 190
Senses and the Intellect, The, 198
Sensations of Tone (Helmholtz), 203
Sense of Truth, The (Xirau), 269
Sentences (Peter Lombard), 109
Sergeant, John, 136
Sermons (Pierre d'Ailly), 111
Sermons (Tauler), 110
Sermons on Human Nature, 153
Sextius, Quintus, 46, 47
Sextus Empiricus, 57, 154
Shaftesbury, Earl of, 148, 158
Sheldon, Wilmon H., 299-300
Sic et Non (Abelard), 87
Sidgwick, Henry, 214
Siger of Brabant, 101
Sigwart, Christoph von, 210
Simmel, Georg, 195, 227
Simplicius, 74
Sin, 67, 69, 71, 117
Six Principles, On (Gilbert), 88
Skeptical Chymist, The (Boyle), 135
Skepticism, 6, 38, 43, 44, 46, 57, 108, 121, 125, 129, 135, 143, 155, 165
Slavery, 35
Smith, Adam, 160
Social Contract, 24, 85, 133
Social Contract, The (Rousseau), 161
Socialism, 179
Society, 5, 6, 35, 41, 62, 100, 152, 159f., 170-173, 181, 186, 192, 202, 205, 209, 214, 219, 224, 229, 231, 233, 246, 254, 257, 263f., 279
Sociology of Religion, Collected Essays on (Weber), 263
Socrates, 16, 19-27, 41, 130

Soliloquies (Augustine), 68
Solomon, 44
Sophist, 17, 19
Sophist (Plato), 27, 284
Sophistical Tests (Aristotle), 31
Sophistry, 18, 22
Sotion, 47
Soul, 12, 16, 25, 26, 27, 28, 30, 34, 40, 42, 43, 45, 55, 59, 61, 62, 67, 68, 81, 83, 85, 90, 91, 95, 96, 99, 105, 108, 114, 116, 120, 121, 122, 131, 132, 133, 149, 157, 164, 165, 167, 171, 178, 184, 185, 198, 201, 209, 211, 212, 218, 219, 228, 229, 256, 268, 275
Soul, On the (Alexander), 59
Soul, On the (Cassiodorus), 73
Soul, World, 119, 122
Sources of Value, The, 304
Sovereign, 133, 141
Sovereign Reason, and Other Studies in the Philosophy of Science, 301
Sozzini, Fausto, 120, 164
Space, 32, 40, 45, 151, 166, 173, 185, 204, 249, 262, 275
Space Perception and Geometrical Illusions (Lipps), 234
Space, Time and Deity, 262
Speculative Mystic Philosophy, 111
Spencer, Herbert, 195, 201f., 213, 215, 225, 232
Speusippus, 29, 30
Spheres, Treatise on, 110
Spinoza, 111, 138, 141, 144, 170, 178, 205, 210, 220, 225, 251
Spir, African, 210
Spirit, 123, 131, 143, 147, 148, 154, 180, 181, 187, 199, 206, 212, 219, 221, 229, 243, 257
Spirit of Medieval Philosophy, 276
Spranger, Edward, 240, 257
Stace, W. T., 273
State, 25-26, 35, 36, 100, 107, 116, 120, 127, 133, 134, 138, 139, 161, 163, 179, 180, 190, 193, 199, 221, 224, 252, 255, 259, 277

Index

Statesman (Plato), 27
Status of the Theory of Objects in the System of the Sciences, 247
Stephen, Sir Leslie, 214
Stern, William, 238, 260
Stewart, Dugald, 172
Stirner, Max, 176, 194
Stoa Poikile, 41
Stobaeus, John, 72
Stoics, 41, 43, 45, 46, 51, 120
Stout, G. F., 231
Strato, 42
Strauss, D. F., 176, 187
Structure of Appearance, The, 294
Struggle, 8, 14, 235, 240
Studies in the Hegelian Dialectic, 233
Study of History, 300
Stumpf, Carl, 220, 271
Stuttgart, 194
Suarez, 123
Sublime, 169, 174
Subsistence, 88
Substance, 15, 31, 32, 34, 132, 139, 149, 173, 197, 210, 211, 216, 246
On Subtlety (Cardano), 120
Suffering, 6, 12, 39
Suidas, 81
Summa Contra Gentiles, 99
Summa Dialecticae (Abelard), 87
Summa Theologiae (Albert), 96
Summa Theologiae (Thomas), 99
Summa Universae Theologiae, 94f.
Summary of Dialectics (Abelard), 87
Summary of Logic (Peter), 101
Summum Bonum, 35, 113
Supernatural, 121, 122
Sura, Gaon of, 81
Sure Footing in Christianity, 136
Surgery (Paracelsus), 118
Swedenborg, Emmanuel, 157
Swift, Jonathan, 155
Sylvester II, Pope, 81
Symbol, 72, 174, 178, 247, 265
Symbolic Logic (Venn), 218

Sympathy, 155, 160, 183, 200
Symposium (Plato), 25, 28, 106
Symposium (Xenophon), 29
Système de la Nature, 163
Systematic Theory of Value, 234
System of Acquired Rights, The, 202
System of Logic (J. S. Mill), 192
System of Logistic, A (Quine), 275
Systematic Theology, 293

Table of the Springs of Action, 296
Tacitus, 152
Taine, H. A., 208
Tarski, Alfred, 238, 273, 274
Tatian, 56, 65
Tauler, John, 104, 110
Taylor, A. E., 238, 244
Teichmüller, Gustav, 195, 211
Tel El Amarna, Letters, 7
Telesio, Bernardino, 120
Temple, William, 228, 275
Terminism, 108
Tertullian, 58
Theaetetus (Plato), 27, 284
Theism and Humanism, 217
Theme of Our Time, The, 266
Themistius, 90
Theodoric, Emperor, 72, 73
Theodoric of Chartres, 88
Theodosius II, 66
Theologia Germanica, 122
Theologia Platonica (Ficino), 113
Theology, 34, 78, 87, 107
Theology of Aristotle (al-Kindi), 79
Theophrastus, 36, 42, 45, 278
Theoria Philosophiae Naturalis, 160
Theory of the Catholic Faith, On the (Alan), 92
Theory of an Ideal and Intelligible World, Essay Towards The, 145f.
Theory of Knowledge (Hobhouse), 232
Theory of Knowledge and Existence (Stace), 273
Theory of Mind as Pure Act, 215

Theory of the Moral Sentiments, 160
Theory of Probability, 275
Theory and Regulation of Love, 146
Three Dialogues (Berkeley), 148
Thomas Aquinas, 76, 84, 88, 94f., 97f., 102-104, 106, 112, 115, 215
Thomas Aquinas, An Introduction to His Personality and Thought-World (Grabmann), 255
Thoreau, H. D., 196
Thought, 14, 41, 61, 143, 185, 196, 209, 218, 220, 233, 235, 253
Thought, Action and Passion, 297
Thought and Reality (Spir), 210
Three Dimensions of Public Morality, 303
Tillich, Paul, 292-293
Timaeus (Cicero), 46
Timaeus (Plato), 28, 64, 65, 85, 106
Timaeus of Plato, On the, 89
Time, 32, 33, 69, 151, 166, 173, 185, 196, 209, 218, 220, 233, 235, 253
Timon, 43
Tindal, Matthew, 152
Toland, John, 143, 146
Toledo, Bishop of, 90
Tolerance, 119, 138, 143
Tönnies, Ferdinand, 224
Topics (Aristotle), 31
Toulmin, Stephen E., 299
Toward Reunion in Philosophy, 286
Toynbee, Arnold, 300
Tractate (d'Ailly), 111
Tractatus Logico-Philosophicus, 265
Traducianism, 85
Tragic Sense of Life, The, 257
Training of a Knight (Pliny), 51
Trajan, Forum of, 66
Transcendentalism, 188, 196
Transcendentalists, The, 290
Transcendental Philosophy, Essays on the (Maimon), 172
Transient and the Permanent in Christianity, The (Parker), 191
Transmigration, 12

Transmutation, 203
Transubstantiation, 78, 82f., 110, 118
Treatise of Human Nature, 154
Treatise on Sensation, 158
Treatise on the Will, 177
Treatises on Government, 141
Trendelenburg, F. A., 176, 190, 221
Trialogus (Wycliffe), 110
Trinity, On the (William), 94
Trinity, On the (Pelagius), 71
Trinity, On the (Richard), 91
Trivium, 71
True Intellectual System of the Universe, The (Cudworth), 140
Truth, 9, 17, 24, 25, 26, 27, 38, 40, 43, 57, 89, 91, 98, 99, 102, 107, 109, 113, 118, 127, 130, 138, 140, 151, 180, 184, 187, 188, 191, 194, 210, 219, 227, 229, 232, 242, 244, 252f., 255, 261, 265, 274f., 279
Truth, On (Anselm), 84
Truth (Lord Herbert), 127
Truth and Reality (Boodin), 254
Truth Concept in Formalized Language, The (Tarski), 274, 303
Truth of Religion, The, 240
Tufts, J. H., 238, 250
Turro y Darder, Ramon, 239, 261
Tusculan Disputations, 46, 68
Twenty Books of Origins or Etymologies (Isidore), 74
Two Brothers, Tale of, 7
Types of Ethical Theory, 221

Ueberweg, Friedrich, 204
Unamuno, Miguel, 238, 256, 266
Unitarianism, 120, 191
Unity of the Catholic Church, 61
Unity of the Intellect, On the, 102
Universal, 21, 63, 80, 81, 86, 87, 88, 95, 96, 99, 108, 270
Universe, On the (Rhabanus), 78
Universe, On the (William), 94
Universities of Europe in the Middle Ages, The (Rashdall), 247

Index

Unreliability of the Principles of Logic (Brouwer), 251
Urbild der Menschheit, Das, 178
Uses of Reason, The, 280
Utilitarianism, 153, 155, 184, 186, 202, 205, 214, 215, 227, 247
Utilitarianism (J. S. Mill), 192
Utopia (More, Sir Thomas), 116

Vaihinger, Hans, 254, 273
Valerian (Emperor), 61
Valoraciones (Korn, ed.), 265
Value, 232, 234, 247, 257, 258, 264, 265, 267, 271, 275, 277, 279, 281
Values for Survival, 282
Vanity of Dogmatizing (Glanvil), 135
Variety of Things, On the, 120
Varieties of Human Value, 303
Various Letters (Cassiodorus), 73
Vasconcelos, Jose, 276
Venn, John, 218
Verifiability of Value, 281
Vespasian, Emperor, 52
Vico, G. B., 151
Victorinus, 65
Vinci, Leonardo da, 114
Vindication of Natural Society, 159
Virtue, 24, 26, 35, 100, 125, 131, 140, 153, 158, 171
Virtue, On (Geulincx), 137
Vischer, Friedrich, 194
Volcanic Islands (Darwin), 200
Void, 32, 33
Volkelt, Johannes, 223, 234
Voltaire, 143, 155, 161, 182
Voluntarism, 236, 265

Wagner, Richard, 223
Wahrheitsbegriff in den formalisierten Sprachen (Tarski), 274
Wahrheitsgehalt der Religion, Der (Eucken), 240
Walden, Or Life in the Woods, 197
Ward, James, 236

War of the Lord, 109
Wartburg Castle, 117
Watson, J. B., 238, 257
Watt, James, 164
Way Things Are, The, 288
Ways of Culture (Huizinga), 271
Ways of Knowing (Montague), 267
Wealth of Nations (Smith), 161
Weber, Max, 238, 263
Weigel, Valentine, 122
Weiss, Paul, 289-290
Wertheimer, Max, 238, 256, 268
Whewell, William, 189
Whichcote, Benjamin, 132
White, Morton, 286
Whitehead, A. N., 238, 245, 267, 269
Wiener, Philip P., 302
Wild, John D., 283-284
Will, 106, 161, 173, 174, 178, 179, 182, 183, 206, 207, 218, 219, 222, 223, 224, 250, 251, 252, 256, 276
William of Auvergne, 94
William of Champaux, 86
William of Conches, 89
William of Moerbeke, 97, 100
William of Normandy, 83
William of Ockham, 108, 111-113, 222
William, Rufus, 83
Will to Believe, The (James), 235
Will to Doubt (Lloyd), 235
Windelband, Wilhelm, 229, 232
Wingless Pegasus, a Handbook for Critics, 289
Wisdom, 120, 125, 157
Wissenschaftslehre (Bolzano), 188
Witelo, 100
Wittgenstein, Ludwig, 238, 261, 265
Wolfenbütteler Fragmente, 162
Wolff, Christian, 151, 162, 172
Wolfson, Harry A., 302
Wollaston, William, 151
Woodbridge, F. J. E., 268
Woodger, J. H., 303
Words of a Believer, 187
Wordsworth, William, 181

Work of the Six Days, On the, 88
Works of Berkeley, 304
World and the Individual, The, 241
World as Will and Idea, The, 182
Wrath (Seneca), 51
Wright, Chauncey, 215
Wundt, Wilhelm, 195, 217, 236, 274
Wycliffe, John, 110

Xeniades, 29
Xenocrates, 30
Xenophanes, 13
Xenophon, 19, 28, 41

Xirau, Joaquin, 238, 269

Yathrib, 76
Yes and No (Abelard), 87

Zabarella, Jacob, 121
Zeno, Eleatic, 13, 14, 33, 162, 228
Zeno, Stoic, 41
Zeno of Tarsus, 41, 43
Zephaniah, 9
Zermelo, Ernst, 238, 246
Zoroaster, 4, 8, 62
Zwingli, Huldreich, 117